# Writing & Speaking FOR Business

## 4TH EDITION

WILLIAM H. BAKER

MATTHEW J. BAKER

**BYU ACADEMIC PUBLISHING**

Managing Editor: Kent Minson
Design and Layout: Kent Minson
Illustrations: William H. Baker, Kent Minson, Jacob Wilson, Matthew J. Baker

Print ISBN: 9781611650211
eBook ISBN: 9781614210009
For more information or permission to use material from this text or product contact:
BYU Academic Publishing
3991 WSC
Provo, UT 84602
Tel (801) 422–4167
Fax (801) 422–0070
academicpublishing@byu.edu

To report ideas or text corrections email us at:
textideas@byu.edu

2nd Printing

# Contents

# Acknowledgments

We are excited about the 4th edition of *Writing and Speaking for Business.* We have put our very best efforts into creating a book that will be of maximum value to all who read it. First, we have included what we believe is the most critical content for communicating effectively, focusing on timeless principles and processes that will endure throughout your career. Second, we have worked hard to present the material in a learner-friendly way to enhance understanding, retention, and application. Finally, we have done everything possible to maintain a budget-friendly price, hoping that you get a great return on your investment.

Many people have contributed to this edition of *Writing and Speaking for Business,* including students and faculty members who have used earlier editions. We appreciate the valuable feedback they have given, and we have implemented their suggestions. Individuals who have made particularly vital contributions to this edition include Nancy Hicks, Central Michigan University; Andy Spackman, Katie Liljenquist, Lisa Thomas, Jonathan Richards, and Julie Haupt, all from Brigham Young University; Sharon Cannon, University of North Carolina; and Ryan Starks, Executive Director of Heber Valley Chamber of Commerce.

We also appreciate the major contributions of Kent Minson, not only for his layout and design work, but also for his content suggestions and his help with the details of production and printing.

Finally, we express our deep appreciation to our wives, Jeannie and Marianne, for help in countless ways. Writing a book is challenging and exacting work that requires an enormous amount of time. Yet during our work on this project, they have been patient, understanding, and encouraging. They have also given critical feedback after reviewing endless pages of drab-looking text, when reading a good novel would have been much more enjoyable.

We hope you like this book and find it to be a useful resource.

—*William H. Baker*
—*Matthew J. Baker*

## CHAPTER 1

# Managing with Communication

Organizations are created to get results. A sports equipment manufacturer, for example, seeks to make products that people will buy so the company can make money. Because of the complexity of manufacturing and marketing sports equipment, the company hires numerous people to help with the process. Someone designs the products, someone creates assembly lines with proper equipment, someone buys supplies, someone arranges financing, many people work on the assembly line, someone advertises the product, and someone ships the product. Each position is expected to get results, and all the small results combine to achieve the overall organization results.

How does everyone get results? Mainly, with effective communication! Communication is the most vital skill of managers. Good planning, organizing, monitoring, and leading all depend on good communication. Financial management, marketing management, operations management, human resource management, and research and develop-

ment all depend on good communication. Communication is the means by which managers manage.

Management communication encompasses how well you speak, write, listen, read, and interact with your fellow professionals, both inside and outside the organization. As a result, your communication skills will have an enormous influence on your advancement, your salary, and your job security. Communication affects everything else in your career.

The first section of this chapter discusses important interpersonal knowledge and skills you need for succeeding in professional organizations. The second section concentrates on the management skills you need for getting results through others.

After you have studied this chapter, you should be able to do the following:

- Demonstrate effective social skills, including conversation, listening, and networking skills.
- Demonstrate commonly expected manners and professional etiquette.
- Apply your knowledge and abilities in working with and achieving success through others.

## INTERPERSONAL AND SOCIAL EFFECTIVENESS

Employers consistently rate interpersonal effectiveness a high priority in hiring new employees. Interpersonal effectiveness is critical at all levels of an organization. This section discusses several vital communication-related attributes and skills.

*Figure 1.1 Effective communication is important at all levels in business organizations.*

## Social Intelligence

The academic and technical knowledge you gain in college and in other training is important for performing your specific tasks, but the relationship aspect of your work must never be overlooked. In fact, Goleman (1995) states that interpersonal and social skills will have a greater impact on business success than academic knowledge. Further, Gardner (1993) suggests four abilities to be socially effective:

|         | What You Sense   | How You Respond          |
|---------|------------------|--------------------------|
| Self    | Self-awareness   | Self-management          |
| Others  | Social awareness | Relationship management  |

### "Self" Abilities

The "self" row in the preceding matrix indicates that you should be aware of your own emotions and manage them appropriately. For instance, if you're in a meeting and someone criticizes an idea you have proposed, your natural tendency is to become angry and lash back at the person. But you can't do that without social consequences. Instead, just say to yourself, "I know I'm angry right now, but I must stay calm and act rationally." By being aware of your own emotions and keeping them under control, you prevent negative consequences and enhance your credibility with your peers.

You should also be aware of how well you are performing your work. Most companies have a formalized employee-evaluation process to give constructive employee feedback. If your company does not have such a process, request performance feedback from your manager, from two or three peers whose opinions you respect, and from your subordinates. Ask about what you are doing well as well as how you could improve. If the feedback isn't forthcoming or is too general to be of much value, ask more specific questions, such as, "In the projects I have been working on during the last three months, what do you think I have done well and what could I do better."

When the feedback comes, be receptive. Never argue or become defensive. After obtaining the feedback, analyze it. Does it seem true? Have you noticed the same thing yourself? Is there consistency across the comments made by different reviewers? After analyzing the information, list the improvements you want to make and then work on them.

In addition to formal verbal feedback, watch for subtle nonverbal feedback. When you talk, do others listen and seem to value your input? Are you included in important

meetings and discussions? Do others ask for your opinions? Do they visit with you in informal hallway conversation? These and other spontaneous cues provide useful feedback. Watch and listen closely to these cues and then work to become better. For instance, if you notice boredom in a meeting you conduct, analyze the cause of that negative feedback and then implement improvements in your next meeting. The ability to self-assess and improve is vital to your professional success.

### "Other" Abilities

The "others" row in the preceding matrix indicates that you should be aware of other people in your social setting and respond to them appropriately. To work effectively with other people, you must be able to empathize; that is, to understand what they are thinking and to sense what they are feeling—to put yourself in their shoes and feel what they are feeling. Then you must know how to respond appropriately. If someone is happy, you share in the happiness. If someone is sad, you lend a listening ear and find out why they are unhappy. If someone is angry, you allow them to vent their anger and then express understanding, followed by offering any appropriate help for dealing with their frustration.

For various reasons, some people lack the ability to sense and interpret the social messages around them. They may talk too much, talk only about themselves, make socially embarrassing comments, ask inappropriate personal questions, or seem oblivious to hints given by others to end a conversation. Their insensitivity can spread to other aspects of their work as well—borrowing without asking, standing too close in a conversation, speaking too loudly in a public place, laughing inappropriately, and committing other social blunders that make their peers uncomfortable. Because subtle hints don't work with these people, you may have to be more bold in giving cues and helping them manage their behavior.

One way to build and strengthen relationships is to work on being more "other-oriented," rather than more "me-oriented." Everyone has a natural tendency to be egocentric, to focus on self, but those who can rise above this natural selfishness find great satisfaction in bringing out the best in others. When they do, they find that they also bring out the best in themselves. Try it for yourself and sense how it changes the way you feel. Here are eight suggestions to help you be more other-oriented:

1.  Be nice! Always be respectful, kind, and considerate. Encourage others; express confidence in them.

2.  Involve others in relationship-building conversation.

Ask questions about things that are important to them. In social conversations, make comments that end with a hook. For instance, if someone asks you about your job, answer the question and then end with a question like, "And what kind of work do you do?" This question will hook the person and give them an open door to talk.

3. Invite others into the conversation. If you're talking with someone at a social gathering and someone else walks up, open up the circle and make appropriate introductions so the new person feels welcome.

4. Sincerely listen when others are sharing their thoughts. Look at them in the eye, nod your head as they talk, and give other nonverbal and verbal encouragement and validation. Don't cut them off or try to "one-up" them with comments about you.

5. Don't talk down to other people, even when you are above them on the company's organization chart. Consider them to be equal to you in terms of importance in the organization.

6. Compliment others as appropriate, but avoid sugary-sweet compliments that sound insincere. Instead, be sincere and compliment something specific.

7. Avoid grapevine gossip—don't pass along information that you would feel uncomfortable saying if the person you're talking about were there to listen.

8. Go out of your way to help others. Perform an act of kindness for someone else every day.

Conversely, a number of me-oriented actions can cause serious problems in business. The following actions will produce bad results:

- Ignoring and not talking to others (stonewalling).

*Figure 1.2 Include others in conversations so they feel welcome.*

- Being discourteous, criticizing, and putting others down.
- Being prideful and arrogant.
- Showing impatience and anger.
- Always talking about yourself and your accomplishments.
- Using flattery as a means of achieving your own ambitions.

The Personal Attributes Chart in Table 1.1 highlights 10 personal attributes that are valued in most organizations. Score yourself on each one to identify where you are strong and where you need work. Higher ratings (4–6) indicate agreement with a statement; lower ratings (0–2) indicate disagreement with a statement. A neutral rating is 3. Ratings in the 4–6 range suggest that a person is more emotionally well adjusted. Ratings below 4 suggest a need for improvement. To improve, set long-term goals and establish specific plans for improvement. Check yourself often to ensure that progress is being made. Remember that the most important element in improvement is a desire to improve.

## Table 1.1 Personal Attributes Chart

| Agree | | | Neutral | Disagree | | | Ten Attributes |
|---|---|---|---|---|---|---|---|
| 6 | 5 | 4 | 3 | 2 | 1 | 0 | 1. Thoughtful and careful rather than impulsive and impetuous |
| 6 | 5 | 4 | 3 | 2 | 1 | 0 | 2. Extroverted rather than introverted |
| 6 | 5 | 4 | 3 | 2 | 1 | 0 | 3. Calm and composed rather than anxious and nervous |
| 6 | 5 | 4 | 3 | 2 | 1 | 0 | 4. Optimistic rather than pessimistic |
| 6 | 5 | 4 | 3 | 2 | 1 | 0 | 5. Respectful and sensitive rather than disrespectful and insensitive |
| 6 | 5 | 4 | 3 | 2 | 1 | 0 | 6. Open and flexible rather than defensive and closed |
| 6 | 5 | 4 | 3 | 2 | 1 | 0 | 7. Patient rather than impatient |
| 6 | 5 | 4 | 3 | 2 | 1 | 0 | 8. Teachable rather than proud and arrogant |
| 6 | 5 | 4 | 3 | 2 | 1 | 0 | 9. Self-confident and secure rather than insecure and apprehensive |
| 6 | 5 | 4 | 3 | 2 | 1 | 0 | 10. Honest and forthright rather than devious and hidden |

## Trust

Everything that happens within and between organizations is based on some type of relationship, and the more the participants can be trusted, the better the relationship will be. The following descriptions apply to those who merit the highest levels of trust.

1. They tell the truth, even when the truth is unpopular. They avoid exaggerating and embellishing the facts.

2. They can always be counted on to fulfill their responsibilities and to complete what they say they will do.

3. They do high-quality work.

4. They work for the good of the team or organization, not for their own selfish interests.

5. They make sound decisions based on careful thinking.

6. They act in a socially appropriate manner, regardless of the setting, and always keep their emotions under control.

7. They are sensitive to the feelings of others.

People who are trusted are chosen to work on important projects, chosen to work on teams, and chosen for promotions. Work to earn and maintain the trust of others throughout your life. Being trustworthy will give you many opportunities to be an influence for good in your profession, in your community, and in your home. Never betray the trust of others, because trust, once lost, is difficult to regain.

Ethics is one particularly important aspect of earning trust. People will not trust individuals who are unethical and lack integrity. Ethics are principle-based standards or codes of behavior. They exist to help ensure that individuals, and businesses, operate in a fair, legal, and moral fashion. When ethical behavior is consistently practiced between two parties, a strong bond of trust develops. When it is not, a feeling of distrust undermines all transactions between the parties.

To prevent employees from acting unethically, many organizations develop a code of conduct that reflects their commitment to ethical behavior. Statements like the following are typical for companies' codes of conduct:

*We promote the interests of our clients and never perform work for competing clients without disclosure.*

*We treat fairly all employees and clients, regardless of their race, religion, gender, disability, age, nationality, or sexual orientation.*

*We honor the confidentiality of our client and employees, disclosing sensitive information only with their consent or because of a legal requirement to do so.*

*We advertise our products and services truthfully and avoid making false statements about our competitors.*

*We refuse gifts or other favors that may compromise integrity and damage credibility.*

Just as companies and organizations write codes of ethical behavior, some individuals do the same. You might consider writing your own code to guide your personal and professional work throughout your life. You can find many examples of individual codes of conduct on the internet.

## Conversation and Listening Skills

Now consider your conversation and listening skills, because today's professionals constantly engage in discussions and conversations, from formal to informal. These interactions can happen in the hallway during work hours, in a parking lot after work, or over lunch. To some people, these conversations may seem to be just time fillers, but they are much more than that. Your ability to converse easily will leave a strong impression in the minds of others, so work to develop this ability. The following guidelines will be helpful.

**Assess the purpose, audience, and context of each conversation.** Be sensitive to the difference between simple chatting and discussing a specific business issue. Be aware of the perceptions of those who might be walking by and overhearing your conversation.

**Show interest in the comments of others.** Eye contact, nonverbal acknowledgment, and paraphrasing are all good ways to show you care about what others say and how they feel.

**Be respectful.** Value other people's comments, and make appropriate validating comments when they finish, such as, "That's interesting," or "I think that's an important point." Avoid aggressive put-downs like, "I don't think that's correct," or "I don't think that's an important issue here." If you must disagree, do it in a positive way. First find agreement on some point and then talk about the related point where you disagree. Also, make sure you understand the intent of the message, in addition to the words. You might find that you can build on the intent and not have to disagree so directly with the words.

**Be optimistic.** Avoid negative comments about others.

Use humor carefully, especially with people you don't know well (e.g., in an interview or during the first few weeks on a job). Avoid comments or jokes that are in poor taste.

**Be appropriately assertive in giving your own comments.** Assertiveness is not being aggressive or abrasive; rather, it is confidently putting forth your comments so your own interests and perspectives are appropriately considered.

**Help keep the conversation going.** Ask "5W2H questions" (who, what, where, when, why, how, and how much). For instance, you might ask, "What is your position in your organization?" "How long have you worked there?" "What are your major products or services?" "Who are your main clients?"

**Help ensure appropriate turn taking.** Don't allow one person to dominate the conversation. Help involve others in the conversation. After your own comments or comments by others, ask another person who has been silent, "What are your thoughts about this topic?" Help bring out all important information related to the topic at hand.

As you participate in conversations, discussions, and meetings, be a good listener. Remember six guidelines as you practice effective listening.

1. Really listen. Avoid fake listening—pretending to listen while thinking about something else. Give the speaker your full attention. Be present, both physically and mentally.

2. Be responsive when you are listening. People will speak longer and more completely if the listener demonstrates nonverbal and verbal responsiveness.

*Figure 1.3  Be verbally and nonverbally responsive when you are listening.*

- Nonverbal: Orient your body toward the speaker, lean forward a bit to show attentiveness, maintain eye contact with the speaker, or nod your head to indicate that you understand.
- Verbal: Make comments like "I see," "I understand," or "That's a good point."

3. Don't interrupt people while they are talking. Doing so is rude, and it prevents speakers from giving their complete message.

4. Listen for facts as well as feelings. What other people say and how they feel about it are both important.

5. Pay attention to both verbal and nonverbal messages. To get the full meaning, use your ears as well as your eyes. With your ears, listen to the words and to voice variations; with your eyes, observe the speaker's eyes, face, gestures, and body movement.

6. Test for understanding. After the speaker makes a substantive comment, paraphrase what you think the speaker is trying to say to you. This technique is called reflective listening or active listening. Paraphrases and questions for clarification can address both content (facts and opinions) and feelings (emotions).

*So you're saying Pat wasn't very receptive to your ideas? [Response to content.]*

*In other words, you're feeling much more optimistic about the sales projections this month? [Response to feelings.]*

After you paraphrase, the speaker either affirms that your understanding is correct or clarifies as needed.

## *Networking*

Your conversation and listening skills will help you in another aspect of professional life—networking. Developing a good social network enables you to extend your social reach and leverage your influence far beyond the people you know personally. For instance, if 150 people are in your network, and each of those people has 150 contacts, you have thousands of people to call on for assistance (see Figure 1.4).

Networks consist of two elements: people and relationships. People in your network can be within your organization or in different organizations, and your relationships can be based on personal, professional, cultural, religious, political, or other connections.

The value of networks is that they can be called on for information, for influence, or for help, such as requesting assistance in finding new employment. However, networks are not just to help you. You are also expected to help oth-

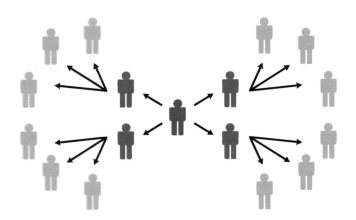

*Figure 1.4  The number of people in a social network increases exponentially with each level of contacts.*

ers. Therefore, approach networking from the standpoint of what you can give, as well as what you can get.

How do you establish a good network? First, consider all events or gatherings as an opportunity to network—workshops, conferences, community events, church events, or social gatherings. Establish new acquaintances at every event you attend. Don't associate just with people you already know, but rather get acquainted with people you don't know.

Second, work on your conversation skills, and stay current on topics typically discussed in interpersonal settings: local, regional, national, and international issues and events; movies and entertainment; industry issues; and sports. Read newspapers or news websites to stay current.

Third, be assertive—greet people and then introduce yourself. Get people talking by asking open-ended questions that can't be answered with a simple "yes" or "no." For instance, ask about where they work, what type of work they do, where they fit in their organization, what their current projects entail, and so forth. Share information about yourself, such as where you work, what type of work you do, and so forth. Engage in turn-taking so you and the other person have adequate opportunity for input.

Fourth, exchange business cards with others so you will have their contact information. Carry a few cards with you wherever you go. Keep your cards current, including your name, company, position, and contact information. Present your card face up and oriented so the other person can read it. As you take the other person's card, take time to look at it and read it, pronounce the person's name, if unsure, and comment on some positive aspect of their organization. After talking with the person, write a memory-jogging note on the business card, such as where and when you met the person and any other information you want to remember.

Fifth, when socializing in large groups, don't stay with one person or group too long. After a few minutes, excuse yourself with a comment like, "Well, it was nice meeting you," and then go visit with another person or group. Look for individuals standing alone or for people in small groups. As you enter a group, listen for a few minutes to capture the essence of what they're talking about and then join in with comments of your own.

Finally, using appropriate online social media (e.g., Facebook or LinkedIn), establish an online network. Enter your own information, including your name, business, position, and other relevant information. Link with others you know so you can maintain contact and communicate with them periodically. Use your network for announcing job openings, finding employment, sending updates about your own employment situation, keeping track of the business activities of others, and congratulating others on their accomplishments.

## Manners and Etiquette

Societies throughout the world have developed different social standards of behavior that encompass good manners and etiquette. Whether these standards and expectations are formally expressed or not, you are expected to abide by them. Failure to do so will result in a loss of credibility and trust. To begin with, understand the following guidelines for social behavior in the United States. As you travel to other countries, consult online sources to teach you about those countries (e.g., www.everyculture.com).

### General

1.  Be on time for social gatherings.

2.  Be courteous and respectful; put the needs of others before your own. Open doors for others.

3.  Thank others whenever they do something for you. Write thank-you notes when others have helped you.

4.  Control your electronic devices in meetings and other social gatherings. Turn off or silence your phone, and avoid using devices when the image on the screen will distract others. If you must answer a phone call during a meeting, leave the room to do so. When talking on your phone in a public area, lower your voice so others don't have to hear your conversation.

5.  Avoid all types of sexual harassment, sexual remarks, unwelcome sexual advances, and all gender-based discrimination. Think carefully before getting involved in workplace romances.

*Figure 1.5  If you must answer a phone call during a meeting, leave the room to do so.*

## Meeting People

1. When you first meet people, listen carefully to their name and then think of a way to remember their name.

2. Shake their hand with appropriate firmness (not too much and not too little).

## Dress and Grooming

1. Dress appropriately for professional events, never less formally than others. Look sharp, even when the dress is "business casual."

2. Avoid excessive jewelry or faddish hair and dress styles that draw attention to you.

## Table Manners

1. Closely observe what others are doing. Take cues from the leader or host. Wait until your host is seated (or invites you to be seated) before you sit down.

2. When you sit down, notice the table setting (see example in Figure 1.6). Use the utensils properly. For multiple utensils, generally use those farthest from the plate and then work inward toward the plate as the meal progresses. After using a utensil, leave it on the plate. Do not put it back on the table.

3. When cutting meat, hold your utensils correctly, depending on American or Continental style. With American-style eating, hold the knife in your right hand and the fork in your left, with the tines facing down. Hold the meat with the fork and cut it with the knife. Then place the knife near the top of the plate, with the blade facing in. Then switch the fork to the right hand, pick up the food, bring it to your mouth. With Continental (or European) style eating, cutting the meat is the same, but the fork remains in the left hand for spearing the food and bringing it to your mouth, with the tines still facing down. At the conclusion of the meal, place your fork and knife in the five o'clock position on your plate to signal to the waiter that you are finished.

4. If you must leave the table during the meal, place the napkin on the seat of your chair. After the meal, leave the napkin on the table (you don't need to refold the napkin).

5. The server will serve you from your left and remove used plates from your right. In tight quarters, you might be asked to help pass an item to someone sitting at the back of the table. Make sure everyone at your table is taken cared of—pass the water pitcher, salt and pepper, dressing, rolls, and other items as needed.

6. In self-serve buffet settings, take smaller portions at first. Make sure everyone has enough food.

7. Before you eat, wait for the host or guest of honor to begin. In a no-host situation, wait until everyone has been served before you begin.

8. Chew with your mouth closed, and don't talk with your mouth full. If you encounter food you cannot swallow, the general rule is to inconspicuously remove it from your mouth the same way it went to your mouth (with a fork or spoon) and place it at the edge of your plate. If others have a problem with food, pretend not to notice. Don't be a fussy eater or complain about the food.

9. In restaurants, remember to leave a tip. In addition to tipping, express thanks to the servers.

10. When you leave, push your chair back to the table.

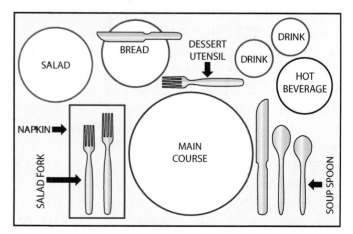

*Figure 1.6  Professionals must understand the rules of etiquette related to a formal table setting.*

# MANAGEMENT EFFECTIVENESS

Many of your workplace tasks will require you to manage and get results through others. The following sections discuss communication skills that will enhance your management effectiveness.

## Understanding Management Basics

Managers work to achieve organizational objectives while striving to minimize resource use and maximize results. Minimizing resource use is referred to as being efficient; maximizing results is referred to as being effective. Obviously, achieving effectiveness and efficiency requires delicate balancing and trade-offs. Sometimes efficiencies must be sacrificed to achieve effectiveness.

Managers are also expected to lead and inspire people to follow them in achieving organizational goals. Different thinking is required for leadership and management activities. On the one hand, leaders look at the larger picture, interpret current conditions, predict future conditions, and creatively chart a course based on their best perception of the future. Leaders develop a vision for the organization. On the other hand, managers focus on organizational operations—on processes and sequences, inputs and outputs, feedback reports and system adjustments, predictability and stability, and efficiency.

As you lead and manage, you can obtain compliance from your followers through both formal power and influence. Part of your power comes from your organizational position, which gives you the authority to make and enforce decisions. Formal power also places you in a position to reward others or to abuse your power through coercion or force. If you abuse your power, you might get short-term compliance, but you will reap long-term problems. Influence is more subtle than power. It comes from having important knowledge and from the trust you have earned from others. When you have important knowledge and high trust, people will follow you without coercion.

Managers are expected to achieve optimum performance and productivity from every resource, especially from people. In performing management and leadership functions, managers must balance their focus on the task (getting the job done) and relationship (maintaining good relationships with people) aspects of the job. Managers who are too task oriented have problems with employee morale, while managers who are too relationship oriented fail to accomplish the task satisfactorily. The most effective managers achieve a good balance between concern for task and concern for people.

## Management Functions

Four basic functions of management include planning, organizing, monitoring, and leading. Communication is critical in all of these areas.

**Planning.** Be proactive. Remain aware of what is happening in your organization, industry, and society, and continually innovate and improve. Set goals. Involve employees appropriately in planning and decision making, particularly when the decision affects them, when buy-in is important, when they have useful knowledge to contribute, or when the experience would be useful for their development.

**Organizing.** Identify units of work and assemble needed resources. Identify roles and responsibilities and then delegate effectively. Explain how and when to report back. Give as much latitude as appropriate. Standardize policies and procedures adequately, without stifling creativity. Show trust; don't micromanage. Provide regular training and development. Foster continuous improvement.

**Monitoring.** Identify and communicate all performance-evaluation measures. Hold regular performance interviews. Discuss responsibilities, agree on objectives, and highlight achievements. Give clear and honest feedback. Resolve performance violations. Solve problems without damaging relationships or morale. Show interest in your subordinates. Visit their work sites. Listen to their concerns.

**Leading.** Clarify your organizational mission. Keep employees informed about company performance. Be honest and build trust with employees. Provide a supportive environment that fosters growth, productivity, and excellence. Empower employees to take needed actions within appropriate guidelines. Give frequent recognition and positive reinforcement. Celebrate accomplishments.

In all management functions, don't forget about your obligations to your own manager and to peers and others in the organization. First, clarify your manager's expectations of you. Second, keep your manager informed about what you are doing. Third, don't talk negatively about your manager. Your negative comments might spread through the grapevine and eventually get back to your manager. Fourth, be honest. Give truthful opinions, but always be tactful. Fifth, be sensitive to your manager's busy schedule. Be efficient with your communications so the time your manager spends reading your emails, reviewing your work,

and answering your questions is minimized. Sixth, give appropriate compliments and expressions of appreciation, both in person and in public.

Regarding all others in the organization, become sufficiently acquainted with them so they know you and know your responsibilities. Keep them appropriately apprised of what you and your group are doing, especially regarding activities that affect their organizational units in one way or another—no one likes surprise announcements that require their time or resources. Finally, always respect the organization's line of authority. Never talk officially with anyone outside your organizational unit without first getting permission from their managers, and never talk with your manager's manager without going through your manager.

### Communication Barriers

Communicating with others sounds easy, but it becomes complicated when it involves large numbers of people in complex organizations. Be aware of several common barriers to communication.

**Organizational Barriers**: The greater the number of employees in an organization, the greater the need for communication to keep everyone informed. Unfortunately, the greater the number of employees, the greater the difficulty in communicating. Every time information is relayed from one person to another, the chance of transmission error increases. Thus, give critical messages directly, not relayed through others.

**Physical Barriers**: Noisy fans, noisy people, distance from the speaker, light on a projection screen, talking by cell phone on a noisy street, and other problems can prevent a person from hearing or seeing important information. Make appropriate changes in the physical setting to eliminate or minimize physical barriers.

**Physiological Barriers**: Communication problems arise when a person may be hard of hearing or visually impaired or when a speaker does not speak clearly. Take action to minimize such communication barriers.

**Language and Cultural Barriers**: Many languages and cultures are represented in today's workplace, creating difficulty in communication. Translate written materials and arrange for interpreters as necessary so people can read and hear in their own language.

**Psychological Barriers**: The human mind causes major communication barriers. For example, emotions overtake clear reasoning in a heated argument as partici-

pants close their minds and become defensive. In such a case, a moderator can step in, clarify concerns, and help calm emotions. Another psychological barrier arises when shy or insecure people feel afraid to express their feelings. To obtain the honest feelings of people, create a safe climate that encourages people to expressing themselves. Still another mental barrier is preoccupation, caused when listeners think so much about another matter that they shut out incoming messages.

**Technical Barriers**: Sometimes messages are sent but not received because of a problem related to technology. Therefore, for critical communications, obtain verification that sent messages have actually been received. For example, "Rick, can you attend a meeting with our senior account executives next Tuesday at 3 p.m. in the Orchard View Conference Room? In that meeting I would like you to take five minutes to describe your analysis of our latest SEO data. Please let me know if you can attend."

## Managing a Team

During your career, you will have multiple occasions to work with teams, some involving only a few people and some, many more. Some of your teams will be in the same department and work face to face, others will be cross-functional teams from different departments, and still others will be virtual teams working across different time zones and in multiple countries with different cultures. Just assigning a group of people to work on a project does not guarantee good results. Careful management is required for success.

As a manager, you must help teams navigate through four stages of development: forming, storming, norming, and performing (Tuckman 1965). Figure 1.7 identifies these four main stages and summarizes what happens in each stage.

### Forming

To select members for a team, look for people with the following types of skills and attributes:

1. **The right knowledge and skills for the task**, including knowledge of the company history, culture, and politics, and skills related to analysis, problem solving, schedule keeping, and communication (writing and speaking).

2. **A strong interest in the specific task** to be completed, assuring a strong emotional commitment.

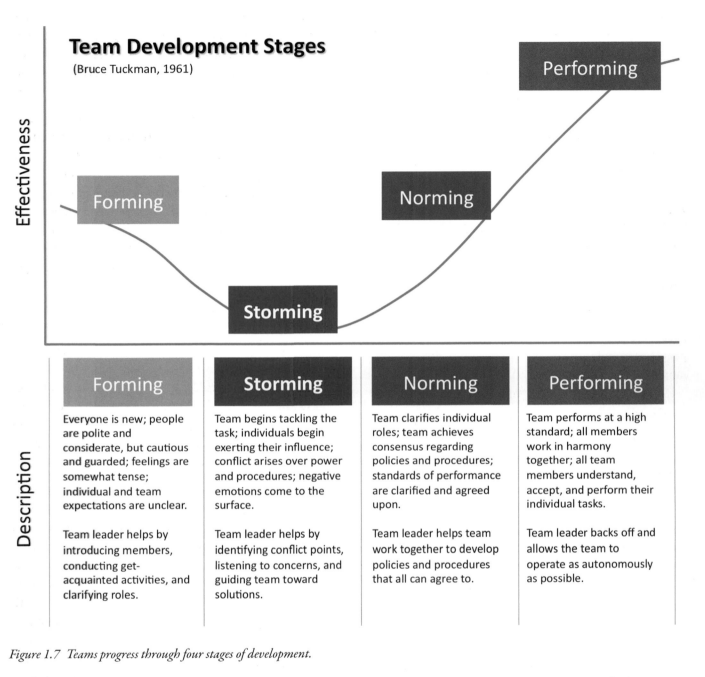

## Team Development Stages
(Bruce Tuckman, 1961)

| Forming | Storming | Norming | Performing |
|---|---|---|---|
| Everyone is new; people are polite and considerate, but cautious and guarded; feelings are somewhat tense; individual and team expectations are unclear. | Team begins tackling the task; individuals begin exerting their influence; conflict arises over power and procedures; negative emotions come to the surface. | Team clarifies individual roles; team achieves consensus regarding policies and procedures; standards of performance are clarified and agreed upon. | Team performs at a high standard; all members work in harmony together; all team members understand, accept, and perform their individual tasks. |
| Team leader helps by introducing members, conducting get-acquainted activities, and clarifying roles. | Team leader helps by identifying conflict points, listening to concerns, and guiding team toward solutions. | Team leader helps team work together to develop policies and procedures that all can agree to. | Team leader backs off and allows the team to operate as autonomously as possible. |

*Figure 1.7  Teams progress through four stages of development.*

Effective teams, especially virtual teams, need people who are self-motivated.

3. **The right personal attributes**. Successful teams require open, honest input; therefore, members must be sensitive to the feelings of each other and get along well with each other. A cooperative attitude, a determination to stay on schedule, and the ability to endure hard times are also critical.

After team members are selected, get them together in a face-to-face setting for an initial meeting. A face-to-face meeting is helpful even for virtual teams, because communication is more difficult when people have never met in person. With no opportunity for face-to-face interaction,

virtual teams may become too task driven, which may produce less creativity, less motivation, lower team cohesion and morale, and an overall less satisfying team experience.

At the first meeting, begin the process of developing good relationships. Invite members to give a detailed self-introduction. Consider having an ice-breaker activity to expose the members' personalities. Ice breakers introduce a social element that is vital in achieving a balance between team tasks and relationships.

Next, move on to the task phase of the meeting. State why the team has been created and what it is to accomplish. Write the team purpose in a document that can provide ongoing guidance.

*Example:* Our team will establish policies and procedures for using social media to market our healthcare products and services, including product research, product introduction, and product feedback.

Describe communication processes. Teams working in close proximity can have frequent face-to-face interaction, experiencing the normal give-and-take conversation that is vital in group work. Virtual teams, however, are limited by the technology available to them for communication. Therefore, clarify how digital interaction and document sharing should occur, such as using services like Skype® or GoToMeeting® and document-sharing sites like Google Drive® or DropBox®.

Discuss work procedures—who will do what work, where the work will be done, when the tasks need to be completed, how the quality will be assessed, and how team progress will be reported. In some cases, management will make these decisions; in other cases, the team members themselves decide. People are generally more supportive of policies and procedures they themselves help develop.

Once team goals, procedures, and standards are agreed upon, consider creating a team charter. A charter states the mission, goals, and objectives of the team—why the team exists and what it is supposed to accomplish. A charter also describes the duties of the team leader and members. It explains critical procedures such as penalties for non-performance, procedures for appointing new members, procedures governing team meetings and communication between meetings, and procedures for processing and evaluating work. Some teams have team members sign the charter. Team charters should be living documents and be revised as needed.

## Storming

The team moves into the storming stage as it begins to actually work on the project together. At this stage, the group members start to feel comfortable with each other, and some individuals may begin to compete for power. Stress the importance of being socially sensitive with one another. Teams that don't get along well will never achieve their full potential. Three general categories of conflict can emerge.

**Content conflict** arises over concerns about how well the team is achieving its assigned purpose. Content conflict is essential in achieving an outcome that meets the highest of standards. Successful teams welcome differing opinions, and members are able to voice differing opinions without relationship conflict. Members of successful teams know they won't always get their way, and they don't become offended or defensive when their ideas are not adopted by the team. Through open dialogue, successful teams make decisions everyone can support. They focus on what is right, not who is right.

**Procedure conflict** involves concerns about what processes to follow. Procedure decisions are best made by dialogue among team members. One vitally important procedure concerns decision making. The most effective teams usually don't make decisions by voting. Instead, they continue in dialogue until they reach a consensus, a solution everyone can support. Not all members may have the same enthusiasm for the decision, but they agree to support it. With successful teams, it is not a matter of *my way vs. your way*, but rather *our way*.

**Relationship conflict** can result from differences in personality, culture, political preferences, or gender differences. Relationship problems are potentially destructive and must be dealt with very carefully. Ideally, relationship conflicts should be prevented by not putting incompatible people together in team assignments and by clarifying assignments. When you have to deal with them, however, always do so with a calm, professional demeanor.

To solve relationship problems, one option is to separate and reassign the people involved. For more serious problems, first interview the people involved to find out the reason for their frustrations. Second, brainstorm for solutions. Ask the individuals for their recommendations. Also, come up with ideas of your own, and get input from others who know about the problem. Third, evaluate all possible solutions, make a temporary decision, and present the idea to each of the parties involved. After getting their input, fine tune the decision as needed. Fourth, implement the decision and follow up to make sure the situation is resolved. If relationship problems become so serious that the two warring parties will never agree to a resolution, you may have to replace one or both of the parties.

## Norming

After storming comes the norming stage, where the team develops efficient and effective ways to work together. Effective norming encompasses the following task, procedure, and relationship factors.

**Tasks:** Team members realize the importance of open, honest discussion about their tasks, and their meetings have a safe atmosphere in which differing opinions are

welcomed and valued. Members are not afraid to disagree, and they do so in a non-confrontational manner.

**Procedures**: Members develop effective procedures for working together—who is to do what, when assignments are to be completed, and how members' work quality will be evaluated.

**Relationships**: Members accept the various team personalities and not only avoid relationship conflict, but also enjoy being together and working collectively on a task they feel strongly about.

## Performing

Once norms are developed for working together, the team enters the perform stage where it becomes most effective. As a united body, the members can accomplish outstanding results. Members feel safe around each other and speak openly and honestly. Diverse opinions are accepted and welcomed. Effective procedures enable the team to perform efficiently and effectively. Quality standards are accepted and self-enforced. Self-motivation is evident in all members, a sense of team pride prevails, and the time needed to oversee the team is minimal.

*Figure 1.8  A sense of team pride prevails when teams reach the performing stage.*

Occasionally teams may become too cohesive, too concerned about group consensus, or dominated by a strong, opinionated leader. Such teams often fall victim to a phenomenon called groupthink (Janis 1972). When groupthink occurs, members hesitate to raise opposing views because they don't want to appear unsupportive, they fear negative peer pressure, or they have too much trust in the team leader or other team members. If left unchecked, groupthink can produce disastrous decisions. Groupthink can be prevented or resolved by maintaining an environ-

ment in which all opinions are encouraged and validated, by methodically examining all viable options, and by controlling dominant team members' influence.

## Managing Diversity

Today's workforce is a rich mixture of people from all walks of life—different genders, different races, different ages, different religions, different nationalities, and different language and cultures. An advantage of this heterogeneity is that input from such a mixture provides a well-rounded perspective. A disadvantage is that some people are bigoted and find it difficult to accept people and ideas that are different from their own.

As a manager, you must rise above this type of behavior and treat everyone fairly and ethically. Hiring and advancement opportunities should be made available to all who are interested, and people should be selected according to their ability to produce the desired results—not on arbitrary factors or prejudices related to their nationality, religion, ethnicity, race, age, gender, or sexual orientation.

In managing diversity, realize that different people use different approaches to achieve the desired results. For example, a woman might be more relationship oriented and a man more task oriented in the way they manage a team, yet both may achieve the desired goals. Avoid becoming too rigid in your thinking, because in many management situations there is no one right way. Your challenge is to bring out the talents and abilities of people in such a way that both the people and the organization achieve the highest and best objectives.

You must also be sensitive to the unique communication needs of individuals, both those within your stewardship and those with whom you deal as customers or clients. Special communication accommodations are often needed

*Figure 1.9  Today's workforce is a rich mixture of people from all walks of life.*

for two specific groups: those with disabilities and those from different areas of the world.

## People with Disabilities

Be sensitive to those who have special communication challenges, such as visual or hearing impairments. The Americans with Disabilities Act (ADA) of 1990 provides legislation to help anyone who has "a physical or mental impairment that substantially limits one or more major life activities" (Department of Justice 2003). The following quotations highlight the critical elements of this legislation regarding communication-related aspects of work.

> Title I of the ADA requires employers with 15 or more employees to provide qualified individuals with disabilities an equal opportunity to benefit from the full range of employment-related opportunities available to others. For example, it prohibits discrimination in recruitment, hiring, promotions, training, pay, social activities, and other privileges of employment. It restricts questions that can be asked about an applicant's disability before a job offer is made. . . .

> Section 255 and Section 251(a)(2) of the Communications Act of 1934, as amended by the Telecommunications Act of 1996, require manufacturers of telecommunications equipment and providers of telecommunications services to ensure that such equipment and services are accessible to and usable by persons with disabilities, if readily achievable (Department of Justice 2003).

As you work with individuals qualifying under the ADA, some may need special accommodations in the communication domain. With visually impaired workers, for instance, you may have to use braille. With hearing-impaired workers, you may have to arrange for a "signing" interpreter. Whenever a new person with disabilities is hired, ask about special accommodations that will be needed.

## International Audiences

You also need to accommodate the communication needs of people from different areas of the world. Be sensitive to their cultural differences, nonverbal communication differences, and language differences.

### Cultural Differences

Cultural variations can be observed in different nationalities, ethnic groups, and geographic regions. When working with an international organization or with people from other countries, consult various resources available on the internet to learn about information such as the following:

1. ***Background***—land, climate, and history.
2. ***Demographics***—population, language, religion, economic factors, education, and employment, and general statistics.
3. ***Customs and Courtesies***—introductions, greetings, social closeness, gestures, visiting, persuading, building relationships, giving gifts (bribes), eating, gender roles, decision making, and dress.
4. ***Means of Exchange***—type of money, exchange rates, electronic purchases, system of weights and measures.
5. ***Lifestyle***—family, dating and marriage, diet, recreation, holidays, and commerce.
6. ***Society***—government, politics, transportation, communication, and health.

By becoming more culturally aware, you can overcome ethnocentrism and learn to appreciate why people from different cultures behave the way they do. For example, Asians prefer to first establish relationships and then move on to the task. Americans and Europeans move more directly to the task. People from Asia and the northern and eastern areas of Europe are more formal in their communication; Americans and southern Europeans are less so. Also, Asians are more concerned than Americans about their organizational and social rank.

### Nonverbal Communication Differences

Nonverbal communication varies significantly from culture to culture. For example, many forms of gesture, posture, social space, and eye contact mean one thing in one culture but something very different in another. For example, children from many Latin American and Asian cultures show respect by avoiding eye contact with an authority figure. In the U.S., this behavior might be interpreted as a sign of disrespect. Further, in areas of the Middle East and South America, people stand very close to each other when

*Figure 1.10  Be aware of social-space differences in other cultures.*

talking. Americans like to have more distance between them when they interact.

Some hand and finger gestures used in a U.S. culture are obscene and taboo in other cultures. For instance, giving a "thumbs up" to a person in the U.S. sends a good-luck message. In the Middle East, it's an obscene gesture. Thus, be careful with finger gestures. The open palm is safe in all cultures, so that should be the preferred form of gesturing in international settings.

### Language Differences

Because of the frequency of international business communications, business professionals need to take great care in creating written messages that cross national borders or that are read by speakers of English as a second language (ESL). Some industries have developed specific rules, grammar, and word choice for international communication. This "controlled English" seeks to eliminate ambiguity and confusion caused by words that won't be understood by international audiences. Remember the following guidelines when writing for international audiences.

*Words:*

- Use simple, concrete words; avoid abstract words and lengthy compound words.
- Use the active voice with strong subjects, vivid verbs, and simple verb tenses.
- Use terms consistently throughout each document. For instance, use the word "transaction" throughout a document, rather than switching back and forth among similar terms like "deal" or "arrangement."
- Avoid slang, puns, abbreviations, and culturally symbolic language. For instance, a worker from the United States likely will understand what a "wild-goose chase" is, but a person from Brazil will not.

*Sentences and Paragraphs:*

- Use simple sentence construction.
- Be careful with question marks (?) and ampersands (&), which are used differently in other languages.
- Keep paragraphs short.

*Visuals:*

- Use internationally recognized icons and avoid any symbolisms and colors that mean different things in different cultures (e.g., black is the dominant color for U.S. funerals; white is the dominant color for funerals in China).
- Create visuals that can be easily understood even without a strong command of the English language.

To ensure that people from the culture, language, or country you are writing for can understand your writing, pilot test your work with a person who is representative of that audience. The extra time and expense will help prevent embarrassing problems.

## Conducting Meetings

Some of the most important business communication occurs in meetings. Here employees engage in presenting, proposing, listening, questioning, defending, and reasoning, and the communication habits and behavior of all participants are played out in public view. Those who can present their ideas well, reason logically, and help bring out the best thinking of the group earn good reputations that work to their advantage in all facets of their jobs. Those who don't present their ideas well, don't reason logically, or get upset when things don't go their way develop a bad reputation. Their social capital erodes, and they find themselves excluded from critical assignments and passed over for promotions and pay raises. Therefore, be on your best behavior in meetings—strive always to make substantive comments, and don't do anything that detracts from the quality meetings.

As a manager, learn how to conduct meetings that bring out the best in the participants and generate the best results. Avoid the following causes of meeting failures.

**Poor planning before the meeting:** Bad meeting time or place, wrong people invited, unclear purpose, or no agenda.

**Poor meeting management:** Too much group input, too little group input, or agenda not followed.

**Poor follow-up after the meeting:** Minutes not distributed, assignments not carried out.

To have effective meetings, pay attention to the details of planning, conducting, and following up after the meeting.

### Plan the Meeting

Good meetings begin with good planning. First, clarify the meeting purpose and describe the results you want the meeting to achieve. Then prepare an appropriate agenda. Arrange agenda items in an appropriate sequence, and make sure adequate time is allotted for items that need significant group discussion.

Arrange an appropriate time and place to meet. Consider people's schedules and work demands. Choose a room that is appropriate in size and that equipped with appropriate technology. As needed, hold an online meeting using remote-meeting technology (e.g., www.gotomeeting.com).

Remote meetings can include a variety of audio and video technology, such as audio devices, screen sharing, or full audiovisual technology that enables participants to see and hear everyone in real time.

Notify all participants. Announce the meeting as far in advance as appropriate, and give all relevant information so attendees can plan and prepare. Appoint a person to take minutes, and send an agenda to each participant. For remote meetings, explain the detailed procedures for making phone or web connections.

Complete any additional planning, such as preparing relevant handouts or slideshow materials and arranging for equipment and food. Develop a checklist to ensure that all planning details are completed.

### Conduct the Meeting

When you conduct a meeting, move methodically through the agenda, paying attention to three parallel tracks of activity: task, procedure, and relationship. The task track focuses on the business items to be covered. The following comments are typical of the task track:

*We've seen a 15 percent increase in product rejects in this part of the plant.*

*What if we merge these two units and have Rob manage them both?*

The procedure track focuses on agenda sequence, voting procedures, time management, and other related issues. Procedural factors may be addressed at any time—whenever it seems appropriate. Comments like the following are common in the procedure track:

*Let's go around the room and have everyone state their key concerns about this strategy.*

*Let's not vote on this today. I think we need some time to think about it.*

*Let's first make sure we understand the causes of the problem and then get into brainstorming.*

The relationship track focuses on people's feelings. Conflicting opinions are appropriate in the task track, but conflict is destructive in the relationship track. Members must learn to interact in a non-abrasive manner. If they don't, people get offended, refuse to go along with group decisions, or sometimes even work against the group. Positive relationship comments validate both the person and the ideas they share, such as the following:

*Ben, how are you feeling about the direction we're going?*

| THREE MEETING TRACKS | | |
|---|---|---|
| **Task** | **Procedure** | **Relationship** |
| Examples: | Examples: | Examples: |
| Define problem | State agenda | Validate a comment |
| Brainstorm | Assign speaking sequence | Paraphrase a comment |
| Evaluate options | Re-sequence agenda items | Draw out a quiet person |
| Develop implementation strategy | Determine closing time | Check on a person's feelings |
| Decide | | |

*Figure 1.11  In meetings you must manage three parallel tracks.*

*Thanks, Samantha. That's an insightful comment.*

Some remarks might cross two or more tracks, such as, "Ryan, you're always well organized; will you be our time-keeper today?" This comment compliments Ryan (relationship track) and implements a time-management element (procedure track) at the same time. Figure 1.11 illustrates these tracks and lists different types of actions that are typical of each track.

One of your major meeting tasks is to facilitate, to skillfully guide the group through a process of problem solving that achieves the best possible outcome. The following list highlights seven facilitation responsibilities.

**Be objective**. Be objective in dealing with opinions, facts, and ideas. Suppress your bias and stress the importance of objectivity.

**Move the discussion forward.** Follow an efficient procedure to launch topics, obtain comments, summarize feelings, and move the group along. Do your best to stick with the schedule and stay on time, but don't be so rigid that you damage the quality of the meeting. To ensure that each agenda item is properly handled, some managers follow a discuss-decide-delegate pattern—an item is discussed, a decision is made, and appropriate tasks are delegated, specifying (a) who (b) will do what (c) by when.

**Foster appropriate divergent and convergent thinking.** Encourage members to express contrary points of view, and use brainstorming to help people be creative and think outside the norm. When sufficient divergent discussion has occurred, move the group to convergent thinking that leads to consensus.

**Create a psychologically safe environment that encourages all members to contribute.** To get full participation, use techniques like a structured go-around,

*Figure 1.12  One of your major meeting tasks is to facilitate effective discussion.*

where every person in turn makes comments about the topic. Bring out the best thinking from everyone.

**Control disruptions.** Meeting disruptions can be caused by cell phones, long-winded talkers, off-topic humor, and more. Work to prevent these problems through appropriate announcement at the beginning of the meeting—turn technology off, keep comments relevant to the task, keep comments concise so all can participate, and so forth. Remind as needed during the meeting.

**Ensure understanding.** Summarize each member's comments to make sure you have understood correctly, and periodically summarize the team's comments to be sure you are accurately assessing overall ideas and feelings.

**Capture critical ideas.** Use a flip chart or a computer with projector to record members' input. Make sure everyone can see and read the comments. Make the text large and legible. Use colors, underlining, and simple graphics to highlight key information.

When the agenda is completed or time runs out, close the meeting. As you conclude, summarize the results of the meeting, restate assignments given, and thank the attendees for their participation.

### Follow Up After the Meeting

As soon as possible after the meeting, distribute meeting minutes with action items highlighted (e.g., highlight individual members' assignments in yellow). Then follow up on assignments to make sure they are completed. Figure 1.13 provides an example of highlighted minutes.

---

**School Relations Committee**
Minutes of Meeting Held on September 12, 20XX

Attending:
- Andy Barton, Chair
- Fabio Giletto
- Kathy Rogers
- Michael Williams
- Cindy Wang
- Megan Waterson

Andy mentioned that our school-contact roster is out of date. Everyone needs to provide all names and contact information for your schools by September 1 to Kathy.

Brooklyn School will be holding its annual Business Leaders  Roundtable on September 26 from 9-11 a.m. Andy, Fabio, Michael, and Megan will attend. You need to arrive at the school by 8:30 a.m. to receive final assignments.

Rod reported that Ashton School wants to hold a case-presentation competition for its graduating seniors. They have asked that we provide case materials for the competition. Cindy will use our recent market expansion project as a basis for that case and present it at our next meeting.

Three seniors from Baskin Heights Community College then gave presentations on their summer internships at our company. All three reported that they had been very pleased with their experience and would strongly recommend a repeat opportunity for three more students next year.

After the seniors were excused, the group discussed their feelings about the internships. Everyone

---

*Figure 1.13  Highlighted meeting minutes serve as a useful reminder of meeting assignments.*

When you conduct a web conference, remember a few extra guidelines. First, prepare well in advance, and send out an agenda to all participants. On the day of the conference, double check the equipment to make sure it is working. Disable pop-ups and other system items that might appear on your screen during the meeting. Also, be sure to start and end on time. At the beginning of the meeting, take time to introduce yourself and everyone else who is involved in the meeting. Finally, make sure everyone has an opportunity to make comments.

## Conducting Interviews

Interviews are like mini-meetings, and many meeting guidelines apply to interviews, including planning, conducting, and following up. Interviews can be held for many reasons, including the following:

- To consider a person for employment
- To obtain information about a problem in the organization
- To request recommendations for solving a problem
- To get a progress report on a project

As you plan an interview, first clarify your purpose. List the items you need to discuss. Arrange the items in a logical sequence. Decide how to record the information you will gather. Arrange for meeting time and place, and notify the interviewee.

As the interview begins, seek for a balance in both relationship building and fact seeking. First, engage in a bit of informal conversation with the interviewee to relax the atmosphere. Then thank the person for coming and indicate the purpose of the meeting. Give adequate background information, and explain the general structure of the interview.

Begin the questioning. Use appropriate questions to obtain the information you need. Avoid disingenuous, leading questions. Leading questions put pressure on the interviewee to answer the way you want, rather than the way he or she really feels. For example, a basic open question might consist of, "How do you feel about Jenny's proposal?" This straightforward question does not divulge your feelings and does not lead the person to answer the way you want. However, if you phrase the question in any of the following ways, the interviewee will feel pressured to give you the kind of response you want:

*I'm not in favor of Jenny's proposal. How do you feel about it?*

*How much of a disruption will Jenny's so-called cost-cutting proposal cause in your department?*

*Don't you agree that we should be cautious about Jenny's proposal so we don't add more stress to our budget during this economic downturn?*

Just as the wording of questions can lead a person to respond in a certain way, your nonverbal communications (facial expressions or tone of voice) can do the same. Both what you say and how you say it are important in obtaining honest communication.

As the interviewee is talking, be responsive, open, encouraging, and nonjudgmental. This will help bring out all the relevant information the person has to give. To ensure that you understand the other person, paraphrase the content and feelings from time to time, such as, "So what I hear you saying is . . ." or "So you feel trapped between . . ."

Avoid letting the interview get bogged down in unproductive side trips or useless details. Keep the discussion productive, providing you with the information you are seeking and moving toward a useful conclusion.

When you feel that you have achieved the purpose of the interview, thank the person and close the interview. If further work or communication is needed, clarify who will do what by when. At the conclusion of the interview, immediately take time to record all facts and feelings that should be remembered for future actions. If you have taken brief notes during the interview, type them in more detail so they don't get "cold."

## Negotiating

Negotiation is an important communication process in business. In spite of its importance, it is widely misunderstood as a process involving conflict between two parties, with one emerging as a winner and the other, a loser. Rather than thinking of negotiation in such negative terms, think of it simply as an interactive process of getting what you want from someone else. It does not, as many people believe, necessarily involve conflict, and it is not a debate, but rather a conversation. Further, it does not always involve money but can involve something as simple as negotiating with your boss to give you the early-morning work shift instead of the late-night shift.

Remember four principles and processes for successful negotiation:

1. Clarify your goal; decide specifically what you want to achieve. State your goal early so it can be an anchoring point for the rest of the conversation. Using this direct approach gets your demands out early, which

influences all subsequent discussion. Make your goal sufficiently high, because if you have high expectations, the outcome will be higher. Conversely, if your goal reflects low expectations, you will usually get far less than you could.

2. Decide what you will not agree to—your deal breaker. For example, if you want a prospective employer to give you an additional $5,000 on your salary, you might decide that anything less than $2,000 will be a deal breaker. Do not divulge your break-deal point during the negotiation, because this will weaken your case. However, do try to find out the other person's break-deal point.

3. Consider alternatives you can turn to if you are unsuccessful in obtaining your goal. For instance, if you have two job offers, you can take the second offer if your preferred offer isn't satisfactory. Mentioning your backup offer gives you additional leverage, because the preferred employer knows that you have another option if your expectations aren't met. Having a good alternative gives you great power; however, don't use it as a threat. During the conversation, focus most of your comments on your desired goal, and hold the alternative in reserve in case you need it when other attempts to persuade have failed.

4. Understand the needs of the other party and then use that knowledge to frame everything in their best interests. Think of negotiation as getting what you want for their reasons. Learn about the other party as much as possible before negotiation begins, but continue to learn as the negotiation proceeds. Throughout the process, try to frame all requests in a way that will achieve the other party's interests. For instance, assume that you have accepted a job offer and want your new employer to pay for a house-hunting trip to the city where you will be relocating. Mention that since you plan to stay with the employer for a long time (which is in the employer's best interest), you want to find the right home where your family will be happy.

If you find that the other person won't budge or is making unreasonable demands during a negotiation, remember that you can always call a "time out" to reconsider what is happening. State something like, "That is very different from what I had been hoping for, so I'll need some time to think about it. Let me call you back in two or three days." You can then think more rationally away from the person and prepare yourself better to address the items you are concerned about.

In all your negotiation discussion with the other person, stay focused on what you want and point out how what you want is also in the person's best interest. Continue to engage in rational discussion, keep your emotions under control, and avoid conflict.

## Holding Difficult Conversations

As a manager, you'll occasionally need to have difficult conversations that you would really rather avoid. Difficult conversations are never easy, no matter how many times you have them. For example, the situation might involve giving feedback to a subordinate whose performance is substandard or talking with an employee whose behavior is causing problems. Your goal, of course, is to achieve a positive change, but this sometimes just doesn't happen. In fact, sometimes difficult conversations make matters worse, rather than better. The following information may help increase your chances of success in your own difficult conversations.

### Factors Involved in Difficult Conversations

Two fundamental factors are involved in most difficult conversations: the attitude and the behavior of the two people involved. The two-by-two grid in Figure 1.14 shows how these two factors affect the conversation.

First, as the red dot indicates, you should have a positive attitude about the other person. Even though the person has behaved inappropriately, you should not think of the person as being bad or having bad motives. Rather, place

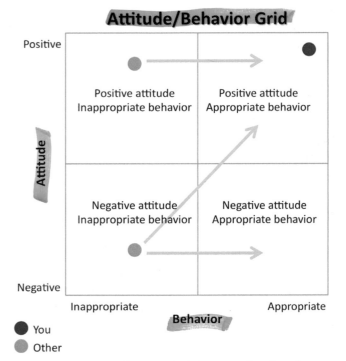

*Figure 1.14 Focus on changing the behavior rather than changing the person.*

## Table 1.2 Negative and Positive Attitudes and Behaviors in Difficult Conversations

| Negative | Positive |
|---|---|
| **Nonverbal communication:** | **Nonverbal communication:** |
| • Anger | • Calmness |
| • Frustration | • Optimism |
| • Defensiveness | • Open mindedness |
| **Verbal communication:** | **Verbal communication:** |
| • Negative comments—sarcasm, blame, put downs, etc. | • Supportive comments—encouragement, compliments, etc. |
| • Attitude-oriented comments | • Behavior-oriented comments |
| • Lecturing about bad behavior | • Questions to seek facts and feelings |
| • Closed-minded listening | • Open-minded listening |
| • Interruptions and put downs | • Paraphrasing to test for understanding |
| • Focus on the negative past | • Focus on a better future |
| • Doubtful comments | • Hopeful comments |

your focus on changing the behavior, not on changing the person. Further, always behave appropriately in the conversation, never allowing yourself to become angry or defensive or to make negative, demeaning comments.

Table 1.2 lists examples of negative and positive communications that can occur in difficult conversations. Because difficult conversations often involve heightened emotions, both you and the other person can easily slip into the negative column, become angry or defensive, and engage in negative communication.

Second, the blue dots in Figure 1.14 show that the other person brings to the conversation either a positive or negative attitude. With a positive attitude, you stand a good chance of getting the person to change and improve as a result of the conversation. In many cases, such a person simply needs to be made aware of the inappropriate behavior, and he or she will change. With a negative attitude, however, your challenge is much greater. You hope for both a change in attitude and a change in behavior, but you might get only a change in behavior with no change in attitude. In fact, if the conversation goes badly, you might get neither a behavioral nor an attitude change. In some cases, the situation can become worse.

### The Difficult Conversation Process

To increase your chance of improved behavioral and attitude changes, start the conversation by thanking the person for taking the time to visit with you. Then explain, "There's a little concern that I'd like to visit with you about today." Describe the context, state your objectives, and explain the problem in behavioral terms: "The issue has to do with our weekly staff meetings. As manager of this group, I'm trying to create a feeling of openness that will encourage participation from you and everyone else in the group. What I see as a problem is that you frequently make the majority of the comments in our meetings, and I'm not getting the benefit of other people's comments." Be sure to frame the problem in a way that it will lead to the outcome you want, and, as stated previously, focus on the person's behavior, not on his or her attitude or character. Obviously, you would not say, "You talk so much in our meetings; how can you be so self-centered and insensitive to everyone else!" Such character assassination will only make a situation worse.

After you have explained the context, the behavior, and the problem caused by the behavior, ask for a response: "I'd like to hear how you feel about the situation." As the person responds, listen carefully to both the facts and the feelings. Then paraphrase to test your understanding: "If I'm hearing you correctly, you sense that the others are hesitant to

participate, so you feel a need to respond more; is that correct?" Continue in open-minded dialogue about the problem until you and the other person both understand each other.

At this point, restate your earlier objective: "As I mentioned earlier, my goal is to create a feeling of openness that will encourage participation from you and everyone else in the group." Then move on to create a plan of action that tells what you and the other person will do: "It seems to me that one way to resolve this situation is for you to hold off a bit on your comments and for me to use a structured go-around to make sure everyone comments." Following that action plan, ask for the other person's response: "How would you feel about that?" Again, listen to the person's comments and paraphrase to test for understanding and buy-in: "So you would feel good about proceeding with this approach in our future meetings?" As needed, engage in additional dialogue to refine the plan for resolving the problem.

When you feel it is time to close the conversation, thank the other person and express your optimism about the plan's effectiveness: "Thanks very much. I really appreciate your taking the time to talk with me today. I think we'll see some nice improvements as a result of our conversation today."

### Additional Guidelines

Before scheduling difficult conversations, plan carefully. Clarify your purpose and objectives, analyze the person and the context, and develop a strategy for a successful engagement. Make a record of the critical facts, including all 5W2H elements (who, what, where, when, how, and how much), and write the purpose as a clear sentence. This statement will serve as an anchor for the conversation. Refer to these notes during the conversation to make sure you cover everything you need to. Because difficult conversations can sometimes get out of hand and stray off the topic, the purpose can be restated to get back on track: "As I mentioned my goal is to . . . so I'd like to get back to addressing that more specifically."

Always make sure your motives are right and are aimed at helping the other person, not just serving your own needs. As you engage in this type of conversation, the other person's first perception may be that you are attacking him or her as a person. However, through constantly seeking for what is mutually beneficial, the other person will hopefully see that your motives are sincere.

As needed during the conversation, eliminate or minimize communication barriers. Apologize if the person points out something you have done to offend. Also, address and try to resolve any inaccurate concerns the other person has about you. An example follows:

*I'm sorry I offended you with my earlier comment. I wasn't saying your input wasn't valuable. In our decision making, I just want to make sure we get as many viewpoints as possible and not overlook any critical input.*

Keep your emotions under control, no matter what—*no matter what!* Even if the other person explodes and lashes out at you in anger, keep your emotions under control. Act, don't react! Be calm, be professional, and continue to move the conversation forward in a calm, confident, and controlled way. Do not cave in to the other person's negative emotions. If you find yourself slipping, however, call a time out and reschedule the conversation for another day so you don't lose control.

Throughout the conversation, maintain a supportive environment in which the other person can feel safe in giving honest responses. Because difficult conversations ask the other person to change, this implies that the person was wrong, and this can damage his or her self-esteem. Therefore, seek for ways to help the other person save face: "I appreciate the good quality of your comments, and I know we can work together to increase the participation by others in the future." As much as possible, make the conversation a positive event, rather than a reprimand. This will help build self-esteem, rather than destroy it.

Sometimes you find yourself placed in an impromptu situation, rather than a planned discussion, where you are asked for negative feedback. When giving this impromptu feedback, do it in a positive, uplifting way. Like serving someone a meal, the quality and taste of the food are important, but the presentation (how it looks on the plate) is also very important. For example, if a colleague asks how you liked the presentation she gave earlier in the day, your negative feedback might be sandwiched between positive comments as follows:

Question: *How did you feel about my presentation this morning?"*

Response: *I liked it a lot. I thought you did an especially good job discussing the need for the proposal. I wondered if perhaps the finance people might have wanted a bit more detail in the budget analysis, but otherwise I thought it was excellent. How did you feel about it?"*

Two final points should be remembered. First, be careful in giving negative feedback to people who are not

under your stewardship. In most cases, negative feedback should come from the person's manager, the one who has the authority and responsibility to give feedback to the person. Second, at any time in a difficult conversation you can call a time out. If the other person isn't being cooperative, or for any other reason, you can say something like, "I think I need a day or two to think about what we've talked about so far. Let's end our discussion for today and get back together on Thursday or Friday."

## CHAPTER SUMMARY

Interpersonal effectiveness is critical at all levels of an organization. Your social intelligence includes being aware of your own emotions and the emotions of others, as well as the ability to manage your own emotions and your relationship with others. Trust is a critical part of interpersonal effectiveness. People who are trusted are chosen to work on important projects, chosen to work on teams, and chosen for promotions. Ethics is one particularly important aspect of earning trust. Companies write codes of conduct to help ensure that employees live according to high standards of ethics.

Develop your ability to participate effectively in discussions and conversations, from formal to informal. As you participate in these interactions, be a good listener. Also, learn about and apply generally accepted social standards of behavior, including good manners and etiquette. Utilize networking to increase the length of your social reach and influence.

Managers work to achieve organizational objectives while striving to minimize resource use and maximize results. Minimizing resource use is referred to as being efficient; maximizing results is referred to as being effective. In performing management and leadership functions, managers must balance their focus on the tasks (getting the job done) and relationships (maintaining good relationships with people) aspects of the job.

During your career, you will have multiple occasions to work with teams, some involving only a few people and some, many more. As a manager, you must help teams navigate through four stages of development: forming, storming, norming, and performing. You must also learn to manage a diverse workforce of people from all walks of life, including those with disabilities and those from different cultures and countries.

As a professional, you will conduct numerous meetings, and you'll need to know how to conduct meetings that bring out the best in the participants and generate the

best results. Interviews are like mini-meetings, and many of the same guidelines apply, including planning, conducting, and following up. You will also need to have difficult conversations from time to time. Two fundamental factors are involved in most difficult conversations: the attitude and the behavior of the two people involved. Focus your efforts on changing the behavior, rather than on changing the person.

## Works Cited

Goleman, Daniel. *Emotional Intelligence*. New York: Bantam Books, 1995, p. 34.

Gardner, Howard. *Multiple Intelligences: The Theory in Practice*. New York: Basic Books, 1993. p. 9. cited in Goleman, Daniel. *Emotional Intelligence*. New York: Bantam Books, 1995, p. 39.

Tuckman, Bruce. *Developmental Sequence in Small Groups*, Psychological Bulletin 63, 1965: 384–99.

Janis, Irving L. *Victims of Groupthink,* Boston: Houghton Mifflin, 1972.

## CHAPTER QUESTIONS

1. List four abilities that Gardner says are essential to social effectiveness.
2. What is stonewalling?
3. List four aspects of trust.
4. How is ethics different from trust?
5. List three ways to improve your conversation ability.
6. Give an example of a 5W2H question.
7. What is a comment with a hook?
8. What is turn taking?
9. What is fake listening?
10. What is reflective listening?
11. Why is networking important?
12. List two guidelines for networking.
13. List five rules of etiquette in the U.S.
14. What is the difference between American and Continental styles of eating?
15. What is the difference between efficiency and effectiveness? Give an example of each.
16. What does "task" and "relationship" balance have to do with management?
17. What is the difference between manageing and leading?
18. List three communication barriers and indicate how to overcome or minimize those barriers.

19. What are the four stages of team development?
20. What is the difference between task conflict and relationship conflict?
21. What is groupthink? How can you prevent it in teams and groups?
22. What is the ADA? How does it apply to business?
23. What is the one safe way to gesture in all cultures?
24. What are the three major tracks of activity that occur in meetings?
25. List three major facilitation responsibilities you have when conducting meetings.
26. What is a leading question?
27. What is negotiation?
28. What is a break-deal point in negotiation?
29. What two major factors are involved in difficult conversations?

## CHAPTER ACTIVITIES

1. Listen carefully to a conversation among your friends, analyze it, and write a report about it. Discuss turn taking and other conversation guidelines given in this chapter.

2. Complete the Personal Attributes Chart. In a small group discussion with several of your classmates, tell about one of your highest- and lowest-scoring social attributes. Share an experience in which these attributes were exhibited. Write a paragraph that describes two or three attributes that you want to improve.

3. Think of a person you trust. Write a paragraph in which you explain what that person has done to earn your trust.

4. Write a code of professional conduct for yourself.

5. Go out to dinner with a group of friends and practice good etiquette. Write a short report about your experience.

6. If you have not already done so, sign up on LinkedIn so you can create an online network.

7. Design a business card for yourself (design guidelines are given in Chapter 11).

8. Your manager has to travel to a different country and has asked you to research that country. Write a one-page memo that summarizes the most important information you find. Conduct research on a country of your choice and write the memo. "(See memo format in Appendix B.)

9. Write five sentences in which you use a figure of speech that would likely be misunderstood by someone from a different culture. Then rewrite the sentences, using wording that would be understood. For example, "The bottom line is that we should adopt the new game plan" could be changed to, "Our conclusion is that we should adopt the new plan."

10. Interview two or three people who are originally from different countries, and ask them to describe the problems they encountered when they first came to your country. Write a short report about their responses.

11. Practice reflective listening in a conversation with another person. Write a short paper describing the impact of reflective listening on your conversation.

12. Analyze your classroom and list the communication barriers you find.

13. Describe a negative experience you have had working in a team setting (such as a sports team or an organizational team). Explain why it was negative, and suggest what could have prevented the problem from occurring.

14. Analyze a time when you have negotiated with someone. Tell what went well and explain what you would do differently if you could do it again.

15. Analyze a difficult conversation you have been involved in. Tell what went well and explain what you would do differently if you could do it again.

# Planning and Organizing Content

**M**any factors can influence the success or failure of your business documents, and one of the most important is how well you plan before you write. Numerous professions develop plans as a normal part of completing their work. Airplane pilots file a flight plan before they fly. Builders require a blueprint before they build. Coaches develop a plan before an athletic competition. Even artists create a preliminary sketch as part of their drawing process. The three images in Figure 2.1 illustrate the progression from a preliminary wire frame to a rough sketch to a finished drawing. Practice using the same basic process in your writing—develop a strategy, create an outline, compose a rough draft, and revise and polish the draft to produce the final document.

*Figure 2.1  Creating preliminary sketches and outlines is important for both artists and writers. (Illustrations by Ward Greenhalgh)*

This chapter covers two parts of that process—planning the writing and assembling and organizing the information. After learning the material in this chapter, you should be able to do the following:

- Perform PACS planning for all of your communications.

- Describe different message strategies and explain when to use each one most effectively.
- Use top-down, bottom-up, and reverse-outlining methods effectively.

## PLAN THE WRITING

Planning is one of the most critical phases in writing. To plan well, complete four steps: determine the purpose of your message, analyze the audience, analyze the context in which the communication will occur, and develop a strategy consistent with the important elements of purpose, audience, and context. This four-step planning process can be remembered with the acronym PACS:

—Purpose
—Audience
—Context
—Strategy

| Strategy | | |
|---|---|---|
| Purpose ↑ | Audience ↑ | Context ↑ |

*Figure 2.2  Purpose, audience, and context form the foundation for developing a strategy.*

To help you understand how purpose, audience, and context factors affect strategy, consider the following three scenarios. First, assume that you are a manager conducting performance reviews. For your first employee you have good news—she will be receiving a year-end bonus. For the second employee, however, you have to tell him that he will not be receiving a year-end bonus. How would that change

the way you approach the two employees? Second, assume that you are talking with a colleague at the water cooler about the new benefits change, and you sense that someone has just come up behind you. You now have a new member in your audience. How would that change your conversation? Third, imagine that you're about to email a client, and you find out that a powerful earthquake just hit where the client is located. How would this new context factor change your communication?

The following sections contain guidelines to help with planning your communications. All four PACS elements are discussed to help you learn the planning process.

## Determine the Purpose

As you plan your communication, make sure you have a clear idea of your purpose—what you want to accomplish. All messages will have one or more of the following three purposes: to inform, to persuade, or to build relationships of trust. Thus, as you plan each message, ask yourself the following three questions:

1. **Inform:** What do I want the audience to know?
   *Example:*  I want the reader to know about my plans to expand my business.

2. **Persuade:** What do I want the audience to do?
   *Example:*  I want the reader to lend me $200,000 to expand my business.

3. **Build relationships of trust:** How do I want the audience to feel?
   *Example:*  I want the reader to feel that I can be trusted and that I am a good credit risk.

Remember these three message aspects by thinking of head, hands, and heart. What information do I want the audience members to know in their head? What do I want them to do with their hands? What do I want them to feel in their heart?

To one degree or another, all messages inform, persuade, and influence relationships, although one of those three purposes will usually be more dominant in a given message. For instance, if you send a note cancelling a luncheon appointment, you inform, but your cancellation also indirectly persuades the person to make alternate plans. In addition, the note might negatively influence your relationship because the person may feel that you considered someone else or something else to be more important.

Regarding the building of relationships, make a habit of sending positive notes to others. Send birthday greetings, congratulations, thank you notes, or appropriate condo-

lences to people in your network. They will do wonders for building and strengthening your relationship with others.

*Happy birthday, Ann. I hope you have a great day. I'm glad you're part of our team.*

*Congratulations, Brandon, on your performance in last weekend's half-marathon. You're great on the job as well as in your personal life.*

*Robert, may God bless and comfort you and your family during this time of grief. Please accept my sincere condolences.*

While sending positive, uplifting messages strengthens relationships, sending negative messages can destroy relationships. Never send a message you have written in anger. Angry messages are rarely forgotten, and they can permanently damage relationships and harm future transactions. If you get an email or social media message that makes you angry, take time to cool down before responding. Then compose a rational message that addresses the topic of concern and that strengthens, not injures, your relationship. Remember especially to be cautious about sending negative electronic messages. They can be quickly created, but once sent they can be on the internet forever. They can be sent and re-sent and re-sent, causing devastating effects that are totally out of your control.

## Analyze the Audience

The importance of analyzing the audience cannot be overemphasized. Each audience has a lens through which it views the world, and the better you can understand what that world looks like to a particular audience, the better you will be able to tailor your message. Don't assume that just writing error-free content will get the job done, because the audience—not the writer—gets to decide whether a message is successful. You may be impressed with a message you have written, but if the audience isn't impressed, the message has failed!

Remember that you might have three levels of audience:

**Primary audience:** The person or persons you are writing to.

**Secondary audience:** People who also need to know or want to know the information you are sending.

**Tertiary audience:** People whom you don't know about but who might receive your message through digital sharing by members of the primary or secondary audience.

For example, Scott Burton is the marketing manager of a small software firm. Scott is trying to develop an online library of articles related to the company's software, so he asks Brianna Gunnell if she will write one of the articles. Brianna writes the article and then sends the article as an email attachment to Scott (the primary audience). Scott shares the article with the company CEO, Kent Swensen (the secondary audience), and then Kent forwards the article to several others who are stockholders and investors in the company (the tertiary audience).

In your first communication with your audience, you might know very little about them, but gather as much information as you can about their demographics, psychographics, and knowledge about your message.

**Demographics:** Demographics can include such factors as occupation, socio-economic status, religion, gender, sexual orientation, political orientation, ethnicity, marital status, and age. Learn where they are in the organization hierarchy, and determine who manages them and whom they manage. Find out how much decision-making authority they have, and what professional networks they belong to.

**Psychographics:** While demographics explain who the audience members are, psychographics refer to why they do what they do. Psychographic analysis examines their interests, beliefs, attitudes, opinions, preferences, and biases, including their feelings about you and your message.

Two opposing forces (positive and negative) may be competing within your audience members' minds whenever they receive a message from you:

Opposing thoughts about your message: If you send a persuasive message to convince them to buy your product, they may want the product (a driving force),

but they might think the cost is greater than the benefit it will provide (a restraining force). If you send them an informative message about a product, they might want to read the message (a driving force), but they might not have the time because of other pressures (a restraining force).

Opposing thoughts about you: Regarding you as a person, they might like you (a driving force) and feel motivated to listen to you just to be nice, but they might think you send them too many emails or stay too long when you visit them (a restraining force).

To be a successful communicator, seek to understand the audience members' wants and needs (their positive, driving forces) and their concerns (the negative, restraining forces). Then tailor your messages appropriately.

**Knowledge:** Regarding audience members' knowledge, find out what they already know about your message and what questions they will most likely ask in connection with your message. Find out also about their technical knowledge and vocabulary so you can know how much you have to educate and what terms and jargon you can use to communicate.

As you have ongoing interaction with people, remember that audience analysis should be ongoing, not just a one-time event. Always keep your eyes and ears open to catch any new information that will enable you to better understand the people you communicate with.

## Analyze the Context

In addition to analyzing the audience members themselves, analyze three aspects of the context in which your communication will occur.

**External factors:** First understand the industry in which the person works. Learn how it operates and understand the challenges faced within that industry. For example, banking, electronics, healthcare, and food-services industries all have different operational concerns. Compliance requirements also play a major role in many industries, such as insurance, banking, financial services, healthcare, energy, building construction, and travel and tourism. Also find out who the organization's major competitors are, and learn about their relative strengths and weaknesses in the industry.

**Internal factors:** In additional to factors external to the company, understand the company itself—its mission,

*Figure 2.3 Learn about your audience and the context in which your communication is occurring.*

history, size, products and services, financial health, challenges, and customers. Learn about its relative strengths and weaknesses among its competitors. Learn also about your audience's department or group—its purpose, products, procedures, problems, and employees, and where it fits within the larger organization.

**Situational factors:** Finally, understand what situational factors will influence your communication. Have you communicated with this person before, or are you initiating the communication? Is this a routine communication or one of high importance? Does this communication involve a large amount of money? Do you want to establish a long-term relationship, or is this a one-time transaction? Answers to these questions, and others of a similar nature, should be analyzed so you can determine how to create your message.

The following information will help you understand the value of knowing as much as possible about your audience. As you read the information, think of how you would use it to shape your communication with this manager, Matthew Good (see Figure 2.3). Matthew works in the home office of a large corporation in California. The company's main product is geographic information systems (GIS) technology. This technology is used by governments and businesses worldwide to analyze geographically related data; the software reveals relationships, patterns, and trends, and produces charts, tables, geospatial maps, and globes. Using the resulting data, organizations are able to improve their decision making and achieve cost savings from greater efficiency.

Matthew's job title is Distribution Manager. In this position Matthew supervises the complex process of shipping products from the company warehouse to over 140 countries throughout the world. All of the thousands of packages shipped out of the country must comply with complex international software, import, and postal laws.

Matthew's office is in the company's warehouse, and he oversees the work of 15 individuals. Part of this group works as a team and is responsible for product assembly, pick-pack-and-ship, inventory cycle count, and outgoing mail. The rest of Matthew's subordinates are responsible for international shipping, in- and out-bound freight coordination, and intracompany shipping, including things such items as computers, monitors, phones, and marketing supplies. Matthew reports, "I monitor email traffic for several of my reporting groups to keep my thumb on the pulse of activity, chime in on anything important, and provide support as necessary." At any time Matthew may receive a query regarding the shipment of a product to any part of the world. Therefore, each shipment must be carefully tracked to ensure timely and safe arrival.

As with all managers, Matthew relies on effective communication to accomplish his work. Every day he receives nearly 200 emails, sends an average of 15 emails, spends two or more hours in meetings, places and responds to additional phone calls, and spends additional face-to-face time dealing with unexpected problem situations that arise. To assist with all these human interactions, the company uses powerful communication software, with screen sharing, instant messaging, virtual meeting, client availability, and phone and voice mail features.

To keep a sense of how everything is going and how everyone is doing, Matthew walks through his department work area several times each day, making himself available if anyone wants to stop him for a question or comment. Further, his office door is always open and his employees know they can drop in at any time and consult with him about their work. Matthew confesses, however, that he is not the "chatty" type of manager—he likes to get to the point, deal with the situation at hand, and get back to work.

Complementing the large volume of communication exchanges, Matthew spends many hours reviewing and analyzing spreadsheet data related to what is being shipped, where it is going, and how much it is costing. He has to be prepared to answer all kinds of shipping questions, such as, "How much of Product X have we shipped in the last six months, broken down by domestic and international?" or "How many customers downloaded Product Y and also requested backup media for it."

With all of this background about Matthew, what aspects of this information are most relevant in communicating with him? If you were an employee in his company,

*Figure 2.3  Matthew P. Good, Distribution Manager.*

how would you interact with him? As a sales representative for another company, how would you approach him?

## Develop a Strategy

Once you have determined the message purpose and have analyzed the audience and context, develop a strategy to achieve the purpose. Developing the best strategy includes both channel choices and psychological choices.

### Channel Strategy

Messages can be sent via different types of communication channels, including face-to-face conversation, paper documents (e.g., letters, reports, and proposals), and a wide array of electronic channels (e.g., phone, text messages, email, instant messages, and social media). Each communication channel can be evaluated on six factors.

**Richness:** Rich channels are those that include the greatest number of message aspects. For instance, face-to-face communication is the richest of all channels, because verbal, nonverbal, and visual messages are exchanged. Similarly, long-distance video conferencing enables digital face-to-face communication, although it is not as rich as face-to-face interaction. A telephone call contains verbal and audio, but no visual component. Text-only messages, such as emails, are the least rich, because they lack the visual component and immediate verbal and nonverbal feedback.

*Figure 2.5  Face-to-face interaction is the richest of all communication channels.*

**Reach:** Both traditional paper messages and electronic messages have the potential for reaching large audiences; however, distributing electronic messages to a widespread audience is much easier than doing the same with paper. Thus, electronic messages have a larger reach. Face-to-face communication is obviously limited in its reach.

**Immediacy:** Electronic channels offer immediate transmission, whereas sending paper through postal services involves delayed transmission and delayed response. Because texting, emailing, and social media offer immediate transmission, they have overtaken the vast majority of messages transmitted in business communication.

**Permanence:** A communication channel is high in permanence if its messages result in a permanent record, whether paper or digital. Permanent messages can be stored and later retrieved for evidence or for review. The importance of permanence varies from one situation to another. For instance, a hallway conversation generates no permanent record, nor is one needed. A thank you note written on paper exists until it is thrown away. However, an electronic message, such as an online complaint about a hotel, is stored permanently on the internet.

**Control:** Control pertains to the degree to which a message sender can manage the audience's use of the transmitted information. Because of the ease of forwarding electronic information, control is difficult, if not impossible.

**Cost:** Communication channels have various costs, such as costs for computers, telecommunications technology, printers, color copies, and postage. Obviously, the lower the cost, the better. In today's world, much of electronic communication is either very low cost or free, which contributes to its widespread use.

So what channel is best overall? It depends! In some cases a single channel may be adequate, but in other situations you will need to use multiple channels. For instance, you might have a face-to-face interview (high in message richness but low in permanence) and then follow it up with a written document (low in message richness but high in permanence) that creates a record of the interview. Also, you might create a slideshow to accompany a face-to-face training presentation you give to your staff, and then you might create a permanent video record of your training and transmit it instantly via email to other departments located across the country.

When sending messages, remember that people are inundated with competing communications—texts, emails, phone calls, blogs, social-media messages, unexpected office visits, endless conversations, and meetings. Hundreds of

messages can be received throughout the day, and people sometimes overlook some of their messages. Therefore, plan an appropriate follow-up, perhaps using a different channel, if your first communication fails.

Also, consider the timing of your messages. For example, phone calls or texts during lunch time or at 5 p.m. are generally not a good idea. Also, sending a thank you note within 24 hours of a special event is much better than sending the same note a few days later. Further, sending a reminder note about an upcoming meeting is a good idea, preferably a day or two in advance so the person can have time to prepare for the meeting.

## Psychological Strategies

In addition to making an appropriate channel choice, you must choose a psychological strategy. Developing an appropriate psychological strategy should take into consideration three key elements: you (the messenger), the message, and the receiver of your message.

**You.** To be most persuasive and effective in your communications, establish trust and credibility, or ethos. As you consistently demonstrate genuineness and diligent technical preparation, the audience will learn to trust you and your expertise. Remember that you must not just *appear* to be trustworthy and credible—you must actually *be* trustworthy and credible.

**The message.** To achieve success you must have a sound message—the message must have good logos. It must have a sound premise, reason, and purpose, all of which must be backed up by sufficient evidence for support. Informational messages must have clear explanations, examples, and details, and persuasive messages must contain convincing evidence and logical reasoning.

**The audience.** Before you can be successful in your persuasion, the audience members must be open to change (and sometimes this is beyond your control). Otherwise, even your best strategy will likely fail. Thus, your persuasion must include appropriate pathos—positive or negative—to achieve the desired emotional response from the audience. Only then will they accept and act on your message.

Take a moment to analyze the psychological state of your audience—their positive and negative feelings about you, their positive and negative feelings about the topic of your message, and their openness to change. Build on their positive emotions (the driving forces) and seek to address and resolve negative emotions (the restraining forces).

After you have analyzed these three factors, consider the following strategic options:

- Direct and indirect approaches
- Head and heart appeals
- Positive and negative appeals

### Direct and Indirect Approaches

With a direct approach you give the main point of the message at or near the beginning, followed by details. With an indirect approach, you give details first, followed by the main point of the message. As a general guideline, use the direct approach for conveying good news or routine messages. Use an indirect approach when you think it would be best to condition the reader's mind before giving the main message, such as with bad-news messages.

For example, if the central message is that a new product will soon be introduced into the market, that message is given at the beginning, followed by relevant details.

*I'm happy to report that our new Product 446 will be officially launched on May 15. It will first be released in New York and Los Angeles on that date, and then on May 20 it will . . .*

However, if the central message is that the company is going to reduce some benefit it offers to employees, the message would first discuss the bad state of the economy and explain that the company is being forced to cut back on expenses. Following a description of the problems (the cause), the main message (the effect) would be given.

*Because of the foregoing problems we are facing, we will be discontinuing our educational assistance program on February 1.*

### Head and Heart Appeals

An appeal to the head is a logos strategy, targeting the logical, rational domain of the reader. With a head appeal, you support your arguments with solid reasons and evidence, along with any other appropriate analyses, explanations, comparisons, and details (including all appropriate who, what, where, when, why, how, and how-much information).

*We should buy Brand X car because it gets better gas mileage than all the rest.*

An appeal to the heart is a pathos strategy. With a heart appeal, you support your arguments with information appealing to the audience's values, beliefs, and emotions, such as fairness, happiness, sadness, pride of accomplish-

ment, or frustration. Citing examples or sharing stories involving emotions is often effective pathos strategy.

> *People need to follow through on their assignments. For example, last Wednesday I had to set my own work aside and spend four extra hours gathering data because the marketing analysts didn't submit their weekly reports on time!*

### Positive and Negative Appeals

Closely related to head and heart appeals are positive and negative appeals. Both positive and negative approaches can be powerful motivators. When you are trying to persuade someone to take a certain action, you can include positive, negative, or both positive and negative reasons. A positive approach focuses on benefits to be gained, whether tangible or intangible. A tangible benefit might be to earn or save more money; an intangible benefit might be to feel better about yourself.

> *Many health benefits can be achieved by eating right and being physically active.*

A negative approach focuses on what the person might lose, such as receiving a costly fine for violation of a law. As with positive rewards, negative rewards can also be tangible or intangible.

> *Obesity leads to an increase in heart disease, high blood pressure, stroke, diabetes, and cancer.*

Table 2.1 can be helpful as you decide on a strategy. Place a check mark in the various boxes that are appropriate for each situation. Check either the direct or indirect order; check one or both of the head- and heart-appeal boxes; and check one or both of the positive- and negative-reasons boxes. Then develop your message according to the boxes you have checked.

#### Table 2.1 Strategy Table

| | | |
|---|---|---|
| ☐ **Direct approach:** Key point first, details after | OR | ☐ **Indirect approach:** Reasons first, key point after |
| ☐ **Head appeal:** Logic and evidence | AND/OR | ☐ **Heart appeal:** Emotion and empathy |
| ☐ **Positive appeal:** What you will gain | AND/OR | ☐ **Negative appeal:** What you will lose |

## ASSEMBLE AND ORGANIZE THE INFORMATION

After completing the PACS planning steps, you are prepared to create an outline. For a variety of reasons, few people create an outline as a preliminary part of their writing. Some feel that it takes too much time, others don't think it will help their writing, and still others have bad memories of trying to outline when they were in high school. Nevertheless, research shows that outlining improves writing and takes no more time than not outlining (Kellogg, 1987).

Obviously, the shorter and simpler your writing task, the less need there will be for a formal outline. For instance, you wouldn't need an outline for a twenty-word email, although a good analysis of the context and audience and clarification of purpose would still be important. For a message consisting of a few lines, however, you could still benefit from jotting down a quick, informal outline that lists in appropriate sequence the content you want to include. Once you create an outline, you can then give your entire attention to composing text and not have to worry about organizational matters.

Developing good outlining skills is useful not only for writing but also for numerous other communication-related activities. A good outline can be used for giving a business presentation, speaking at community or church meetings, providing training, conducting an interview or meeting, recording a lengthy voice mail, and even developing a website. Once you develop good outlining skills, you'll find numerous occasions to use them.

When you're ready to begin outlining, choose from three general approaches: top-down outlining, bottom-up outlining, and reverse outlining (see Table 2.2). Top-down outlining starts with the major topics (categories) and moves to the details. It is most useful when your information has an obvious structure. Bottom-up outlining first lists the details and then groups clusters of related details into major categories. It is most useful when an appropriate structure is not obvious. Reverse outlining extracts an outline from text that is already written. It is useful when evaluating the structure of existing text.

#### Table 2.2 Three Outlining Methods

| | |
|---|---|
| **Top-down outlining:** | From categories to details |
| **Bottom-up outlining:** | From details to categories |
| **Reverse outlining:** | Extracted from existing text |

Because most people are best acquainted with top-down outlining, they see outlining as a process mainly to organize content and not a process to discover, create, or invent content. However, effective outlining can indeed help generate new content and new relationships, yielding value in both the creation and the organization of information. After all, writing is always easier if you have something to say! The following sections provide more information about top-down, bottom-up, and reverse outlining, followed by a method to show you how to test the structural soundness of outlines.

## Top-down Outlining

Two effective methods for top-down outlining include traditional outlining and mind-map outlining. Traditional outlining is the method most people are familiar with, but mind mapping has become much more popular in recent years. Whereas traditional outlining involves working exclusively with text, mind mapping includes text as well as visual elements (most often circles and lines).

### Traditional Outlining

To create a traditional outline, first list the main categories and then list supporting elements beneath them. Identify the main categories with Roman numerals and supporting elements as shown in the following example:

Title: Need for Company Training Director
I.   Increase in staff
   A.   45 % increase in staff turnover
   B.   118 % increase in new order-fulfillment staff
II.  Increase in number of transaction errors
   A.   Financial errors
   B.   Order-processing errors
      1.   Wrong product
      2.   Wrong contact information
         a.   Wrong name spelling
         b.   Wrong address
III. Overburdened line managers
IV.  Need for Training Standards

An advantage of traditional outlining is its familiarity—most people learn it as they go through the public school system. A disadvantage is that some people find it too rigid and confining. Also, traditional outlining is totally textual, and some people prefer to use methods that are more visual.

### Mind Map Outlining

Mind mapping is another top-down process. It is a top-down process because it begins with the big idea and extends down to smaller ideas. A mind map is a graphic representation of the information, somewhat resembling a spider web. You write the main topic inside a circle in the middle of a page and then draw lines to connect the main circle to the first level of categories, which may also be circles (or even other sketches of objects related to the topic). These first-level categories can be used as the primary headings in the final document. The first-level categories are then further connected with subcategories by additional lines (see Figure 2.6). This process of adding more connecting lines and more details can go on for as many levels as desired.

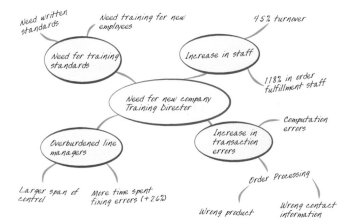

*Figure 2.6  A mind map is a graphical form of top-down outlining.*

Many people like mind mapping because of its visual nature and its flexibility. Because the mind map is visual, the circles may be changed to rectangles or other shapes if desired. For instance, a mind map for a document that will evaluate four different vendors could include the vendors' logos inside four first-level categories. Because they are flexible, mind maps allow for additions in a somewhat random nature as thoughts come to the author's mind.

Visual outlining can also be easily modified to fit the needs of different situations or to meet the preferences of different writers. For example, a tree-shaped mind map can begin from the bottom of a paper and grow branches upward to the top of the page. Or a mind map can be created like a pedigree chart, growing from left to right. Another mind map (fishbone diagram) serves to analyze causes of problems—it puts the causes of the problem as the bones of the fish and the effect of the causes as the head. You could also create visual maps that symbolize a wheel, a house, a family, a three-legged chair, or dozens of other

structures. Creativity is the only limitation on different ways to use visual outlines as information maps.

## Bottom-up Outlining

Sometimes you'll encounter writing situations that involve content that doesn't have an obvious structure. If you try to use traditional top-down outlining in such situations, you might well find the process to be time consuming, frustrating, and ineffective. A much more efficient and effective approach is to use bottom-up outlining.

Bottom-up outlining works just the opposite from top-down outlining. It consists of three steps: (1) Create an unorganized free list of details, (2) categorize the items, and (3) sequence the categories. The final result can then be easily used as a traditional outline.

### Create a Free List

Before you can create an outline, of course, you must have information to include in the outline, and sometimes this can be the most challenging part of the entire composition process. At the beginning of the process you might wonder, "Where do I even start!"

One of the best ways to jumpstart your thinking is to develop a free list. A free list is an unstructured listing of information you think might be appropriate to include in the message. When creating a free list, remember to consider all you learned in your PACS planning. Think of the information needed to answer all relevant 5W2H questions: who, what, where, when, why, how, and how much. Be thorough and detailed in your thinking.

If your main purpose is to inform, think of information that helps to present the content clearly, such as facts, explanations, reasons, definitions, comparisons, examples and non-examples, and stories. If your purpose is to persuade, think of information that shows causes and effects, problems and solutions, trends, data, research, practices of other successful organizations, testimonials, relationships, and costs and benefits. While creating a free list, don't worry about sequence or organization—just add the ideas to the list as they come to your mind. You'll organize them later.

Two other methods of creating content are free writing and summary writing. With free writing, you create full sentences instead of just a list. For example, if you were having difficulty thinking of the best way to solve a problem, you could engage in free writing. You would just put your fingers on your computer keyboard and write the first thought that enters you mind, and then the next, and the next, and so forth, until you run out of ideas. After creating

free-writing text, you would examine the content, looking for ideas that could be expanded, ideas that seem useless, or ideas that could be connected. Gradually you would transform the material into a plan for writing the entire composition.

Summary writing is more structured than free writing because you write the summary in the sequence you would plan to follow in the final document. After writing the summary, you would simply add details to each part of the summary until it becomes a full report. For example, if you need to write a report to recommend one of three individuals to hire, your summary could be as follows. "I have interviewed three people: James, Sami, and Nathan. I like James the best because he has the best experience and skills. Sami is second, with good experience but with some skills that need to be developed. Nathan is in 3rd place because of his lack of experience. Thus, I recommend that we hire James."

### Categorize the Information

After creating a free list, classify all the items into categories. Examine all the items and determine commonalities among them. As you find two or more closely related items, choose a name that describes the items and use that name as the category label. If you are struggling to identify categories, consider the 5W2H words (who, what, where, when, why, how, and how much). All of the information you need to share with other people can be classified into one of those seven categories.

If you have a few ideas that don't fit in any category, you can take one of three approaches. First, if the ideas seem unnecessary, discard them. Second, if they seem important, continue brainstorming for additional categories. Third, if the remaining ideas seem necessary and no additional categories have emerged, place the ideas in a "miscellaneous" category.

To perform the classification process on a computer, type each category name below the main list as the name comes into your mind. Then move related items from the main list down to a position below the category name. Continue this process until all items on the main list are placed in a category or eliminated from the list.

### Sequence the Information

After the categorization process, arrange the categories and the information within them into an appropriate sequence. If your purpose is to inform, the overall sequence could be (a) known information followed by (b) new information. If your purpose is to persuade, the overall sequence could be (a) problem followed by (b) solution.

When deciding on the sequence, think of information as being either non-chronological or chronological in nature. Non-chronological information is stationary, unmoving, and somewhat like a photograph. For instance, you might describe three different laser printers you are considering for purchase. Describing static information involves telling about something at a specific point in time, not over a period of time. A description of three different printers, for example, would probably include their price, reliability, efficiency, print quality, and so forth.

For non-chronological information, arrange the items in a topical order, alphabetic order, quantitative order, spatial order, or comparative order, depending on the information and the needs and expectations of the audience.

**Topical order:** The protein segment of the food pyramid contains the following groups—meat, poultry, fish, dry beans, eggs, and nuts.

**Alphabetic order:** The five sections of the food pyramid are dairy, fruits, grains, protein, and vegetables.

**Quantitative order:** An adult male should consume three cups of dairy products, two to three cups of vegetables, and two cups of fruit each day.

**Spatial order:** For our serving table, we will place items in the following sequence: vegetables, fruits, grains, protein, and dairy.

**Comparative order** (also known as compare and contrast): In our research on dietary deficiencies, we found that Person A lacked in all areas except protein, Person B lacked in fruits, vegetables, and grains; and Person C lacked only in vegetables.

Chronological information consists of a series of happenings, somewhat like a movie. It involves different events that happen over time, such as a few minutes, a few days, or even a few years. It is narrative—one thing happening after another. For example, you might describe the increase of traffic through an intersection over a five-year period, during which a neighborhood grows from just a few houses to a few hundred houses.

**Time-series order:** The average per capita availability of beef in 1970 was 79.6 pounds; in 2005 the amount was 62.4.

**Problem-solution order:** Americans consumed 8.1 ounces of grains per person per day, but only .9 ounces were whole grains; therefore, Americans need to reduce their intake of refined grains and increase their consumption of whole grains.

**Cause-effect order:** If Americans don't adhere to the FDA food consumption recommendations and be more physically active, the trend toward more obesity will continue.

**Narrative:** She began her health-improvement program by adopting the general guidelines of a Mediterranean diet. Then she reduced the size of her portions and eliminated between-meal snacks. Finally, she began a regular exercise program, which included walking four days per week, for a total of 10 miles per week. In six months she lost over 65 pounds and said she felt better than she had done in many years.

No information sequence is right or wrong, but rather is more or less appropriate. Therefore, consider the context of each situation and choose the sequence that seems to be best for the situation.

Now that you understand the three steps in bottom-up outlining, consider the example of Jenny Baxter, a software developer, who has just attended a public hearing in her community. The public hearing did not go well for city council members who tried unsuccessfully to persuade the citizens to accept their proposal for dealing with a troublesome issue. As Jenny leaves the public hearing, she is frustrated with the city council and wonders why they didn't get input from the citizens earlier. Then a thought comes to her mind—why couldn't the city use technology to deal with this problem! When she arrives home, she creates a free list on her computer, quickly typing her thoughts as they come into her mind (see Figure 2.7). She doesn't worry

**FREE LIST**

Technology could be used for public input
People get blindsided at public hearings
City gets pushback b/c it doesn't get early input
25 citizens appointed by mayor
Name: Citizen Advisory Council
Would get citizens involved early
Better decisions
Better buy in and less resistance
City IT group distributes emails, analyzes feedback
Need approval from city council to make it happen
City identifies a problem or proposal it is working on
Sends out request for feedback from CAC
City acts on CAC counsel

*Figure 2.7  A free list is the beginning of bottom-up outlining.*

**CATEGORIES**

<u>Solution</u>
Technology could be used for public input
25 citizens appointed by mayor
Name: Citizen Advisory Council
City IT group distributes emails, analyzes feedback
City identifies a problem or proposal it is working on
Sends out request for feedback from CAC
City acts on CAC counsel

<u>Problem</u>
City gets pushback b/c it doesn't get early input
People get blindsided at public hearings

<u>Implementation</u>
Need approval from city council to make it happen

<u>Benefits</u>
Would get citizens involved early
Better decisions
Better buy in and less resistance

*Figure 2.8  Place the individual free-list items into categories.*

**SEQUENCE**

<u>Problem</u>
City gets pushback b/c it doesn't get early input
People get blindsided at public hearings

<u>Solution</u>
Technology could be used for public input
Name: Citizen Advisory Council
25 citizens appointed by mayor
City identifies a problem or proposal it is working on
Sends out request for feedback from CAC
City IT group distributes emails, analyzes feedback
City acts on CAC counsel

<u>Benefits</u>
Would get citizens involved early
Better decisions
Better buy in and less resistance

<u>Implementation</u>
Need approval from city council to make it happen

*Figure 2.9  Sequence the categories and the items within the categories.*

about sequencing the thoughts at this time—she can do that later.

Once the free list is created, Jenny knows that she must organize all the thoughts into categories. After a few minutes of analysis, she decides to place them into four categories: solution, problem, implementation, and benefits (see Figure 2.8).

At this point, the list is looking more organized, but Jenny knows the current sequence of ideas doesn't seem logical. But what would be the best order? To make this decision, Jenny needs to have a specific purpose, and she decides that she will write a proposal to persuade the city council to organize a 25-member citizen advisory council (CAC). Using an online discussion board, the CAC would give input whenever the council begins discussing new ideas or solutions to city problems. This feedback would improve the quality of the city council's decisions and achieve greater acceptance by citizens.

Knowing that her purpose is to persuade, Jenny decides to organize her material in a problem-solution order. Therefore, she first sequences the overall categories and then sequences the free-list items within each category (see Figure 2.9). With the information in this form, Jenny can now begin to write a well-organized and persuasive proposal.

## Reverse Outlining

In addition to top-down and bottom-up outlining options, you will find occasions to use reverse outlining. Whereas top-down and bottom-up outlining are used before writing the first draft, reverse outlining is used after writing the first draft—which is the reverse of the normal sequence. For example, assume that a colleague gives you a copy of her analytical report and asks for feedback. To evaluate the overall structure of the report, you would like to see an outline, but she says she didn't create one. Therefore, you go through the report paragraph by paragraph and make a list of the content you encounter. That list is a reverse outline. You can then evaluate the outline and make various suggestions, such as rearranging the content, expanding or deleting content, or adding useful headings for easier reading.

You can also use reverse outlining to help you better comprehend the structure and key points of long professional papers, for analyzing the structure of websites, or for capturing and organizing information given in a long speech. Anywhere you are faced with a large amount of text, you can employ reverse outlining to help analyze, understand, or improve it.

## Structure Tests for Outlines

Sometimes you'll work on projects that involve complex structures, such as developing websites, writing user manuals, or writing policy and procedure manuals. Such cases can benefit from a careful evaluation of the information structure. To evaluate the structural soundness of such outlines, you can use a relatively simple five-step procedure (Baker 1994) that methodically examines each outline cluster, or family (a family is one group of parallel categories, such as I, II, III or A, B, C, D). This is a top-down process that starts at the first-level categories and then progresses family by family to the most detailed level of the hierarchy.

The five outline tests are as follows:

1. **Inclusion** (or presence) test: Given the title, heading, or parent of a family, are all appropriate items (children) included? If not, add the missing items or restrict the scope of the title or heading to fit the items that are present. Make sure every family contains at least two children (e.g., A *and* B, 1 *and* 2).

2. **Exclusion** (or absence) test: Given the title or heading of a family, are all inappropriate items excluded? If not, delete the inappropriate items, or expand the title or heading to fit all the items in the family.

3. **Hierarchy** (or horizontal) test: Are the items in the family hierarchically parallel in the correct generation? If not, shift the nonparallel items to the appropriate level (e.g., from the A, B, C level to the 1, 2, 3 level), and make other adjustments necessary to ensure hierarchical parallelism. In most cases you'll find no specific right or wrong hierarchy, because most subject matter can be organized in a variety of

ways. Just decide which organization seems most logical in each circumstance.

4. **Sequence** (or vertical) test: Are the items in the appropriate sequence? Determine whether the family is a noun or verb type, and then decide which sequence seems to be most appropriate for each family. Make this decision from the perspective of the audience.

5. **Language** (or parallelism) test: Are the items in the family grammatically parallel? If not, change the wording to achieve parallelism. Test 5 is important only if the items are used as headings in the final text. If they are not, you may skip this test.

Remember these tests by thinking of presence and absence (Tests 1 and 2), horizontal and vertical (Tests 3 and 4), and wording (Test 5). The five tests can be easily understood when applied to a real family, as illustrated in Table 2.3.

Remember one additional guideline when working with outlines. Try to limit the number of items in each family to six or seven. The human brain cannot easily process long lists. If you have too many items in a family, reorganize the material and place the information into a few categories that can be processed more easily.

This outline-testing procedure is a comprehensive, yet relatively simple, writing tool. The five tests encompass every type of change you can make in an outline: (1) addition, (2) deletion, (3) horizontal movement, (4) vertical movement, and (5) change of wording. Tests 1 and 2 help ensure that the proper content is included in each family; tests 3 and 4 make sure the items are properly located (horizontally and vertically), and test 5 guarantees proper language parallelism.

### Table 2.3 Five Tests to Evaluate the Structural Soundness of Outlines

| Test 1: Presence | Test 2: Absence | Test 3. Horizontal | Test 4. Vertical | Test 5: Parallelism | Final |
|---|---|---|---|---|---|
| Parents: K. & T. Cox | Parents: K. & T. Cox | Parents: K. & T. Cox | Parents: K. & T. Cox | Parents: K. & T. Cox | Parents: K. & T. Cox |
| Brooklyn Williams | Brooklyn Williams | Brooklyn Williams | Brooklyn Williams | Sam | Sam Cox |
| Ethan | Ethan | Ethan | Ethan | Emily | Emily Cox |
| Anthony | Anthony | Anthony | Anthony | Brooklyn Williams | Brooklyn Williams |
| Madison Hyer | Madison Hyer | Madison Hyer | Madison Hyer | Ethan | Ethan |
| Emily | Emily | Emily | Emily | Anthony | Anthony |
| Abbey | Abbey | Sam | Sam | Madison Hyer | Madison Hyer |
| Sam | Sam | Jasmine | Jasmine | Jasmine | Jasmine Cox |
| | Jasmine | | | | |
| *Are all children present? No. Add sibling Jasmine.* | *Are all non-family members absent? No. Delete Abbey, a neighbor girl.* | *Are all members siblings? No. Ethan and Anthony are grandchildren.* | *Are all children in the best sequence? No. Arrange in chronological order by date of birth.* | *Do all the names have parallel structure? No. List all last names.* | *The Cox family now passes all tests. The next-generation Williams family now needs to be tested.* |

# CHAPTER SUMMARY

Before beginning a writing project, complete a four-step PACS plan. Determine your purpose for communicating, including informing, persuading, and enhancing your relationship with the audience. Analyze the demographic, psychographic, and knowledge factors related to the audience, the people with whom you will communicate. Analyze both external and internal factors of the context, the situation in which the communication will occur. Finally, develop channel and psychological strategies that will enable you to achieve your purpose.

As you conclude your PACS planning, move on to assemble and organize the information. For easily structured information, use a top-down outlining approach. For unstructured information, and when you still need to brainstorm your content, use a bottom-up outlining approach. For previously written text that you want to perform a structure examination, use a reverse-outlining approach. For more complex outlines, test the structure to make sure it is complete and architecturally sound.

## *Works Cited*

Kellogg, R. T. (1987). Writing Performance: Effects of Cognitive Strategies. *Written Communication*, 4 (3), 269–278.

Kellogg, R. T. (1988). Attentional Overload and Writing Performance: Effects of rough draft and outline strategies. *Journal of Experimental Psychology: Learning, Memory, and Cognition*, 14(2), 355.

Baker, William H. (1994) How to Produce and Communicate Structured Text. *Technical Communication*, 41(3), 456–66.

# CHAPTER QUESTIONS

1. What are the three main purposes of business messages?

2. List three categories of factors to consider in audience analysis.

3. What is the difference between demographic and psychographic analysis?

4. Explain primary, secondary, and tertiary audiences.

5. List two general categories of factors to consider in context analysis.

6. What is message richness?

7. Explain ethos, logos, and pathos.

8. When would you use a direct approach? An indirect approach?

9. What is the difference between head and heart appeals?

10. Give an example of a positive appeal and an example of a negative appeal.

11. What is the difference between top-down and bottom-up outlining?

12. What is reverse outlining? When is it used?

13. Should you create an outline for all written messages? Why or why not?

14. What is a mind map? How does it differ from a traditional top-down outline?

15. List the three steps in creating a bottom-up outline.

16. What is the difference between free listing, free writing, and summary writing?

17. What are the two broad categories of sequencing?

18. What is spatial order?

19. What is the difference between the inclusion and exclusion structure tests?

# CHAPTER ACTIVITIES

1. Assume that you want to sell your personal car, bicycle, or motorcycle to another student. Perform an audience and context analysis and then develop a strategy that you think be most effective. Submit all of this information in a one-page report to your instructor.

2. Assume that you want to persuade an older relative or friend to contribute $100 to the general scholarship program at your college. Perform an audience and context analysis and then develop a strategy that you think would be most effective. Submit all of this information in a one-page report to your instructor.

3. Assume that you want to persuade the other students at your school to vote in the next election. Perform an audience and context analysis and then develop a strategy that you think would be most effective. Submit all of this information in a one-page report to your instructor.

4. How would you sequence each of the following types of information?

   a. An analysis of your school's win-loss record in last year's basketball games

   b. An analysis of the busiest automobile-traffic intersections in your city

   c. An evaluation of the ten best MBA programs in the country

   d. A description of the parks in your city

e. A description of the two finalists in a national athletic competition (e.g., NCAA basketball)

f. The enrollment trend in your college during the past 10 years

g. A description of a traffic accident that you witnessed first hand

h. A description of the benefits of going to college

i. A description of the steps to take in preparing for a telephone job interview

j. A description of the effects of cigarette smoking

5. Create a table that shows the relative message richness of email, telephone conversation, and face-to-face meetings. List the message-richness factors in the left column of your table, and list the three options across the top row. Rate each of the options on a scale of 1 to 5, with 5 being the highest rating.

6. Using a bottom-up approach, develop an outline for writing a public-relations document on the benefits of attending your college or university. Assume the audience for your message is high school students throughout your state.

7. Create a visually rich mind map that you could use as an outline for describing your favorite sport or hobby to a person who knows nothing about the topic.

8. Describe the channel and strategy you would use in each of the following situations:

a. You are a college student; convince a friend to go play golf with you on Saturday.

b. You are a college student; tell your friend why you cannot go play golf with him or her on Saturday.

c. You are a manager; tell a person you interviewed last week that you are not going to hire him.

d. You are a manager; tell a person you interviewed last week that you are going to hire him.

e. You are a banker; tell a college student that her application for an auto loan has been disapproved.

f. You are a college graduate; persuade an employer whom you don't know to hire you.

g. You are the president of a student club; persuade a local business leader to speak at a club meeting.

9. The following football-concussion outline is taken from Wikipedia[1]. Using the five outline structure tests, analyze and evaluate this outline. Then develop your own outline that you think is superior and tell why you think it is superior.

Title: Concussions in American Football

I. Concussions in the National Football League
    1. Federal NFL Concussion Litigation
    2. Kansas City Chiefs concussion lawsuit
II. Concussions in college football
III. Concussions in other leagues
    A. Canadian Football League
    B. Arena Football League
    C. Youth football
    D. Concussions in high school football
IV. Prevention efforts
    A. NFL
V. Screening procedures
VI. Recovery efforts

---

1 Outline taken from http://en.wikipedia.org/wiki/Concussions_in_American_football, 11 February 2015.

# Composing Business Messages

Chapter 3 builds on the planning process explained in Chapter 2. The focus is on composing—the work of creating sentences out of words, paragraphs out of sentences, and complete messages out of paragraphs. Just as great oil paintings require the artist to apply thousands of tiny paint strokes, a written document also requires someone to create the text word by word, with each small detail making a contribution to the total document. Obviously, the more words you have in your vocabulary, the more options you have for expressing your thoughts.

Good writing, however, is not just about choosing words. It can involve hours of pondering and multiple attempts at composing, deleting, adding, revising, and proofreading. It can involve all kinds of emotions, from frustration to satisfaction. And after all that, it is the reader, not the writer, who determines whether all the words, sentences, and paragraphs succeed or fail.

*Figure 3.1 The reader, not the writer, determines whether a message is successful.*

In spite of all the complexities of composition, good writing is based on timeless procedures and principles that can be learned. As you learn and apply those procedures and principles, your writing effectiveness and efficiency will improve.

After studying this chapter, you should be able to do the following:

- Follow appropriate writing patterns, including OABC, in writing messages.
- Use direct and indirect approaches effectively.
- Write well-constructed paragraphs.
- Strengthen the content in both informative and persuasive messages.

## FOLLOW AN APPROPRIATE PATTERN

Composing business messages can be enhanced by following an effective writing pattern. A pattern is like a generic outline, and knowing about different patterns can increase your composition speed and improve the quality and readability of your messages. Rather than embarking on each writing task as a brand new adventure, you'll find that a few common patterns can be used again and again, saving you time and enhancing your writing effectiveness. The details of each situation will be different, but the generic information structure does not need to be.

For very short messages, patterns are simple and uncomplicated, such as those sent on mobile devices or through social media. For one-sentence messages, the main

message will, of course, be included in that one sentence. For short messages of a few sentences, you should usually give the main message at the beginning. Then follow with any necessary details.

The following short text messages illustrate the direct approach, with the main message or idea coming first and any supporting details coming afterward.

*Matt, may we reschedule our Thursday 2 p.m. meeting to Friday at 2? My dad is in town on Thursday, and I want to spend the afternoon with him.*

*Jake, please send me your thoughts re. Elena Alexander's interview yesterday. Do you think she fills our requirements? I am especially interested in your comments re. her interpersonal skills.*

*Julie, sorry I won't be able to join you for lunch today. I just got assigned to write a news release with a 2 p.m. deadline.*

*Caitlin, I'm going to be about 15 minutes late for our 4 p.m. meeting. Stuck in slow traffic at 43rd Street. Will get there ASAP.*

Notice that each of the messages is direct, clear, conversational, and cordial. They all provide answers to the critical 5W2H questions—who, what, where, when, why, how, and how much.

Microblog messages will be much the same length. However, they will not be as personal because you are broadcasting before a somewhat unknown large audience, hoping to get a response from a few.

*Last chance for 25% off smart-phone desk stand. Expires tonight at midnight. Use code SMART-2BUY.*

*Enhance the effectiveness of your personal networking. Don't push your qualifications until you first build a relationship.*

In cases where you need to give some explanatory details before the main message, use an indirect approach, as shown in the following messages.

*Jenna, I received the attached email from a potential customer in Virginia. I think you are better equipped to answer her message than I. Will you take it from here?*

*Andrew, thanks for your invitation to your personal finance seminar on June 11. Unfortunately, I'm going to be in England from June 3 to June 16 so I'll not be able to attend. I hope it goes well for you.*

*Juan, I have been asked to be in charge of planning our annual department summer party to be held Saturday morning, July 18. I need a good assistant to work with me on this project. Would you be willing and able to help me with that?*

These messages give relevant background information before the main message, because giving the main message first might be a bit too abrupt, as shown in these openings:

*Jenna, will you answer the attached email?* [Jenna initially thinks, why me? What a strange request! You should answer your own email. I don't know what you're talking about.]

*Andrew, I can't attend your seminar.* [Andrew initially thinks you just don't want to attend.]

*Juan, will you be my assistant for our upcoming party?* [Juan initially thinks, I don't know what you're talking about. What party?]

You can see that giving background information first is the best option in some cases. Thus, as you write very short messages, decide whether to follow a direct or indirect pattern. Then just fill in the relevant 5W2H details. The resulting message should be clear, logical, and effective.

For longer messages, you have more details to include and, as a result, more pattern options. Table 3.1 gives a list of some of these different options.

Most of these patterns can fit neatly into a more generic, easy-to-remember pattern called OABC—opening, agenda, body, and closing. The opening, obviously, is the first item in all types of messages, including all those listed in Table 3.1. The agenda is a preview, or forecast, of the information to be given in the body. The body gives the details promised by the agenda (e.g., details, reasons, explanations). The closing gives an appropriate ending, which varies according to the nature of the message (e.g., action ending, benefits, recommendations). The OABC pattern may not be a good fit for all messages you write, but it will be helpful for many (see Table 3.2).

Most writers include an opening, body, and closing in their messages, but few include an agenda after the opening. Including an agenda helps the writer to create messages that are clear and well organized, and it helps the audience in reading and understanding the message. The following section gives more detail about the OABC writing pattern.

## Opening

The opening presents background and context information to the reader. It indicates why you are writing and

## Table 3.1  Optional Writing Patterns

| Situation | Writing Pattern |
| --- | --- |
| To give good news | Good news → Details → Closing |
| To give bad news | Neutral opening → Reasons → Bad news → Closing |
| To ask a person to speak at a professional meeting | Request → Explanation of 5W2H details → Action ending |
| To persuade a vendor to cancel an incorrect billing | Request → Reasons → Action ending |
| To summarize the minutes of a meeting | Chronological narrative of agenda item 1, 2, 3, etc. |
| To teach someone a new process | Big picture → New procedure → Benefits |
| To return a faulty product and request a refund | Purchase information → Problems → Refund request |
| To write a sales letter | Attention → Interest → Desire → Action ending |
| To report the results of a performance audit | Results → Positive and negatives → Recommendations |
| To recommend a change in processing orders | Current process → Problems → Recommendations |

explains why the message is relevant to the reader. Openings may contain any of the following kinds of information:

- Background information related to the topic
- Justification or reason for the text
- An attention getter, or hook

For routine and good-news messages, use a direct approach and get to the point quickly. For example, you might begin with (a) the reason for the message, (b) a recommendation you are making, (c) an answer to a previous communication, or (d) other information appropriate to the situation. Here are four example openings that immediately address the main idea:

*I am happy to provide you with answers to the employment questions you asked in your July 13 letter.*

*Since February 1, we have lost three major accounts because of our late product deliveries. I'm convinced that we need to implement the procedures used in our Atlanta operations.*

*After months of work, I'm pleased to report that the details have been finalized for our new retirement program.*

*Since talking with you in Omaha last week, I have thought a lot about the idea of acquiring the Bronson property. At this point, I'm not convinced that such a move would be in our best interest.*

For bad-news messages, use an indirect approach which refers to the reason for the message but does not give the bad news. An opening like "Thank you for writing about the problems you've had with the ABC printer" would be followed by the reasons for the bad news, which would then be followed by the bad news. Table 3.1 provides some general guidelines for various types of business messages.

Remember that different writing situations require different kinds of openings, both in content and length. Therefore, develop your opening to fit the purposes of your message, context, and audience.

## Agenda

The agenda is a preview, or road map, of the body of the message. If you create a good outline before you write, the agenda can come directly from the main points of the outline. Agendas provide a smooth bridge, or transition, to the subsequent text.

Agendas can (1) quantify—tell the number of key content units; (2) identify—specify the subject matter that follows, like a small table of contents; (3) organize—explain the order or arrangement of the following content units; or (4) symbolize—create a visual mental image. The following examples illustrate these four types of agendas.

1. **Quantify.** Disaster can occur night or day and without warning. It can force you from your neighborhood or confine you to your home. It can result in loss of water, gas, electricity, or telephones and cause major disruptions in normal daily routines. Local public safety officials and relief workers can be called on to help, but they cannot reach everyone right away, especially if the disaster is widespread. The following information describes *three* steps your family can take to prepare for disasters.

## Table 3.2 Types, Approaches, and Guidelines for Composing Correspondence

| Message Type | Approach | Examples | Guidelines |
|---|---|---|---|
| **Good news** | Direct | Announce a promotion<br><br>Grant a request<br><br>Announce the achievement of a sales goal | **Opening:** Give the main idea.<br><br>**Agenda:** As appropriate, forecast the body text, revealing its content and/or structure.<br><br>**Body:** Develop the body content.<br><br>**Closing:** Close as appropriate, perhaps referring back to the good news given at the beginning. |
| **Routine** | Usually direct | Ask for clarification about a policy or procedure<br><br>Announce an upcoming meeting<br><br>Request permission to attend a conference<br><br>Request permission to make a purchase<br><br>Deny a minor request | **Opening:** Give the main idea, sometimes giving a sentence or two of appropriate introduction before the main idea.<br><br>**Agenda:** Forecast the key body information, revealing its content and/or structure. Consider enhancing the visual access of the agenda items with (a), (b), (c), etc.<br><br>**Body:** Develop the body information to fulfill the agenda.<br><br>**Closing:** Close with content appropriate to the subject matter. |
| **Sales or mild persuasion** | Usually quite direct | Convince a person to buy your product or idea<br><br>Convince a person to make payment on a financial account.<br><br>Persuade a person to accept a different point of view on a matter that has limited risk | **Opening:** Hook the reader's attention with content that interests the reader. Then introduce the key message.<br><br>**Agenda:** Use an agenda if appropriate (such as introducing key features and/or benefits explained in the body).<br><br>**Body:** Develop the key features and/or benefits, and include logically or emotionally persuasive content as appropriate.<br><br>**Closing:** Emphasize the action you want the reader to take. |
| **Difficult persuasion** | Usually indirect | Convince people to change their mind about a difficult issue<br><br>Persuade people to participate in something in which they have little interest<br><br>Convince people to take action on a controversial issue | **Opening:** Effectively frame the troublesome issue or problem being addressed, but don't give the key message yet.<br><br>**Agenda:** Use an agenda if appropriate to provide structure for the body content.<br><br>**Body:** Explain your reasoning or other relevant content; then state your key point. Highlight the positives and minimize the negatives of your argument. As relevant, highlight the negatives and minimize the positives of other perspectives.<br><br>**Closing:** Reinforce the key message, and request appropriate action. |
| **Bad news** | Usually indirect | Deny a person's employment request<br><br>Announce the elimination of an employee benefit<br><br>Announce the firing of an employee<br><br>Place an employee on probation<br><br>Deny a product-adjustment request | **Opening:** Begin with content appropriately related to the main idea, but don't give the bad news yet.<br><br>**Agenda:** Omit the agenda (or give a very general agenda).<br><br>**Body:** Give your reasoning that logically leads to the bad news. State the bad news with as little negative language and negative feeling as possible, perhaps visually burying it in the middle of a paragraph. Highlight any positive information as appropriate.<br><br>**Closing:** Try to suggest possible alternatives to help the reader, or give other relevant content that is as positive as appropriate. |

2. **Identify.** Prepare for potential disasters by (a) *identifying the risks*, (b) *developing a plan*, and (c) *rehearsing the plan on a regular basis*.

3. **Organize.** The following text describes the steps you should take to be prepared, given *in order of occurrence*.

4. **Symbolize.** The following text describes the steps you should take to be prepared, given as *three points on a triangle*.

Figure 3.2 provides an example of a good-news message that employs a direct approach and includes all parts of the OABC pattern. It begins with the good news, which is followed by an agenda that forecasts two body parts. Following the two-part body, the message closes on a positive note that reinforces the good news.

Figure 3.3 shows an agenda being used in an email. This agenda quantifies the body parts and uses an acronym (DOCS) as a symbol to prepare the reader's mind for receiving the body information.

Another option is to combine agenda types, such as, "The following information describes three steps your family can take to prepare for disasters—identify the risks, develop a plan, and rehearse the plan—given in order of occurrence." This example combines three agenda types (quantify, identify, and organize) into a single agenda.

For bad-news messages, you might decide not to use an agenda at all. If you do include one, however, be sure not to state anything specific about the bad news that will follow:

No:  The following reasons explain why we decided to deny your request.

Yes:  The following information explains what we found when we analyzed your claim.

As you can see, all agenda types prepare the reader's mind to receive the body information in the systematic way you present it. After reading the agenda, the audience is better prepared to read, process, and understand the information in the body.

Another advantage of using an agenda is that it fits with reader behavior in today's fast-paced, too-much-email-too-little-time business environment. Many readers read the first few lines of an email to get the essence of the message

---

To:  Jarret Bender

From:  Samuel H. O'Brien
Vice President, Public Relations

Date:  October 3, 20XX

Re:  EMPLOYEE OF THE YEAR

*Good news at the beginning*

I am pleased to announce that you have been selected as our *20XX Employee of the Year*! I congratulate you on being chosen for this prestigious award. Your award will be announced on November 13 at our annual employee awards banquet, held in the Marriott Hotel Grand Ballroom. An opening reception will be at 6:00 p.m., to be followed by the banquet at 6:30 p.m.

To give you appropriate recognition, our awards committee needs two items:  — *Agenda*

*Body*

First, a member of our public relations staff will interview you and write a short biographical sketch for the printed program. During the interview she will give you additional details about the awards banquet.

Second, our company photographer will call to arrange for a photo shoot in the next two weeks.

I again congratulate you on this prestigious award. You have been a valued contributor to our company's success for 14 years, and we are happy to be able to honor you in this way.

*Closing*

Attachment: Copy of last year's printed program

*Figure 3.2 An OABC message includes an agenda that forecasts the body of the message.*

To: Tony Martinez

Cc:

Bcc:

*Specific subject*

Subject: Report of Business Writing Workshop

Attachments:

Tony, —— *Name makes email personable*                    —— *Cordial opening*

Thank you for allowing me to attend the recent business-writing workshop in Dallas, Texas. Because of my responsibilities in customer service, the training was very beneficial. Here are four key highlights of the training, captured with the acronym DOCS. —— *Agenda*

*Paragraph headings in all caps for easy reading*

DESIGN. Written messages are more than just words on paper— messages should be visually enhanced to help them achieve good "eye appeal." Using appropriate headings, art and visuals, typography, and spacing will provide for an improved reading experience.

ORGANIZATION. Written messages should be well organized. While disorganized messages create confusion in the minds of readers, well-structured messages provide a clear architecture for understanding.

CONTENT. The content of messages should be clear, complete, correct, and compelling. Further, the content of paragraphs should meet the highest standards of excellence.

SENTENCES. Sentences should be edited and proofread so they reflect good structure, comply with punctuation rules, avoid grammar errors, utilize appropriate language style, and avoid excessive length.

Thanks again for your support in my work. I hope my new learning will enable me to achieve even higher levels of job performance.

Robyn Perkins —— *Name indicates end of email*

*Figure 3.3 Multiple agenda types may be combined into one message agenda.*

and then only skim the remaining text. Using an "identify" type agenda, you can quickly highlight the key supporting points of a persuasive message or the relevant detail points of an informative message.

As you consider the use of agendas, remember three additional guidelines. First, write your agendas so they don't interrupt the flow of communication. The first of the following three agenda examples is wordy and mechanical sounding; the second and third examples flow more smoothly and reflect more stylistically effective approaches:

*Wordy and mechanical:* I will now cover three main topics in this email. They are as follows: (a) social security, (b) health care, and (c) personal savings.

*Acceptable style:* When you plan for retirement, evaluate your social security, health care, and personal savings.

*Acceptable style:* When you plan for retirement, evaluate the three areas of social security, health care, and personal savings.

Second, if you want to emphasize the agenda, consider

the following three examples, with each example increasing in emphasis:

*Use bolding and/or italics:*

Let me explain the *knowledge, skills,* and *experience* required for the supply-chain manager position.

*Insert alphabetic or numeric markers in front of each agenda item:*

Let me explain the (a) knowledge, (b) skills, and (c) experience required for the supply-chain manager position.

*Arrange agendas vertically, with each agenda item preceded by a bullet* (this would be most appropriate for long reports):

Let me explain the three categories of requirements of the supply-chain manager position:

- Knowledge
- Skills
- Experience

Third, in addition to using agendas in your writing, consider using them in other communication situations— in phone calls, interviews, meetings, formal business presentations, and numerous other situations. For example, as you plan a phone call, take 20 seconds to jot down the two or three main points you need to communicate. Then as you make the phone call, whether you talk to the other person directly or leave a message, you will be fluent and well organized. Consider this phone message:

*Hi, Mia; this is Adrian Silva. Sorry I missed you. I just need to mention two things. First, I'm planning a staff meeting for next Monday at 9 a.m. That is one hour earlier than we usually have the meeting. Second, in that meeting would you be willing to share what you learned at last week's SHRM conference in Dallas? If you could just take about 10 minutes to highlight a handful of your key take-aways from that conference, I would really appreciate it. Give me a call when you get this message. Thanks.*

This message inserts an agenda at the beginning and then follows with the use of "first" and "second" to mark the

two segments of the conversation. Following this approach will help Mia easily understand and remember the message, and she will appreciate how clear and easy the message is to follow. The same approach can be used in other situations mentioned, such as beginning an interview or meeting with, "Today we need to cover three main items. . . ." As you learn how to use agendas, you'll find countless situations where they can help you be clear and well organized in your delivery. Further, you'll often find that your well-organized messages are answered by well-organized replies, which will make your own reading easier.

## Body

The body follows the agenda and usually comprises the largest portion of the text—often as much as 80 to 90 percent of the total. The body logically follows the agenda, and the content comes from your outline. For example, an agenda forecasting a trend analysis might be followed by numeric data organized in chronological order (year 1, year 2, year 3, etc.). An agenda that forecasts an evaluation of three job applicants might be followed by three paragraphs describing the applicants in best, second-best, and third-best order. Finally, a bad-news agenda would be followed by the reasoning that leads to the bad news.

### Information Standards

Because the body contains such vital information, make sure the information meets the highest of standards, including the following five:

**Clear**: The message must be logical, well organized, coherent, and easy to understand.

**Complete**: The content must include all the 5W2H details needed by the audience, without violating the principle of conciseness.

**Correct**: The information must contain no misleading information or factual errors, and it must appropriately cite the source of all borrowed material.

**Considerate**: The writing should be cordial and do everything reasonably possible to help the reader.

**Convincing**: The material must be relevant and persuasive, and it must achieve the purpose of the message.

Having someone else read your messages will help ensure that your information is meeting all five of these important standards, especially if you ask them to review the material from the audience's perspective.

### Paragraph Standards

To help you compose organized paragraphs for the body of a document, remember five important standards: organization, unity, coherence, development, and length (arranged differently, these standards can be remembered with the acronym CLOUD).

#### Organization

Generally use a direct approach in paragraphs, with a topic sentence leading the way. In a way, you can think of a topic sentence as a mini-agenda for the paragraph. Feel free to also add a summarizing sentence at the end of the paragraph as appropriate. To check your document for direct-paragraph organization, skim through the document and read only the first sentence of each paragraph. As you do this, see if you obtain enough of the critical information to understand generally what the document is about. If you don't, go back and write better topic sentences for each of the paragraphs.

The following paragraph illustrates the direct approach, with a topic sentence at the beginning; it also contains a summarizing sentence at the end.

*Two flexible work arrangements—flextime and compressed—can help reduce employees' childcare concerns.* First, flextime work schedules allow workers flexibility in their work times. With this arrangement, days are divided into core time (hours when employees *must* be at work) and flextime (the earlier morning and later afternoon hours when employees have flexibility). Second, compressed work schedules allow workers to work more hours during some days and fewer or no hours on others. For example, a person could work for ten hours a day Monday through Thursday and then take Friday off. *Both of these flexible arrangements are welcomed by employees with children.*

The next paragraph uses an indirect approach:

With flextime work schedules, days are divided into core times (hours when employees must be at work) and flextime (earlier morning and later afternoon hours when employees have flexibility). Compared to flextime, compressed work schedules allow workers to work more hours during some days and fewer or no hours on others. For example, a person could work for ten hours a day Monday through Thursday and then take Friday off. *Both flextime and compressed work schedules give work-time flexibility to employees, and they are welcomed by employees with young children.*

If you read only the topic sentence of the preceding indirect paragraph, you would miss the information about the compressed work schedule. Only the direct-approach

first sentence includes information about both flextime and compressed work schedules.

Because many people read in detail only the first few lines of a document and then just skim the rest of the message, good topic sentences are critical for body paragraphs. Topic sentences produce a two-fold benefit—they will help you be a better writer, and they enhance readability for your audience.

For bad-news messages, the first body paragraph can often benefit from an indirect approach, such as the following:

> After receiving your appeal request, we analyzed the information you included to determine whether an exception to policy should be granted. We found that your level of income is within the required guidelines, but the amount of your current debt exceeds the maximum amount allowed. Because of the debt problem, we have determined that it would be best not to grant an exception.

In this case, the main idea comes at the end of the paragraph, which requires the audience to read the first part of the paragraph before finding the bad news. Hopefully, the first part will convince the reader that the decision to deny was appropriate. Also, the indirect approach de-emphasizes the bad news by moving it from the highly visible beginning to a de-emphasized position in the body of the message.

If you wish, you may choose to bury the bad news even more by placing it in the middle of a paragraph, rather than at the end, as follows:

> After receiving your appeal request, we analyzed the information you included to determine whether an exception to policy should be granted. Your level of income certainly falls within the required guidelines, but your current debt exceeds the maximum amount allowed. When your debt can be adequately reduced, we would again welcome the chance to consider your application.

### Unity

Be sure that all sentences in a paragraph are unified—they should all refer to the content introduced in the topic sentence. For example, if the topic sentence is about vacation days, the paragraph content should be about vacation days. If the writer wants to talk about vacation days and sick days, the topic sentence would need to mention both vacation days and sick days. Notice the difference in the content of the following two paragraphs.

No: Many businesses are recognizing the importance of having employee fitness programs. Often a fitness trainer is hired, either full or part time. Obesity is becoming a major issue in our country. Many people are unhappy and unfulfilled at work, and this leads to high levels of turnover in some industries. Having a good fit between a person's talents and interests is important in long-term employee satisfaction.

Yes: Many businesses are recognizing the importance of having employee fitness programs. This trend is happening because many people fail to get enough exercise and to eat well, thus contributing to an increasing percentage of our citizens who are out of shape and overweight. Employee fitness programs often include onsite gym facilities, a fitness trainer (either part-time or full-time), health improvement seminars, exercise programs, and financial rewards for employees who complete the exercise programs. As a result of these programs, many companies are finding positive results even beyond improved employee health, including reduced health insurance costs, higher morale, and added recruitment incentives.

The first paragraph lacks unity because the content strays outside the scope of the first sentence. The content in the second paragraph reflects good unity because it stays within the employee fitness scope of the first sentence.

### Coherence

Make sure sentences flow logically from one sentence to the next. Coherence is achieved through systematic progression from one related idea to the next. Notice the difference in coherence between the following two paragraphs.

No: During the early years of a new business, expenses are high and income is low. They often operate at a loss for many months. They have to have a good product or service to succeed. If customers don't like the product or service, they will shop elsewhere. The main reason businesses fail in their infancy is lack of ability to make money. Roughly 50 percent of new businesses fail in the first five years. They have to advertise successfully. The main cause of failure is that they don't make enough money early enough in the life of the business. It takes a lot of money to start most businesses.

Yes: Roughly 50 percent of new businesses fail during the first five years of operation. The main reason is their lack of ability to make a profit. Even if they have a good product or service, income is limited and expenses are high during these early years, including high advertising

costs, high personnel costs, and high production costs. Thus, successful businesses must have a solid source of financing to endure their years of infancy.

In addition to logical coherence, be sure your sentences have appropriate cohesion. Whereas coherence refers to the logical and rational interconnection of ideas, cohesion focuses on specific words that clarify the relationships among the ideas. Cohesion words can occur both within and between ideas. In the following example, the second sentence needs a transition bridge to connect with the first sentence.

No:  As the deadline approached for implementing the new federal requirements, company executives became increasingly anxious. Many executives hired outside consultants for assistance. [Writing is somewhat choppy.]

Yes:  As the deadline approached for implementing the new federal requirements, company executives became increasingly anxious. *This anxiety prompted* many of them to hire outside consultants for assistance. [The cohesion words clarify the relationship between the two sentences.]

The following samples show different types of cohesion words.

**Addition:** *In addition,* she is an LPN. *Further,* she has six years of experience.

**Comparison:** *Similarly,* Gavin also worked as a systems engineer at A & B, Inc.

**Consequence:** *Because* his father passed away on Sunday, he will not be traveling with us to New York.

**Condition:** *If* we can get the Williams contract, *then* we'll gain a greater foothold in the market.

**Example:** *For instance,* she received a recommendation letter from the company president.

**Forecasting:** Her outstanding education is complemented by the *following* three key experiences.

**Numeration:** *First,* write your name; *second,* write your age.

**Place:** *At the conference in Raleigh,* we can review your redesign plans.

**Time:** *Later,* we'll go to dinner.

## Development

Be sure to give adequate information to support the topic sentence. You can develop the main point of a paragraph in many ways, as shown in the following examples.

*Applications:*

Past: "The finance department tried this approach last month. . . ."

Future: "You could use this method in a variety of situations, including . . ."

*Evaluations:*

Comparisons: "Let's compare the two approaches side by side. . . ."

Ratings or rankings: "In the latest product rankings, Brand X was . . ."

*Explanations:*

Definitions: "The initials PDF stand for . . ."

Description: "I'll first describe this process and then be happy to answer any questions."

Details: "Let me explain each of these factors in more detail. . . ."

Logic: "We first observed a 46 percent decline in X; then we noticed a large decrease in Y. Therefore, we concluded that . . ."

*Instances:*

Examples: "For example, last week two employees complained about . . ."

Stories: "Last week I had an experience that intensifies the need for urgent action. . . ."

*Research:*

Statistics: "In a research study of the 100 largest hospitals, over 60 percent . . ."

*Testimonials:*

Authority opinion: "The head of our main manufacturing operation says that . . ."

Quotation: "Mark Twain, the great American author, stated . . ."

Notice the difference in the development in the next two paragraphs.

No:  Good business writers should know how to

compose effective paragraphs. Paragraphs are usually the combination of several sentences related to the same topic.

Yes:   Good business writers should know how to compose effective paragraphs. Effective paragraphs should exhibit five major attributes. First, paragraphs should begin with a topic sentence, which gives the focus of the paragraph. Second, the content of all sentences should relate to the topic sentence. Third, the content of each sentence should logically follow the content of the preceding sentence. Fourth, the topic of the paragraph should be adequately explained and developed. Fifth, the paragraph should be short enough that it looks easy to read. Paragraphs that possess these five attributes will be easy to read and understand.

The first paragraph is underdeveloped, leaving the reader with inadequate information about composing effective paragraphs. The second paragraph gives more substantive content to support the topic sentence. Granted, you can always write more and more about any topic, so you have to learn to judge when enough is enough.

### Length

Avoid writing paragraphs that are so long that they look difficult to read. Many people suggest line counting as a way to determine maximum paragraph length, such as five or six lines for routine messages or eight or nine lines for long reports. Perhaps a more reliable method is to just trust your eyes—if a paragraph looks long and uninviting to read, it is too long! When you encounter a paragraph that is too long, find the most logical breaking point and divide the paragraph in two.

And remember—sometimes a one-sentence paragraph is best!

With a good understanding of the five attributes of effective paragraphs, you should be able to evaluate the quality of any paragraph you encounter. Test your ability as you read the two following paragraphs. Identify the specific CLOUD strengths and weaknesses in each.

Kerry's work has been a problem ever since he was hired. I have talked with him on three different occasions about the need to improve, but nothing has happened. I plan to let him go on July 11. His work affects at least a dozen other employees. His performance record and my notes are attached.

I have decided to terminate Kerry's employment, effective July 11. The main reason for this decision is his inability to keep up with the assembly line. He consistently holds up

the line, causing delays for at least a dozen other employees whose work is affected by his slow speed. I have talked with Kerry on three separate occasions about the need to increase his output, but no significant improvement has occurred. Kerry's performance record and the documentation of my interviews are attached.

You probably noticed that the first paragraph fails three of the five paragraph tests. To its credit, it is not too long and it does have unity, but it has problems with organization, coherence, and development. For example, it does not begin with a good topic sentence (the idea that Kerry is being fired). It also bounces from one idea to the next and reflects a lack of coherence and cohesion. Further, it fails to develop the case for Kerry being fired.

The second paragraph reflects good strength in all five paragraph standards. It begins with the main point, achieves unity by sticking with the topic of discussion, moves logically through the reasoning behind the decision, gives sufficient detail to understand the reasoning behind the decision to terminate, and maintains appropriate length.

### Closing

After writing the opening, agenda, and body with CLOUD paragraphs, close the message. The closing may summarize the document's key points, draw appropriate conclusions, recommend certain actions, or provide some other closing relevant to the situation. For example, the following closing summarizes the body of the document:

FEMA's Family Protection Program and the American Red Cross's Disaster Education Program have identified three steps that have helped families survive disasters most effectively. First, families have determined the disasters that could happen, such as floods, fire, tornadoes, and chemical spills. Second, they have created a disaster plan for each of the disaster types. Third, they regularly practice their disaster plan several times each year to ensure that everyone is prepared. We hope you will implement these steps in your family.

This next closing gives a strong emphasis for action:

To minimize the impact of a disaster to your family, implement these three steps as soon as possible. Don't be caught unprepared!

This third closing includes a cordial offer to help and invites additional communication with the reader.

Thank you for your interest in this information. Please contact me at XXX–XXX–XXXX if you have any additional questions.

Each closing must be uniquely tailored to the message it concludes. As you create the closing of each message, make sure it helps achieve the purposes of the message. For instance, informative messages will often have a summary closing, whereas persuasive messages often have a call for action, such as, "Please let me know by Friday if you can attend this meeting." Bad-news messages may have a more subdued closing that does not invite additional communication: "Thank you again for writing about your concerns. We hope the alternatives we have suggested might be of help to you."

As you might expect, short documents usually have short closings, and longer documents have longer closings. For example, business reports often end with conclusions and recommendations sections, as shown below.

**Conclusions**: Three main conclusions can be drawn from this preliminary study: (1) Students perceive parking to be a major problem at the university, (2) students think public transportation is only a partial solution to the parking problem, and (3) students state that they would be willing to pay higher parking rates for a high-rise parking facility closer to campus.

**Recommendations**: Because of the foregoing conclusions, we recommend that the university take the following action:

1.  Continue to pursue inexpensive public transportation options for students.

2.  Enhance the quality of public transportation options to better meet students' pick-up and drop-off needs.

3.  Conduct a financial analysis to determine the feasibility of constructing a three-level parking terrace on Parking Lot G on the northwest side of campus.

Figures 3.4 and 3.5 give examples of messages that apply the OABC pattern.

In addition to the major OABC sections in an overall document, you may use an OABC pattern within subsections of a longer document. For example, an auditing firm's proposal might have major sections about the tasks to be

Dear Mr. Matthews:

Thank you for your resume and letter expressing interest in our Recruiting Specialist position. The duties of this position vary during the year, depending on recruiting demands. Therefore, a knowledge of all aspects of human resource management is required, including HR law, compensation and benefits, training and development, staffing, and job design.

The position requires exceptional people skills, especially in working with college-age students. Good written and oral communication skills are essential, including interviewing and giving informative presentations. Candidates must have advanced skill in using presentation software and creating professional slideshows. A minimum of three years' business experience in HR is required. Experience is also helpful in organizing interview schedules, planning trip itineraries, and working with travel-management software.

If your schedule allows, we would like to meet with you at 10 a.m. on April 23. Please call Paula, my executive assistant, at (803) 357–87XX to confirm this appointment. We look forward to meeting you.

Sincerely,

Sydney Smith, HR Manager

*Figures 3.4 A sample message with a direct opening and OABC.*

Dear Mr. Matthews:

Thank you for your resume and letter expressing interest in our Recruiting Specialist position. The following paragraphs provide information regarding the (a) knowledge, (b) skills, and (c) experience required for this position.

**Knowledge.** The duties of this position vary during the year, depending on recruiting demands. Therefore, a knowledge of all aspects of human resource management is required, including HR law, compensation and benefits, training and development, staffing, and job design.

**Skills.** The position requires exceptional people skills, especially in working with college-age students. Good written and oral communication skills are essential, including interviewing and giving informative presentations. Candidates must have advanced skill in using presentation software and creating professional slideshows.

**Experience.** A minimum of three years' business experience in HR is required. Experience is also helpful in organizing interview schedules, planning trip itineraries, and working with travel-management software.

If your schedule allows, we would like to meet with you at 10 a.m. on April 23. Please call Paula, my executive assistant, at (803) 357–87XX to confirm this appointment. We look forward to meeting you.

Sincerely,

Sydney Smith, HR Manager

*Figure 3.5 A sample message using OABC and paragraph headings.*

completed by the firm, the task deadlines, the audit team, and the cost of the audit. A mini-OABC could also be used at the beginning of the audit-team section of the proposal. The opening and agenda for that section might be as follows:

> [Opening] We will send to your site a team of experienced and well-trained professionals, ensuring that the work performed will meet your highest expectations. [Agenda] The following paragraphs introduce the audit team, along with their professional credentials.

After the body, which introduces the team, the closing might read as follows:

> [Closing] As you can see, this team of auditors has both the experience and training to perform a thorough audit of your operations. This team will assure that your audit report will provide the information needed for effectively managing your firm and meeting IRS requirements.

As mentioned throughout the preceding sections, bad-news messages do not follow the same OABC approach as good-news or routine messages. In some cases, bad-news messages can still follow OABC if a general agenda is used, but in other cases, the agenda may be omitted. In either case, an indirect approach will enable you to prepare, or condition, the reader's mind before giving the bad news, thereby minimizing the shock when the bad news is given.

Remember the following guidelines when you write messages that deny requests:

1. Open by mentioning the topic of the message, but don't give the bad news yet.
2. Skip the agenda, or include a general agenda that does not reveal the bad news.
3. Explain the reasons for your decision to deny.
4. Give the bad news, which should appear as a logical extension of the information given in step 3. You can use various writing tactics to de-emphasize bad news by (a) avoiding negative words like *can't, won't,* and *unfortunately,* (b) writing the bad news in passive voice, and (c) burying the bad news in the middle of a paragraph.
5. If possible, suggest alternative solutions. Whenever possible, go the second mile to be helpful.
6. Close the message as positively as is appropriate.

Figure 3.6 provides an example of a bad-news message that employs an indirect approach and a modified OABC pattern.

Note that using an indirect approach for giving bad news does not mean that you open the message with unrelated fluff and then give the bad news abruptly, such as the following adaptation of the message in Figure 3.6.

> Dear Chris,
>
> Thank you for writing about the problem you have had with your camera. We are always glad to hear from our customers, and we thank you for purchasing one of our products. We try always to meet the needs of our customers.
>
> Unfortunately, we cannot repair or replace your camera free of charge....

Perhaps this response to Chris could qualify as indirect, but it is misleading and inappropriate. It begins on a positive note, implying that the reader's request will be granted. Then it abruptly changes from positive to negative and denies the request. Chris would likely be upset at receiving such an insincere message. Remember that indirect messages should have a neutral, but related, beginning.

## STRENGTHEN THE CONTENT

Once you get your message organized into an appropriate and effective pattern, consider how you might further clarify informative text and strengthen your persuasion.

### *Clarify Informative Text*

The goal of informative text is not to persuade the audience to take any action, but rather to help the audience understand. As a result, the text explains, describes, discusses, analyzes, evaluates, illustrates, or uses other information required to achieve understanding. The following list gives examples of informative tasks:

- Explain our company's benefits package.
- Describe the new employee.
- Discuss the advantages and disadvantages of merging with another company.
- Compare television advertising and social media advertising.
- Analyze credit card fraud.
- Evaluate the financial strength of Company A.
- Illustrate how we fulfill orders for our products.

Faced with the task of creating informative messages, you should complete two major steps. First, analyze the information, and second, package the information in the most brain-friendly way possible.

**Picture Place**

*1490 Lakeside Drive*
*Anywhere, US XXXXX*
*Phone: 1-800-229-XXXX*
*Web: pixplace.com*

July 18, 20XX

Chris Shen
8834 Riverside Drive
Somewhere, XX 83924

MALFUNCTIONING K305 CAMERA

*Indirect approach*

We have received your K305 camera and your description of the recent problems you have had. Our technicians have carefully examined the camera to determine the cause of the problems. Here is what they found. —— *For bad news, avoid using an agenda that reveals the bad news.*

First, our technicians discovered a hairline crack in the body of the camera, perhaps due to the camera being accidentally dropped. Second, they found numerous sand particles around various camera buttons and the lens, perhaps from use in windy, sandy conditions. The sand could be cleaned from the various camera parts, but the damage from the crack cannot be repaired. We are returning the camera to you in a separate package.

If these problems had occurred during our manufacturing process, we would have been happy to replace your camera free of charge. Because the problems were caused after purchase, we can offer you a new camera for $89.95 (35 percent lower than the suggested retail price). The new camera will have the same 90-day guarantee you had with your other camera and will capture photos of the same quality you enjoyed in the past.

Before September 1, please call 1-800-229-XXXX to let us know if you would like to take advantage of this offer. With proper care of the new camera, you'll be able to enjoy many years of rewarding photography.

*Jen Alta Villa*

JENNIFER ALTA VILLA—CUSTOMER SERVICE SPECIALIST

*Content focuses on what you can do, not what you can't.*

*Bad news is placed in the middle of a paragraph for de-emphasis*

*Bad news is given after the reasons*

*Figure 3.6  This bad-news message employs an indirect approach and uses modified OABC pattern.*

## Analyze the Information

When you write to inform, strive to present the information in a way that it can be easily understood. However, achieving understanding is easier with some messages than with others, because some information is inherently difficult to explain and understand. Table 3.3 lists 10 factors that affect information difficulty.

Using this table, you can analyze a passage of text and rate its difficulty with the 10-point rating scale. The more high ratings you give, the more difficult the text will be to comprehend. You can compute an overall difficulty score by adding all the ratings (highest possible score is 100).

## Make the Information Brain Friendly

Readers will appreciate your efforts to make the information easy for them to process—to make it brain friendly! You can approach this effort both by simplifying the information itself and by presenting the information in a logical way.

First, to simplify the information, consider where the text has higher ratings from the previous table, and take appropriate action to mitigate the difficulty. Consider each of the 10 factors individually, and work to make the text match the easy-to-understand description on the left, rather than the difficult-to-understand description on the right.

- When you describe new and unfamiliar information, use clear descriptions and add redundancy (examples, illustrations, stories, etc.).

- For conceptual information, use a visual or metaphor to make it more concrete. People are primarily visual learners.
- With a large amount of information, break it down into smaller bite-size chunks; with long lists, combine some items if possible—short lists can be remembered better than long lists.
- If you encounter text with high information density, rewrite and redesign the text so it doesn't overwhelm the reader with too much information too fast.
- If you encounter information with unclear meaning, rewrite it to be clear.
- Where you find unfamiliar words, define them or use synonymous familiar words in their place.
- Where you encounter disorganized information, place the main point at the beginning (direct approach) and organize the information logically.
- Where you encounter long passages of difficult-looking text, insert headings, visual signposts (numbered items or other visual markers), and enhanced typography (bold or italicize important words).

As you implement several individual improvements one by one, you'll see the overall reading and comprehension improve. For example, to explain a new government reporting requirement, you could explain the reason for the requirement; give a basic explanation of the requirement, broken down into small chunks; illustrate the compliance process with a visual diagram; give an example of how it will

### Table 3.3. Factors that Affect Reading Comprehension

| Factors Making Information Easy to Understand | Rating | Factors Making Information Difficult to Understand |
|---|---|---|
| Familiar topic | 1 2 3 4 5 6 7 8 9 10 | Unfamiliar topic |
| Redundant, repeated information (examples, applications, stories, etc.) | 1 2 3 4 5 6 7 8 9 10 | Non-redundant information (no repetition of important ideas) |
| Concrete information | 1 2 3 4 5 6 7 8 9 10 | Conceptual, vague information |
| Smaller amount of information | 1 2 3 4 5 6 7 8 9 10 | Larger amount of information |
| Moderate information density | 1 2 3 4 5 6 7 8 9 10 | Information density (high rate of content words vs. total words) |
| Information with clear meaning | 1 2 3 4 5 6 7 8 9 10 | Information with only implied meaning |
| Familiar words | 1 2 3 4 5 6 7 8 9 10 | Unfamiliar words |
| Main point at beginning (direct approach) | 1 2 3 4 5 6 7 8 9 10 | Main point in the middle (indirect approach) |
| Well organized, coherent information | 1 2 3 4 5 6 7 8 9 10 | Poorly organized, disjointed information |
| Headings and visual signposts; enhanced typography | 1 2 3 4 5 6 7 8 9 10 | No headings or signposts; no enhanced typography |

be carried out in your organization; and insert headings to make the text skimmable.

Second, you have various options for logically organizing the information. One option is to go from the known to the unknown, beginning with a reference to what the reader already knows and following with an explanation of the new information. For example, to explain a new marketing concept, briefly refer to the current marketing strategy (the known), and then give a conceptual explanation of the new strategy (the unknown), followed by an example of the concept in a real-world application, a comparison of the new concept with the current strategy, and a list of the benefits that would be achieved by adopting the new concept.

In addition to the known-to-unknown approach, informative messages can often be organized around one or more of the 5W2H factors (who, what, where, when, why, how, and how much). For example, a "when" oriented informative message might be organized as follows:

> Our training retreat next Tuesday will include the following sessions. We'll begin at 9:00 a.m. with a welcome from our president. From 9:30 a.m. until noon, we will receive training on the new federal tax laws pertaining to information privacy. After lunch, from 12:00 to 1:00 p.m., we will receive two hours of training on the new changes that have been made to our computer-input screens. Following a half-hour break at 3:00 p.m., we'll participate in a fun team-development activity that will run until 5:00 p.m.

A "why" oriented informative message might look something like this:

> I have organized next Tuesday's training meeting for three main reasons. First, our new company president wants to have an opportunity to meet all of us and give us his vision of the next five years. Second, we all need more training on the new tax laws and on our new computer-input screens. Third, we could benefit from some team-building activities to help us become more effective in working together.

Further, a "how" oriented message could explain the actions taken by various people in the creation and marketing of a new product, and a "where" oriented message could describe the sales effectiveness of different markets across the U.S. (e.g., Northeast, Southeast, Midwest, etc.).

Following your writing of an informative message, ask colleagues or friends to read the message and give you feedback regarding its clarity and effectiveness. If your material is clear, the readers should be able to explain the concept clearly to someone else.

## Strengthen Your Persuasion

Unlike informative messages that require no audience response, persuasive messages seek for audience response. Through persuasive messages you influence other people to change their minds—to think the way you want them to think, to do something you want them to do, or to be what you want them to be. Much of your success in life will depend on your ability to persuade people.

The need to persuade usually grows from a problem that you feel needs to be solved or from an opportunity that you feel should be pursued. Problems or opportunities are usually revealed through a three-step process that involves analysis, evaluation, and synthesis. Remember this process with three simple questions: What? So what? Now what?

1. **Analysis** (What?) is the process of disassembling something piece by piece so you can understand each part. Asking all the 5W2H questions (who, what, where, when, why, how, and how much) helps to complete the analysis step.

2. **Evaluation** (So what?) is the process of judging the relative goodness or badness of something. Asking "so what" helps to isolate the implications of each part of the analysis. Whereas analysis can often be more quantitative in nature, evaluation is more qualitative. Evaluation usually involves some established system for rating, such as textual rating (excellent, good, satisfactory, marginal, unsatisfactory), numeric rating (5, 4, 3, 2, 1), numeric ranking (1st, 2nd, 3rd), or actual measurement (3.06, 6.93, 8.77, 10.41).

3. **Synthesis** (Now what?) is the process of putting things together in a new and better way. It develops a solution to the problem. Asking "now what" helps to generate creative thinking about how to improve the current situation.

An example will help illustrate the what, so-what, and now-what process. Assume that you supervise the work of five people. To understand "what" the employees are accomplishing, you analyze their work and discover that Persons A and B are producing an average of ten units per day, Persons C and D are producing an average of seven units per day, and Person E is producing three units per day. Moving on to the "so what" question, you judge the work of Persons A and B to be very good, the work of Persons C and D to be fairly good, but the work of Person E to be poor. In response to the "now what" question, you decide to reward Persons A and B with a higher wage, provide additional training for Persons C and D, and terminate the employment of Person E.

After the problem or opportunity is identified, you

move on to the actual process of persuasion. The following three sections explain the basic steps of persuasion, describe different persuasion strategies, and discuss various fallacies in logic.

## Follow the Steps of Persuasion

For simple persuasive situations, a short, simple approach is adequate—just choose either a direct approach (what followed by why) or an indirect approach (why followed by what). The direct approach gets right to the point, whereas the indirect approach gives reasons before recommending action. Both direct and indirect approaches are illustrated as follows:

> Direct approach, with the action (the *what*) preceding the reason (the *why*):
>
> **Action:** We need to hire someone to replace Marilyn, *because* . . .
>
> **Reason:** She is quitting next month. That will leave a vacancy on the assembly line.

> Indirect approach, with reasons (the *why*) preceding the action (the *what*):
>
> **Reason:** Our employee Marilyn is quitting next month. That will leave a vacancy on the assembly line.
>
> **Action:** *Therefore,* we need to hire someone to replace Marilyn.

For more complex and difficult persuasive situations, five steps are usually involved. The steps follow a more indirect approach, which research has shown to be effective when persuading a person to accept a controversial idea (Frischknecht & Baker, 2012). These five steps can be adapted to fit various persuasive situations, whether involving written or oral communication.

1.  The first step in the process of persuasion begins with framing the problem or issue. For instance, assume that you live in an apartment with a swimming pool. However, you noticed today that the pool is closed for repairs—again! It has been closed for repair 18 days during the months of June and July, making it impossible for you to enjoy the pool during nearly three weeks of two warm summer months. As a result, you decide that you want to move to another apartment with a working pool. To do so, however, you would have to break your one-year lease contract (it ends on October 20) and pay a penalty. You want to

get the apartment manager to allow you to break the lease and move without penalty.

How you frame the problem is very important, because it serves as the basis for your persuasion and establishes the scope of your argument. For instance, you could frame the problem in one of the three ways:

A.  The apartment pool is not usable.

B.  I want to move.

C.  The landlord has not kept his part of the lease contract.

If you choose option A, your argument would be that if the landlord fixes the pool, the problem would be solved, which is not exactly what you want. Choosing option B would logically lead the landlord to say, "Yes, you may move, but you have to pay a penalty." Again, this is not what you want. If you choose option C, you would argue that because the landlord has not kept his part of the agreement, the contract is now broken and you are not obligated to stay or to pay a penalty.

Option C seems to be the best choice, although you could frame the problem so its solution will also generate some benefit to the landlord. In this case, the landlord's reputation for kindness and understanding would be enhanced by allowing you to move without penalty.

2.  In the second step, state your proposed solution—what you think is the best way to solve the problem. In this case, your solution is to move on August 1, cancel the contract, and not have to pay a penalty.

3.  Step 3 provides information to support your argument. In this case, it could be something like the following: "One of the main reasons I rented this apartment is that it had a nice pool. Further, the contract stated that the landlord would 'keep up on all needed repairs in a timely manner.' Because the pool has not been kept up in a timely manner, I have not been able to enjoy it for 18 days of the warmest months of the year. Therefore, I feel that my best option is to move to another apartment with a working pool."

4.  Step 4 is the place for resolving concerns, downplaying competing proposals, or giving a rebuttal to counterarguments. Lewin's force-field theory (Mind Tools, 2015) states that persuasion to change is accompanied by two opposing forces—reasons arguing for change and reasons arguing against it. As you try to persuade people, identify both the positive and the negative forces, and then work to strengthen the pos-

itive forces and to eliminate or weaken the negative forces.

In this case, the landlord's two opposing forces are as follows:

Why I should comply: The pool has indeed been a problem, and this tenant has been good about paying rent and keeping the apartment clean. I also like to be as sensitive to tenants' concerns as possible.

Why I should not comply: The tenant signed the one-year contract, and if the tenant leaves, I will lose money and have to put forth effort to find a new tenant. Also, if I relax the contract requirements for this tenant, other tenants might ask me to do the same thing.

At this point, the negative forces are winning, persuading him to deny your request. Therefore, you will need to strengthen the reasons he should comply and weaken his reasons not to comply. Thus, you might write, "The landlord's attempts to fix the pool have failed to resolve the problem, leaving us with no pool to enjoy. Because this is a violation of our housing contract, I plan to move out on August 1, without paying a penalty."

5. Step 5 requests the audience to act—in this case, to accept your proposal. You want the landlord to write back and grant your request. Thus, you write, "Because I have a day off work next Thursday, may I meet with you at 10 a.m. in your office to complete this arrangement? Please email or call me at (XXX-XXX-XXXX) to confirm."

After your persuasive message is delivered, you wait for a response. That response will let you know whether your message has been successful. Even if he doesn't respond, however, that is still a response—it lets you know that you will have to make a second attempt to arrange a meeting with the manager.

## Apply Persuasion Strategies

Throughout the five steps of persuasion, you can use a variety of persuasion strategies. The evidence you present may be logic based or emotion based—appealing more to the analytical mind or to the feeling heart. Often you will include both logic- and emotion-based strategies. The following lists give a variety of strategic options.

### Logic-based Strategies

**Analogy** strategy compares two somewhat similar things.

*If a contractor agrees to paint a house and then fails to do so, the homeowner would not be obligated to pay. Neither should I have to pay for apartment service I haven't received.*

*Airlines give incentives for frequent flyers; therefore, our restaurant should do the same for our repeating customers.*

**Cause-and-effect** strategy shows how some cause leads to some effect. Research and statistics can be used effectively with this strategy.

*Your swimming pool has been closed 18 days, and this problem has caused me to want to move out of my apartment.*

*Installing this new technology will result in a savings of 20–25 percent on your phone bill.*

*Over 80 percent of our income comes from repeat business. Our bottom line will suffer significantly if we don't take care of these customers.*

**Generalization** strategy says that what happened in one case can be generalized to other situations.

*A friend of mine had a similar situation in another apartment, and she was allowed to move without paying a penalty. Therefore, I should be able to do the same.*

*Four other branch offices in our company have adopted this marketing strategy and have experienced an increase of 15 percent in their market share. I'm confident that the same thing will happen if we adopt this strategy.*

**Legal** strategy discusses adherence to laws or contracts.

*You have violated your part of the contract; therefore, we will discontinue our participation in this project on August 1.*

*According to our city's building code, you may not take occupancy until the home passes the final inspection.*

### Emotion-based Strategies

**Morality,** ethics-based strategy centers on doing what is right and good. For instance, fair-play appeals can be used to appeal to the hearts of customers who don't act responsibly.

*Ethically, the proper action would be for you to cancel my contract because of the pool problem.*

*We completed the engineering work on the project according to the agreement; now it is your turn to complete your part of the agreement.*

*We issued your credit card to help make purchasing easier for you. Now you have an obligation to pay your bills on time.*

*We all have a responsibility to protect the environment of this community.*

**Pride** strategy appeals to a person's ego or to a desire to associate with popular trends or popular individuals.

*Imagine how you'll feel driving to work in your new car.*

*Your friends will be impressed with your ability to stay so well organized.*

*Olympic winner Sara Smith uses product XYZ.*

*Nearly two-thirds of Fortune 500 companies are using this product.*

**Reciprocity** strategy argues that because X has done something for Y, Y should reciprocate by doing something good for X in return.

*I have paid my monthly rent faithfully and kept my apartment clean; therefore, you should waive the penalty and let me get out of the contract.*

*We have had a good working relationship for many years, and I hope you'll be patient with us during this short-term delay in our services.*

**Safety** and **fear** strategies appeal to the basic human need to avoid risk and to be physically and emotionally safe.

*This ladder has been UL tested to ensure maximum safety in your working environment.*

*If you're not satisfied with the first issue of this publication, just call our toll-free number and let us know. We'll cancel your subscription and you'll owe nothing.*

*The federal government used our software for its last major census.*

*International consultant Brad Baumann endorses our product and says it's the best he has seen.*

*If we don't soon provide this service, we might lose some of our best employees.*

As is illustrated in the preceding examples, strategies can involve either positive or negative results. Positive strategies focus on what the audiences will gain if they take the recommended action. Negative strategies highlight what they will lose if they don't take the recommended action. "Your customers will trust you when they find your products have been safety tested with us" is a positive strategy. A negative strategy is, "Potential customers will do business with other vendors if you don't safety test your products with us." Because humans are motivated by a desire for personal gain and by a fear of loss, both types of strategies can be used effectively. Understanding your audience will help you determine whether to use positive or negative appeals.

In some persuasive situations, the persuader is able to include tangible or intangible (psychological) incentives to increase the likelihood of persuasion. A word of caution is needed when dealing with tangible incentives. In some countries, the giving of bribes or gifts in return for special favors is somewhat common, but not so in the United States. Accepting gifts creates a conflict of interest that impairs a person's ability to make objective and fair decisions involving the giver of the gift. Many companies have strict policies against receiving gifts from vendors or contractors, so always check your company's gifting policy before offering or receiving gifts.

Whatever persuasive situation you may encounter, think creatively about how to build your case. Pull together all the evidence you can, and choose a strategy that combines your best appeals, including such elements as facts, statistics, case studies, credible opinions, and examples. For instance, an argument might provide convincing quantitative data, quote experts, and cite examples to support a claim. It might also include visually oriented elements, such as photographs and diagrams, to create a strong visual impression to help with the persuasion. Make sure everything works together to achieve the desired objective—to change the person's mind to your way of thinking.

Keeping in mind the foregoing information about persuasion, read the messages in Figures 3.7, 3.8, and 3.9 to see how various persuasion steps, strategies, and incentives are used.

## Avoid Fallacies in Logic

Whenever you attempt to persuade, the audience will evaluate your arguments to see if they make sense and are relevant to their situation. Non sequiturs (Latin for "it does not follow") are errors in logic that can arise from illogical or careless thinking, and they weaken your persuasive appeals. The following list provides examples of non-sequitur thinking.

To:      All Employees

From:   Amanda Turner  *AMTurner*
         Corporate Wellness Coordinator

Date:   October 1, 20XX

**Re:     Stay Healthy Campaign**

The flu season is fast approaching, and we again face the potential of production delays caused by absenteeism due to illness. The U.S. Center for Disease Control and Prevention reminds us of the severity of this disease:

> "The flu is a contagious respiratory illness caused by influenza viruses that infect the nose, throat, and lungs. It can cause mild to severe illness, and at times can lead to death. The best way to prevent the flu is by getting a flu vaccine each year."

To help protect everyone against the flu and maintain a healthy workforce, we have arranged for healthcare professionals to come and provide flu vaccinations for all employees. The details are as follows:

**What**:   Flu vaccination
**Who**:    Everyone
**When**:   October 20, 9 a.m. to 12:00 and 1:30 to 4:30 (supervisors will communicate the specific times
             for each team)
**Where**:  South Conference Room
**Cost**:   Free—covered by our health insurance

The U.S. Center for Disease Control and Prevention states that getting vaccinated typically reduces the risk of having to go to the doctor for flu treatment by nearly 50 percent. Although flu vaccinations cannot protect against all strains of flu, they do increase your likelihood of staying well and help us prevent work delays during the flu season.

Our company president will be the first to be vaccinated on the October 20, and we strongly encourage everyone to join him in our "***Stay Healthy***" campaign. As an added incentive, everyone who participates will receive a *free* "Stay Healthy" T-shirt and water bottle.

Please note that if you have an allergy to eggs or to any ingredients in the flu vaccine, you should not get a flu shot. Also, if you have any other concerns about your health status as related to the flu vaccine, please talk with your doctor before October 20.

Last year's flu-season absenteeism was better than the year before, but we hope for even better health this year. We will appreciate your efforts to do all you can to help in our campaign.

*Figure 3.7  A persuasive message to convince employees to get flu shots.*

256 West Center; Orem, UT 84057 ❖ Phone: 801-717-3499
Online: goreact.com ❖ Email: info@goreact.com

March 4, 20XX

Professor Maria Dumitrescu
4783 44th Avenue
Anywhere, US 839XX

Dear Professor Dumitrescu:

As an instructor of speech communication, you can give your students more than just a video recording of their presentations and a few written comments. Now you can capture video **and** embed time-stamped comments that students can view online immediately after their presentations. And you can have these advantages for FREE!

Announcing GoReact, a real-time, video-based presentation coaching system! This amazing technology offers numerous advantages for enhanced student involvement and improvement.

| Yes ... | No ... |
|---|---|
| *Capture video with online software,* using only your computer or mobile device, a webcam, and an internet connection. | No more hassle with expensive video cameras or other technology. |
| *Capture instructor's feedback during the presentation,* and time-stamp the comments to the specific points in the presentation where they were given. | No more handwriting of comments on paper for you, and no more mental disconnect between comments on paper and subsequent viewing of presentations for your students. |
| *Capture fellow students' feedback during presentations* so they can be involved both in giving their presentations and in coaching their peers. | No more disconnected, passive endurance while students wait their turn to present. |
| *Provide immediate video and time-stamped feedback* to students after their presentations. | No more delay in getting instructor feedback or waiting for video media to be produced. |

If you would like to improve the precision and effectiveness of your feedback, and to provide the feedback online for viewing immediately following students' presentations, GoReact is the program for you. Using GoReact, you'll see improved performance more quickly, and you'll give your students a distinct edge in their business careers.

Here is what students are saying after they use GoReact:

- I loved being able to watch myself present. I have never had that opportunity before, despite being involved with many presentations. Now I can be a part of my own audience and evaluate how I can improve my skills.
- GoReact helped me actually see what I was doing from the audience's perspective.
- The "line" rating system is great. I loved being able to see exactly how well my presentation was being received.

*Figure 3.8  A two–page sales letter using a direct approach.*

8. Write a complaint letter to a business organization regarding a problem you have had with one of its products or services. Ask for some specific action, such as a refund of your money or a replacement of the product. Write the letter twice, once using a direct approach and once using an indirect approach.

9. Read an editorial in a newspaper and analyze the logic it uses to persuade.

10. Identify a problem on your college campus. Write a message that attempts to persuade the appropriate campus leader to solve the problem.

11. Analyze five different television ads and discuss how they attempt to persuade.

12. A local politician is proposing a new recreation center, police station, library, park, or other facility (you choose which one to respond to). Write an editorial piece that tells why this is either a good or bad idea (you choose which point of view to take). Use all appropriate steps in the persuasion process, as well as all appropriate persuasion strategies.

13. Go to the federal government's website www.plain-language.gov and review the government's guidelines for readable writing. Write a short essay on how you think the guidelines for plain writing in government also apply to writing for business.

14. You work as a customer service agent for MidWest Airlines. On January 1, 20XX, you received the following letter (today's date is January 4). Write an appropriate letter to this individual, but do not grant his request for a free flight.

> On December 23, 20XX, I was flying MidWest Airlines from Calgary to Chicago on flight 268 with a stop off in Minneapolis. The flight was delayed 2 hours because of bad weather. I took that particular flight because it did not require me to de-plane in Minneapolis. To prevent hassle between flights, I thought this would be the best option, but when we arrived in Minneapolis your people told me the Chicago flight had been cancelled. After much rudeness from your staff I was put up in a hotel for the night.
>
> Then when flying home on Dec. 26, 20XX, the flight I scheduled from Chicago to Calgary was late by two hours. Then when I arrived in Minneapolis, I again found the flight to Calgary had been cancelled. Again after much rude behavior by your staff, I was given a hotel for the night. I then called my family in Calgary to let them know that I was not coming in that night and they had told me that when they called the airline to find out if the flight was delayed, the airline told my family that the flight had landed in Calgary. This was very odd since I was stranded in Minneapolis. I must say that the entire experience flying on your airline was a total nightmare. I will think twice before ever flying with

you again. I would like the airline to accept responsibility for bad service and unacceptable behavior from their staff. A free flight would be nice.

> Tom Martin
> 328 Thornhill Road NW
> Calgary, AB T2E-6S6

15. Your position is Director of Personnel Benefits for Southwest Clothing Mills, located at 2883 Industrial Way, Oklahoma City, OK 73132. Your company has a tuition-assistance program (TAP) that helps employees complete educational degrees. The company will pay up to half of the tuition for educational programs for employees whose applications are approved. To obtain company participation, an employee must submit a letter describing the intended educational program and asking for assistance. The letter must be accompanied by a recommendation letter from the employee's supervisor. This procedure must be repeated each semester; for subsequent semesters, the employee's letter must include the grades earned for the previous semester. If a participant doesn't maintain a 3.0 GPA, no funds will be made available until that participant's semester GPA once again reaches the 3.0 level—the participant may then reapply for tuition funding.

### *Letter 1—Bad News*

Dave Wheeler, one of your company's accounting clerks, has just completed his bachelor's degree at University of Oklahoma. His degree is in accounting, and you gave him educational assistance for three semesters while he was working on that degree. Now he wants to pursue an evening MBA degree, also at OU. Tuition for the night program is $3,850 per semester. Write him a letter denying his request. Your TAP budget for next semester has reached its limit. Plus, you have a policy of helping out with undergraduate programs first and then with graduate programs *if funds permit.* Dave is a good employee (he gets high marks from his supervisor), and you don't want to destroy his motivation, either for his job or for his educational pursuits. Therefore, be very careful in wording the letter.

> Mr. David J. Wheeler
> 7834 Maple Lane
> Broken Arrow, OK 73155

### *Letter 2—Good News*

Julia Lockhart has also applied for funding from TAP. This is her first application, and she wants to complete her undergraduate degree in computer science at the University

of Central Oklahoma. She has approximately three semesters left, and her GPA for her prior work at the University of Central Oklahoma is 2.89. Grant her request, and indicate that a check for half of the tuition amount will be sent to her as soon as she sends a copy of her tuition billing statement to you. Remind her that for future funding, she must earn at least a 3.0 GPA for the previous semester. Julia is an administrative assistant in the Public Relations Department and has been given a good recommendation by her supervisor.

Ms. Julia Lockhart
835 North First Avenue
Edmond, OK 73028

16. Obtain an employment resume from two of your classmates.

Letter 1—Bad news. Write a bad-news letter to one, indicating that he or she will not be hired. Without offending, give one or more reasons for your refusal.

Letter 2—Good news. Write a good-news letter to the other, stating that he or she will be hired, and explaining the appropriate starting date, starting salary, starting position, supervisor, and department.

# Enhancing Messages Visually

Perhaps you have heard the statement, "A picture is worth a thousand words." People make this comment because a picture can communicate information in a way that words cannot. So why don't we just communicate with pictures? The reason is that just as pictures have certain advantages over words, words also have certain advantages over pictures. With words you can analyze, evaluate, explore, explain, defend, and discuss in ways that pictures cannot. Thus, in some situations one picture might be worth a thousand words, but in another situation a thousand words might be better than a picture. Both words and visuals are important, and in each writing situation your task is to use both of them in a way that will produce the best results.

Long passages of text, with no visuals, look boring and uninviting, and research has shown that undifferentiated text is less effective than text with headings, business graphics, and varied typography (Frischknecht & Baker 2011).

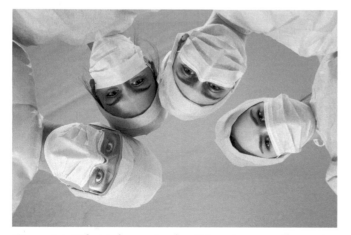

*Figure 4.1 What is happening here? Is a picture really worth a thousand words?*

In spite of this evidence, many writers ignore the need for visual enhancement. Short emails and memos are generally acceptable without visual polish because they require so little time to read, but for all other messages you write, spend a bit of time to enhance their visual presentation.

In addition to enhancing the visual presentation of a message, you can use visually oriented words and metaphors to create a picture in the reader's mind. Consider, for example, the following two descriptions of a small tool kit.

1. *Example A:* This tool kit gives you everything you need for your next emergency repair . . . and it is amazingly small!

2. *Example B:* This tool kit gives you everything you need for your next emergency repair . . . and it fits easily in your glove compartment!

The first example relies on nonvisual text; the second example uses visually oriented wording. "Amazingly small" is helpful, but "fits right in your glove compartment" gives readers something they can see in their mind.

Consider another example of symbolism: "We got the perfect pitch but struck out." This sports metaphor is a symbolic way of saying, "A good opportunity came to us, but we didn't take advantage of it." However, anyone who doesn't know about baseball wouldn't understand. Therefore, when using a metaphor, make sure the audience will understand.

Chapter 4 describes a four-step procedure to help you enhance the visual effectiveness of your writing. This procedure, represented by the acronym HATS, stands for headings, art, typography, and spacing (Baker 2001). After reading this chapter, you should be able to do the following:

- Insert headings to show the structure of documents.

- Augment text with appropriate art and visuals.
- Use appropriate typography for headings and body text.
- Insert appropriate external and internal space throughout each document.

## HEADINGS

Headings are helpful in both long and short documents. Headings enhance information access—the degree to which important information is easily accessible to the reader. Just as people use links to navigate through internet sites, they use headings to navigate through business documents. Remember, however, that people's use of headings is unpredictable. Therefore, even though you insert headings in your documents, compose the text before and after headings as though there were no headings. Doing so will ensure good coherence even if people skip over headings and read only the body text.

Remember two important purposes of headings: they serve as signposts and they reveal textual structure.

**Signposts**. Reading a document is like driving down the interstate highway, and the headings of the document serve as signposts announcing each upcoming city. Thus, include enough headings to keep the audience aware of what is coming next. Messages are made up of individual information chunks, and each heading announces a new chunk. Headings are also helpful when readers want to skim a document, stopping only in selected spots for more detailed reading.

**Structure**. For long documents, use headings to reveal the structure and hierarchy of the information. Headings reveal to the reader your writing outline, now embedded within the text. To help the reader see the message structure, designate first-, second-, and third-level headings by varying typography (font, alignment, bold, italics, case, and size) and placement (side, center). The following example shows font and placement variations for different heading levels:

# ANALYSIS OF DATA

## Financial Data

### *Third-quarter Changes*

**Phoenix Plant.** In our Phoenix plant we noted a 23 percent increase in inventory between the second and third quarters. This increase was most likely caused by . . .

*Major heading:* Arial, centered, bold, all capitals, 16 point

*Second-level heading:* Arial, left-aligned, bold, initial capitals, 14 point

*Third-level heading:* Times New Roman, left-aligned, bold, italic, 12 point

*Paragraph-level heading:* Bolded body font with the heading on the first line of the paragraph.

Choose the words in the headings carefully. The wording can take one of three forms: topic, statement, and question. Topic headings are the most commonly used form; they are a concise description of the topic that follows. Statement headings are like topic sentences for a section. They convey more information than topic headings, and they convey useful information even if the audience doesn't read the subsequent text. Question headings help emphasize issues being considered and provide a useful guide for readers who want quick answers to specific questions. The headings, thus, ask questions, and the subsequent text provides the answers to the questions. The following examples illustrate the differences in the three heading forms.

*Topic Heading:*

**Analysis of Inventory**

*Statement Heading:*

**Inventory Increased Slightly in Third Quarter**

*Question Heading:*

**What Changes Occurred in Inventory?**

When working with headings, remember three additional guidelines. First, be consistent in the heading form that you use, thus ensuring parallelism in wording. For instance, don't mix topic and statement headings. Use one or the other, not both. Second, avoid contiguous headings (a subheading following a heading with no text in between). Insert at least a bit of text between the two headings. Often this text will introduce or announce the upcoming information. Third, you may put more white space before a heading than after. For instance, if you have one blank space after a heading, put one and a half or two blank spaces before the heading. The white space provides a visual break and visually associates the heading with the subsequent text.

## ART

In the HATS acronym, art refers to the use of all types of visual treatments to make information easier to find and

process. At a very basic level you can format several parallel items as a numbered or bulleted list. Compared with text buried in the middle of a paragraph, a list is easier for the reader to find and process.

Graphic representations, such as tables, bar charts, maps, organization charts, and photographs, can also make information easy to find and easier to understand. Table 4.1 gives some options for communicating information visually. Notice that tables and charts are the major options for illustrating quantitative data (such as financial data), while many other options are available for illustrating non-quantitative information (such as organizational hierarchies, spatial information, and procedures).

## Table 4.1
## Visual Communication Alternatives

| Information Type | Effective Ways to Present |
| --- | --- |
| Who | Photographs, organization charts |
| What | Line drawings, photographs, concept maps |
| Where | Geographic maps |
| When | Flow charts |
| Why | Cause-and-effect drawings |
| How | Process charts, line drawings, concept maps |
| How much | Tables and charts (bar, line, pie, area, scatter plots, surface, bubble, radar, etc.) |

Too often writers use only text to convey their message when they could more effectively communicate the information with a combination of text and graphics. To illustrate the difference between presenting data as text and or as a visual, assume that you need to communicate information about the salaries of biological science graduates in the United States. Which of the following three examples do you think works best—the standard paragraph, the table, or the bar graph?

*Text example:*

In 2014 there were 960,000 people with B.S. degrees, and their projected work-life earnings were $2,288,000. Approximately 420,000 held M.S. degrees, with projected work-life earning of $2,757,000. Roughly 455,000 had earned a professional degree, with a projected work-life earning of $5,435,000. And with 255,000 holding doctorate degrees, their projected work-life earnings amounted to $3,511,000, over 50 percent above those with just a B.S. degree.

*Table example:*

| Degree | Number of Graduates | Projected Work-life Earnings |
| --- | --- | --- |
| B.S. | 960,000 | $2,288,000 |
| M.S. | 420,000 | $2,757,000 |
| Professional | 455,000 | $5,435,000 |
| Doctorate | 255,000 | $3,511,000 |

*Graphic example[1]:*

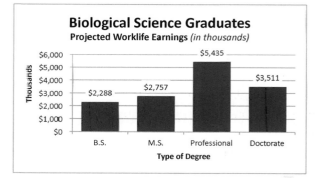

The differences among the three methods of communicating information are obvious. Presenting quantitative information in paragraph format is ineffective, because the human brain is not very good at processing raw quantitative values in that form. A table format makes the mental processing is a bit easier, but it is still difficult because you can't easily spot trends or relationships when numbers are presented in paragraphs or tables. With a bar chart, however, trends and differences are immediately apparent. Text and tables enable the audience to read the data, but graphics enable the audience to see the data! Visuals are the language of the eye, and your challenge is to shape data so it is visually meaningful to the reader. Often the best option is a combination of text and visuals. For instance, a bar chart can provide a powerful visual impression and an accompanying paragraph can give additional analysis.

Whenever you insert a visual item, such as a table or chart, in a document, remember three "I's"—introduce, insert, and interpret. First, introduce the visual with a statement like, "Figure 3 illustrates the differences between Site A and Site B." Second, insert the visual within the text as soon after the point of introduction as possible. Third, interpret the visual. The purpose of the interpretation is to answer the visual's "so what" question. You don't present data just to present data; you present data to make a point. Thus, be sure to tell the audience what the visual item means. For instance, you might say, "Figure 3 shows

---

1  Source: www.census.gov/library/infographics/biological_majors.html

that the earning potential for professional graduates (such as doctors and dentists) is nearly twice that of graduates with M.S. degrees." The introduction should always come before the place where the visual is inserted, but the interpretation may come before or after, depending on the space constraints of the page where the graphic is placed.

Remember the following additional general guidelines for visuals:

**Titles.** Develop a descriptive title for each visual. Instead of using an overly brief title like "20XX Sales," create a title like, "20XX Worldwide Sales of Leadership Training Materials" or "Sales of Leadership Training Materials Increased in 20XX."

**Numbers.** Number visuals consecutively. For instance, number tables as Table 1, Table 2, etc. Number other visuals as Figure 1, Figure 2, etc. If a document has only one table or only one figure, no numbering is necessary.

**Placement.** Be consistent in placing figure and table numbers and titles. Traditionally, the number and title of tables should be at the top, and the number and title of figures should be at the bottom. If you encounter variations of these guidelines, however, you may need to adapt to the practices of that organization.

**Typography.** Generally use a sans serif font for visuals (fonts are discussed later in the chapter).

**Simplicity.** Keep visuals simple and easy to understand. Avoid clutter and don't try to communicate too much information in one graph.

**Highlighting.** Use appropriate legends and callouts. A legend is an explanatory list of the symbols or colors used in a chart. A callout is explanatory text placed beside a graphic, with a line going from the explanatory text to the part of the graphic it is explaining (see Figures 4.5 and 4.12). Legends and callouts are particularly helpful with complex tables or graphics. You may also add trend lines, color, and any other visual enhancements to highlight the key points of your graphics.

**Attribution.** Cite appropriate source information in a footnote at the base of the graphic or table. Don't be guilty of plagiarism.

The following sections give additional instruction for including tables, bar charts, line graphs, scatter plots, pie graphs, photographs and clip art, maps, organization charts, flow charts, and infographics in your business documents.

## Tables

Tables consist of an information grid, with vertical columns and horizontal rows containing numeric or alphabetic information. Because of their flexibility in displaying many kinds of data, tables are widely used in business documents. Depending on their use, tables can be very simple or complex. For instance, if you are trying to decide whether to buy a bicycle, you can use a basic T chart, which is a simple, but useful, two-column table (see Figure 4.2).

### Should I buy a bicycle?

| PROS | CONS |
|------|------|
| Price is reasonable | Might get stolen |
| Will save on gas | Cold riding in the winter |
| Low maintenance costs | Less safe than a car |
| Parking is always good | Hard to carry large items |

*Figure 4.2  A T chart can be helpful in making simple decisions.*

If you are trying to choose between two or more bicycles, you can use a decision table that provides for decision factors, for factor weights, and for all options (see Figure 4.3). Notice that this table employs boldface type to make the headings and total row more visible.

| Decision Factors | Weight (10-point scale) | Option 1: Giant FastRoad SLR | Option 2: Trek Madone 2.1 |
|---|---|---|---|
| Comfort | 10 | 10 | 8 |
| Cost | 7 | 6 | 4 |
| Color | 5 | 4 | 4 |
| Dealer proximity | 2 | 2 | 1 |
| Model in stock | 1 | 1 | 0 |
| **Total** | **25** | **23** | **17** |

*Figure 4.3  A decision table is helpful in choosing between multiple options.*

Figure 4.4 illustrates an even more complex table with additional rows and columns, as well as braced headings (major headings over secondary headings).

Remember the following important guidelines as you create tables.

**Labels.** Label each column and row, and use typographic enhancement for emphasis, such as boldfaced headings.

| Table XXX. Usage of Social Media by Online Adults (Online Users 18+ Years of Age) | | | | |
|---|---|---|---|---|
| Social Media Site | 2013 | | 2014 | |
| | Men (%) | Women (%) | Men (%) | Women (%) |
| Facebook | 66 | 76 | 66 | 77 |
| LinkedIn | 24 | 19 | 28 | 27 |
| Twitter | 17 | 18 | 24 | 21 |
| Instagram | 15 | 20 | 22 | 29 |
| Pinterest | 8 | 33 | 13 | 42 |
| Average | 26 | 33.2 | 30.6 | 39.2 |
| Source: Maeve Duggan, Nicole B. Ellison, Cliff Lampe, Amanda Lenhart, and Mary Madden, "Social Media Update 2014," Pew Research Center. January 9, 2015: www.pewinternet.org. | | | | |

*Figure 4.4  Complex tables can include numerous columns and rows, as well as braced headings.*

**Order and Sequence.** Put columns to be compared next to each other, and sequence the data in some logical way, such as alphabetical or high to low. When comparing the financial performance of seven branches, for example, sequence the branches from highest to lowest.

**Numbers.** When working with numbers, generally limit to two decimal places and align columns of numbers by their decimals. Also, if exact numbers are not absolutely necessary, considering rounding for easier mental processing.

**Cell Contents.** Table cells typically contain either alphabetic or numeric data, although you could, if appropriate, include a graphic element in a cell. As a general rule, leave no empty cells. If data is missing for a cell, type a dashed line, type N/A (not available), or fill the cell with black or gray, thus letting the reader know the data omission was intentional.

**Footnotes.** As appropriate, add footnotes beneath tables, either to give additional explanation or to document the information source.

**Page Breaks.** Try to keep the entire contents of each table on one page. If you have to divide a table across pages, however, type "continued from page x" and repeat the column headings for easy reference.

**Highlighting.** If you have long columns of data, consider highlighting every other row with a light color to aid the reader in tracking from left to right across the rows.

## Bar Graphs

Bar graphs are one of the most common visuals used in business and government. The bars may be either vertical or horizontal (if the bars are vertical, they are often called column charts). Bar charts are a great option for comparing two or more quantities, because the human eye can easily discern differences in lengths of the bars. For vertical bars the Y axis (vertical axis) represents a quantity, such as money, and the X axis (horizontal axis) represents some other factor, such as time, geographic areas, organizational units, or commodity types. Many types of bar charts can be used, including simple, multiple bar, subdivided, and 100-percent charts, all illustrated in Figure 4.5.

Pictograms are sometimes used as a creative alternative to bar graphs. Instead of showing data as a bar, a pictogram uses small visual symbols (see Figure 4.6). If you use pictograms, use symbols that are easily recognizable and that clearly represent the subject.

Several guidelines are important to remember as you prepare bar charts:

**Titles.** Include titles for X and Y axes, and include a legend when you have more than one data series.

**Sequence.** Logically sequence the bars (e.g., alphabetically or high to low).

**Widths.** Keep all bars the same width, and keep the space between the bars the same width, such as one-half the width of the bars.

**Color.** For a single data series, make all the bars the same color, unless you want to visually highlight one or more of the bars for emphasis. For multiple-bar charts, avoid placing red and green bars beside each other,

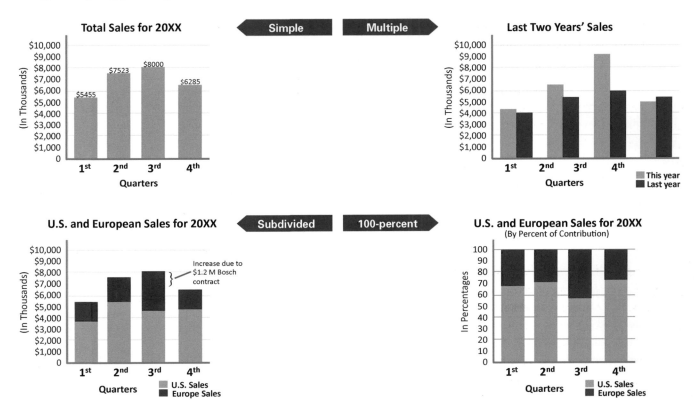

Figure 4.5  *Samples of simple, multiple bar, subdivided bar, and 100-percent bar graphs. Notice the callout in the subdivided bar chart.*

because color-blind readers cannot tell the difference. Avoid using too much color, and be sensitive to the cultural meaning of various colors.

**Dimension.** If you use three-dimensional bar charts, limit their depth to avoid confusion about the real height of the bars.

**Data Labels.** Consider using data labels (i.e., numbers at the end of the bars), except when too many data labels would make the chart look cluttered.

**Deception.** Avoid deceiving your audience by distorting graphics to your advantage. For example, keep equal time increments along the X and Y axes of charts, and keep the height or length of each bar in exact percentage proportion to other bars. For instance, a bar showing 25 percent should be exactly half as long as a bar showing 50 percent. For pictograms, use multiple small images to represent quantity differences, rather than using a small and a large size of the same image. As you can see in Figure 4.7, the larger image is twice as high as the smaller, but is also twice as wide. Consequently,

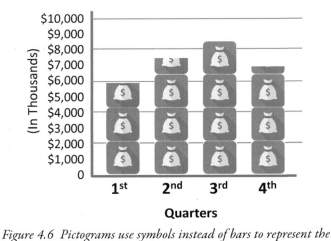

Figure 4.6  *Pictograms use symbols instead of bars to represent the data.*

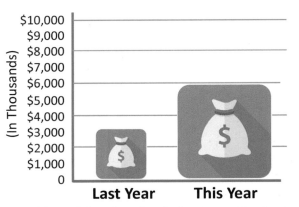

Figure 4.7  *The symbol on the right is both twice as tall and twice as wide, giving a visual impression of more than a 100 percent increase.*

the larger image is four times the size, creating confusion as to the actual difference between the quantities represented.

From time to time you might have to report data that touches humans in a particularly sensitive way, such as the number of deaths caused by automobile accidents. In such a case, you might include a footnote that acknowledges the sensitivity of the data or include a few brief stories of how the families' lives have been tragically affected. Always be sensitive to what the numbers represent.

## Line Graphs

Line graphs are useful for showing data changes over a period of time. The human eye can easily discern slopes, and so upward and downward trends can be easily spotted with line graphs. As with bar charts, the vertical axis (Y axis) of the graph represents some quantity, either actual amounts or percentages. The horizontal axis (X axis) usually represents time. Several variations of line charts can be used, including simple one-line charts, multiple-line charts, and area charts.

Remember the following guidelines as you work with line graphs:

**Multiple Lines.** Avoid including too many lines, because doing so makes the chart look cluttered and makes the information difficult to comprehend.

**Line Differentiation.** Differentiate between lines with line-style variations or color, and include a key (legend) to identify each line.

**Titles.** Include titles for both X and Y axes for clarification.

**Proportional Axes.** Keep horizontal and vertical axes proportionate to avoid distorting the data. With distorted X or Y axes, you can increase or decrease the slope and make the data look either better or worse than it is in reality.

**Color.** For multiple-line charts, remember that color-blind readers often have trouble distinguishing between red and green.

Figure 4.8 illustrates a line chart with number of units sold on the Y axis and years shown on the X axis. Figure 4.9 illustrates the same data in an area chart, which is a line chart with the area below the lines filled in with a color or shade. Area charts should be avoided if some of the lines cross each other, because the data points below

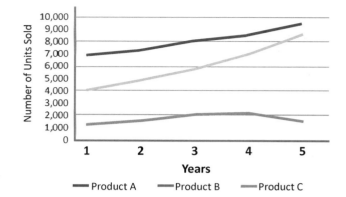

*Figure 4.8 Line charts show changes in quantities over a time period.*

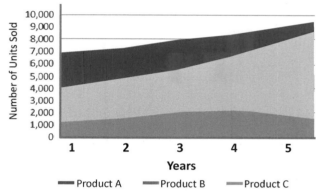

*Figure 4.9 An area chart shows the same data as a line chart but with filled areas.*

the crossed lines will be hidden behind the area with the higher numbers.

## Scatter Plot Charts

Scatter plots are similar to line graphs in that they use a horizontal X axis and a vertical Y axis to illustrate data. Rather than plotting change over a period of time, however, scatter plots are used to plot two sets of data, such as a person's weight and height. Scatter plots show how one variable correlates (or does not correlate) with the other. Three general types of correlation are possible:

**Positive correlation.** When one factor goes up, the other also goes up, such as that shown in Figure 4.10. (Example: "When we increase our advertising budget, sales rise.")

**No correlation.** The rise or fall of the two data sets shows no correlation with one another. (Example: "When interest rates rise, our sales do not move in a predictable direction.")

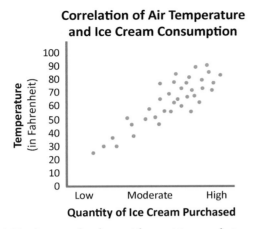

Figure 4.10  *A scatterplot chart with a positive correlation.*

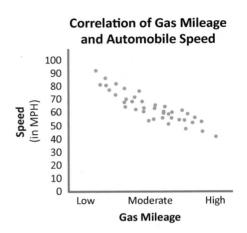

Figure 4.11  *A scatterplot chart with a negative correlation.*

**Negative correlation.** When one factor goes up, the other goes down, such as is shown in Figure 4.11. (Example: "When we increase the price, sales go down.")

## Pie Graphs

Whereas bar graphs show quantity by bar length and line graphs show quantity by line height, pie graphs show quantity by area (see Figure 4.12). Unfortunately, the human eye does not easily distinguish between the size of two similar areas as well as it does between the lengths of different bars or the heights of different lines. As a result, bar and line graphs are often preferred over pie graphs. Nevertheless, pie graphs are very common and you need to know how and when to use them. Remember the four basic guidelines.

**Single Series.** Use pie charts for showing percentages or proportions of one number series, such as the breakdown of this year's budget, rather than the breakdown of several years' budgets. If you want to compare the breakdown of this year's budget with last year's budget, however, don't use two pie charts. Instead, use a bar chart.

**Sequencing.** Arrange the segments from largest to smallest in clockwise order (beginning at the 12 o'clock point), except that the miscellaneous segment should always come last.

**Labels.** Label the quantity for each segment of the pie.

**Emphasis.** If you wish to emphasize one segment, explode it (detach it and slide it away from the rest of the segments), as shown in Figure 4.12.

## Photographs and Clip Art

As you work with photographs and clip art, you will encounter two different file formats: vector and raster (also known as bitmap). Vector images are made up of basic geometric lines and shapes and are created by a mathematical formula inside the computer. The formula dictates the shape, size, and color of the object. Vector images cannot display the detailed natural qualities of photographs. Figure 4.13 shows vector and raster graphics side by side to contrast the difference.

Raster images are comprised of rows and columns of

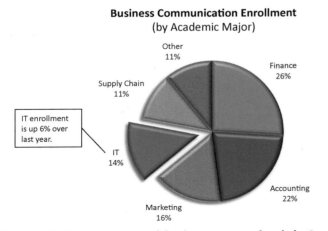

Figure 4.12  *Pie charts are good for showing parts of a whole. Segments can be exploded for emphasis.*

Figure 4.13  *Vector graphics (left) are often used for drawings; raster graphics (right), for photographs.*

tiny pixels (a word coined from the words picture and element) on a computer screen. Each pixel can be a different color, so computers can display highly defined color photographs with millions of colors. Because computers must store the attributes of all the dots in an image, raster files are often very large. Vector images, by comparison, are usually much smaller.

Even though raster images can portray a rich texture of color, they cannot be enlarged without a loss of resolution, or picture quality. When you enlarge a raster image, you enlarge each of the pixels so the image becomes jagged in appearance, or pixelated. Thus, when you plan to enlarge a photograph, shoot the original photo in high resolution (which will result in a larger file size). Vector images, by comparison, retain the same resolution, or image sharpness, regardless of their size, so you can vary the size of a vector graphic without losing any image quality. Because they are scalable, vector images will retain the same resolution for something as small as a business card or as large as a billboard.

Raster images are used primarily for photos, and Adobe Photoshop and Microsoft Paint are raster-editing programs. Conversely, Adobe Illustrator is a vector-drawing program and is used for creating simpler images like logos. Vector images can be displayed on the internet as SVG files. Many projects, such as creating a pamphlet, require the use of both raster and vector images.

When raster graphics are displayed on the internet, they are usually in JPEG, GIF, or PNG format. Photos are usually saved as JPEG files; simpler graphics, such as logos, are often saved as GIF or PNG files. All of these file types involve file compression; that is, if a 3.4-megabyte BMP or TIFF graphic (uncompressed formats) is subsequently saved as a JPEG, it will be reduced (compressed) in size, perhaps to about 350 K. Smaller file size results in shorter internet-transmission time, which means less waiting time for internet users.

With drawing software, you can create vector graphics of your own (as shown in Figure 4.14). Drawing tools in Microsoft PowerPoint and Microsoft Publisher include lines, connectors, block arrows, flowchart symbols, stars, banners, call outs, and action buttons. These software packages also contain tools to align, distribute, rotate, and flip images. Using a combination of four basic shapes—a line, circle or oval, square or rectangle (with squared or rounded corners), and triangle—you can draw a variety of simple objects to use in documents or slideshows. After drawing the various parts of an object, you can group all the parts so they stick together and become as one graphic, rather than

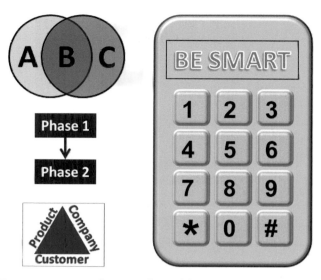

*Figure 4.14  Vector shapes can be used for drawing simple objects.*

as a number of individual parts. Then you can add special effects provided by the software you use.

You can also use basic shapes for developing concept maps. As the name implies, concept maps are visual representations of the various parts of a concept or idea. These representations typically use lines to connect circles or boxes, showing relationships between the various elements of the concept. Figure 4.15 shows a concept map of the main parts of this chapter. As this figure illustrates, a mind map is an example of a concept map.

Clip art is created with vector software, but clip art is not used often in business or government documents because it often looks amateurish. Thus, if you use clip art, make sure it looks professional and does not detract from your message. Also, avoid using different styles of clip art in the same publication. For example, two pieces of clip art created by the same artist will usually show similar artistic style, but two art pieces drawn by different artists will not. As with all graphics, get appropriate legal clearance from the creator before using it.

Because you will use photographs often in newsletters, handouts, slideshows, and reports, work to improve your

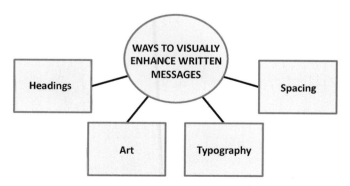

*Figure 4.15  Vector graphics can be used to create concept maps.*

photographic skills. The following photo-composition guidelines will help you get the most out of the photos you take.

**Message Clarity**. Decide what message you want the photo to communicate. Remove any items that might distract from that message. Remove any background items that might appear inappropriately attached to the main subject. For instance, if a man poses exactly in front of a small tree, it might look like the tree is growing out of his head.

**Photo Orientation**. As a general guideline, photograph tall and narrow objects in portrait (vertical) mode; shoot short and wide objects in landscape (horizontal) mode. In other words, turn your camera to the side (portrait mode) to shoot one or two people, but leave it in landscape mode for photographing a group.

**Light**. Use light appropriately. Usually the sun or other light source should be shining on the front of the object (such as a person's face), rather than on the back of the object. When photographing people outdoors, bright overcast days are better than sunny days that cast harsh shadows. If you photograph people on a sunny day, use a camera flash to reduce the darkness of shadows on their faces.

**Cropping**. Move or zoom in to fill the picture with the subject matter, although not too close—you need to leave a bit of a border around the subject matter. You can perform additional cropping with your photo-editing software.

**Rule of Thirds**. Because the human eye prefers photographs that are not totally symmetrical, try to apply the rule of thirds to enhance the photograph's composition.

Imagine a tic-tac-toe grid on your photo. Place the subject at one of the places where the lines intersect, rather than right in the middle of the photograph. Figure 4.16 shows the same photo, but the photo at the right has been cropped to position the man's face near the upper-right one-third intersection.

**Editing**. Edit photos to improve the contrast, brightness, and colors and to eliminate problems such as red eye and other imperfections.

Once you have your photographs ready to insert in a document, you have just three additional tasks to complete. First, if any outside part of a picture is white (e.g., a white cloud in the sky), place a black hairline border around the picture. The border will create a distinct line between the white part of the picture and the white page. Second, if you include a caption with your printed photo, use a font different from the font used for surrounding body text. For instance, if the body text of a report uses 11-point Times New Roman, you could use 10-point Times New Roman italics for the photo caption. Finally, if you obtain your photo from the internet, get legal clearance to use it.

## Maps

Maps are useful for giving directions in a geographic area, as well as for presenting data that is spatially related, such as population comparisons among various states. For directions, travelers have become accustomed to using GPS (global positioning system) software for finding their way to their desired destinations, but you may also use common vector software to draw the layout of a room or to place textual instructions or directional shapes (e.g., arrows) on a raster map of your city.

*Figure 4.16 The photo on the right demonstrates the rule of thirds. The man's face is now at the upper-right one-third intersection, which draws your eye to it.*

## Single-family Housing Starts
### West Coast States—2013

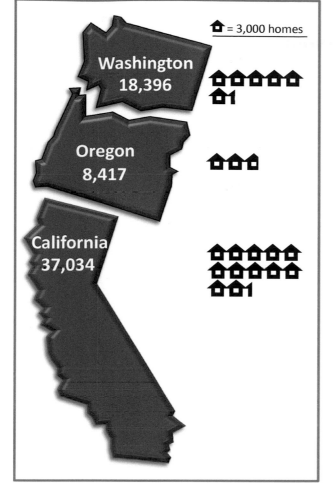

*Figure 4.17  Maps are useful for showing directions and for showing data.*

For data maps, you can obtain geographic maps online and then place your data on those maps (see Figure 4.17). While the data could be placed in a standard table, it can be understood much easier in visual form. As you create maps, make sure they accurately represent the right shape and relative size. Also, use appropriate colors, labels, and legends to communicate quickly and clearly.

### Organization Charts

Organization charts show people or positions in their hierarchical location on the organizational tree. Usually the CEO (chief executive officer) will be at the top of the chart, with vice presidents under the president, and so forth down to the lower level supervisors and personnel.

Also feel free to draw additional dotted lines that reveal frequent communication pathways or to insert additional helpful information. Figure 4.18 illustrates a basic organization chart.

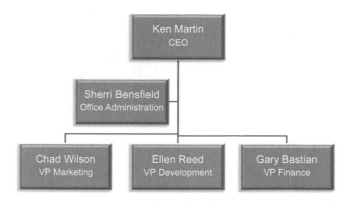

*Figure 4.18  Organization charts show the management hierarchy in businesses.*

### Flowcharts

A flowchart (sometimes referred to as a flow process chart) is a graphical representation of the steps involved in some process, such as the process of manufacturing a product step by step along an assembly line. Flowcharts help in the analysis of work flow, resulting in the identification and elimination of waste. Flowcharts are also used in computer programming to show the logical steps of software and for drawing concept maps to represent sequential reasoning.

To create a flowchart, first list all the tasks in chronological order. Identify any decisions that must be made along the way, as well as any approvals that are required. Once you have a complete list, place each step, each decision, and each approval step inside an appropriately shaped figure. You can find standardized flowchart figures on your computer's software or online, but for most flowcharts you may use rectangle or whatever shapes seem to be most appropriate for the task. Connect all the shapes with a directional arrow, moving in a general left-to-right, top-to-bottom direction. Once the flow chart is completed, check it carefully—make sure the sequence is accurate, that the textual descriptions are clear, and that the chart achieves its intended objective. Figure 4.19 shows a sample flow chart.

### How to Plan a Meeting

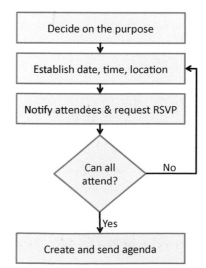

*Figure 4.19  Flow charts show steps and sequences in a process.*

## Infographics

Infographics (short for information graphics) are typically comprised of multiple graphs and explanatory text that combine to communicate a message in a highly visual way. While all the business graphs and charts previously discussed are relatively standard ways of representing data, each infographic is uniquely designed. They may include standard graphics, but they go far beyond that and use a variety of text, typography, shapes and symbols, tables, arrows, and anything else that will help communicate the complex information quickly and clearly (see Figure 4.20).

As you design infographics, first clearly define your purpose. Then analyze the audience and context and develop your design strategy. Brainstorm wildly and use your best imagination to present the information in a way that captures attention and communicates the information clearly. Make sure to have an obvious doorway, or entry point, to the infographic and then a clear path for moving through the information. You can find numerous examples of infographics by searching "creative infographics" online.

As you create infographics, always make sure the purpose drives the design. The design should complement, not compete with, the purpose. Remember the importance of simplicity and clarity. Several design principles are given in Chapter 11 of this book, and you can find online guidance and software at canva.com, www.easel.ly, and infogr.am, as well as at other related sites.

# TYPOGRAPHY

The third element of HATS is typography. The most important aspects of typography are reflected on the tool bar of your software, including the font, size, style, and alignment. When deciding on typography, consider the audience and the context in which the text will be read, whether on a computer screen, on a small mobile device in the bright sunlight, or on a page.

## Font (typeface)

Font recommendations are different for paper documents and electronic documents. For paper, Serif fonts (such as Times New Roman) are often preferred for body text because the serifs (the little finishing marks at the end of their strokes) make each letter more unique and easy to recognize.[2] Sans serif fonts (such as Arial) are sans (with-

out) such distinguishing little flourishes. Sans serif fonts are often used for headings because they usually have a thicker stroke. This blockier weight makes them easier to read in larger point sizes or from a distance. Because of these differences, sans serif fonts are more easily read than serif fonts in small groups, such as headings or titles, but are not as easy to read as serif fonts in large groups such as paragraphs.

For electronic documents, the font recommendations are different. Sans serif is usually the recommended font for body text. Because visual resolution (clarity) is lower for screens than for paper, serifs can get in the way of visual clarity. Thus, Calibri, Arial, Helvetica, and Tahoma fonts are used often for electronic documents.

Professional designers recommend the use of only two primary fonts (typefaces) for most documents, one serif and one sans serif. For example, a paper document could use a serif font for body text and a sans serif font for headings, and an electronic document could use a sans serif font for body text and a serif font for headings. The two faces can then be varied for different levels of headings and different effects in body type.

In addition to serif and sans serif categories, decorative and script typefaces can be used to add personality and flair to a document. However, these are best considered like strong spices in cooking. A small amount sprinkled carefully and with thoughtful intent can add pleasing flavor to a document, but dumping in a random selection can overpower a document's purpose. If you are not sure about including another font, it is better to leave it out.

From the thousands of fonts that are available, use those that fit the situation. For example, use an informal font for something like a company party announcement. Use a formal font for a formal reception. Use a neutral font for routine memos and reports.

### Come to our department party!
(Comic Sans font)

*You are invited to a reception to honor . . .*
(French Script font)

This memo will introduce a new procedure . . .
(Times New Roman font)

Finally, don't forget that your purpose is to communicate. An interesting or eye-catching font like the following won't strengthen your document if people can't read it.

DOES THIS HELP COMMUNICATE?

---

2 The body text for this book is set in 11 point Garamond.

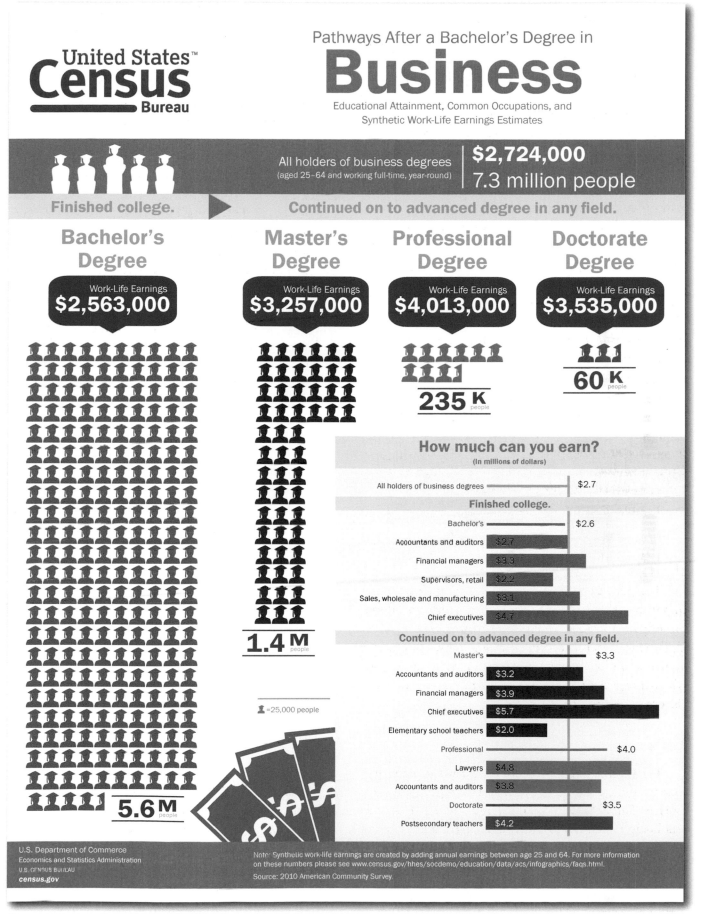

*Figure 4.20  An infographic from the U.S. Department of Commerce shows academic options after a bachelor's degree.*

## Size (height)

Typography height is measured in points, with 72 points equaling one inch. Normally, for paper and computer screen, use 10–12 point type for general audiences. For an elderly audience, increase the type size. For text on mobile devices, use a larger font to ensure readability. For slideshows viewed by a large audience, also increase the type size appropriately so everyone in the audience can see and read the text easily.

Vary the type sizes for different levels of headings, such as 22-point type for first-level headings, 16-point for second-level headings, and so forth.

# Calibri 22-point

## Times New Roman 16-point

## Style

You can enhance basic type in several ways to make it more noticeable, including the two most commonly used treatments—bold and italic. You can also put white type on a black background, called reverse type. When you use reverse type with serif fonts, you may need to bold the text so the thin strokes of each character are wide enough to be clearly visible.

> **Reverse type usually gets noticed!**

In most cases, avoid underlining text because the line cuts through the descenders of lower-case letters like j, q, g, and y, detracting from their appearance (e.g., <u>typography</u>) and making them more difficult to read. You can also use occasional **color** for emphasis, or use ALL CAPITAL LETTERS for headings. Do not use all capitals for body text, however, because text in all capitals is hard to read. Use moderation with all typographic enhancement, because too much emphasis is distracting.

## Alignment

Type can be aligned on the left, center, or right. It can also be aligned on both left and right sides, called full justification. For most paper and electronic business documents, use left alignment (also called ragged right). Left-aligned type is easier to read than fully justified type. The following samples illustrate different text alignment.

This is left-aligned text, also called left justified text. Left-aligned text is easier to read when you have a wider text block (more than about 4 inches wide).

- All lines of bulleted text should be left aligned with the first line of text, not with the bullet. The space between the bullet and the first word should be about the width of a capital M.

This is centered text. It has ragged left and right sides and is centered on the middle of the text line. Centered text is most often used for headings and formal invitations.

This is right-aligned text, also called right justified text. It aligns text on the right margin and is used infrequently. However, it may be used in tables or charts for columns of numbers.

This is fully justified text. Both left and right sides of the text are aligned with the margins. An advantage of fully justified text is that it gives a polished, formal appearance. However, if it creates too much space between words in the lines of text, it can inhibit readability and look unprofessional.

In addition to alignment concerns, typography experts suggest that readability can be impacted by the length of text lines. If the average number of words or characters is too long or too short, readability may decrease. Use formatting options like adjusting the width of the side margins, changing the font size, or using a multi-column layout to create line lengths that produce good readability.

## SPACING

You can often improve the visual appearance of business documents by adding more white space in strategic places. Having plenty of white space is important because pages with many lines of text without a visual break look gray and uninviting. White space gives visual relief, prevents reader fatigue, and enhances reader friendliness. Space also divides and frames elements on a page or screen. For instance, white space placed around a block of text or a graphic divides it from neighboring elements.

Check two aspects of spacing in your documents: external and internal. External spacing refers to the margins around the edges of the page. For most routine documents, a one-inch margin is standard, but don't be afraid to allow margins of more than an inch for text-heavy documents.

Internal spacing is the space within the text. Pay attention to three aspects of internal spacing. First, generally leave more space between paragraphs than between the lines of text within paragraphs. Second, leave at least one line of space before and after tables and graphics. Third,

leave enough space between the lines of text (line spacing) that the white space guides the eye as its returns from the end of one line of text to the beginning of the next. The longer the line length, the greater the amount of line spacing is needed. (See more spacing guidelines in Appendix B.)

After considering external and internal spacing, be aware of stray textual elements such as headings, orphans, or widows. A heading should always be followed by at least two lines of body text before a page break. An orphan is a paragraph's first line left by itself at the bottom of a page; a widow is a paragraph's last line left by itself at the top of a page. Where possible, avoid both by making sure at least the first two lines appear at the bottom of the first page and at least the last two lines appear at the top of the next page.

The two following memos show the impact of the HATS procedure on a routine document. Figure 4.21 suffers from the following design problems:

*Headings:* No headings are used in the body of the text.

*Art:* No visual techniques are used to make the information easier to read and understand.

*Typography:* All type is 10-point Arial, a sans serif type. Type style variation is not used to emphasize important text. Alignment of the text creates an unhelpful and uninviting block shape.

*Spacing:* Internal spacing is too tight, giving the memo a dark, gray appearance which repels rather than attracts the reader.

The redesigned memo in Figure 4.22 incorporates the following improvements:

*Headings:* Three headings are added in the body of the memo, clearly showing the text structure and reflecting the three main parts of the text.

*Art:* The financial information is displayed in a bar chart, showing a clear visual comparison between the two sales-to-staff ratios.

To: Western Region Store Managers
From: Sara Howard, FastFood Operations Manager
Date: June 10, 20XX
Re: Recruiting, Hiring, Scheduling, and Retaining Employees
    On a recent visit to Las Vegas, I found a FastFood store that is getting and keeping a quality work force, a goal which, as you know, is an ongoing problem for our industry. The manager, Carl Wallace, shared with me the success strategy.
    Carl has determined that the standard FastFood staff figure of one employee for every $2,500 of monthly sales is not optimal. After experimenting, he found the best figure to be $1,800. At this level, more employee flexibility is achievable.
    Maintaining adequate staffing levels is an industry-wide challenge. To solve this problem, Carl has organized his workforce into three teams. Each team is given a $100 monthly budget to use in recruiting, interviewing, and training new employees. If the team's staff level is maintained at 10 throughout a quarter, each member of the team receives a $100 bonus. Another industry problem is employee retention. Annual turnover at Carl's store has decreased 151 percent since implementing his program. Four incentives have helped improve employee retention: Monthly free-food days; 30-day wage evaluations for new employees, quarterly wage evaluations for all employees; monthly performance reviews for all employees; and "Buddies" and other programs to ensure employee satisfaction.
    Because of Carl's success, I strongly recommend that you consider implementing one or more of these approaches as appropriate in your store. Please send me an email response to this memo by the first of next month to let me know your specific plans.

*Figure 4.21 Messages with no visual enhancement are gray, uninviting, and often hard to read.*

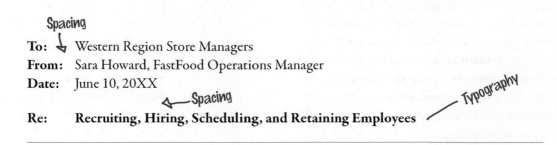

**To:**      Western Region Store Managers

**From:**    Sara Howard, FastFood Operations Manager

**Date:**    June 10, 20XX

**Re:**      **Recruiting, Hiring, Scheduling, and Retaining Employees**

On a recent visit to Las Vegas, I found a FastFood store that is getting and keeping a quality work force, a goal which, as you know, is an ongoing problem for our industry. The manager, Carl Wallace, shared with me the success strategy, and I recommend it to you for implementation. Carl's strategy includes (a) determining appropriate staff levels, (b) finding qualified staff, and (c) retaining employees.

**Determining Appropriate Staffing Levels.** Carl has determined that the standard FastFood staff figure of one employee for every $2,500 of monthly sales is not optimal. After experimenting, he found the best figure to be $1,800. At this level, more employee flexibility is achievable (see accompanying chart).

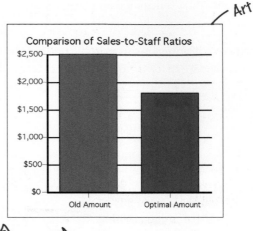

**Finding Qualified Staff.** Maintaining adequate staffing levels is an industry-wide challenge. To solve this problem, Carl has organized his workforce into three teams. Each team is given a $100 monthly budget to use in recruiting, interviewing, and training new employees. If the team's staff level is maintained at 10 throughout a quarter, each member of the team receives a $100 bonus.

**Retaining Employees.** Another industry problem is employee retention. Annual turnover at Carl's store has decreased 151 percent since implementing his program. Four incentives have helped improve employee retention:

- Monthly free-food days
- 30-day wage evaluations for new employees, and quarterly wage evaluations for all employees
- Monthly performance reviews for all employees
- "Buddies" and other programs to ensure employee satisfaction

Because of Carl's success, I strongly recommend that you consider implementing one or more of these approaches as appropriate in your store. Please **send me an email response** to this memo by the first of next month to let me know your specific plans.

*Figure 4.22  Headings and other visual enhancements make messages more inviting and easier to read.*

*Typography:* The subject line is bolded, as are the headings in the body. The individual agenda items are set off with alphabetic markers (a, b, and c). A bulleted list has been created in the fourth paragraph, making the information easier to find. Also, the entire document has been typed in 11-point type, a good size for general audiences. Further, the memo body is left aligned, making the text easier to read than fully justified text. The left-aligned body also gives the memo a more friendly appearance. Finally, the response request is bolded in the last paragraph, helping to ensure that the reader doesn't miss the return-requested information.

*Spacing:* Needed space has been added between the paragraphs, as well as between the various parts of the main headings at the top of the memo. The subject line has been framed in white, quickly revealing the content of the memo. The horizontal space between the bullets and their associated text is closer than word processors' default tabs allow, reflecting a close relationship between the bullets and text.

The HATS design process offers three key benefits.

1.  HATS can be easily remembered because of the obvious acronym.

2.  HATS provides a general standard for both designing and editing documents.

3.  HATS improves the audience's reading experience, enhancing both efficiency and effectiveness.

As you develop a good understanding of headings, art, typography, and spacing, you will be able to apply the HATS principles and techniques in your own written documents. These design steps may take a bit of extra time, but they will produce a better document for your audience and will enhance your professional reputation.

## CHAPTER SUMMARY

Long passages of text, with no visuals, look boring and uninviting. For all substantive messages you write, invest a bit of time to enhance their visual design. HATS (Headings, Art, Typography, and Spacing) will help you do this. First, headings are helpful in both long and short documents, because they enhance information access—the degree to which important information is easily accessible to the reader.

Second, art refers to the use of all types of visual treatments to make information easier to find and process. Graphic representations, such as tables, bar charts, maps, organization charts, and photographs, can also make information easy to find and easier to understand. Tables consist of an information grid, with vertical columns and horizontal rows containing numeric or alphabetic information. Bar charts are a great option for comparing two or more quantities, because the human eye can easily discern differences in lengths of the bars. Line charts are good for showing data changes over a period of time. Scatter plots show how one variable correlates (or does not correlate) with the other. Line graphs show quantity by line height. Pie graphs show quantity by area.

Vector images are comprised of basic geometric lines and shapes and are created by a mathematical formula inside the computer. Raster images are comprised of tiny pixels on a computer screen. With drawing software, you can create vector graphics of your own. Clip art is created with vector software, but clip art is not used often in business or government documents because it looks amateurish.

Maps are useful for helping people find their way, as well as for communicating information that is spatially related. Organization charts show people or positions in their hierarchical location on the organizational tree. A flow chart is a graphical representation of the steps involved in some process, such as manufacturing a product step by step as it moves along an assembly line. Infographics (short for information graphics) typically include a variety of creative graphs, along with appropriate text, that combine to communicate the desired message.

The third element of HATS is typography. The most important aspects of typography are on the tool bar of computer software—the font, size, style, and alignment. Two fonts are recommended for most paper documents—one serif and one sans serif. The best font size for most office settings is in the 10–12 point range. Left alignment is best for most routine documents.

The final element of HATS is spacing. Leave appropriate spacing for the outside margins and for spacing between paragraphs, visuals, and lines of text.

### *Works Cited*

Baker, William H. "HATS: A Design Procedure for Routine Business Documents." *Business Communication Quarterly* 64, no. 2 (2001): 65–76.

Frischknecht, Sierra Sloan and William H. Baker. "Enhanced vs. Undifferentiated Text: A Study to Assess the Effects on Readers." *Proceedings of the 76th Annual Convention of the Association for Business Communication.* Montreal, Quebec, Canada. Association for Business Communication (2011), 19–22.

## CHAPTER QUESTIONS

1. What words are represented by the acronym HATS?

2. What are the two main headings factors to remember?

3. What is a question heading? When should it be used?

4. What are the three "I" rules to remember for including visuals in text?

5. What is a legend? A call out? A braced heading?

6. What is a T chart used for?

7. What segments are in a decision table?

8. Compare the similarities and differences of bar charts and line charts. Why are line and bar charts generally preferred over pie charts?

9. What is a pictogram? How does it compare with bar charts?

10. What is a scatter-plot chart?

11. What is the difference between positive and negative correlation?

12. Where should the miscellaneous data be shown on a pie chart?

13. Describe two limitations of pie charts.

14. Describe the differences between vector and raster graphics.

15. What is a flow chart? How is it used?

16. What is an infographic? What is its purpose?

17. In photography, what is the rule of thirds?

18. Explain two guidelines for photographing people outdoors on sunny days.

19. Describe the difference between serif and sans serif fonts.

20. How many typographic "points" are in an inch? What is the ideal type size for most audiences?

21. Which text alignment should be used with most office documents?

22. What are widows and orphans? Why should they be avoided?

23. What is white space? What are the two main functions of white space?

## CHAPTER ACTIVITIES

1. Obtain some quantitative data from the U.S. Census Bureau website or other government or business site approved by your instructor. Using this data, create an original bar chart and an original table. Cite the source of your material at the bottom of the chart and table.

2. Write a memo that includes and explains one of the graphics you created for Activity 1. Apply the three "I" guidelines and include the graphic in your document.

3. Visit the website www.pewresearch.org. Select a chart and transform it to a different type of graphic. For example, change a line chart to a bar chart or transform data from a bar chart to a pie chart. Submit both the original and your new chart to your instructor.

4. Take several pairs of digital photos. For each pair, violate one of the following photography principles for one photo and apply it in the other:

   a. Correct lighting

   b. Portrait or landscape orientation

   c. Rule of thirds

   d. Distracting items

5. Create a flow chart that shows the steps involved in some process with which you are familiar. Include at least 10 steps and include at least one decision step.

6. Find a one- or two-page document on the internet or elsewhere. Evaluate its design, and then re-create and redesign the document so it includes effective use of headings, art, typography, and spacing.

7. Using the draw tools of PowerPoint or other program, create a concept model for a topic of your choice.

8. Using the draw tools of PowerPoint or other program, create a logo for yourself or someone else.

9. Using PowerPoint or other program, create a one-page infographic of one of the chapters in this book.

# CHAPTER 5

# Reviewing and Revising

Think of the times in your life when you have read something that was hard to follow or hard to understand. How did you feel about it? How did you feel about the writer? Now consider your own writing—do you ever write essays, reports, or messages that are less polished and effective than they should be? Good writing is demanding work, and as you compose documents containing hundreds of words, so much can go wrong. You can misspell words, make comma mistakes, forget to capitalize a word, write disjointed sentences, create poorly organized paragraphs, fail to explain something clearly, get facts wrong, omit important information, or commit other errors that will make your messages less effective than they could be.

When people in business send poorly written messages, several consequences can occur. For writing that is unclear, the reader must take extra time to understand it, and for writing that contains factual errors, the reader may draw improper conclusions. But the writers of the poorly written documents also pay a price—their credibility suffers because the reader assumes they either don't know how to write well or are simply careless. Further, they may be passed over for promotions and other opportunities that require good writing skills.

Now is the time for you to develop effective writing and revising habits that will serve you well throughout your career. As you do, opportunities will come your way, and you might even find that others will come to you for help with their writing.

After learning the material in this chapter, you should be able to do the following:

- Work effectively with others in getting and giving good writing feedback.

- Use the four-step DOCS review process to revise and edit written documents.

The first section of this chapter discusses factors to consider before revising; the remainder of the chapter walks you through the comprehensive DOCS review process that will guide you in your revision efforts.

## PREPARING TO REVIEW AND REVISE A DOCUMENT

All messages, whether long or short, can benefit from revision. As much as you would like to be able to write first-time-final text, it won't happen very often. As you compose the first draft of a message, you have to think about what you want to say, how to structure the sentences, what words to use, what punctuation to use, and so forth. You have so much information to be processed at once! But after you get the first draft created, you can sit back and examine the document from a different perspective.

One important revision consideration relates to the importance of the document. For routine messages, you can perform the review-and-revise process alone. However, for more important documents, consider having others review the documents, because other people are usually better than you at reading a document from the perspective of the intended audience.

Some people hesitate to ask others to review their writing—they may not want to impose on others, they may not want to take the extra time to obtain more feedback, or they fear letting others see their writing. Without obtaining needed feedback, writers increase their risk of sending inef-

fective or inaccurate messages. When you write an important document that could benefit from having another person check it, overcome your hesitation and ask for help. Choose reviewers who are knowledgeable and who will be forthright in their feedback. Be open and express appreciation for the feedback they give you. Never become defensive, even if you disagree with some of their suggestions. After all, you are not required to apply all the suggestions they give. Just use the ones you think will help your message, and then disregard the rest.

As you review a document, whether for yourself or for others, do it from both the writer's and the reader's perspectives. Consider all important PACS information, as explained in Chapter 2. (If you're reviewing someone else's writing, be sure to obtain the PACS information from them.)

- Understand the *purpose* of the message.
- Understand the *audience* and all relevant demographic, psychographic, and knowledge factors.
- Understand all relevant *context* factors that will affect how the message is received and acted upon.
- Understand the *strategy* being applied to achieve the purpose.

When others are reviewing a document for you, make your expectations clear. Too often other people will perform only a cursory review, looking for any spelling or grammar problems, and then return the document with a comment like, "It looks pretty good to me; just a grammar item or two that you might want to fix." Such feedback is not very useful. Ask for feedback on all design, organization, content, and sentence issues, but also tell the reviewer that you are mostly interested in whether the document will achieve its intended purpose. After all, revising is more than just fixing grammar errors. Good revision is aimed at helping the

*Figure. 5.1 A good reviewer will read each document from the perspective of the audience.*

writing to get the desired results. For example, if you write a collection letter that doesn't collect, it hasn't achieved its purpose. After all, the most important thing is not what the authors think of their writing, but what the readers think and how they respond.

Reviewing can be performed with either electronic or paper copies, although many authors feel that reviewing paper copies is better.

## Screen Reviewing

For screen reviewing, use your software tools to catch writing errors. Spell checkers are helpful in catching many spelling errors—although not all. Grammar and style checkers are also helpful in catching many sentence weaknesses—although not all. Further, technology doesn't always make the right recommendations for correcting the errors. Nevertheless, software editing tools are right much of the time, so use them.

When reviewing electronic copy for others, use your word processor's track-changes function. For example, Microsoft Word's track-changes feature records all suggestions made by reviewers and displays the comments of each reviewer in a different color. Thus, the system keeps everyone's suggestions separate, so the writer can see who recommended what.

When including multiple reviewers, the writer may email a copy to each person or share the copy electronically on a cloud network, giving each person the ability to edit, comment, or just view. Editing capability allows various reviewers or authors to make changes to the same document simultaneously. For example, if Dave, a technical writer, creates a document, he can save it on Google Drive and share it electronically with others. Dave can give three levels of sharing rights:

**View** enables the other person to view the document but not make comments or change it.

**Comment** enables the other person to view the document and add comments on the side, but not change the document itself.

**Edit** enables the other person to view and revise the document.

When Dave extends editing capability to others, confusion can result when Person A makes a change and then Person B changes the change made by Person A. Thus, Dave should keep an original version on his own drive then make the changes he feels are best.

## Paper Reviewing

Paper reviewing is recommended for longer documents and for more important documents. When reviewing paper copy, you can use standard proofreaders' marks (see Figure 5.2), supplemented with additional notes in the margins. The main point is to communicate clearly to the author how the writing could be improved or how an error should be fixed.

When reviewing and editing a document, you can improve your effectiveness by reading the document out loud meaningfully to force you to concentrate on each word. When reading silently, people typically read clusters of words, without giving adequate attention to individual words. If the text doesn't sound good, revise it until it does.

You can also improve your reviewing and revising effectiveness by using a ruler or piece of paper to cover the text below the line you are reading. This technique helps you to consider individual lines and words instead of larger clusters.

Finally, remember that errors often go undetected in titles, headings, captions, and other areas away from the body text. Therefore, make a quick pass through the document to check for these elements.

# REVISING DESIGN, ORGANIZATION, CONTENT, AND SENTENCES

A good review of professional workplace documents will include four separate phases. Remember the four phases with the acronym DOCS:

Phase 1—Review the Design

Phase 2—Review the Organization

Phase 3—Review the Content

Phase 4—Review the Sentences

A rubric is provided at the end of the chapter to guide the DOCS review process.

| **DOCS** |
| --- |
| Design |
| Organization |
| Content |
| Sentences |

As you go through the four phases of review for a paper document, compliment the writer on the aspects that are good, and jot down the major factors that need improvement. To help organize your review comments, write the letters D, O, C, and S down the left side of a paper. As you complete the first review for design, write your suggestions under the D. Then do the same thing for the organization, content, and sentences reviews. When you complete the process, you will then have a comprehensive, well-organized list for improving the document's design, organization, content, and sentences (see Figure 5.3).

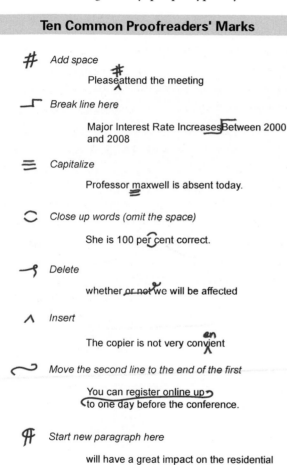

*Figure 5.2 Standard marks help reviewers communicate efficiently with authors.*

```
                    DOCS
        ─────────────────────────────
    D   + Good format
        - Need headings for major sections

    O   + Good OABC
        - Use direct approach

    C   + Message is clear & coherent
        + Good evaluation of options
        - Check topic sentences for paragraphs

    S   - Review comma rules
        - Hyphenate compound adjectives
```

*Figure 5.3   Give a well-organized summary of strengths and suggestions.*

## Phase 1—Review and Revise the Design

The first step in the review process is a high-level examination to check the document for correct formatting and good visual appeal. If your organization has a style guide, become familiar with it. A style guide is a document with writing and design standards to assist everyone when they produce written materials. Margin widths, typography (font, size, and alignment), use of the company logo, company colors, line spacing, use and formatting of headings, and language style can be included. Style guides help ensure that the company puts forth a consistent brand and voice in all of its materials that go out to the public.

To accurately assess document design, become familiar with formatting expectations and standards for the type of business document you are reviewing. Then check the document for adherence to those standards. For instance, an email should follow email formatting standards, an employment resume should follow formatting standards for resumes, and a report should follow generally accepted standards for reports. Typical formatting factors include the width of the top, bottom, left, and right margins; the spacing and alignment of text; the placement of the writer's and reader's names; and so forth. In essence, a business report should be formatted as a business report, and a proposal should be formatted as a proposal. Document formatting guidelines are presented in Appendix B.

After ensuring that the right format has been followed, examine the document to see whether appropriate visual elements have been employed. Initially, glance at the docu-

ment and ask yourself whether it looks "reader friendly." If it looks uninviting and difficult to read, make appropriate changes in the use of HATS (headings, art, typography, and spacing) as explained in Chapter 4.

```
        ┌─────────────────────┐
        │       HATS          │
        ├─────────────────────┤
          Headings

          Art & Graphics

          Typography

          Spacing
        └─────────────────────┘
```

**Headings**. Make sure headings and subheadings enable skimming and adequately reveal the message structure.

**Art**. Bulleted and numbered lists should be used appropriately. Visual techniques (e.g., tables, charts, or photographs) should be used to make important information stand out.

**Typography**. Appropriate typefaces should be employed for headings and body text (e.g., for paper documents, many experts suggest using a serif font for body text and a sans serif font for headings). Determine if the font size is appropriate (usually 10–12 point type height for general-audience documents). See if the text is properly aligned (left alignment for most documents). Determine whether bolded or italicized text is used appropriately.

**Spacing**. Check to see if pages have appropriate outside margins, with adequate white space between lines and paragraphs. Determine whether enough white space is placed around table, charts, photographs, and other visuals. For multipage documents, check for any widowed or orphaned headings, captions, or sentences.

Figure 5.4 shows a message from an administrative unit in a municipal organization, including a reviewer's comments about the design aspects of the document.

## Phase 2—Review and Revise the Organization

As you review the organization, first check to see whether a direct or indirect approach has been used. Remember, the direct approach places the key message at or near the beginning of the message. The direct approach is used for most routine and good-news messages, and it should be used in the majority of messages. The indirect approach places the key message a bit later—following information that is needed to condition the reader's mind.

**Align**

**Boldface x4**

**#**

To: Ken morgan
From:    Jane Sanders
Date: April 9, 20XX
Re: Request for input

DESIGN

Ital

*Break text into short paragraphs to increase white space*

*Use paragraph headings (in sans serif)*

Thanks for requesting my thoughts regarding Midwest City's General Plan. I believe we should work on establishing neighbor hood pocket parks wherever possible. They could contain picnic tables and open areas for throwing a frisbee or football. The parks would make small playgrounds quickly accessible to families and youth groups and would add a nice touch of green among our ever increasing miles of asphalt and concrete.

*Use serif font for body text*

Other cities have had great success with the pocket-park idea, and I think our citizens would like the idea as well. I also think Midwest's most pressing problem is poor traffic flow in a north south direcion. State Street and Arlington Boulevard seem to carry most of the traffic volume in this direction, citizens need several other alternate routes and I know there are probably 3 other routes that should be addressed, also. We also should work on nieghborhood lighting so our streets are not so dark at night. With gang-related problems edging upward, improved lighting would be welcomed by most residents. For many years we have discussed this project, and I think we should now take action.

*Include a map*

Thanks again, Ken, for allowing me to give input as you develop the General Plan. I hope my recommendations will help in this process. Please let me know if you would like to discuss any of these items in detail.        *Top and bottom margins are too narrow*

*Figure 5.4  A memo that has been reviewed for design.*

The indirect approach is used less frequently and is reserved mainly for bad-news and difficult persuasive messages.

Second, check to see if an OABC pattern (or other appropriate pattern) is used and, if so, whether information in the agenda matches the information in the body. OABC may be used as an overall document pattern as well as a pattern within sections of longer documents.

**OABC**

Opening

Agenda

Body

Closing

Third, consider the structure and sequence of all the information chunks throughout the document. Just as an architectural supervisor checks a subordinate's house plans to make sure the rooms are well laid out, so should you check the architecture of a document's information chunks. For shorter documents, a quick skim will reveal to you the information chunks. For longer reports, however, you need an outline. If a table of contents is not provided, you can create a reverse outline to reveal the structure.

For example, an analytical report might include five major information chunks: introduction, research methods, analysis of findings, conclusions, and recommendations. Within these major chunks you may find smaller chunks that should be examined to ensure that they are organized logically. The standard sections for scientific journal articles often follow what is called the IMRAD pattern (Introduction, Methods, Results, And Discussion).

Following an analysis and evaluation of the organization, make appropriate changes. For instance, the main recommendations may need to be moved to the beginning, complying with most managers' preference for direct order. Also, the research findings might need to be rearranged from most to least significant, and the recommendations might need to be sequenced according to implementation order. Figure 5.5 shows the same document as in Figure 5.4, this time with a reviewer's comments about the document's organization.

## Phase 3—Review and Revise the Content

The third phase of review focuses on the content. As you revise the content, seek to write not only so you can be understood, but also so you cannot be misunderstood! In this review, make sure that the content is five-C compliant and that the paragraphs are CLOUD compliant.

To: Ken morgan
From:   Jane Sanders
Date: April 9, 20XX
Re: Request for input

ORGANIZATION

*Add agenda*

¶

Thanks for requesting my thoughts regarding Midwest City's General Plan. I believe we should work on establishing neighbor hood pocket parks wherever possible. They could contain picnic tables and open areas for throwing a frisbee or football. The parks would make small playgrounds quickly accessible to families and youth groups and would add a nice touch of green among our ever increasing miles of asphalt and concrete.

Other cities have had great success with the pocket-park idea, and I think our citizens would like the idea as well. I also think Midwest's most pressing problem is poor traffic flow in a north south direcion. State Street and Arlington Boulevard seem to carry most of the traffic volume in this direction, citizens need several other alternate routes and I know there are probably 3 other routes that should be addressed, also. We also should work on nieghborhood lighting so our streets are not so dark at night. With gang-related problems edging upward, improved lighting would be welcomed by most residents. For many years we have discussed this project, and I think we should now take action.

*Move this text to first body paragraph*

¶

*Break into 3 paragraphs*

Thanks again, Ken, for allowing me to give input as you develop the General Plan. I hope my recommendations will help in this process. Please let me know if you would like to discuss any of these items in detail.

*Good use of direct approach*

*Figure 5.5  A memo that has been reviewed for organization.*

## The Five C's

The content of a document should be clear, complete, correct, considerate, and convincing. To examine the five-C aspect of the content, read the document carefully—sentence by sentence and paragraph by paragraph. As you read the content, remember the author's purpose, but read mainly from the reader's perspective.

| 5 C's |
|-------|
| Clear |
| Complete |
| Correct |
| Considerate |
| Convincing |

### Is it Clear?

A message is clear when it is easy for the audience to read and understand. Is the message clear, with no unanswered questions? Are the key points of the message emphasized and obvious? Are the words clear to the intended audience, with technical words defined as needed? Are sufficient examples and explanations given? Does the information flow logically from beginning to end?

### Is it Complete?

A complete document includes all the content that is relevant to achieving its purpose. Does it answer the basic 5W2H questions (who, what, where, when, why, how, and how much)? Does it cover the subject matter in appropriate depth? Does it examine all issues and consider alternate viewpoints?

Completeness also pertains to the exclusion of irrelevant material. Content that does not contribute, or, worse yet, that distracts from the central message, should be eliminated. Does the document contain too much detail? Does it contain information that is beyond the scope of its purpose? Are some examples or explanations unnecessary?

### Is it Correct?

Correctness refers to the accuracy of the content. Is it factual and free from bias and error? Are all financial and other quantities correct? Can all statements of fact be proven? Are all sources properly cited? Does the document contain any ethical violations, such as misrepresentations or exaggerations of the truth, intentional withholding of relevant information, or making of promises that cannot be fulfilled? Does the message contain any false or malicious statements about competitors' products or practices? Does it include any false or malicious statements that would

constitute defamation? (Defamation is the dissemination of untrue information about another person, resulting in damage to that person's reputation. Defamation can come from both libel and slander—libel is written defamation; slander is spoken defamation.)

### Is it Considerate?

Considerate writing is cordial, kind, and gracious writing, not inconsiderate, demeaning, or condescending. Considerate writing also reflects what is sometimes called "you attitude." It is the opposite of writing with a "me attitude," which considers only the writer's needs. Has the writer tried to meet, or exceed, the reader's expectations? Does the writing help build a relationship of trust with the audience?

### Is it Convincing?

Convincing content is content that achieves the purpose of the message. Does the content achieve the intended purposes of informing, persuading, and building trust and goodwill? Are audience concerns anticipated and resolved? Are the logical and emotional appeals persuasive?

### The Paragraphs

After evaluating the overall content of the document, check the individual paragraphs, especially body paragraphs, for CLOUD compliance. First check each paragraph's organization ("O") and then check the C, L, U, and D aspects.

**CLOUD**

Coherence

Length

Organization

Unity

Development

### Organization

A direct approach is preferred for paragraphs (especially for body paragraphs), with the first sentence stating the topic of the paragraph and the second and succeeding sentences developing or supporting the topic sentence. The sequence of the sentences should follow appropriate chronological or non-chronological order. As needed, a summary sentence may be added at the end of a paragraph.

### Unity

To meet the unity standard, all sentences in a paragraph should relate to the same topic. If the paragraph is about computer software, it shouldn't include information about computer hardware. If you want to include both software and hardware in the paragraph, introduce both in the opening sentence.

### Coherence

To meet the coherence standard, each thought in a paragraph should flow logically from the thought that precedes it. Thus, sentence 1 should lead logically to sentence 2, which should lead logically to sentence 3, and so forth. Further, the relationships among the ideas should be made clear with appropriate cohesion phrases or words (e.g., therefore, but, also, likewise, after, in addition, and because).

### Development

To meet the development standard, a paragraph should include all the information the audience will need to know about the topic introduced in the first sentence. A paragraph may be developed with statistics, examples, explanations, stories, quotes from authorities, and anything else that will help the audience fully understand.

### Length

To meet the length standard, paragraphs should not be too long. Rather than relying on a specific line or word length as a standard for paragraph length, trust your eye to tell you. If a paragraph looks hard to read when you first glance at it, it is probably too long. Break long paragraphs into two or more shorter paragraphs, or put some of the content in a bulleted or numbered list to add some white space and break up the text.

Figure 5.6 illustrates an application checked for the five C's and CLOUD standards.

## Phase 4—Review and Revise the Sentences

The fourth review phase consists of checking sentences. In the previous three review phases, writing quality is judged mainly on principles and guidelines. In the sentence-review phase, writing must conform to rules as well as guidelines. In Appendix A you will find basic writing guidelines and rules organized under the acronym SPELL (structure, punctuation, errors, language, and length).

To: Ken morgan
From:    Jane Sanders
Date: April 9, 20XX
Re: Request for input — *Make subject line more specific*

*CONTENT*

*underlining in CLOUD indicates weak areas.*

Thanks for requesting my thoughts regarding Midwest City's General Plan. I believe we should work on establishing neighbor hood pocket parks wherever possible. They could contain picnic tables and open areas for throwing a frisbee or football. The parks would make small playgrounds quickly accessible to families and youth groups and would add a nice touch of green among our ever increasing miles of asphalt and concrete. — *CLOUD*

*such as?* *CLOUD*

Other cities have had great success with the pocket-park idea, and I think our citizens would like the idea as well. I also think Midwest's most pressing problem is poor traffic flow in a north south direcion. State Street and Arlington Boulevard seem to carry most of the traffic volume in this direction, citizens need several other alternate routes and I know there are probably 3 other routes that should be addressed, also. We also should work on nieghborhood lighting so our streets are not so dark at night. With gang-related problems edging upward, improved lighting would be welcomed by most residents. For many years we have discussed this project, and I think we should now take action. — *What are they?* *CLOUD*

Thanks again, Ken, for allowing me to give input as you develop the General Plan. I hope my recommendations will help in this process. Please let me know if you would like to discuss any of these items in detail. — *Restate the three recommendations*

*Figure 5.6  A memo that has been reviewed for content.*

| SPELL |
| --- |
| Structure |
| Punctuation |
| Errors in Grammar |
| Language |
| Length |

## Structure

Make sure all sentences have a clear structure. Well-designed sentences are easy to follow, and they don't have to be read twice to be understood. Remember SVC (subject, verb, complement) as you evaluate the structure of each sentence.

**Subject:** Use strong, clear subjects, generally avoiding "it" and "there" as subjects.

**Verb:** Remember two V's—vicinity and voice. Place each verb close to (in the vicinity of) its subject. Also, use active voice, rather than passive voice (unless you want to emphasize the action or de-emphasize the actor).

**Complement:** Make sure the remainder of the sentence (the complement) is clear and easy to follow. Avoid sentence clutter caused by too many add-on phrases. Make sure all relative pronouns (e.g., her, his, they, and this) have clear references, place all modifying words close to the words they modify, and ensure grammatical parallelism for words in a series and other structurally parallel phrases.

Identify any awkward wording structures. Where you find problems, reconstruct and improve the sentence. For example, you might put secondary information in an introductory phrase or subordinate clause and then place the primary information in a main clause.

Employ appropriate sentence variety. Readers get tired of multiple sentences with similar length and structure.

## Punctuation

Review each sentence for appropriate punctuation. Be especially mindful of the following punctuation rules that are frequently violated:

- Place a comma between all items in a series.
- Place a comma after introductory phrases to make meaning clear.
- Insert a hyphen between two or more words that act

jointly to modify a subsequent noun or pronoun (e.g., high-priced product).

- Place commas and periods inside quotation marks at the end of a quote.
- Use a period with a polite request that asks for an action.

## Errors in Grammar

Check each sentence for case, agreement, tense, number, and capitalization rules. Be especially watchful for the following rules that are violated frequently.

- Use "me" or "I," rather than "myself." ("Submit the report to David or me, and then he and I will distribute the copies," rather than "Submit the report to David or myself, and then he and myself will distribute the copies.")
- Use "me" and "I" correctly. ("They invited Sami and me to attend," rather than "They invited Sami and I to attend.")
- Use "him/her" and "her/she" correctly. ("Elias and she talked with Marty and him," rather than "Elias and her talked with Marty and he.")
- Make subjects and verbs agree. ("One of our websites is down this morning," rather than "One of our websites are down this morning.")
- Use relative pronouns (who, which, that) properly with embedded essential and nonessential clauses. ("The transaction that was cancelled is for $586.22," rather than "The transaction which was cancelled is for $586.22.")
- Use adjectives and adverbs correctly. ("You did well in today's meeting," rather than "You did good in today's meeting.")
- Don't include an apostrophe in the possessive form of

"its" ("The car crashed when its tire blew out," rather than "The car crashed when it's tire blew out.")

- Generally, spell out numbers one through nine; write as numerals everything larger than nine. Be aware of the numerous exceptions to this basic rule. ("I gave 12 cookies to the six employees," rather than "I gave twelve cookies to the 6 employees.")

## Language

Evaluate word usage throughout the document.

- Use words that are appropriately precise, rather than general and ambiguous.
- Use words that are easily understood by the audience; jargon may be used if it will be readily understood or if it is defined.
- Make sure all words are correct in usage (e.g., principle vs. principal, affect vs. effect).
- Spell all words correctly (e.g., receive, precede, questionnaire, separate).

Check the wording of sentences to ensure appropriate tone. Use words that are considerate and conversational, yet professional.

No:  We can't ship your parts until March 1. [Wording is negative; focuses on what you can't do.]

Yes:  We will ship your parts on March 1. [Words focus on the positive—states what you can or will do.]

No:  Your order was received today. It will be shipped in two days. [Words are mechanical and uncaring.]

Yes:  We appreciate your order and will ship it to you within the next 48 hours. [Words are warm and friendly.]

*Figure 5.7  In writing, as in speaking, your tone should be appropriate for the situation.*

No: Per your request that we scrutinize the various purported illegalities suggested in the management audit report, we hereby submit the attached. [Words are too pompous and arrogant; not conversational.]

Yes: Here is our management audit report that analyzes three illegal actions. [Words reflect conversational language.]

## Length

Avoid long, wordy sentences that cause readers to lose their way. Ask yourself, "How can I say what needs to be said with as few words as possible?" You can reduce sentence length and wordiness in the following ways:

Omit useless words.

No: In my mind I thought I would be rehired again.

Yes: I thought I would be rehired. ["In my mind" and "again" are redundant.]

Condense wordy passages of text.

No: I made the assumption that she was planning to be in attendance.

Yes: I assumed she would attend.

No: The negative effect of the pay cut in the marketing department was severe in its motivational impact. [Sentence has too many prepositional phrases.]

Yes: The pay cut greatly reduced the marketing employees' motivation.

Consider splitting long sentences into two.

No: The foregoing standards and OMB Circular A-133 require that we plan and perform the audit to obtain reasonable assurance about whether or not noncompliance with the types of compliance requirements referred to above could have a direct and material effect on a major federal program.

Yes: The foregoing standards and OMB Circular A-133 specify our audit criteria. These criteria require that we determine if any noncompliance could directly or materially affect a major federal program.

Figure 5.8 shows a business memo reviewed at the sentence level.

After you have finished the four-phase DOCS review, revise as needed. Improve the design, make needed organizational changes, improve and strengthen the content, and fix all sentence-level flaws. Then make one final pass through the document to make sure everything is acceptable. Figure 5.9 shows the revised memo.

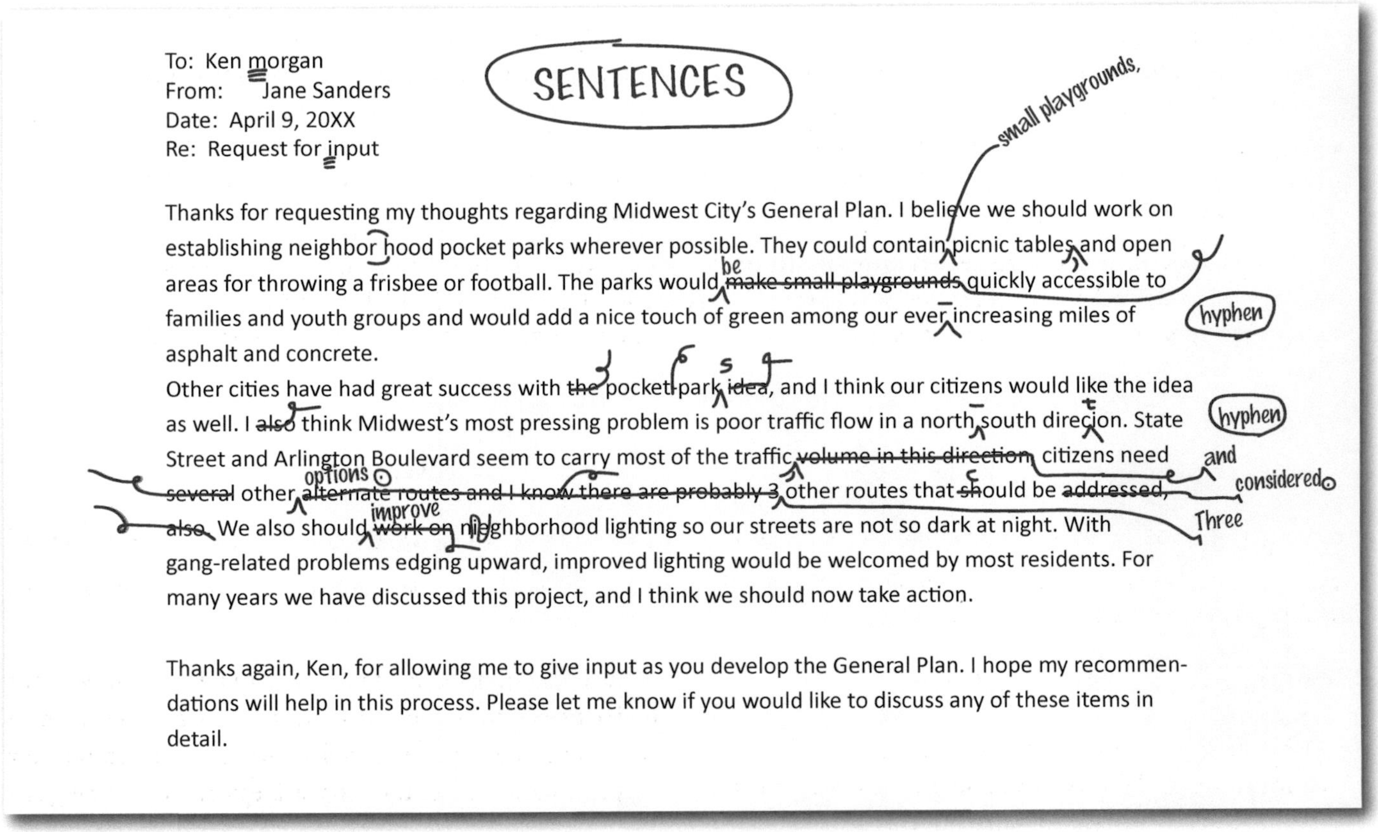

*Figure 5.8 A memo that has been reviewed for sentence quality.*

**To:** Ken Morgan
**From:** Jane Sanders
**Date:** April 9, 20XX

**Re:** **Request for Input on Midwest City's General Plan**

Thanks for requesting my thoughts regarding Midwest City's General Plan. From my perspective, the three most pressing needs are to (a) improve traffic flow, (b) install neighborhood lighting, and (c) build pocket parks.

**Improve Traffic Flow**

I think Midwest's most pressing problem is poor traffic flow in a north-south direction. State Street and Arlington Boulevard carry most of the traffic, and citizens need other options. I have attached a map showing the following three routes that could be considered.

- 800 East from 1200 South to 1600 North
- 1200 West from 800 South to 1600 North
- 800 West from 800 South to 1600 North

**Install Neighborhood Lighting**

We should also improve neighborhood lighting so our streets are not so dark at night. With gang-related problems edging upward in our city, improved lighting would be welcomed by most residents. For many years we have discussed this project, and I think we should now take action.

**Build Pocket Parks**

In addition to improving traffic flow and neighborhood lighting, I believe we should establish neighborhood *pocket parks* wherever possible. These small parks could contain small playgrounds, picnic tables, and open areas for throwing a frisbee or football. The parks would be quickly accessible to families and youth groups and would add a nice touch of green among our ever-increasing miles of asphalt and concrete. Other cities, such as Westmore and Johnsonville, have had great success with pocket parks, and I think our citizens would like the idea as well.

Thanks again, Ken, for allowing me to give input as you develop the General Plan. I hope my recommendations to improve traffic flow, improve neighborhood lighting, and establish pocket parks will help in this process. Please let me know if you would like to discuss any of these items in more detail.

*Figure 5.9 Compare this revised memo with Figures 5.4, 5.5, 5.6, and 5.8. As you can see, a methodical DOCS review can result in a significantly improved document.*

## CHAPTER SUMMARY

Writing is a complex process, and good writing is demanding work. Most errors and writing weaknesses can be fixed with rigorous review and revision. Revising is more than just fixing grammar errors; it is mainly about achieving the communication purpose. Before reviewing a document, the reviewer should understand all important purpose, audience, context, and strategy factors. Editing can

be accomplished with paper or electronic copies. Software can provide assistance in reviewing and revising documents.

A good review of professional workplace documents will include four separate phases: design, organization, content, and sentences. First, the design review is a high-level examination to check the document for correct formatting and good use of visual elements, including headings, art, typography, and spacing. Second, the organization review checks to see if the appropriate direct or indirect approach has been used and to see if an appropriate pattern has been followed. Many messages can benefit from following an OABC pattern (opening, agenda, body, and closing). Third, the content review examines the document to see if it is clear, complete, correct, considerate, and convincing. The content review also examines CLOUD factors (coherence, length, organization, unity, and development) in paragraphs. Fourth, the final review examines individual sentences for structure, punctuation, grammar errors, language, and length.

## CHAPTER QUESTIONS

1. What does the acronym PACS refer to?

2. When people read a poorly written message, what two assumptions might they make about the writer?

3. Why are some writers hesitant to ask others to review their documents?

4. What should be the main focus of revising?

5. How can computer software assist in the process of reviewing and revising a document?

6. Describe two techniques that can help improve proofreading accuracy.

7. What does the acronym DOCS stand for?

8. Explain the four phases of document review.

9. What factors should be considered in the design review?

10. What does the acronym HATS stand for?

11. What two factors should be considered in the organization review?

12. What are the five "C" factors of content?

13. Describe the five CLOUD factors of paragraphs.

14. Explain the difference between unity and coherence.

15. What does the acronym SPELL represent?

16. Why should subjects and verbs be kept close together?

17. What two words should generally be avoided as sentence subjects?

18. What two "v" factors should be checked when reviewing sentence verbs?

19. Why is sentence variety important?

20. Why is the tone of a message important?

## CHAPTER ACTIVITIES

1. Review all the rules and principles in Appendix A, and then revise the following sentences.

   a. It is hoped that the new security measures will prevent further break-ins.

   b. There is a chance that the Federal Reserve will increase interest rates by early June.

   c. The new employee-wellness program that was introduced last week is creating a lot of excitement among the employees.

   d. Our new employee-recognition committee will be led by Marissa McFaddin.

   e. The analyst became convinced that the problem in the stitching-machine segment of the assembly line that occurred during last Thursday's night shift was caused by an electrical short.

   f. Rachel paid the bills for office rent, for office utilities and telecommunications services.

   g. Before he approved the car repair on Monday he checked with the insurance agent.

   h. The building manager evacuated the entire building, even though the fire was confined to an upper floor apartment.

   i. The new policy not only affects tenants in this building but also tenants in other Office One tenants throughout the city.

   j. Please submit your expense requests for your travel, your hotel accommodations, and conference registration fees.

   k. What this company needs is more money for updating old equipment.

   l. Joseph's brother said he would help the Johnson's move their computers this Friday.

   m. Complaining loudly, the manager told the fired employee why he had been terminated.

   n. Our training activities have had the overall effect of decreasing the average length of emails and increasing the number of emails using a direct approach and OABC structure and bullet lists.

   o. In the event that you encounter a situation that appears to be suspicious, check with the HR manager before taking any action.

p. Each manager should keep himself up to date on all employment laws.

2. Critique and revise the following paragraph, using CLOUD as your standard.

When Paula took over the accounting function in the office, things were in total disarray. Some bills had been left unpaid; others were paid the wrong amount. Landlords were calling constantly to find out when their rent would be paid. Everyone in the office had access to the petty cash box. Rents were being paid to several vacated apartments. Over $300 from petty case was missing, with no record of where the funds had gone. And the files containing bills and receipts were totally unorganized. The former accountant in the Memphis office left suddenly three months ago, without any forewarning. Proper procedures are now in place and things are running smoothly. The former accountant moved to San Francisco.

3. Critique the SPELL and CLOUD factors of the following paragraph. Then write an improved paragraph.

Cycling has many advantages. Bikes don't require gasoline to operate. They also generate no air pollution. They provide good exercise. They also reduce traffic congestion. But they can be dangerous in traffic. They are also less costly to park. They are also highly maneuverable. Flat tires can also be a problem on bikes. They also offer no protection from the weather during storms or cold spells.

4. Critique and revise the following message, checking all design, organization, content, and sentence factors:

Thanks you for your order of 6 training videos. "If Only They Were More Motivated," "Send Me an Email," and "Oh, No, Not Another Meeting" have been sent. "Slideshow Tips and Techniques," "Performance Appraisal that Really Improves Performance," and "Hiring Employees: Your Most Important Work" will be sent by Mar. 25. With each video you'll receive a companion booklet to assist your trainers in maximizing the value of the video in your organization. We want you to be 100 percent satisfied with the materials you receive from us. The booklets contain participant materials that may be freely copied for your in house seminars and workshops. We're also enclosing our latest catalogue that includes over fifty new training videos. As with all our training materials, the new videos carry a thirty day, no questions asked return-policy. Thank you again for your order, we appreciate your patronage.

5. Critique and revise the following summary paragraph:

The U.S. Department of State's (State) Bureau of Overseas Building Operations (OBO) officials made decisions during the construction or renovation process in Sarajevo, Bosnia and Herzegovina; Belgrade, Serbia; and Helsinki, Finland to lease facilities off-site versus build on-site, but they did not provide a clear explanation of how those decisions were made in the documents they used to plan and track the construction and renovation of embassy compounds. OBO's planning documentation for the three embassy compounds provided general information on the construction projects and changes to the planned scope, schedule, and cost. However, GAO was unable to determine from the documentation the reasons for the decisions. Without complete documentation, as directed by State's guidance, GAO could not verify how OBO makes decisions, informs future decision makers about the basis for these decisions, or maintains institutional knowledge in the face of staff turnover. (Source: http://www.gao.gov/products/GAO-15-472R; 27 April 2015.)

6. Conduct a design review of the report on Hispanic employment at the following website: http://www.gao.gov/assets/90/86274.pdf. Evaluate of the report's use of headings, art and graphics, typography, and spacing. Make specific recommendations for improvements.

7. Select a long paragraph in a textbook you are using this semester and evaluate it for CLOUD compliance. Rewrite the paragraph so it is CLOUD compliant.

8. Ask two friends to review a document you have created. Inform your reviewers about the document's purpose, audience, context, and strategy. Compare the reviewers' feedback, and answer the following five questions. What feedback is similar? What feedback is different? What feedback do you agree with and disagree with? Do the reviewers' suggestions focus more on design, organization, content, or sentences? What type of suggestions do you value most?

9. Volunteer to provide feedback on a friend's writing. Before reviewing, request information about the writer's purpose, audience, context, and strategy. Review the document four times, first for design, second for organization, third for content, and fourth for sentences. Give appropriate feedback for each of the DOCS factors.

## Rubric for Evaluating Writing

Writer_____    Topic_____

Evaluator_____

| Rating (10-1) | **Evaluation Factors**<br>Circle (strengths) underline weaknesses, add +/- comments |
|---|---|
| **Design** | —*Format:* appropriate for document type<br>—*Visual appeal*<br>  • *Headings:* enable skimming, show information structure<br>  • Art: appropriate tables, graphs, photos, bullet/number lists, etc.<br>  • Typography: appropriate font, size, style, alignment<br>  • Spacing: appropriate margins, text spacing<br>*Comments:* |
| **Organization** | —*Approach:* appropriate direct/indirect approach<br>—*Structure:* appropriate agenda and information architecture<br>*Comments:* |
| **Content** | —*Clear, complete, correct, considerate, convincing*<br>—*Paragraph standards:* coherence, length, organization, unity, development<br>*Comments:* |
| **Sentences** | —**Structure:** subject, verb, complement<br>—**Punctuation**<br>—**Errors in grammar:** case, agreement, tense, numbers, capitalization<br>—**Language:** spelling, word choice, formality, tone<br>—**Length:** conciseness<br>*Comments:* |
| _____/40 Total | |

## CHAPTER 6

# Communicating with Social Media

Looking back in history, consider the time it has taken for people to communicate with each other over long distances. Messages sent by foot could take weeks to arrive at their destination, messages sent by horseback could decrease that time to days, and messages sent electronically by telegraph could speed that process to minutes. Today, electronic technology delivers messages instantaneously.

Consider also the history of information accessibility. Early societies relied heavily on person-to-person oral communication to pass along knowledge and ideas. Some early information was also written on clay tablets, metal plates, and papyrus scrolls, with each of these media offering accessibility to only a small portion of the population. Later, movable type revolutionized printing, which greatly improved information access, although distributing the documents was still a challenge.

Eventually, electronic communication developed, and with it came almost limitless opportunities for information access. Thanks to advances in transmission speed and increased numbers of communication channels, you now have almost endless opportunities to stay in contact with people in your network, to access up-to-the-minute information for decision making, and to let your voice be heard on any topic of your choosing.

With today's increased speed come increased challenges, such as the ability to post messages in haste or in anger, to take messages out of context, and to forward sensitive messages to unintended audiences. Electronic communication also introduces numerous paradoxes. It enables you to network, which can also interfere with your work. It can get you hired but also get you fired. It can help you win a customer but also lose a customer. It is indispensable to younger generations but intimidating to older generations. It enables you to send messages to many people you know, yet prevents you from knowing to whom your messages are being forwarded.

Given these great opportunities and challenges, you need to understand and apply effective communication principles more than ever before. This chapter focuses on these critical principles, specifically those related to social media. The focus is less on specific technologies that are constantly changing and more on timeless principles that apply even as more technologies come into existence.

After reading this chapter, you should be able to do the following:

- Apply the PACS framework (purpose, audience, context, strategy) in creating social media messages.
- Build online credibility and trust in your social network.
- Create engaging online content, with sensitivity to social contexts.
- Use social media tools effectively.

Social media communication involves the intersection of people, tools, content, and networks. People use online tools such as Twitter®, Facebook®, LinkedIn®, and YouTube® in order to share content. This content, live or delayed, includes text, video, audio, or images. While some tools specialize in sharing one specific type of content, most tools enable you to share multiple types with your network. Your network might include friends, classmates, colleagues at work, and customers. As you use tools to communicate content to this network, be sure to plan your social media strategy by considering your purpose, audience, and context.

## DETERMINE THE PURPOSE

The purposes of social media communication are similar to communication of all types. However, social media communication differs from other communication because of its heavier emphasis on credibility, engagement, and relationships. Consequently, this section will discuss the three common communication purposes of informing, persuading, and building relationships of trust as they are adapted specifically to social media.

### *Informing*

Informative, useful content is the foundation of social media as individuals and organizations create and share information in the form of blogs, tweets, posts, chats, updates, videos, and podcasts. Informative content is what keeps people coming back. This content draws people online as they search for product reviews, stock market updates, weather forecasts, news, word definitions, or status updates from friends and colleagues.

With social media, you are not only a consumer of information, but also a creator of information. However, just because you post content on social media doesn't mean that people in your network will automatically pay attention to it or value it. Audiences make decisions about what information to consume based on several factors, but especially the credibility of the content and the credibility of the writer. These two elements of credibility are highly interconnected and highly positively correlated—when the credibility of one increases, the credibility of the other also increases. Thus, improve your content credibility to improve your personal credibility, and improve your personal credibility to improve your content credibility. Here are three suggestions for how to improve credibility.

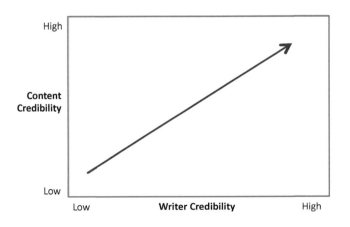

*Figure 6.1 A high positive correlation exists between content credibility and writer credibility.*

### Create High-Quality Content

As with all audiences, your network audience is constantly asking the WIIFM question: "What's in it for me?" In other words, they want content that will have high value for them. For example, you might decide to create a blog that analyzes current trends in your industry. As you write professional posts that are well researched, balanced, accurate, helpful, and well designed, your network of followers will begin to recognize you as someone they can turn to for valuable information. Conversely, if your posts are unprofessional, poorly researched, biased, inaccurate, unhelpful, or designed poorly, your credibility erodes.

Some companies such as klout.com or www.kred.com generate measures of an individual's credibility and influence online. These scores are determined by the impact of the content that you create. Such outcomes include the number of times your content is liked, tweeted, or shared. Although such measures can be helpful guides, avoid falling into the trap of placing your primary focus on the pursuit of a higher and higher credibility score based on these outcomes. Instead, keep your focus on creating high-quality content, and high credibility will naturally follow.

### Share High-Quality Content

While the content you *create* influences your network's perception of your credibility, the content you *share* also influences that perception. Consequently, as you share content created by others, make sure it is accurate and professional. If you suspect that anything about an image, news story, or video isn't accurate or professional, avoid becoming associated with that content by sharing it with your network. To increase the likelihood of sharing high-quality content, consider these suggestions:

- Take time to do your own research on content you share. If something seems too good to be true, it probably is.

- Make sure you have at least an adequate understanding of the information you are sharing. If you feel the need for additional context or background information, do not share the information until you become comfortable with all aspects of the issue.

- Consider the content's currency, authority, reliability, purpose, and point of view. Review the questions from Chapter 9 in relation to information quality.

- Be wary of information and perspectives you read from only one source. Generally, important content will be somewhat widely shared.

- Consult your compliance and public relations departments about questionable content to gain their

approval. This practice becomes especially important when you are posting on behalf of your company or organization.

Remember that once you post questionable content, everything you have posted in the past and everything you post in the future will be suspect. Credibility and trust, once lost, are difficult to regain.

## Become an Expert

Just as the content you create or share affects your personal credibility, your personal credibility influences content credibility. For example, imagine you are listening to an interesting podcast on personal fitness. At the end of the episode, the presenter invites you to subscribe to the podcast. Will you subscribe? Maybe, but maybe not. Then the presenter mentions that she is a three-time Olympic gold medalist. Given what you now know about the presenter, are you more or less likely to subscribe? Most likely your perception of her will greatly influence your perception of her content.

Therefore, as you become an expert on a certain industry, production method, software tool, investment strategy, or other subject, you begin to establish a personal brand that can be trusted. With your increased knowledge, you will be able to provide deeper and more useful information, your content will be recognized more widely, and others will begin to follow or turn to you as a credible source in the areas of your expertise.

## Persuading

As you work to make your social media messages persuasive, recognize that your audience is inundated with a flood of email, tweets, and other types of electronic communication that compete for attention. Thus, before you can persuade people online, you must capture their attention by making your content engaging.

Engaging information is content that is watched, read, and shared by networks. As a company's social media content engages customers, the content makes an impression that increases the likelihood that the customers will purchase the company's goods and services. Social media strategists use the term "engagement" to refer to the number of shares, tweets, likes, views, and other measures that signal how an audience is receiving a company's social media content.

Because of the connection between impressions and purchasing, companies use software tools to track and analyze their customers' engagement with their content (see Figure 6.2). These tools measure the number of times the content is viewed or shared, analyze the sentiment (positivity or negativity) of people who are discussing the company online, show the location of people who engage with the company's content, and calculate the number of customer impressions that convert into sales.

As an individual, you can also capture analytics of your own social media content. For example, if you post an update on Facebook, you can count how many likes

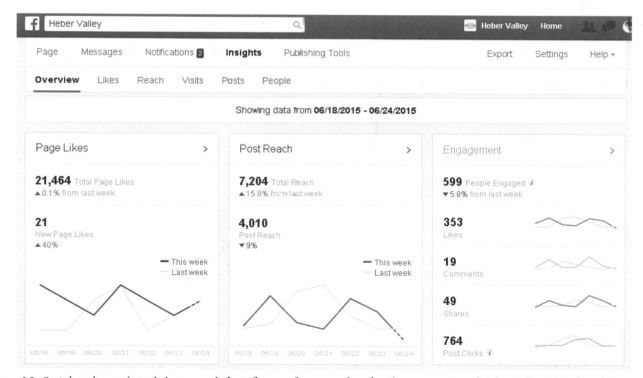

*Figure 6.2  Social media analytics help you track the influence of your social media. (Image courtesy of Heber Valley Chamber of Commerce.)*

you receive. If you create a blog on wordpress.com, you can access a dashboard of site statistics that shows such data as the following:

- How many people are viewing your site.
- When they viewed your site.
- What cities, states, and countries these visitors are from.
- What search terms they typed into a search engine (e.g., Google) to find your site.
- What they clicked or commented on.

Because you can measure these statistics, you can use them to increase your audience's engagement with your content. For example, analyze your blog posts that generate the most comments or shares, and then create more related content. When you see the number of people viewing your blog diminish, add another post in order to keep traffic returning to your site. If you see that most people visit your site during the morning, create and post new content during the evening so it is ready for visitors the next day.

Here are six additional suggestions that can help you create engaging content:

**Think visual.** When you are posting text, visually enhance it with headings, pictures and other visuals, typographic variation, and spacing. While these enhancements will improve your content, recognize that online audiences see immense amounts of text as they scroll through endless updates and news feeds. Therefore, in addition to posting text, consider adding an interesting picture, infographic, or video. In this way you can differentiate your content and better capture your audience's attention.

**Think sharing.** Make your content as shareable as possible by providing links where individuals can tweet it, post it, pin it, or otherwise share it. Consider condensing large amounts of text into an infographic or other easily accessible and shareable format. Your audience can then share your content with others in their networks, expanding the scope and reach of your network, content, and influence.

**Think consistency.** Imagine that a local grocery store you visit frequently runs out of bread, milk and eggs. Further, often when you visit, many of these products have passed their expiration date. Will you keep returning to the store? Similarly, your audience expects fresh content that is restocked on a consistent basis. When they can count on you regularly posting new content that they like, they will keep returning and engaging.

**Think stories.** Regardless of whether they are told in print or online, stories have a unique way of engaging audiences. Use stories to capture your audience's attention up front, to set the overall organization of your content, or to illustrate points.

**Think advertising.** Remember that for your content to be viewed and shared, you must let people know it is there. For example, if you have posted a new video on your company website, tweet the link to your followers on Twitter. You might also provide a link to the video in an email newsletter to customers. Further, you could mention the video in an update on LinkedIn. You thus inform multiple networks of people who will likely engage with the content when they know it is there.

**Think clarity.** As you write for social media, pay careful attention to your writing style. Use a direct approach—get to the point early in all of your posts. Also, for longer texts, ensure good content structure by following an OABC pattern. As you compose text, use words that are easy to understand, make sure your sentences are concise and structurally sound, and follow CLOUD standards for paragraphs. Finally, employ a comfortable, conversational writing style that radiates a nice human touch.

## Building Relationships of Trust

As you communicate with customers and potential customers through social media, the interim return on your investment is the relationships you develop. These relationships form the substance of your network. As you build relationships with people, you gain their trust and loyalty, and this trust and loyalty can then help to sway customers when they are making purchasing decisions.

For example, imagine that you are reserving a flight, and you have narrowed your choice to three airlines, all offering their airfares at the same price. One way to make your decision is to ask friends and family members which airline they prefer. Because of the relationship you have developed with these people, you trust their opinions as you make your decision.

Imagine now that the last time you flew with one of the companies, your luggage was lost. However, you sent a tweet to the company's customer service, and your bags were quickly located and delivered to your home. By responding quickly to an event that could have severely damaged a relationship of trust, the employees of that airline increased the likelihood that you will fly with them

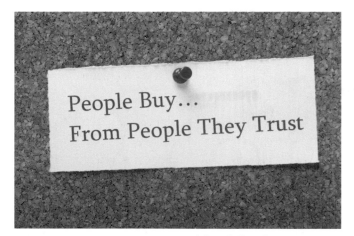

*Figure 6.3 Just as you turn to trusted friends for advice when making purchases, consumers turn to trusted companies.*

again. Customer service is an old-fashioned concept, but it is still alive and well today—people do business with those they trust.

Here are a few tips to help you establish relationships of trust within your social network:

**Assist others in your network.** Remember that for a network to stay healthy, it must be cultivated. People must be contributing to the network, in addition to calling on the network for help. Consequently, when people post questions or ask for help, do what you can to help where possible. For example, if someone in your network posts a question on LinkedIn about current industry practices related to a topic you are familiar with, respond with your own experiences or reply with a link to a helpful article that relates to the question. By assisting others when you are able, you increase the likelihood that your network will help you when you are in need.

**Ask for nothing in return.** Social media networking is full of paradoxes that sometimes seem counterintuitive. One of these paradoxes is that as you help others in your network, do not ask for anything in return. For example, as you create and post informative content related to your business, seek to teach and instruct rather than to sell your product. As you maintain a motive of service, your network will sense that you have their best interest in mind. Then when they are shopping for products or services that you sell, their trust in you will influence their purchasing decision.

**Do more than simply "like."** Social media sites offer different levels of engagement with the content of others. For example, if someone posts an update in Facebook about a new job promotion, you can either "like" it or respond with a comment. While "liking"

an update may be the best strategy for some situations, consider engaging more fully by adding a thoughtful comment or sending a direct message that shows you really took notice of the update. Further, don't be afraid to move offline and give the individual a personal call. In this way, you show a genuine interest in people that will strengthen their trust in you.

One of the core purposes of social media communication is to grow your social network, and establishing trust is only one way to grow your network. One additional way is to simply add others into your network. Here is an example of how one city's chamber of commerce follows this simple principle.

Businesses, non-profit organizations, and government entities use social media as a communication tool to provide instant updates, promotions, and other public notices. The Heber Valley Chamber of Commerce, a non-profit business networking organization, has seen tremendous benefits from using Facebook, Twitter, Instagram, and Pinterest (see Figure 6.4). At one point, the Heber Valley Chamber of Commerce had 2,304 followers on its Facebook page. Through a series of regular posts and promotions, the number grew to 21,400 in just a few years.

The Heber Valley Chamber of Commerce demonstrates the power of online networks. For example, when the chamber's Facebook and other social media pages were first created, the organization's leaders decided to "like" as many other similar organizations as possible. This step resulted in increased exposure from followers and fans of other social media pages.

Now, Facebook, Twitter, Instagram, and Pinterest all link to the chamber's website so the social media user will have another landing place with additional pertinent information. Additionally, the chamber launched a customized

*Figure 6.4 Social media has helped make thousands of people aware of Heber Valley's natural beauty and recreational opportunities.*

newsletter to its mailing list with the intent of promoting key messages to its members. Likewise, the newsletter contains links to the chamber's websites and social media pages. In essence, all social media channels and pages, including the chamber's website, cross-promote other social media platforms to capture as many fans and followers as possible. To further enhance its digital footprint, the Heber Valley Chamber of Commerce also launched a free mobile app which ties into the organization's social media pages and website, www.gohebervalley.com.

## ANALYZE THE AUDIENCE

In social networking, your audience consists of all the people in your primary network, as well as all the people in your network's network. You have little control over your social media messages after you post them, and some of your messages might be forwarded to thousands, even millions, of people. As a result, performing an accurate audience analysis for social media is difficult. Nevertheless, analyze your primary and secondary audiences as you normally would do, and then be aware of the potential tertiary audience that might see your message. Keep in mind that your manager or future manager might be an unanticipated member of that tertiary audience.

Also, recognize that your audience transcends time and may also include people who will link to your network in the future. For example, the messages you posted when you were 18 years old might one day be viewed by your colleagues when you are 24 years old. And these same message might be read by your customers when you are 40 years old. In such cases, remember that in your audience's eyes, your personal life influences the credibility of your professional life. Consequently, avoid posting anything that will erode the relationships of trust that you and your company (or future companies) have worked hard to establish with clients and customers.

As you analyze your audience, recognize that current social media communication builds on a foundation of a many-to-many communication model (see Figure 6.5). In the early days of the internet, companies created and displayed content on their websites for consumers to view, basically as a one-to-many type of structure. Presently, companies may still display content on their websites, but that content is then commented on, shared, critiqued, and analyzed by customers and competitors in online product reviews, Wikipedia, news sharing sites, blogs, and other social media sites. The internet is thus a dynamic place with content being created and shared about your company all

*Figure 6.5 Today's social media networks enable many-to-many communication.*

the time. You can either let your audience create that content without your influence, or you can step in and influence what is happening.

As was explained in Chapter 2, audience analysis involves gathering information about demographic and psychographic factors so you can later develop an appropriate communication strategy.

### Demographics

Social networking use appears to be extremely consistent across many demographic factors, including sex, education levels, and income levels (Pew Research Center 2015). However, because older members of society grew up before the internet emerged, they are, on average, less likely to use social media (see Figure 6.6). In fact, many older people are intimidated by computers and the internet. Those who do use the internet tend to rely more on email or other more traditional forms of communication. In contrast, younger people not only use computers and the internet far more often, but also use social media, more than email, for communicating. Thus, if your target social media audience includes people from all age categories, you will need to think carefully about how to reach older generations.

Another demographic factor to consider is the country in which the audience resides. If your audience consists of individuals from your own country, you will already be aware of the language, culture, and other similar factors. For international audiences, however, you will need to adjust the message for differences, such as language (English vs.

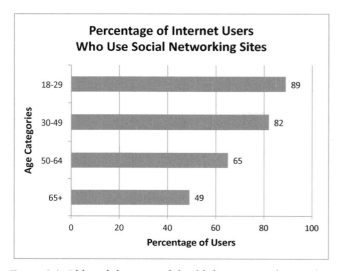

*Figure 6.6  Older adults are much less likely to use social networking sites. Source: Pew Research Center.*

Spanish), culture (American vs. Latino), monetary systems (dollars vs. pesos), and weights and measures (pounds vs. kilograms).

## Psychographics

Because of the diverse nature and number of people in social media audiences, a precise psychographic profile is perhaps impossible. Nevertheless, certain methods may be employed to improve your understanding of the audience. In fact, the very network that you use to transmit your content can be used to gather information about your audience. The following paragraphs explain how conversation and social media analytics can help in this process.

### Invite Conversation

One way to gather information about your network audience is to invite interaction with them. Because your audience can speak back to you in the many-to-many structure of social media, make the effort to establish two-way conversations with people. For example, on your company website, invite consumers to give feedback about their experience with your goods and services. Then follow up and address the problems you learn about. On your Twitter feed, search for times your company is mentioned positively by customers, and retweet what they post. Further, establish an instant messaging feature where consumers can chat with employees from your company in real time.

As you work to open up these two-way conversations with your audience, realize that you can encourage or discourage these conversations. For example, you can disable or enable posting comments on blogs, or you can reply or not reply to tweets that mention your company. In addition,

you can encourage people to provide information about their needs by listening well, asking them about their needs, going the extra mile, and responding respectfully. The more respectfully you engage in conversation with your audience, the more they will likely engage with you (see Figure 6.7).

Remember that although online networks are made up of computers, laptops, tablets, servers, routers, and cables, social networks also include people. Because of the human element involved in social networks, most social media audiences expect to communicate with real people. To meet this expectation, be authentic in your social communication, showing that you are a person with typical human concerns. In addition to posting about work-related topics, mention other interests in a professional way, showing you have a life outside of your work and organization. This authenticity builds trust with people, and most customers relate better to real people than they do to impersonal organizations or companies.

Whatever channels you set up for two-way communication, make sure to maintain them. Customers become frustrated when they send a message and don't get a reply. Some forms of social media communication, like instant messaging, are synchronous, which requires that both the sender and receiver be available at the same time. Other forms like tweets and status updates are asynchronous, which can be read and replied to when convenient. Obvi-

*Figure 6.7  Respectful conversation fosters continuing conversation.*

ously, synchronous channels require more attention because someone must be present to respond immediately to messages. As you make plans for encouraging conversations, recognize that conversations take time to sustain, so make sure you have adequate resources.

To set up a two-way conversation with your audience, you must enable your audience to find you online. Part of an audience's search for you may involve their searching the internet through search engines like www.google.com, www.bing.com, or www.yahoo.com. These sites use computer programs to parse and index your website's text content. When searching for your site on these search engines, customers then type or voice in the keywords that they associate with your site, and your page ranks higher or lower depending on the presence or absence of those keywords. While your site's page rank varies according to other criteria as well, you should create content with terms that your audience will use in their search for you. Lastly, remember that mobile users most frequently want to know opening and closing times for businesses, so make sure your social network sites and website include that important information.

### Use Social Media Analytics

A second way to learn about your social media audience is to use social media analytics. For instance, network-activity data tells you something about their needs and interests, channel data lets you know about their social network channels, time data tells you when they are most active on the internet, and location data tells you where they live (see Figure 6.8). Further, tracking and analyzing the search patterns of audience members lets you know the content and products they are searching for, and from this data you can infer their wants and needs. This data can then provide the basis for designing human, technological, and logistical systems to respond to those wants and needs in the most efficient and effective ways possible.

# ANALYZE THE CONTEXT

The context in which social media communication occurs is vitally important to understand. People are heavily influenced by their individual worlds, and the better you can understand what their worlds are like, the better you will be able to tailor messages that fit. In addition to understanding the contexts of others, you must also analyze your own context. The following sections discuss the important aspects of analyzing your own internal context and the external context of your audience.

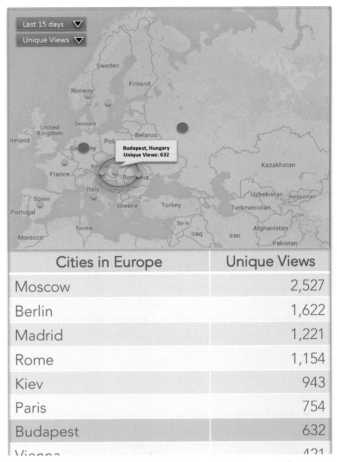

| Cities in Europe | Unique Views |
|---|---|
| Moscow | 2,527 |
| Berlin | 1,622 |
| Madrid | 1,221 |
| Rome | 1,154 |
| Kiev | 943 |
| Paris | 754 |
| Budapest | 632 |
| Vienna | 421 |

*Figure 6.8  Social media analytics help you learn more about your audience.*

## *Your Own Context*

As you plan to create and send social media messages, make sure you understand what is going on in your own industry, company, and department. Remain aware of the issues, challenges, and trends of your industry by reading trade publications. Keep in mind your company's mission and purposes, values, code of ethics, and current strengths, issues, and challenges so you can represent your company well. As you craft social media messages, make sure they are consistent with these organizational factors and the image your company wants to establish.

If you are creating social media messages for your department or company, stay aware of your company's current relationships and previous communication with its customers. For example, if a customer recently accused your company of breaching a contract and you post information about the company on one of your social media accounts, someone from that company could misinterpret that information and cause problems for you personally and for your company. Therefore, as much as possible stay aware of all internal company news.

## *Audience Context*

In addition to staying aware of internal company news, stay aware of broader social and political news. Because of the many-to-many structure of social media communication, much social media content becomes open and available for public scrutiny. As a result, your content must be sensitive to the external social and political context where it could be read by your customers, your competitors, the press, and others among your public audience.

To adapt your communication to this broader social context, become aware of social issues that might get you in trouble or that might harm your credibility. Stay current on local and national news, paying attention to topics generating the most discussion online. Frequently, sensitive social issues relate to topics generally avoided in interviews, including "race, color, religion, sex (including pregnancy), national origin, age (40 or older), disability or genetic information" (U.S. Equal Employment Opportunity Commission 2015). These topics frequently become the focus of controversy, so think carefully before posting content about these issues.

Remember that if you post content related to a particular issue, you associate yourself with that issue in your audience's minds. Before taking a stand, ask yourself whether you are willing to stake your reputation and career on the issue. If not, avoid posting the content. Sometimes silence is the best strategy. At other times you'll want to speak out, possibly losing customers as the price of achieving a greater social good.

Here are some additional tips for posting socially sensitive content:

- Don't post anything that is defamatory or inappropriate.
- Don't post in anger.
- Balance your content by considering all points of view.
- Don't post anything you wouldn't want published on the front page of a national newspaper.
- Provide adequate context so your messages are more likely to seem reasonable.

Applying these tips in a short online product review, you would be truthful in your appraisal, yet avoid writing anything that is defamatory, sarcastic, or inappropriate. Your review would consider both negative and positive comments to ensure fairness, and you would feel comfortable having your review appear on the front page of a newspaper. An example follows:

On January 18, 20XX, I stayed at the Motel ABC in Lincoln, Nebraska. I travel frequently for work, so I stay in motels at least 25–30 days each year. My positive comments and suggestions for improvement are as follows. The clerks were efficient and friendly as I checked in, and I found the room to be clean and in good order. The bed was very comfortable, and the shower was one of the best I have experienced. I also found the rate to be very reasonable for the area. Only two aspects of my accommodations were not as good as I had hoped: a slow internet connection and a fairly sparse breakfast. Other than these two items, my stay at Motel ABC met my expectations, and I would have no hesitation about staying there again.

If you happen to make a mistake and post something you wish you hadn't, take responsibility and do your best to correct any misperceptions that might have occurred. As much as possible, don't let your mistakes cause you to stop conversing on social media. Also, the news contains numerous stories of people who have posted inappropriately and lost a job or lost their good reputation as a result. Don't let these stories of others drive you into silence. Instead, learn from their mistakes and be careful, tasteful, and professional with your own content.

Three additional factors should be considered as you create and share content: timing, location, and channel.

### Timing

Timing can play an important role in the context of social media communication. For example, imagine that you work for a pharmaceutical company that produces allergy medication. As you receive information about the pollen levels in various locations around the world, you can target your online social messaging to those specific locations. You need to get your messages out in a timely manner or they lose their effectiveness.

Although timing must be a priority, messages should not be posted in haste. For example, if you become upset with someone after reading some of their communication, that is not a good time to post a reply! Take time to cool down, letting more rational thinking rule.

Further, space your social media messages far enough apart that you don't inundate your network with messages. Consider using a social media calendar to strategically plan when and what you will post to your social networks.

### Location

Location can also plan an important role in the context of some social media communication, especially for content

viewed on mobile devices. Many mobile phones include global positioning system (GPS) technology that enables companies to adapt content to their customers' physical location. For example, people may search for restaurants close to where they are and then read product reviews of others who have eaten in the area. Other sites enable users to check in at a particular location and receive special promotions or services. If you consider using location-based services as part of your social media communication, recognize that not everyone with a mobile device in the area will receive your messages—some people will block this feature because of privacy concerns.

*Figure 6.9  Location-based services enable you to adapt your content to your audience's physical context.*

## Channel

The social media channels you choose determine the richness of your message. For example, online video provides great channel richness because you can see people's facial expressions and observe their gestures. In contrast, online text messages limit the richness of expression and may further restrict expression because of message-size limitations. Nevertheless, you still need to provide enough background information so your messages aren't taken out of context. With a tweet, for example, that may mean sending the main idea in one message and additional contextual content in subsequent messages. The ability to write concisely is obviously a great advantage in a communication situation such as this.

The social networking sites you use to share your content also influence the message context. In fact, they become part of the message context. For example, LinkedIn is generally perceived as a professional web application where individuals share work-related content and ideas. Facebook, in contrast, is perceived less as a professional

site and more as a personal site for staying in contact with family and friends in personal networks. Therefore, people generally share their personal information on Facebook, whereas on LinkedIn they share business content, such as employment and career information.

Social networking sites vary in the number and kind of features and options they offer. For example, on a given site, you can share with family, friends, and professional contacts different types of content—instant messages, blogs, files, forum posts, images, and videos. Further, social networking sites offer a range of privacy options, such as making all their content visible to everyone or restricting content to certain designated individuals or groups. Users can also choose whether to have their profiles searchable. Further, social networking sites are interactive. Users can indicate whether they "like" the content, comment on the content, and share the content with their own network. The amount of engagement with followers gives an indication of users' social influence.

### Social Networking Sites

The following paragraphs illustrate various types of social networking sites that may influence the context of your messages.

**Facebook** (facebook.com) is the world's largest social networking site, with over a billion users. Facebook requires you to create a personal profile, after which you may invite others to be Facebook "friends." The friend status gives them access to information that might be restricted to others. Facebook provides a "wall," which is essentially a virtual bulletin board, or forum, where you can post text, photos, and videos. In addition to posting your own content, you can share others' content in the form of microblogs, photos, videos, and events.

**Twitter** (twitter.com) is a microblogging service that enables users to broadcast concise posts called tweets. Each tweet is restricted to 140 characters, making it ideal for mobile applications. Twitter is the most popular site for real-time sharing of political, cultural, and other news. Twitter uses a hashtag, which consists of the pound sign (#) plus trailing letters and alphabetic characters. The hashtag accomplishes two purposes. First, it designates a content category. Second, the hashtag becomes a searchable link. For example, you might insert #mcdonalds as your hashtag, followed by a comment about your recent experience at the restaurant. Other people could then search on #mcdonalds

*Figure 6.10  Social media is ideally suited for mobile devices.*

and find your tweet, along with the tweets of others who have used the same hashtag.

**LinkedIn** (linkedin.com) is a social networking site for professionals. On LinkedIn, you create a personal professional profile, including education and work experience, after which you can connect with other professionals, promote yourself and your business, apply for jobs, post employment ads, and participate in group discussions. LinkedIn also features LinkedIn Pulse, which includes business articles on current business issues and topics to help professionals keep current.

**YouTube** (youtube.com) is the largest site for organizing and playing videos. Owned by Google, YouTube is one of the largest search engines on the internet. It offers users the means of sharing videos, music, movies, and vlogs (video web logs). Your videos can be created to share with family and friends, or you can use the videos for business purposes, such as providing online training.

**Pinterest** (pinterest.com) is a social bookmarking site or "pinboard," that enables you to collect, organize, and share images and related information by "pinning" images onto various "boards." These images usually link users to the information source on another website. In addition, you can interact online with other Pinterest users.

**Instagram** (instagram.com) is a photo-sharing mobile application. It enables you to take, edit, and share photos or videos. In addition to posting the photos or videos on Instagram, you can post them to your other social media accounts, such Facebook and Twitter. As with other social networking sites, followers can "like" and comment on others' posts. Instagram provides various photo-editing tools that enable special effects, frames, and captions. You can also search for other online photos using a hashtag, as with Twitter.

You can find much more information about these and many other social networking sites online. In addition, many more sites will come online in the future. Social networking and sharing are in their early stages of development, and competitors will undoubtedly emerge with new options and features.

### Functions of Social Networking Sites

Social media networks provide a variety of tools and options to assist you in performing various actions online. The following 10 functions are listed in alphabetic order.

**Blogging:** Blogs are websites written in conversational style and added to regularly. The term "blog" is a word created from the words "web log." Thus, a blog is often a log of activities or a series of thoughts written over time about a particular topic. Popular blogging sites are often built from wordpress.com or blogger.com.

**Discussing:** Online forums, or message boards, are online bulletin boards where people leave original messages, read messages from others, and comment on messages left by others. For example, many news, blogging, and social networking sites include a comment feature, enabling users to post comments back and forth to each other about their views.

**Messaging:** Messaging tools enable you to send text, images, or other media, to a person or group of people. Email, instant messaging, and other forms of text messaging fall into this category.

**Microblogging:** Microblogs allow subscribers to broadcast short messages about any topic of interest. A major appeal of microblogs is their immediacy. As soon as some noteworthy event occurs, a microblog can be sent to notify the world. Microblogs can be posted on a website or distributed to a specific group of followers. Further, they may be sent as an SMS text message or as an instant message (IM). Most microblogs include only text, but video and audio posts are available. With Twitter, the most well-known microblogging site, a user can "tweet" an original message and can "retweet" a message received from others.

**Networking:** Networking sites enable individuals to maintain existing connections or to create new con-

nections with other people. For instance, Jana knows Natalie, but doesn't know Natalie's friend Paula, and Natalie doesn't know Paula's friend Rachel. Nevertheless, as Jana links with Natalie, who links with Paula, who links with Rachel, all four individuals can connect with each other. Major players in this arena are Facebook and LinkedIn.

**Organizing:** Some sites provide for sharing and discovery of content as a result of people organizing that content around a topic or media. This act of organizing takes on various forms, such as curating, bookmarking, and tagging. For example, the site del.icio.us enables users to curate by selectively submitting web links and tagging those links with keywords. These tags can then be searched, enabling users to view all related links. Pinterest also enables users to bookmark by "pinning" images found on the internet to "pinboards" dedicated to a topic. As users browse images by topic, they can follow a bookmarked image back to its original location on the internet. Twitter users also tag and organize their tweets by hashtag (e.g., #socialmedia), enabling others to find tweets related to these user-defined topics.

**Reviewing:** Once content is posted, some sites enable users to review it. For example, the review feature on sites like amazon.com enable users to review products and provide feedback for other users who might be looking to purchase the same product.

**Sharing:** Many sites enable people to share a wide variety of content, including videos, images, or sound. YouTube and Vimeo are popular video-sharing sites, Flickr and Instagram are popular image-sharing sites, and iTunes is a popular platform for sharing sound in the form of podcasts.

**Voting:** Similar to reviewing, some sites enable people to vote on content or links. Social news sites such

*Figure 6.11 Social networking enables communication with audiences around the world.*

as digg.com or www.reddit.com enable users to vote content up or down, thus influencing what news displays most prominently on the site. Other sites, such as do-it-yourself.com or other help sites enable users to vote on the effectiveness of user-generated solutions to problems.

**Wiki creating:** Wiki sites enable users to collaborate in creating content. Wikipedia is the most popular online wiki-creation site.

All this context information underscores the technological richness of today's audience context, along with its complexity. Today's professionals must maintain their awareness of the social media marketplace so they can develop appropriate strategies for exploiting the best of all networking options.

## DEVELOP A STRATEGY

After determining your purpose, analyzing your audience, and analyzing the context, you can strategically adapt your message and its delivery. While many strategies have already been covered in the previous sections of this chapter, this section includes additional information related to channel strategies and psychological strategies.

### Channel Strategy

Choosing a channel for social media communication involves both the selection of the content medium (e.g., text, video, image) and the method of delivery (e.g., Facebook, LinkedIn, Twitter). As you make these choices, consider the following channel factors.

**Richness:** Videos and images provide the richest content on social media, while text-based messages provide the least. Real-time (synchronous) communication and delayed (asynchronous) communication also exhibit varying levels of richness; real-time seems richer to audiences since it mimics real-life conversation, but it can also take more resources to sustain.

**Reach:** As noted earlier in the chapter, Facebook currently reports the most users out of all social networking sites in the world and may thus generate the most views of the content you post. However, a large number of users does not automatically produce the engagement you desire since different audiences may prefer to receive their content through sources other than Facebook. Thus, to reach these audiences, you'll need to use

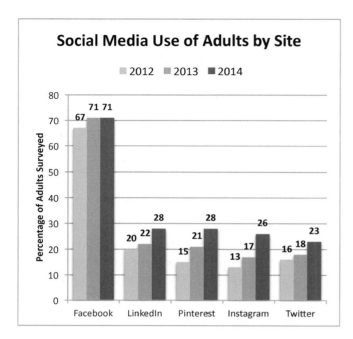

*Figure 6.12 Facebook has by far the largest number of adult users of its social media site. Source: Maeve Duggan, Nicole B. Ellison, Cliff Lampe, Amanda Lenhart and Mary Madden, "Social Media Update 2014," Pew Research Center (January 9, 2014): http://www.pewinternet.org/2015/01/09/social-media-update-2014.*

their preferred channel (see Figure 6.12). For example, your audience may check Facebook infrequently, but log on to LinkedIn numerous times per day. Also, recognize that some audiences, especially mobile audiences on the go, have varying levels of bandwidth and screen size that limit access to certain types of content.

**Immediacy**: Most social media sites allow immediate delivery of content, so you are generally restricted only by your own ability to prepare your content for publication online and by your strategic decisions of when to release new content. For example, if your company is scheduled to make a new product announcement that you plan to record and make available online, be sure to schedule enough resources to make the recording available within the time frame you promise customers. In addition, recognize that an audience's engagement with content generally peaks and then falls within about 24 hours. If you are working to maximize audience engagement, you will need to regularly post new content to maintain your audience's engagement levels. That said, if your analytics show that engagement is high with previously posted content, avoid posting new content until engagement levels fall.

**Permanence**: Because you have little control over an audience's sharing, reposting, downloading, or cap-

turing content on their screens, you should always consider the social media you create or share to be permanently public. With this mindset, regardless of the method you use to deliver your content, you will be more careful about the content you post. However, recognize that you can delete messages or entire accounts on most social networking sites. In addition, while your request may not always be granted, you can ask that sites remove your content that other users have posted.

**Control**: Regardless of the site you choose, your control of social media communication is limited. Therefore, focus on the aspects of your content delivery that you can control or at least influence. For example, most sites include privacy settings that you can use to your advantage when posting content. Creating and sharing high-quality content, engaging your audience in conversations, and building relationships of trust with your audience can also influence the ways that your audience chooses to critique, criticize, praise, or promote your content.

**Cost**: Most social networking sites require no fee for businesses to create and maintain accounts. Instead, these sites charge businesses only if the organizations choose to advertise or otherwise promote their content, products, or services on the site. By providing these free accounts, social networking sites grow the site's network and encourage businesses and individuals to generate more network content. This network effect generates more traffic on the site, and this increase of traffic results in more revenue.

As you consider your medium of delivery, recognize that some forms of content will cost more in terms of money or time to produce. For example, video can be more expensive to produce, even though mobile video or inexpensive animation sites such as goanimate.com may enable you to minimize video production costs. In contrast, text can cost much less to produce, especially for short messages and updates. When cost is not an overriding issue, recognize that sending the same message in multiple formats and through multiple channels may increase the reach of your message.

## Psychological Strategy

In addition to determining a channel strategy, you should consider psychological strategies as well. Two strategies to consider include convergence and push and pull.

## Convergence

As people read interesting content online, they make decisions about its credibility. For example, they may stumble upon a valuable online coupon offered by your company. To establish whether the coupon is real, they may then turn to the internet to see if they can find other sites offering the same coupon. If other reputable sites are offering the same content, then the credibility of the content increases; if the content is offered on only one potentially questionable site, then the credibility of the content decreases.

To assist your network in determining whether your content is credible, post your content across multiple social media channels. By sending a consistent message through multiple channels, you increase the likelihood that your audience will find multiple sites converging on the same message, resulting in content that your audience will deem more credible. The earlier example of the Heber Valley Chamber of Commerce's social media strategy illustrates effective use of convergence, with all of its social network sites and pages linking back to, or converging back to, the company web page. Also, the sites interweave and refer to each other, thus converging together in a coherent whole, while still accessing the audiences of different social networking sites and pages.

## Push and Pull

As people make decisions about the information they consume online, they naturally turn to their trusted network for recommendations. By receiving recommendations from those they trust, people decrease the risk that they will read or watch something they would prefer not to. As you create your social media communication, seek to promote your content through networks when possible. To do so, recognize the difference between push and pull strategies.

With a push strategy, you deliver your content directly to your audience without their seeking out your content. For example, you might pay a social networking site to place an ad for your content on the sidebar of users of the site. You have high control of the content pushed to these users since you controlled both the creation and delivery of the message. However, the audience may view your ad content as less credible since they recognize that it was delivered to them by a potentially biased content creator.

With a pull strategy, your audience originates and delivers your content for you. For example, a customer may experience exceptional service at your restaurant. This service prompts the customer to post a positive online review of your restaurant. In this way, you have somewhat less control since the customer controlled both the content posted

and its delivery. However, the content will seem more credible to other people searching for a restaurant since the content originated from someone outside the company.

While you may have less direct influence over the content your audiences share with a pull strategy, you do have indirect influence. For example, by providing superior service you increase the likelihood that customers will positively review your company online (see Figure 6.13). Also, by creating high-quality content, you increase the likelihood that your videos, infographics, or newsletters will be shared and reshared through your audience's personal networks. A pull strategy builds on the core principles that make up social media communication—credibility, engagement, and a network of people who believe in you and your product.

This chapter provides a foundation and framework for understanding, analyzing, and explaining social media communication. The best way for you to continue learning is to apply what you have learned by producing social media communication of your own. Start by following or connecting with influential people or companies in your industry. Listen in on their conversations, gaining a better understanding of social media trends in your field. When you have something to contribute to the conversation, consider your purpose, audience, and context, and then strategically

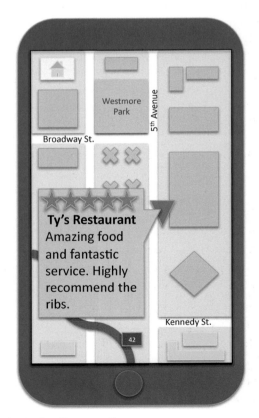

*Figure 6.13 An effective pull strategy generates customer compliments with great persuasive power.*

post your own content by starting a blog, writing a product review, or contributing to a wiki. Analyze the response of your network to your content, and then update your strategy accordingly. As you gain more experience, experiment with new social media channels to increase your network and to stay current on technology trends.

## CHAPTER SUMMARY

Thanks to advances in transmission speed and increased numbers of communication channels, you now have almost endless opportunities to stay in contact with people in your network, to access up-to-the-minute information for decision making, and to let your voice be heard on any topic of your choosing.

Social media communication involves the intersection of people, tools, content, and networks. People use online tools such as Twitter, Facebook, email, and Skype to share content. This content, live or delayed, includes text, video, audio, or images. While some tools specialize in sharing one specific type of content, most tools enable you to share multiple types with your network.

The purposes of social media communication are similar to communication of all types—to inform, to persuade, and to build relationships of trust. To inform, you must create high-quality content, share high-quality content, and become an expert. To persuade, you must create engaging content—content that is watched, read, and shared by networks. To build good relationships, you must assist others in your network, ask for nothing in return, and do more than simply "like."

Audience and context analysis is more difficult with social media networks because of the long reach of social media. Because electronic messages can be passed on and on, you can't really know who your audience may be. Nevertheless, you can use social media itself to gather information about your audience and their context.

Numerous social networking sites are present in today's social media marketplace, and the dynamic nature of social media phenomenon makes it impossible to know what the world will be like in the near future. Major features of social media networks include the capabilities to blog, discuss, instant message, microblog, share, network, and many more. Both channel and psychological strategies must be carefully implemented to achieve the greatest success with social media, with convergence, push, and pull strategies being among the most common.

## *Works Cited*

Pew Research Center. 2015. "Social Networking Fact Sheet." Accessed June 24. http://www.pewinternet.org/fact-sheets/social-networking-fact-sheet/.

U.S. Equal Employment Opportunity Commission. 2015. "Prohibited Employment Policies/Practices." Accessed June 24. http://www.eeoc.gov/laws/practices/.

## CHAPTER QUESTIONS

1.  What are the three main purposes of social media?
2.  Why is content credibility so important in social media?
3.  Describe how social media analytics are used in relation to social media networks.
4.  What demographic factor is most different in the use of social media?
5.  What is the difference between synchronous and asynchronous communication?
6.  How do your credibility and your content credibility interrelate with each other?
7.  List three guidelines for writing social media content.
8.  What role does online conversation play in social media?
9.  Briefly describe five different social networking sites.
10. What are the two main functions of hashtags?
11. Describe the differences between blogs and microblogs.
12. What role does a wiki site play in social media?
13. List three factors to consider in choosing a social media channel.
14. Describe the one-to-many and many-to-many concepts as they pertain to content distribution.
15. Describe push and pull strategies.

## CHAPTER ACTIVITIES

1.  Applying secondary research principles from Chapter 9, become an expert on a current industry trend. Write a 300-word summary on your research and post it on a social networking site of your choice. Respond to any comments you receive from your network in response.
2.  For an extended period of time, create and lead a blog. Using the principles discussed in this chapter, apply strategies to increase your audience's engagement with your content. For example, add visual elements

to your posts, sharing links, or a story. Post consistently, and advertise your posts on other social media channels. Ensure that your writing style is clear.

3.  While completing Activity 2, periodically check the site statistics on your blog. Experiment with various engagement strategies and measure the resulting change in the analytics. Write a memo to your instructor about how the various strategies worked. Include a visual of your analytics data.

4.  Determine a product that you can review online and write a 200-word product review. Apply principles learned in this chapter.

5.  Find a company of interest that maintains pages on multiple social media communication sites. Compare the content on each site, and write a brief memo analyzing the differences and similarities of the content posted on each channel.

6.  Follow a company of interest on Facebook, Twitter, and LinkedIn for a week. Write a brief memo analyzing the topics posted by the company on each channel. What can you infer about the company's purpose, audience, and context based on the content it posts?

7.  Analyze the social media communication of multiple companies in different industries. Try to find companies in both B2B (business to business) and B2C (business to consumer) industries. Analyze their social media use. What are the similarities among industries? What are the differences? What contextual factors do you think explain those differences?

8.  Find a company's Twitter account that handles customer service. For example, look at @DeltaAssist or @ComcastCare. Examine some of the tweets from customers and the replies from the company. What strategies does the company use for responding to negative messages? For positive messages?

9.  Find a current online news or magazine article related to your major or job. Share the article with your network on a social networking site of your choosing. Join the conversation by adding your own critique of the article when you post it.

10. Write a memo to your boss about a current business topic. Transform the memo into a blog post. Adapt the post to share it on Facebook. Condense the post into a tweet or series of tweets. Using the original content, write a transcript for a podcast and audio record it if possible. Then create an infographic. Write an analysis of your experience, discussing how your purpose, audience, and context influenced your content decisions.

11. Follow an industry leader on Twitter for an extended period of time. Report on what you learn about the industry from your experience.

## CHAPTER 7

# Communicating for Employment

Many people view job searching as a vague, ill-defined process filled with uncertainty and anxiety. First comes the challenge of finding employment openings that match their skills and that offer an adequate salary. Next comes the stressful process of interviewing and securing the position. After that comes the challenge of learning a new job and learning how to get along with new work colleagues. The entire process consumes large amounts of time, as well as physical and emotional energy.

In spite of the stress involved in securing employment, work is an exciting and important aspect of life. It provides opportunities to develop and use an art or skill in a productive way, to make money and provide for yourself or a family, to work with interesting people, and to contribute to the betterment of society. It provides a way to escape dullness and boredom, and it gives you a sense of purpose and satisfaction.

This chapter will help you better understand and prepare for the employment process, so you will be more confident and competent in this important aspect of your life. After reading this chapter, you should be able to do the following:

- Prepare a professional resume.
- Write effective employment messages, such as cover letters, thank-you letters, and recommendation letters.
- Perform well in a job interview, including sharing effective PAR stories.
- Conduct effective employment interviews.

## CHOOSING A CAREER

Before focusing on obtaining long-term employment, first choose a satisfying career path in which you can find fulfillment for many years, along with receiving satisfactory compensation and good benefits. As you consider specializing in a particular field, think seriously about the following questions:

- Am I interested in this field (e.g., finance, advertising, entrepreneurship)?
- Could I use my natural abilities and talents in this field (e.g., math, language, or science)?
- Would I enjoy doing this type of work day after day for many years?
- Do I have the money and time to invest in the education needed for this career?
- Would I have opportunities to continually learn and progress throughout my career?
- Is there adequate short- and long-term demand for workers in this industry?
- Would my salary be high enough for my needs?
- Would this career enable me to live and travel where I would like?
- Would I enjoy working with the people who would be my colleagues in this career?
- Would this career give me appropriate work-life balance?

If you are unsure of your career, make a plan to learn about different professions that might be suitable for you. Go visit with a career counselor. Take an aptitude test (free tests are available on the internet). Arrange for an infor-

mational interview with one or more people who work in fields you are interested in. Ask them what their careers are like, what they do during a typical day, and what skills and educational backgrounds are most important. Also, visit internet sites that give information about occupational trends, job openings, and salaries.

For example, the United States Bureau of Labor Statistics provides the *Occupational Outlook Handbook* and other useful career information on www.bls.gov. You can also find useful information at various websites, such as www.glassdoor.com, www.vault.com, and www.monster.com. The glassdoor.com website, for instance, provides average salaries of different jobs at specific companies, along with employee reviews of companies as employers. Further, the vault.com website reviews and ranks employers, with a focus on business careers, such as rankings of consulting firms.

## FINDING JOB OPENINGS

Once you settle on a career and qualify yourself for employment in that career, you will begin seeking specific employment. First, visit your school's career services office where you will be assisted in your information search. There you can also learn about companies coming on campus for interviews and career fairs. In addition to visiting your career services office, you should visit online recruiting sites, such as those in Table 7.1.

### Table 7.1 Sites for Employment Assistance

| Website | Web Address |
|---|---|
| Career Builder | www.careerbuilder.com |
| Careeronestop | www.acinet.org |
| Internship Programs | www.internshipprograms.com |
| Indeed | www.indeed.com |
| JobFox | www.jobfox.com |
| Jobster | www.jobster.com |
| Monster | swoop.monster.com |
| Monster College | www.monstertrak.com |
| NetTemps | www.net-temps.com |
| Riley Guide | www.rileyguide.com |
| SimplyHired | www.simplyhired.com |
| The Bridgespan Group | www.bridgespan.org |
| USAJobs | www.usajobs.gov |

In addition to these websites, search online for "employment" or "employment in X state," and visit the websites that are of interest to you.

*Figure 7.1 Wherever you are, let others know you are looking for employment.*

Ask people in your online and interpersonal networks to help you. Thousands of jobs go unadvertised and are filled by people who hear about them by word of mouth. Sometimes people are embarrassed to admit they are unemployed, yet they know they would be happy to help a friend who is unemployed. Therefore, overcome any hesitation you might feel and call on your friends and contacts for help. Send them a copy of your resume, highlighting your experiences, education, and strengths that make you a good candidate for the type of work you are seeking.

The most well-known online business networking resource is LinkedIn, but you can also call on your friends on Facebook and other social media. In addition to utilizing your online networks, don't forget your family, neighbors, and close friends. Let them know you are looking for employment, tell them what type of position you are seeking, give them your contact information, and ask them to let you know if they hear of any job openings that might be a good fit for you. In addition, join professional online groups, such as those you'll find on LinkedIn. Be sure to write a thank-you note to those who help you.

You can also be proactive in taking advantage of impromptu opportunities to self-promote with new people you meet. Prepare a 30-second speech that briefly describes your desired employment and highlights your preparation for that employment. Some people refer to this as an *elevator speech*, implying that it can be given in the amount of time it takes to ride in an elevator. Wherever you are, you can share your elevator speech and ask for help in finding employment. This brief speech is especially useful for career fairs. Consider the following two examples as models for your speech:

*Hi, I'm (give your name) and I'm a senior graduating in accounting from ABC University. I was president of our accounting club at ABC, and I completed*

*an internship last summer with Grant Thornton. I also have a 3.89 GPA. I'd like to work in the Northwest for a CPA firm, with an emphasis in tax. If you know of any openings in a regional or national firm, I would appreciate hearing about them. Here's my card with my contact information. I'd appreciate anything you can do to help.*

*I am (give your name) and I'm looking for a position as a full-time web developer. I'll be receiving a bachelor's degree in computer science in May and have put myself through four years of school by programming websites for several clients. I also speak and write Spanish, so I'm comfortable working with clients in a multicultural setting. Do you know anyone who might be looking for someone with my skills?*

In these two examples, notice that the information is succinct, yet filled with content relevant to the job-seeking process. Sharing concise, well-planned messages like these also shows that you have good self-confidence and communication capability.

Further, develop your own social media sites and put them to work for you. On your profile page include your education, relevant work experience, community service work, and skills. List any other information that might be useful, such as projects you have worked on, honors and awards received, special certificates and licenses obtained, and other noteworthy achievements. Keep all information up to date, and make sure it is accurate and free of errors. Make sure nothing on your site detracts from the professional image you are trying to portray.

Remember also that anything you have ever posted on the internet can be found by prospective employers and can disqualify you from employment. Many companies now conduct detailed web searches to see if anything you have ever posted would make you suspect. Using text analytics and data-mining capabilities, recruiters can gather all the information from your Facebook and LinkedIn pages, as well as all of the product reviews, blog posts, and comments that you have ever written anywhere on the web. With this information the software can then create an applicant psychological profile, based on what, where, and how you have written (including grammar), what you like and dislike, what kinds of friends you have, and so forth. If you have a record of writing numerous negative product reviews and use bad grammar, that history might disqualify you from getting an interview.

# PREPARING EMPLOYMENT DOCUMENTS

Seeking employment involves a variety of written and oral communications, and the materials in this chapter include instructions and samples to help you compose application letters, resumes, follow-up letters, and recommendation letters. You will also learn how to prepare for employment interviews. As with all communications, complete a thorough PACS plan to guide you in all your employment-related activities.

**Clarify your purpose:** Prepare your own job wish list, including your ideal type of work, your ideal salary, your preferred location, and anything else that is important to you.

**Analyze the audience:** Understand the people with whom you will be dealing, including human resource personnel, managers, and recruiters.

**Analyze the context:** Understand the context factors that will influence the outcome of your employment search, so you will be able to respond specifically to those factors. Study each job description and each company carefully.

**Develop an appropriate strategy.** Keeping in mind the audience and the context, develop a strategy to achieve your purpose. Show in detail how your credentials match the required knowledge, skills, and abilities. Include specific job-description terminology in your cover letter and resume, and customize your job documents for each position.

## *Application Letters*

Application letters (also known as cover letters) are addressed to the person or organization you want to work for. As is the case with many business messages, this letter seeks to inform, persuade, and build goodwill. You inform the employer about your interest in obtaining employment, you persuade him or her to contact you for an interview, and you begin building goodwill and a relationship of trust.

Cover letters are one of two types—letters that respond to a specific job posting and letters that inquire about possible job openings. Letters that respond to specific job posting obviously have a much greater chance for success because there is a real need and because you can tailor your letter precisely to that need. Letters of inquiry rarely gener-

ate any good job prospects. Therefore, focus your efforts on finding real job openings and applying for them.

As you write a cover letter, show how your qualifications match the job description. Write the letter from the employer's perspective, and explain how you can help the employer meet his or her needs. The following paragraphs explain the OABC parts of an application letter. (Sample cover letters are given in Figures 7.2 and 7.3.)

### Opening

Hook the reader and connect with the company. To make yourself stand out from all other job applicants, begin the letter with something more engaging than just, "I'm graduating from college and am looking for a job." Such an opening focuses totally on you, not on the employer's needs. Therefore, write your opening with the employer's needs in mind. Be original in your opening, but don't be so creative that it comes across as gimmicky and insincere. Consider the following examples:

*Share your passion for the work*: "For the last two years I have been working hard to prepare myself for work in human resource management. I have loved all my HR classes and now feel prepared to start a lifelong career in this vital part of business. After comparing the HR job postings of several companies, I am hoping to put my skills to work as an HR analyst at ABC, Inc."

*Show a good fit with your education*: "My degree in human resource management included coursework in HR law, compensation and benefits, employee training and development, and workforce planning—all of which are requirements for the compensation specialist position you have posted. Please consider me an applicant for this opening."

*Share your experience with their product*: "Last month I downloaded the free demo of your software and have enjoyed working with it since that time. I would love to become a developer in your firm and work on this and other products in your software line."

*Mention your acquaintance with an employee:* "A year ago I had an information interview with Nora Gray, an employee in your Ft. Worth office. She told me about her work in the finance department of your company. Now that I have completed my degree, I would love to put my skills to work in ABC's finance department as well. Please consider me an applicant for the financial analyst opening you have posted."

### Agenda

After the opening, include an agenda if you want to use an OABC pattern. For a tax accountant position with a CPA firm, your agenda could be, "I believe my academic emphasis in tax accounting, my internship experience performing actual tax work, and my communication skills and abilities are a good fit for your open tax position."

### Body

Show how your qualifications match the job description. The middle paragraphs are the persuasive part of the message, so include your most convincing information in these paragraphs. If you don't use an OABC pattern, compose one or two paragraphs that tell how your qualifications match the job requirements, perhaps using a bullet list for emphasis (see Figure 7.3).

If you use OABC, organize the body of your letter to match the agenda. For instance, in the second paragraph, highlight the tax knowledge you learned in your coursework; in the third paragraph, tell about last summer's tax internship, and share a brief example of what you achieved in that position; and in the fourth paragraph, include information about your communication skills (written, oral, and interpersonal). Another option for the body would be to include several bullet points, each one containing a line or two of information that shows you to be a good match for the employer's specific job requirements.

In your resume you provide a list of your experience and accomplishments, but in the cover letter you can go beyond these basic facts and add some color to your qualification statements. For instance, describe your passion for the work, highlight your effectiveness in working with a team, or explain how you have been willing to go the second mile in difficult situations.

### Closing

In the last paragraph, refer the reader to your resume. Then close with an action ending, such as, "I look forward to hearing from you about the possibility of an interview to discuss your needs and my qualifications in more detail.

## Resumes

A resume is a self-promotion document to help you obtain a job interview with a prospective employer. Sample resumes are shown in Figures 7.4, 7.5, and 7.6, but you should modify your resume as needed to effectively market yourself for each employer. Study the employer's job requirements carefully, and then design your resume to

# Melinda Miller

17 Hillside Road, Sunset City, US 835XX   •   (947) 663-92XX   •   melmill@email.com

March 11, 20XX

Mr. Matias Garcia
Big West LLP
778 East 4th Street
Northwest City, XX 638XX

Dear Mr. Garcia:

While I was at home for Christmas last December, I talked with Kevin Fillmore, an auditing manager in your local office. He mentioned that you would be hiring several new staff accountants in June, and he encouraged me to apply. In May of this year, I will graduate from Northbrook University with a master's degree in accounting and would like to be considered for one of those positions. The following paragraphs summarize my education, experience, and personal attributes that will enable me to contribute to the auditing function of Big West.

*Accounting Education.* I have worked hard to gain the education needed for success as a professional accountant. In addition to completing the basic accounting coursework at Northbrook, I have completed courses in general auditing, advanced auditing, and forensic accounting. In each of these courses I earned an A grade. I am confident that I can quickly learn the auditing methodology used by Big West and become a productive member of the audit team.

*Accounting Experience.* To enhance my professional preparation, I have worked part-time as an accountant in a local construction company. Also, last summer I completed an intensive summer internship with a CPA firm in Seattle. My responsibilities with both companies gave me first-hand experience with a wide range of accounting issues, which will be helpful in performing auditing work for Big West.

*Personal Attributes.* To complement my accounting education and experience, I have developed effective communication skills, both written and oral. I also work well with people and am a team player. I am the former president of our on-campus accounting club, and I increased the club's membership by nearly 35 percent during my tenure. I enjoy the challenge of setting high goals and working to achieve them. I am confident that my communication skills and interpersonal attributes would fit well in the professional culture of your firm.

The enclosed resume gives additional details about my qualifications. You are welcome to contact my former managers or professors and ask about my work performance. After you have reviewed the resume, I would appreciate the opportunity to talk more about how I might put my skills to work at Big West.

Sincerely,

*Melinda Miller*

Melinda Miller

Enclosure: Resume

*Figure 7.2   Application letters should show how your qualifications match the job requirements.*

# David R. Rosenthall

423 West 47th Street, Midcity, US 36229  •  (724) 369-5327  •  brwat@email.com

January 24, 20XX

Ms. Michelle McFarlain
Metro Properties, Inc.
431 West Avenue
Central, US  123XX

Dear Ms. McFarlain:

As a son of a landlord with numerous apartment rentals, I became involved with various aspects of property management at an early age—performing building maintenance, fixing electrical and plumbing problems, and talking with renters. To build on that foundation, I have completed a Bachelor of Science degree and have worked to develop the skills needed for a career in commercial property management. Please consider me for your Property Manager Specialist position.

As the position description requires, I have a degree in business management. In completing this degree, I excelled in my business finance, entrepreneurship, marketing, and accounting courses. I also took additional information systems courses to strengthen my computer skills. I am familiar with the AppFolio, MRI, and other property management software. I believe my educational background is a good fit for your major job specifications.

During my last two years of college, I have worked part-time with a local property management company. In this work I have gained experience with many of the responsibilities listed in your job description:

- **Attract tenants.** I have 16 months' experience using various media, including social media, to advertise vacancies.
- **Establish rental rates.** I performed two major rental surveys to help determine company pricing structures.
- **Manage financial transactions.** I have two years' experience performing financial transactions using property management software and resolving financial disputes with renters.
- **Resolve tenant complaints.** I have resolved dozens of tenant complaints, ranging from maintenance and repair issues to disputes between neighbors.

The enclosed resume gives additional details about my qualifications and background. After you have reviewed the resume, I would appreciate the opportunity to talk more about how I might contribute to the success of Metro Properties.

Sincerely,

*David Rosenthall*

David R. Rosenthall

Enclosure: Resume

*Figure 7.3  Application letters are marketing documents and should be modified for each unique job you seek.*

# Aaron B. Dobson

(829) 400-23XX  -  abdobs@email.com  -  http://www.linkedin.com/in/aarondobson

**Summary**

**Experience**: Three years' work experience in beverage industry analyzing brand distribution, customer trends, and sales results and opportunities

**Administrative skills**: Excellent quantitative, communication, and interpersonal skills; fluent in Spanish; worked in cross-functional teams in results-driven environment

**Computer skills**: MS Excel, Word, PowerPoint, Publisher, and SPSS

**Education**

**Master of Business Administration, Marketing Emphasis**          Apr 20XX
Drucker University, Midwest, US
- Awarded graduate scholarship
- Scored in 90th percentile on GMAT
- Served as president of MBA Marketing Association
- Developed training presentation for instructor's website

**Bachelor of Science, Statistics, Business Analysis Emphasis**          Aug 20XX
Minor, Business Management
State University, Anywhere, US
- Secretary of Student Chapter of American Society for Quality

**Experience**

**Product Management Intern**          May 20XX – Aug 20XX
Big Freight Trucking, Inc.; Southeast, US
- Developed and applied segmentation guidelines for 75,000 small business customers and co-developed marketing campaign targeting key segments of small business market
- Implemented new incentive offer and performed industry analysis for two regional campaigns to direct sales team in customer focus and retention
- Created two promotional offers for international campaign to increase trans-border shipments and promote next-day capabilities

**Sales Analyst**          Oct 20XX – Aug 20XX
Soft Drink Bottling Group; Big City, ST
- Developed and implemented Excel tool that tracked distribution voids of 70+ innovative SKU's for 2,200 retail, convenience, and food-service customers
- Assumed full responsibility in development and execution of all incentives for sales representatives; increased success rate of incentive targets achieved by 30 percent
- Received Customer Service Award, awarded to only 10 employees each year who exemplified the company's customer-service initiative
- Built yearly volume plans of 8.5 million cases for 4 territories and 60+ routes, and analyzed sales and out-of-date, breakage, and sellable returns on daily basis

**Course Assistant**          Jan 20XX – Aug 20XX
Department of Statistics; Big City, US
- Conducted weekly training meetings for 5-10 department teaching assistants
- Graded exams, homework, and quizzes, and maintained grade database of 200 students
- Assisted professor in lectures for introductory statistics class
- Ranked in top 20 percent of TA's in student ratings

**Service**

Volunteered with Annual United Way Day of Caring          Sep 20XX, Sep 20XY
Helped struggling statistics students in statistics lab          Sep 20XX – May 20XY

*Figure 7.4  A sample resume submitted for a posted position. Employment resumes should reflect careful attention to content and design.*

match those requirements as closely as possible. In your resume, try to match the wording in the position description.

Design your resume to match the company's system for processing resumes, whether human or machine. For humans, remember that human resource managers often have so many resumes to examine that they will spend only 20 or 30 seconds skimming each one. Therefore, make your strengths easy to find. List your major strengths early in the resume, and use formatting and typography enhancements to make your most impressive information stand out. To help employers match your resume and cover letter, use the same letterhead on both documents.

To improve your chances of being selected with machine scans, include keywords that are used in the job posting. When your resume will be scanned by resume-management software, avoid all typographic and visual enhancements (such as bolding, italicizing, and underlining) that might make your resume unrecognizable. Make sure to put your name on the first line and your contact information on the next line. Further, use just one font throughout the document to avoid the chance of error by the scanning software.

As you decide what information to include in your resume, be honest. Deception in resumes is a real problem. Of course you should highlight your strengths, but if you embellish the facts and say things that aren't really true, you are being unethical and dishonest. If you lie in any of your employment documents and your dishonesty is discovered after you are hired, you will likely be dismissed and find yourself out looking for another job—this time with a black mark on your record!

You can follow one of two basic resume patterns—chronological or functional—as explained in the following two sections. The chronological format is the one most commonly used.

### Chronological Resume Guidelines

Most job applicants use a traditional chronological resume format, shown in Figures 7.4 and 7.5. With this type of format, most of the content is listed in reverse-chronological order. Most employers are familiar with this format, and most prefer this format. Following are guidelines for chronological resumes.

#### Heading

Create a heading that lists your name, telephone number, and email address as the first items on the resume. You may also include a web address if you have one. Type your name in a larger font for emphasis. Use this same heading at the top of your cover letter, perhaps reducing the font size of your name for the letter.

#### Summary

Create a professional summary, skills, or strengths section that captures your main attributes and job qualifications, such as "Ten years programming experience, . . ." or "Word, Excel, PowerPoint . . ." For unsolicited applications, you may include an "objectives" statement that clarifies the type of job you are seeking, such as, "Seeking marketing analyst position where I can apply my statistical and analytical skills."

#### Education and Experience

List your education and experience, with the more impressive section first. In other words, if your education is more impressive than your experience, list your education first. Also, list your education and experience entries in reverse-chronological order—with the most recent degree or most recent job first.

For each college you have attended in the past but have not graduated from, include the dates of attendance. Where you have graduated or will graduate, list the month and date of graduation. Also list the degree you received, your major field of study (and minor if applicable), and other pertinent information. At this point you may also include specific classes you have taken that help qualify you for the job you are seeking, academic awards or scholarships you have received, or professional academic clubs or organizations you have affiliated with. As a general rule, do not include high school information.

For each job you have held, list the job title, employment dates, company name and address (city and state), job responsibilities, and the results you achieved. To the extent possible, tie your responsibilities and results in your previous jobs to the knowledge, skills, and abilities required in the job you are seeking. Use words that match those included in the position description. Wherever possible, include impressive results that you achieved. Employers are much more impressed with results than with bland responsibility statements like, "Responsible for vendor payments," or "Responsible for regional market reports." Also, try to include quantifiable results and responsibilities to show the size and scope of your work.

*Provided telephone support for over 130 computer and telephone products.*

*Conducted and analyzed market research with over 30 focus groups.*

# *Emily R. Bowen*

339-461-28XX   ❖   mleb@email.com   ❖   http://www.linkedin.com/in/aarondobson

## *Education*

**Bachelor of Science**, Brandon University (projected graduation: May 20XX)
*Major: Accounting* (3.8/4.0 GPA)
Academic Scholarship; Dean's List
Member Beta Gamma Sigma and Beta Alpha Psi
Relevant course work:
- Completed: Business Communication, Introduction to Financial Accounting, Cost Accounting, Income Tax Accounting, and Business Law
- Currently enrolled: Auditing, Accounting Information Systems

## *Experience*

**Staff Accountant** (June 20XX - January 20XX)
*TNU Department of Visual Communications*, Big City, ST
- Identified weaknesses in AIS that led to recovery of over $10,000 in revenue
- Suggested and implemented billing policies that saved time and increased accuracy by 15%
- Helped plan and submit $5,000 yearly budget

**Teacher's Assistant** (September 20XX - May 20XX)
*BU Department of Accounting*, Metro City, ST
- Graded homework, quizzes, and exams of 350 students
- Conducted daily help sessions for beginning accounting students
- Created over 100 PowerPoint slides for professor

*Figure 7.5  Where appropriate, quantify the scope of your responsibilities and the results you have achieved.*

# *Emily R. Bowen*

Page 2

## *Volunteer*

**Training Consultant** (September 20XX-December 20XX)
- *Center for Service and Learning*
  Worked with small team to evaluate center's recruiting and training practices, implemented policy changes, redesigned brochure, and recommended more effective recruiting media

- *Stone Soup After-School Program (January 20XX – April 20XX)*
  Instructed minority and underprivileged children on improving study habits and social skills

## *Computer Skills*

- *Accounting*: QuickBooks, NetSuite
- *Microsoft*: Access, Excel, PowerPoint, Outlook, Word
- *Adobe*: Acrobat, Illustrator, Photoshop

*Figure 7.6  Your resume might exceed one page later in your career. Subsequent pages in a resume should have a header that includes the page number.*

*Managed transaction history for 16 different payroll accounts.*

*Increased annual income by 146 percent by restructuring company business plan and sales model.*

*Created streamlined system to maintain digital transaction records for over 5,000 customers.*

When you describe your results, begin the statements with strong action verbs, such as the following (use present tense for current employment and past tense for past employment):

| Strong Action Verbs | | | |
|---|---|---|---|
| Achieved | Developed | Managed | Proposed |
| Arranged | Directed | Operated | Reduced |
| Assisted | Implemented | Organized | Reorganized |
| Completed | Improved | Performed | Resolved |
| Coordinated | Increased | Planned | Supervised |
| Created | Initiated | Presented | Trained |

### Additional Sections

Include one or more additional sections as needed to include awards, special achievements, volunteer service, or other relevant information. Volunteer service in your community is always looked upon favorably, so seek for opportunities to get involved in activities of this nature. Get involved also in professional clubs related to your major, such as an accounting club or a finance club.

### Length

Keep your resume to one page, especially when you are early in your career. Later on, if you have good information that warrants two pages, use two pages. Put your name and the page number at the top of any subsequent pages, as shown in Figure 7.6. Leave two blank lines between the page number and the next line of text in your resume.

### Proofreading

Make sure your resume is perfect in spelling, grammar, and punctuation.

### Design

Pay attention to appearance. Use an attractive format (unless your resume will be machine scanned), and use high-quality stationery for a professional image.

## Functional Resume Guidelines

Some applicants choose a functional-resume format, shown in Figure 7.7. The functional-resume format emphasizes a person's skills and competencies and de-emphasizes the career path. This format is most appropriate for individuals who wish to make a career shift, who want to de-emphasize their older age, or who don't have an impressive career path. The following paragraphs provide guidelines for functional resumes.

**Heading.** Create the heading section just as you would with the traditional chronological format. Include your name, telephone number, email address, and so forth.

**Objective.** For unsolicited resumes, you may include an objective that states the type of employment you are seeking.

**Relevant Content.** Create a section that highlights the knowledge, skills, and abilities that are relevant to the employment you are seeking. Organize this information under appropriate headings, such as team skills, communication skills, project management skills, or programming skills. As with chronological resumes, include specific results you have achieved, and quantify results and responsibilities whenever appropriate.

**Additional Sections.** Create any additional sections that will be of value to the employer, including a brief listing of educational degrees and employment experience, professional memberships, awards received, and so forth.

Other guidelines regarding typography, spacing, length, proofreading, and so forth are consistent for both chronological and functional resumes.

In addition to developing a resume for paper or email distribution, you may wish to post an online version. For both email and online versions, save them in PDF format to ensure proper formatting. Your online resume may be attached to your own social media site or to other organizations' online job boards. As an alternative, you may also create a unique version using the formatting options provided by some online employment services, such as LinkedIn and VisualCV (www.visualcv.com).

With LinkedIn, for example, you choose a template and then your resume content is automatically pulled from your profile and formatted according to that template. You can then customize the resume according to your preferences. Afterward, you can give prospective employers a link that will take them directly to your LinkedIn resume. With online services you also have the option of including a port-

# Trevor L. Carter

592.738.45XX  •  tlc95@.email.com  •  http://www.linkedin.com/in/tlc

## OBJECTIVE

Community health professional seeking challenging career opportunity as Health Educator.

## PROFESSIONAL SKILLS

**Communication Skills**
- Presented to large groups using professionally designed PowerPoint slides
- Participated in Jefferson County Health Department Speakers Bureau
- Developed facility with Spanish language; performed health coaching in Spanish and assisted with translation in office settings
- Wrote comprehensive evaluation report of Walktober program and made recommendations for improvements in future events
- Created and designed weekly newsletters for Walktober participants

**Interpersonal Skills**
- Acquired donations from various companies through successful verbal and written communication
- Demonstrated proficiency in teaching and informing target population on pertinent topics
- Resolved landlord/tenant disputes, taking legal action when necessary
- Demonstrated competence as team leader, ensuring that team objectives were met
- Demonstrated strong interpersonal skills with individuals from various cultural backgrounds

**Leadership Skills**
- Served as Chair of Walktober program at Jefferson County Health Department and oversaw all details; over 250 employees participated
- Raised over $5,000 of donations in kind from various companies
- Successfully trained new employees; taught efficiency in problem solving and time management
- Managed property for 210 self-storage units; responsible for coordinating maintenance and repairs

**Technical Skills**
- Assisted in financial management and budgeting for large self-storage company
- Demonstrated competence in assessing needs and developing programs to meet those needs
- Demonstrated excellent technical-writing skills; wrote three successful grant proposals
- Demonstrated critical thinking, ability to analyze and solve problems, and ability to make effective decisions
- Demonstrated proficiency with Microsoft Office software: Word, Excel, PowerPoint, Publisher

## EDUCATION

**Bachelor of Science in Community Health (Health Education Emphasis)**          Dec 20XX
Achiever State College, Somewhere, US (3.68/4.0 GPA; Dean's list – 4 Semesters)
*Related Coursework:*
- Principles of Marketing
- Community Health Program Development and Evaluation
- Modifying Health Behavior
- Foundations of Health Education
- Human Diseases/Pathophysiology

## EMPLOYMENT HISTORY

**Assistant Manager** – Alamo Storage; Port Arthur, TX                    Dec 20XX - Present
**Intern** – Jefferson County Health Department; Beaumont, TX              May 20XX - Aug 20XX
**Home Health Aide** – Southwest Home Care; Beaumont, TX                   Aug 20XX - Dec 20XX

## PROFESSIONAL MEMBERSHIPS

**THEA** – Texas Health Education Association
**NSNA** – National Student Nursing Association

*Figure 7.7  A functional resume emphasizes the applicant's qualifications, rather than the employment and education history.*

folio of additional electronic documents (such as certificates, writing samples, and letters from previous employers) and multimedia elements (such as presentations). Be sure to do your very best design work when developing additional materials to post on the internet.

## PREPARING FOR INTERVIEWS

As you prepare for employment interviews, you should realize that the employee selection process may include several stages. In the earliest stage, employers will perform a resume review and will eliminate all who are clearly not qualified. This includes those whose education or experience don't qualify and those whose resumes are so poorly created that they reflect a lack of attention to detail and insensitivity to standard business practices. Where large numbers of job seekers have applied, this phase may reduce the list of candidates by as much as 90 percent, yielding a short list of perhaps 8 to 10 people.

Next, employers will conduct screening interviews of those on the short list to identify the two or three strongest candidates. This is the first opportunity for employers to meet with candidates in a video or face-to-face interview. For college students, screening interviews will often take place on their college campus. Employers will be interested in learning more about candidates' technical qualifications, as well as about their communication and interpersonal skills.

The final employee-selection stage may include multiple interviews with both HR and technical managers, usually at the employer's site. During this stage, employers will examine candidates' technical and interpersonal qualifications in great depth. Also, this stage may involve candidate testing, stress interviews, conversations over lunch, presentations by the candidates, and other selection procedures. Finally, a decision will be made, and an offer will be extended to the candidate judged to be the best qualified.

During your years in business you will find yourself on both sides of the desk—sometimes being interviewed by others and sometimes interviewing others. The following sections give tips to be successful in both roles.

### When You Are Being Interviewed

Like written business messages, interviews have an opening (sometimes with an agenda), a body, and a closing. The opening of first interviews typically includes a warm-up phase, a questioning phase, and a closing phase. In the warm-up phase the interviewer often asks one or two open-ended questions to get the conversation going. A typical opening question is, "Tell me about yourself." With this question you have the freedom to take the conversation in whatever direction you want. Remember, however, that even though interviewers may not be looking for a specific answer in this phase, they are receiving strong first impressions about you. The impression you make during the first minute or two of the interview is often a lasting impression. One way to answer the tell-me-about-yourself question is to give an adaptation of your 30-second elevator speech:

> *I am seeking a position as a full-time web developer with your company. I'll be receiving a bachelor's degree in computer science in May and have put myself through four years of school by programming websites for several clients. I also speak and write Spanish, so I'm comfortable working with clients in a multicultural setting. After reviewing the requirements for this position, I believe my background is a good fit, and I would really like to be considered for that position.*

Once the conversation is underway, the interviewer will move to the body of the interview and ask questions that are more specific. The goal is to determine whether you can perform the work adequately and whether your personality and attributes are a good fit for the job. The body of the interview will occupy the greatest amount of time and will give you the opportunity to go into more depth about your background and preparation for the job. After the body, the closing phase will conclude the interview. Often it will include an invitation for you to ask questions and a statement regarding what to expect next, such as, "We'll get back to you by next Friday to let you know our decision."

The following guidelines will help you make a good impression in interviews. Review these guidelines and practice your interview with someone who can effectively represent an interviewer.

1. **Do your homework.** Learn about the organization by searching the internet, looking in the library, or studying information provided by a college placement center. Learn about the organization's history, products and services, organizational structure, locations of home office and branches, industry challenges and trends, competition, and financial standing. If possible, contact someone inside the organization, and request information that will help you prepare for your interview. Also, visit competitors' websites and social media sites so you know as much as possible about the company's competition.

2. **Be prepared and be on time.** Be prompt—leave early for the interview so an unexpected delay won't make

you late. Take an extra copy of your resume, as well as paper and pen for making notes either during or after the interview.

3. **Dress appropriately.** Appropriate dress for an interview depends on the position you are seeking, but assume a dark-colored conservative business suit. (If you are unsure, call the company and ask about the dress code.) For men, wear a white shirt—or solid-colored shirt for less formal situations—and a conservative tie. For women, wear a white or light-colored blouse, with a skirt that does not come above the knees. Avoid low necklines and any jewelry or accessories that draw attention to themselves.

   If you have been told to wear business casual, be aware that this does not mean *casual*! Rather, business casual is a classic, well-groomed look that is a step below a full business suit. For men it usually involves khakis or slacks and a short-sleeved polo shirt or collared long-sleeved shirt, typically with no necktie. For women it includes nice slacks or knee-length skirts, and an appropriate blouse or collared shirt. For both men and women, it may include a jacket or blazer. Always avoid faddish clothing and hair styles and visible tattoos.

*Figure 7.8 Dress appropriately for interviews.*

4. **Be sensitive to body language.** At the beginning of the interview, shake hands with appropriate firmness. During the interview, be alert, interested, and pleasant. Smile as appropriate. Maintain good posture and eye contact. Avoid nervous mannerisms with hands and feet. Watch for nonverbal cues from the interviewer and adjust your behavior accordingly.

   Try to be sensitive to nonverbal messages that leak from your voice and body language. Many of the impressions you make on the interviewer are formed through your nonverbal communications. Through these unspoken messages, the interviewer senses whether you have ambition, passion, confidence, clarity of vision, and a sense of humor, as well as whether you are authentic, prepared, creative, clear in your expression, and willing to take risks. If possible, video record one or two practice interviews and then afterward critique your nonverbal messages—your voice, your eyes and face, your gestures, and your body posture. Get help from a communications coach to help you improve in these areas.

5. **Speak confidently and clearly.** Show confidence in your answers, but don't be cocky! People are generally unimpressed with arrogance. Maintain good vocal energy, and don't speak in a flat, monotone voice. Answer questions fluently, and avoid awkward pauses that communicate, "I'm not prepared." Listen carefully to the questions and answer them completely, yet concisely. Don't dominate the interview with long answers and explanations.

6. **Be honest; don't pretend to be something you're not!** Be truthful; never lie. Be yourself; be genuine. Don't exaggerate. If you are always honest, you never have to worry about people finding out something that conflicts with what you have said.

7. **Tie your answers to the knowledge, skills, and abilities required for the job.** Remember to sell both your technical qualifications and your human attributes. For instance, you might be asked a question like "What are your two greatest strengths?" Regardless of how you answer this question, tie your answer to the job requirements. For example, describe two job-related strengths, and state how you think they help qualify you for the open position. Avoid giving extreme or controversial viewpoints, and avoid wandering off the subject with your answers.

8. **Strengthen your content.** If your answers are informative, interesting, and convincing, they will have great mental "stickiness" and be remembered by the interviewer. If your answers are vague and general, they will be quickly forgotten.

   Be especially well prepared for behavioral questions, such as, "Tell me about a time when you were a member of a team." PAR (problem, action, result) stories are effective for answering behavioral questions. Therefore, as you plan for interviews, prepare a PAR story for each of your major skills and abilities, such as your ability to solve problems, your ability to assume a leadership role, or your skill in using computers effectively. Also, prepare PAR stories for such things as your greatest achievement in life and your greatest challenge in life.

   As you create PAR stories, (a) describe a problem situation you were in, (b) explain what action you took to deal with the problem, and (c) highlight the

results you achieved. Rehearse your PAR stories so you can tell them smoothly, effectively, and concisely. Don't make them too long. Here is an example of a PAR story:

Problem: "Our systems analysis department had an old project that should have been completed six months earlier, but the analyst assigned to the project just hadn't delivered. So my boss asked me to take it on."

Action: "I first went to the client to make sure I knew what he wanted. I then went to my boss and requested the full-time service of another analyst for three months. Next I gathered all the data we needed for the project. Then the other analyst and I went to work."

Result: "We finished the project in three months, and the client and my boss were very happy with the results."

If you are asked a negative question that could work *against* you, try giving an answer that works *for* you. For instance, you might be asked, "What is one of your greatest weaknesses?" To such a question you might respond with the following PAR story:

Problem: "Well, my dad was an army officer, and so we had to move a lot. This meant I was uprooted from my friends every few years, and I became a bit quiet and hesitant to get involved socially."

Action: "But in high school I realized that I needed to change my attitude and be more outgoing. As a result, when we moved to St. Louis at the beginning of my junior year, I went out of my way to develop new friendships."

Result: "A few months later, I was elected as vice president of my senior class. So even though I didn't particularly like all those moves my family had to make, I have become more resilient and adaptable as a result."

PAR stories are great for answering behavioral questions, but they can be used effectively at any point in an interview. For example, if you are asked to tell about your greatest challenge in life or to tell about your responsibilities in your previous job, you could include a PAR story as part of your answer.

9. **Have questions to ask the interviewer.** Job interviews are not just one-sided conversations where the

employer does all the asking and the job seeker does all the answering. Rather, both parties should come to the interview with a list of information they want to gather. Thus, when you are being interviewed, determine beforehand what questions you want to ask about the company. Some of your questions may be answered during the normal course of the interview; for those that are not, you may ask them at the end. However, don't ask too many—typically not more than two or three. Sample questions are listed as follows:

*What are the specific functions and responsibilities of this position? How has it evolved in the last few years?*

*What training opportunities are provided for new employees?*

*What are the typical challenges for a person working in this position?*

*What have other people in this position done to be most successful?*

*What do you like best about working for this organization?*

*Tell me about the organizational culture here.*

*Tell me about your organization's management philosophy.*

*What is a typical career path for someone in this position?*

10. **Expect some surprise questions.** Despite your best preparation, you may be asked some unexpected questions. When these questions are asked, stay calm and take a few seconds to plan your answer—it is better to take a moment of silence and give a coherent answer than to respond instantly without forethought. For some surprise questions, the interviewer may be looking more for how you think and respond under pressure than whether you give an exact answer.

If quantitative data is involved, use round numbers for easier calculation. For instance, assume the interviewer asks, "How many gas stations are there in the U.S.?" To respond, pause for a moment and think about the process you might follow to obtain a reasonably close answer. Then you might say something like, "Well, if we have roughly 300 million people in the country, and if we assume two cars for every three people, that would give us about 200 million cars. And if we assume there is one gas station for every

1,000 cars, that would give us about 200,000 gas stations."

Sometimes you may be interviewed by telephone. Telephone interviews enable employers to reduce travel costs and employee selection time. As you prepare for a phone interview, arrange for a quiet location, possibly at your college career center. Some career centers have quiet rooms, as well as special communication equipment, that you can reserve for telephone or video-based interviews. Also, if you will be using a cell phone, make sure it is well charged before the interview.

Preparing for a phone interview is much like preparing for a regular interview, including researching the company, preparing your PAR stories, and so forth. The actual interview, however, is different, so you need to be prepared for these differences.

With phone interviews involving just audio, you can't see the person or people you are talking with, so you miss out on facial expressions and other nonverbal cues that help set the tone of the interview. Equally important is the fact that they can't see you, so they miss out on your nonverbal cues. Thus, be sure to listen very carefully. When you are responding to a question, speak clearly, speak with enthusiasm (but don't speak too fast), answer every question fully, smile and let your personality come through in your voice, and be respectful. In addition, even though you can't be seen, consider dressing up for the interview—being professionally dressed will help you remember to act professionally and to speak at an appropriate level of formality.

With telephone interviews you may have various documents spread out in front of you for quick information access. For example, on a table or desk in front of you, place a copy of your resume, a list of questions you want to have answered, key points you want to emphasize during the interview, PAR stories you want to tell, names of people

*Figure 7.9  Let your voice convey your personality and enthusiasm during telephone interviews.*

who will be interviewing you, and any other information that might be relevant. Also consider having your computer in front of you, with the company's website displayed. Further, be prepared to take notes during the interview, capturing important information immediately, rather than having to wait until after the interview. Finally, have a glass of water nearby in case your mouth gets dry from stress.

If you are interviewed via Skype or other video-based system, you will be able to see your interviewers, although video-based interviewing is still not as rich with feedback as is face-to-face interviewing. Because of the media involved, the interpersonal turn taking may be a bit more awkward, so listen carefully and be sensitive to the communication cues given by the interviewers. Be sure to speak clearly, be pleasant, and let your personality come through in both your face and your voice.

With video-based interviewing, arrange the setting carefully. Make sure that nothing within the camera's range distracts. As with audio interviews, you may arrange a few documents in front of you, but out of the camera's range. Also, dress as you would for a face-to-face interview. Your dress has an important influence on your behavior and on the interviewer's impression of you.

## When You Are Interviewing Others

When you are in the role of a manager and need to conduct an employment interview, first gather all relevant information about the job, such as job title, job qualifications, job description, organizational placement, salary, and full- or part-time status. Write a detailed job-requirements list for evaluating all applicants. Recruit widely to ensure that you can find the best-qualified candidates—include your own organization, employment agencies, college and university placement centers, online, and word-of-mouth.

Once you receive resumes from job applications, conduct an initial screening. Using the list of job requirements, quickly skim each resume and eliminate the candidates who are obviously not qualified. Rate all remaining candidates according to how closely they meet the job requirements. Then create a short list of people to interview. Contact the candidates, invite them to an interview, and communicate all appropriate logistics, such as date, time, place, duration, and so forth. Some out-of-town applicants may need to be interviewed via audio- or video-based technology. Sometimes employment interviews will have to be conducted after regular work hours to accommodate the full-time work schedule of a candidate.

In preparing for the actual interview, invite the right people to participate. To select a new manager, for example,

a subordinate, a colleague, the manager over that position, and an HR representative might be a well-rounded interview team. Arrange seating that will make the candidate feel comfortable. Sitting directly across the desk or rectangular table from a candidate is a confrontational setting. A better arrangement would be to sit at an angle cross the corner of a desk or around a small round table.

With the list of job requirements as your guide, create the interview questions that you will ask to all candidates. Remember that all questions must comply with civil rights employment law and must pertain to bona fide occupational qualifications (BFOQs). Avoid questions that illegally discriminate, specifically those related to race, religion, age, gender, sexual orientation, nationality, marital and family status, and military status.

Be aware of biases that may occur. For example, you may be inclined to hire someone who is just like you. Remember, however, that appropriate diversity can play an important role in the workplace. Remember also that if you have a very poor interview, the next person will likely seem impressive by comparison, no matter who it is. To help eliminate bias that may occur as you interview different people, create a rubric for scoring interviewees' answers to your standard questions.

The following guidelines will help you conduct an effective employment interview.

1.  **Prepare well.** Review the resume thoroughly so you'll know as much as possible about the person before the interview begins. Also, prepare your questions in advance (all individuals being interviewed for the same position should be asked the same questions).

2.  **Take good notes and record your impressions during or immediately after the interview.** Evaluate each person against the factors you are using in making the selection decision. Document each interview carefully to protect your firm in case a passed-over person decides to take you to court.

3.  **Start out with a brief warm-up phase to put the interviewee at ease.** For example, ask about a hobby or something else the person feels comfortable talking about.

4.  **Be a good listener.** First, be responsive and encouraging as the interviewee speaks. Provide encouraging nonverbal communication, including maintaining good eye contact, smiling, and nodding your head. Give verbal encouragement as well, such as saying "yes," "I understand," or "Tell me more about . . ." Second, use reflective listening as needed to make sure you understand the person's answers. Third, listen to

*Figure 7.10 Listen to both verbal and nonverbal messages.*

the person's nonverbal messages given through tone of voice and body language.

5.  **Use closed and open questions effectively.** Closed questions can be answered with a yes or no or other short answer; open questions require greater explanation. Open questions require more explanation, and they often inquire about feelings, opinions, and values.

    *Closed questions:* Could you begin employment by next Monday? Do you speak Spanish? How many years did you live in Germany?

    *Open questions:* How much experience have you had with project management? How would you recommend that we improve sales of product X? What did you like best about your previous job?

6.  **Use probing questions appropriately.** A common problem with employment interviews is that interviewees often give shallow answers. Probing questions enable you to obtain more in-depth information. They dig beneath the surface of general answers and obtain answers that are richer in meaning.

    *Example:* Could you give me more details about the product-testing technology you're working on?

7.  **Use behavioral questions appropriately.** A behavioral question is an open question that asks the respondent how he or she acted in a specific situation. The ideal answer for behavioral questions will be given in a problem-action-results (PAR) format, but often the interviewer will have to keep probing until a detailed answer is given.

    Note the difference in the quality of information

given by Allen, the interviewee, for each of the following questions asked by Holly, the interviewer.

*Closed question that yields almost no useful information:*

*Holly:*  Are you good at handling irate customers?

*Allen:*  Yes, I have had to do that a lot.

*Open behavioral question that generates a shallow answer:*

*Holly:*  Tell me about a time you had to handle an irate customer.

*Allen:*  Well, I worked at a car rental place for a year, and I had to handle a lot of upset customers in that business. They would have problems with the car, like mechanical troubles, or stuff like that. And I'd have to deal with it.

*Open behavioral question, followed by probing questions to generate specific information:*

*Holly:*  Tell me about a time you had to handle an irate customer.

*Allen:*  Well, I worked at a car rental place for a year, and I had to handle a lot of upset customers in that business. They would have problems with the car, like mechanical troubles, or stuff like that. And I'd have to deal with it.

*Holly:*  Tell me in detail how you handled one of those cases.

*Allen:*  Well, this one guy came in and the car he had rented had overheated on the highway, and he missed an important appointment or something like that. They're supposed to call us if they have problems, but I guess he called a towing company and had it towed to a repair shop. He had to spend two or three hours waiting for it to be fixed, and then he had to pay over two hundred bucks out of his own pocket. So he was pretty steamed by the time he got back to us.

*Holly:*  So, specifically, how did you handle the situation?

*Allen:*  Well, he was yelling and carrying on, and so I just called my manager and turned it over to

him. I didn't want to get involved. He was so mad.

In this third case, the interviewer finally has something to work with. Allen's first answer was shallow, so Holly kept probing until Allen gave the specifics she wanted. Because of her effective questioning, she now knows that Allen doesn't listen carefully (he didn't answer the questions directly), he doesn't know how to sell himself, and he doesn't know how to handle an irate customer by himself. All of this information was missed in the first case involving the closed question, "Are you good at handling irate customers?"

## Sample Interview Questions

To help you prepare for interviewing, and for being interviewed, the following sample questions are provided.

*Personal Characteristics*

Tell me about yourself.

What are your two greatest strengths? Tell me about an instance that called for you to apply those strengths.

What percentage of your college expenses did you earn?

Why should we hire you over someone else?

Define success, and explain how successful you have been in your life?

What has been your greatest challenge in life? Your greatest accomplishment?

*Experience*

What did you like best and least about your previous job?

Why did you leave your previous job(s)?

Tell me about your greatest success in your previous job.

What motivates you on the job?

*Relationships*

What kinds of people are most frustrating to you?

If I were to call two or three of your friends/previous employers/fellow employees, what would they tell me about you?

What leadership positions did you have in college?

*Education*

Why did you choose your particular major? If you could start college over again, would you choose a different major? Why or why not?

Were you an active participant in class discussions? Why or why not?

What was your GPA? Is it a fair assessment of your abilities?

What were your toughest and easiest college classes? Why?

What were your most valuable and least valuable college classes? Why?

*Career Plans*

Where do you see yourself 10 years from now?

Describe your ideal career path.

*Knowledge About the Company*

Why do you want to work for our organization?

What do you know about our organization?

Who are our biggest competitors, and how can we increase our share of the marketplace?

*Problem-solving Ability*

You've been out of town for a week. You return to find your in-basket full. How would you handle this situation?

You have an irate customer standing at your work station complaining about the poor service he has been given. How would you handle this person?

You are now in charge of marketing a new type of running shoe. How will you proceed with this task?

*Behavioral Questions*

Tell me about your best and worst team experiences and the role you played in each.

Tell me about a time when you had to meet a deadline under difficult circumstances.

Tell me about the greatest challenge you have had to deal with in life and how you dealt with it.

# PREPARING FOLLOW-UP LETTERS AND RECOMMENDATION DOCUMENTS

Two additional documents are involved with many employment-seeking situations—thank-you letters or emails and recommendation letters. The following short sections give guidelines for these important documents.

## Thank-you Letters or Emails

Send a letter or email thanking the person who interviewed you, preferably within 24 hours. An effective thank-

you message is a great way to differentiate yourself from your competition. To ensure that you have contact information for those you interview with, ask for a business card at the end of each of your interviews. When you write your thank-you message, include (1) a sincere thanks, (2) something about the interview that you appreciated, found interesting, or particularly enjoyed, and (3) a statement or two reaffirming your interest in working for the organization. Keep the message short. Something as simple as the email in Figure 7.11 will suffice, as will the typewritten thank-you letter shown in Figure 7.12.

Thanks for interview

To: crandersen@email.com

Cc:

Bcc:

Subject: **Thanks for interview**

Signature: None

Message Size: 31 KB

Dear Mr. Andersen,

Thank you for the opportunity to visit with you today about employment at XYZ Corporation. I appreciated your discussion about the company's five-year plan and the part I might play in it. I do believe that my strong work ethic, my academic preparation, and my experience make me a good candidate for the staff accountant position you are trying to fill.

As you requested, I am attaching the paper I wrote on international accounting standards. I hope you enjoy reading it.

Thanks again for a very enjoyable interview. I look forward to hearing from you.

Talia Meyer

International Standards 22 KB

*Figure 7.11  A carefully worded thank-you message should be sent soon after the interview is completed.*

**Karen L. Walker**

668 South Maple ▪ Hometown, US 846XX ▪ (842) 555-12XX ▪ kwalker@email.com

February 28, 20XX

Mr. James Colucci
Big Four Marketing
882 Washington Avenue
West City, US 338XX

Dear Mr. Colucci:

Thank you for the opportunity to meet with you about your staff accountant position. I found the interview to be very enlightening, and I appreciate the time you took to visit with me.

I believe my qualifications and professional goals would mesh well with Big Four's mission and culture. As I mentioned in the interview, I am willing to relocate wherever my services can be best used. Because of my familiarity with the German language and culture, I could also be considered for European assignments.

Thanks again for the opportunity to talk with you. I look forward to hearing from you soon.

Sincerely,

*Karen L Walker*

Karen L. Walker

*Figure 7.12 Thank-you letters should be concise and should re-emphasize your qualifications for the position.*

## Recommendation Letters

When job seeking, you will often be asked to provide the names of individuals who are willing to serve as references—people who will vouch for your qualifications and competence. As you select these people, choose those who know you well and with whom you have had successful interaction, such as former employers, teachers and professors, and professional colleagues.

Ask permission from each of your references before giving their names to prospective employers. For example, you might say something like, "I am applying for employment at ABC Company, and they are asking for letters of recommendation from people who know me well. Is that something you would feel comfortable doing, and if so, would you have time to do that within the next couple of weeks?" If they can't answer positively to both questions, eliminate them from your reference list and ask someone else. Whenever you ask someone to write a recommendation for you, provide them with a description of the job you are seeking and a list of your qualifications that make you a good fit for that job. Give them a copy of your resume, and highlight the areas that have relevance to the job you are seeking.

When you are asked to write a recommendation letter for someone else, ask for this same information: a description of the job being sought and a list of the person's specific qualifications for that job. When planning the recommendation letter, use bottom-up outlining. First, develop a list of everything you can think of to include. Next, select the most relevant items and place them into categories and sequences. Finally, compose the letter, using an OABC pattern and enhancing the document with HATS (see Figure 7.13).

---

**Department of Business**
**ABC University**
8800 Campus Drive
Somewhere, US 462XX
XXX-XXX-XXXX ❖ abcuniv.edu

28 February 20XX

Mr. Anthony L. Gallucci
Director of Human Resources
Successful Industries, Inc.
28973 Commerce Drive
Anywhere, US 394XX

RECOMMENDATION FOR JAMIE LEWIS

I am pleased to recommend Jamie Lewis for a marketing position in your company. Two years ago she was a student in my business communication class and earned an "A" grade. Since that time I have visited with her on several occasions, and she says she has done equally well in her other business classes. Three major attributes became apparent as I observed her performance during the semester she was my student.

*Writing Ability.* First, Jamie is an excellent writer. As the daughter of a high-school English teacher, she seems to have natural ability with the English language. Her written assignments always reflected good content and good writing. Her arguments were always well supported, and her conclusions were sound. She was one of the top scorers in a spelling activity we held in class, and she was one of three students selected to share her outstanding writing in a paragraph-writing activity held on another day.

*Presentation Skills.* Jamie is also an excellent presenter. Her team analyzed online complaints filed against a major airline, and then they developed recommendations for resolving those complaints. Jamie helped present the final oral report, which earned a high grade, and she helped develop a superb PowerPoint slide show and handout that accompanied the presentation. She also earned an A grade on her individual oral presentation that featured her library research.

*Interpersonal Skills.* Finally, Jamie is outstanding in interpersonal situations. Throughout the semester she worked in a team setting, and she was always an active participant. She was not afraid to speak her mind, but she was also sensitive to the interpersonal needs of others. She has a sense for knowing when to lead and when to allow others to take the lead. Jamie was well liked and well respected by her team, and there was an obvious spirit of comradery in her team throughout the semester.

I am confident you would be pleased with Jamie's performance in your organization. With her strong communication and interpersonal skills and her ability to solve problems and reason well, I believe she would be a great asset to your company.

*RAWhite*

RUSSELL A. WHITE—PROFESSOR OF BUSINESS COMMUNICATION

---

*Figure 7.13  The OABC pattern works well for writing recommendation letters.*

# NEGOTIATING AND ACCEPTING EMPLOYMENT OFFERS

When you are given a job offer, your work may still not be quite finished. Before actually accepting the offer, take time to consider several factors. First, make sure the job offer is in writing and that the document explains your job responsibilities, financial aspects, start date, and deadline for accepting or rejecting the job offer. If you plan to take a week or more to decide, send an immediate thank-you

response for the offer, and indicate that you will respond by a certain date.

Think about your job responsibilities and consider whether they will give you the type of experience that will be best for your career. If your long-term goal is to be an investment advisor and the job being offered does not move your career in that direction, you should consider waiting until a better fit comes along. If you would like to see some modification in the responsibilities explained in the offer letter, talk with the employer about the possibility of such an adjustment.

Examine also the complete financial package, including the benefits package, any relocation or signing bonuses, and salary. Benefits are usually standard for all employees within a given company, but you'll find significant differences between companies. If you have more than one job offer, carefully examine doctor, hospital, and pharmacy co-pays; prescription coverages; dental and eye-care plans; health club plans; and so forth. Retirement plans, vacation time, and flextime options can also vary greatly.

Examine the salary in light of the cost of living in the area and in comparison with what is being paid for similar work in other companies in the area. If the salary seems too low, consider negotiating for an increase. Some people feel uneasy about taking this action, but such a request is common in business. Also, remember that you'll never get what you don't ask for. As you approach the employer about a higher salary, frame your request in a logically justifiable way, such as, "I've noticed that the median salary for this type of work in your area is about $5,000 higher. Making at least the average salary would help my family better meet our needs." If you have a higher pending offer from another company, you might say, "I have been offered $XX,XXX from XYZ Company, but long term I see a better fit with your company. If an adjustment could be made to match the other offer more closely, that would make it easier for me to turn down the other offer."

Consider the deadline for accepting or rejecting the job offer. If you are waiting for a job offer from another company and the deadline for the current offer comes before you expect the other offer, talk with the employer and see if the deadline can be extended. If it can't, talk with the other employer and see if that offer can be extended sooner.

The starting date for new employment is often flexible and should also be carefully considered. If you need to finish school before starting or have any other upcoming events (including a vacation) that might conflict with the starting date, decide what would be your preferred date, and negotiate with the employer to modify the date.

When you decide to accept a job offer, call the employer and give your decision orally. Mention that you will be following up your phone call with an acceptance in writing. Include something like the following in the acceptance letter:

> Dear Mr. Sanders:
>
> It was exciting news to receive your offer of employment as assistant purchasing agent for ABC Corp. I am pleased to accept your offer at an annual salary of $XX,XXX, plus standard benefits. As we agreed, my starting date will be June 1, which will allow me to complete my business management degree and find an apartment in your area.
>
> With this position, I understand that I will complete an eight-week training program in Chicago and that my status will be probationary during my first six months on the job.
>
> Thank you again, Mr. Sanders, for offering me the opportunity to work with your company. I pledge my very best efforts to help ABC achieve its goals of providing exceptional financial services to clients throughout the country.
>
> Please let me know if you need additional information in advance of the starting date to facilitate required paperwork.

Once you accept a job offer, remember that you are legally obligated to keep your commitment! Under no circumstance should you change your mind and back out, even if you get a better offer from someone else. If you were to back out, your unethical action would damage your reputation, as well as the reputation of the school you graduated from. Therefore, be true to your commitment.

## CHAPTER SUMMARY

Work is an important element of life, but many people end up in unsatisfying careers. You should plan carefully so you can increase your chances of enjoying a lifetime of fulfilling work. Many resources are available for finding employment, from your school's career services office to many online sources. Seeking employment involves a variety of written and oral communications, including letters, resumes, follow-up letters, recommendation letters, and interviews. As with all communications, complete a thorough PACS analysis to guide you in all your employment-related activities. As you prepare your resume, you may choose either a chronological or a functional format, with the chronological format being the most widely accepted.

When you are being interviewed, dress appropriately, be on time, and develop good PAR (problem, action, result) stories. PAR stories contain powerful results messages and

leave a memorable impression with interviewers. After you are interviewed, write a sincere thank-you message. When you are interviewing others, prepare your questions in advance, use appropriate open and closed questions, listen effectively, and avoid bias and illegal discrimination. After you receive an employment offer, evaluate the position carefully, negotiate as needed, and then accept the offer if you feel the offer is best for you.

## CHAPTER QUESTIONS

1. List three important factors to consider in choosing a career.

2. What is the most well-known online business networking resource?

3. What is an elevator speech? How long should it be?

4. Why should you be careful with what you post on the internet?

5. What is the purpose of an application letter?

6. What type of information should be included in the first paragraph of an application letter? In the body paragraphs? In the concluding paragraph?

7. In what sequence should your job history be arranged?

8. List two guidelines to follow for resumes that are going to be read by resume-management software.

9. What is the main difference between a chronological resume and a functional resume?

10. Should your resume be limited to one page? Why or why not?

11. What is appropriate interview dress for most interviews (for men and women)?

12. Why is honesty important in an interview?

13. What is a PAR story? Why are PAR stories effective in interviews?

14. List three guidelines to help you with a telephone interview.

15. What is a BFOQ?

16. What types of questions are illegal to ask in a job interview?

17. Give an example of a closed question, an open question, and a behavioral question.

18. When should you write a thank-you letter or email?

19. What factors should be considered in accepting a job offer?

20. What part does negotiation play in accepting a job offer?

## CHAPTER ACTIVITIES

1. Prepare an attractive letterhead to use with your resume and cover letter. Include your name, address, telephone numbers, and email address.

2. Prepare an employment resume for the job you would like to obtain when you graduate from college. Consult the examples in this chapter for ideas, but customize your resume to fit your unique employment situation. First, create a brainstorm list of everything in your background that might relate to employment: education and training, employment, languages spoken, computer skills, service, leadership, teamwork, special achievements, awards, talents, and attributes. Then find a job that matches your qualifications. Next, using the job description as a guide, create a polished resume, and prepare a cover letter to accompany your resume.

3. Write three short PAR stories. Label the problem, action, and results section of each story. Also, identify the knowledge, skills, abilities, or attributes illustrated in each story.

4. Interview two or more of your peers and have them interview you. After each interview, discuss what went well and what could be improved.

5. Write a thank-you message to one of the people who interviewed you in Chapter Activity 4. Write an offer letter to one of the people you interviewed. Write a rejection letter to one of the people you interviewed.

6. On the internet, browse the Occupational Outlook Handbook on the U.S. Government's website (http://www.bls.gov/ooh/). Read about the outlook for the type of profession you are interested in. Also, visit five of the employment websites listed at the beginning of this chapter. Write a short memo about what you find.

7. Contact someone who works in a career you are interested in, and see if you can arrange an information interview to learn about the person's job. Prior to meeting with the person, research the person's company and create a list of questions you would like answered. Keep the interview brief. After the interview, send a thank-you note to the person.

8. Create a list of your top three educational, work-related, or life achievements. Describe the achievements to a family member or friend, and together brainstorm at least five personal attributes that were required to accomplish each achievement. Analyze those personal attributes. Do you notice any patterns that could be interpreted as your strengths?

## CHAPTER 8

# Solving Problems and Writing Proposals

Problems are a normal and common part of organization life, and most of your communication in organizations deals with some aspect of problem solving. For some people, problem solving seems difficult and tedious; however, others view problem solving as a great opportunity for progress and improvement. For example, you may have a problem if you lose your job; however, you may also have an opportunity to transition to the career you have always wanted. As you view problems as opportunities throughout your career, you will find yourself more willing and eager to take on challenges that can positively define your professional life.

As you engage in the problem-solving process, you will frequently need to request resources from others. The way you make such a request is to create a proposal. Consequently, Chapter 8 contains two major sections focusing on solving problems and preparing proposals. After learning the material in this chapter, you should be able to do the following:

- Apply six steps to analyze problems and implement solutions to problems.
- Explain the proposal-writing process and write a persuasive proposal.

## SOLVING PROBLEMS

While you will solve many problems throughout your career, not all problems are of equal importance or of equal urgency. Table 8.1 shows four general types of problems. Less effective managers find themselves spending most of their time on the problems located on the left. While urgent problems will surely demand your attention as a manager, be sure to reserve time in your workday to focus on problems that are important, but not urgent. For problems that are not important and not urgent, become comfortable letting those go unsolved.

Such urgency may cause managers to feel that they need to solve a problem quickly, without considering all of the stakeholders affected by the problem's cause or solution. All problems affect people, so take sufficient time to analyze problems so your solutions are sensitive to all stakeholders.

### Table 8.1 Types of Problems

| Important and urgent | Important, but not urgent |
|---|---|
| Not important, but urgent | Not important and not urgent |

Problems surface in a variety of ways—formal and informal. Formal ways might include routine reports, continuous improvement committees, annual performance reviews, or employee suggestion boxes. Informal ways might include suggestions posted by customers, grapevine communication, personal observation, or unexpected emergencies. All are important information sources, so be alert to information from all areas of your work that signal problems needing your attention.

These six general steps can help you effectively solve problems:

1. Define the problem
2. Analyze the problem
3. Develop alternative solutions

4. Select a solution
5. Implement the solution
6. Evaluate the outcome

To one degree or another, these six steps apply to all problems, complex or simple, and to all organizations, large or small. You, as a problem solver, must possess sufficient wisdom to know what specific actions are appropriate for completing these steps in different settings.

## Define the Problem

What is a problem? Think of it as the difference between what you think *should be* and what *is*. As noted previously, an opportunity can also be thought of as a problem—it is the difference between what *could be* and what *is*. For example, if you think you *should be* or *could be* making $80,000 a year but your salary *is* currently $40,000 a year, then you have a $40,000 problem. Using these approaches, you can define problems in the following manner:

1. Identify what you think *should be* or *could be*.
2. Identify the current status—what *is*.
3. The problem is the difference between 1 and 2 (what *should be* or *could be* vs. what *is*).

As you define problems, recognize that problems may relate to you on individual, team, or organizational levels. Generally, you will have the most influence to correct problems relating to you individually, and you will need to work more closely with others as you resolve team- or organizational-level problems.

## Analyze the Problem

Once you define the problem, you must gather and analyze additional information so you can perform a proper diagnosis. Too often, people start developing solutions before clearly understanding the problem. Before attempting to solve a problem, take time to analyze and diagnose it, breaking it down into small pieces that can be examined in detail. To assist in this process, this section provides multiple suggestions for analyzing problems.

Simple problems may need very little data analysis for proper diagnosis, but complex problems usually require significant amounts of data and analysis. The data can be either qualitative or quantitative in nature, and both types can help you better understand the problem. Organized into the five M's of management resources, here are some examples of qualitative data that you could analyze for insight:

**Manpower:** Negative employee attitudes, declining morale, ineffective training methods

**Money:** Spending of funds on questionable purchases, lack of financial oversight, lack of budget planning

**Machines:** Outdated computers, uncontrolled purchasing of new technology, inappropriate use of new technology

**Methods:** Job duplication, job overlap, or lack of needed cross training among different tasks

**Materials:** Outdated appearance of products, environmentally unfriendly products, inappropriate management of waste products

For qualitative data, write down and analyze what you find, yielding information such as the following:

- Common themes or categories
- Recurring key words, stories, or grapevine communication
- What is said vs. what is done
- Company policy vs. employee behavior
- Job descriptions vs. actual work completed
- Customer compliments vs. customer complaints
- Company's written values vs. company reputation

In addition to analyzing qualitative data, take time to think of available quantitative data that may provide insight:

**Manpower:** Increasing employee turnover, increasing customer complaints, slow response time to customer requests

**Money:** Worsening financial ratios, declining sales revenue, escalating cost of production

**Machines:** Increasing equipment breakdowns, increasing equipment costs, decreasing efficiency of equipment

**Methods:** Slow manufacturing processes, increasing numbers of product defects, flawed security measures

**Materials:** Poor reliability of product line, increasing number of flaws in raw materials, short shelf-life of products, shortage of production parts

For quantitative data, develop a spreadsheet and run appropriate calculations, yielding information such as the following:

- Comparative averages
- Rankings (high to low)

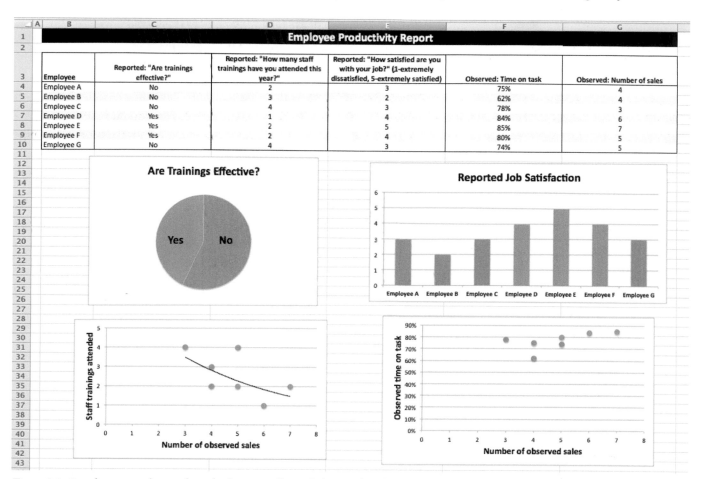

*Figure 8.1 Developing graphics to show the data visually can help you identify trends, trouble spots, and opportunities for improvement.*

- Trends over various time periods
- Forecasts vs. actual performance
- Budgeted vs. actual performance
- Year-to-date performance (e.g., monthly, quarterly)
- Company vs. industry performance

Also, from quantitative data, develop bar charts, line charts, and other graphics that enable you to analyze the data visually. For example, without the aid of the graphics in Figure 8.1, people have a difficult time seeing the trends and relationships in the data. Once visualized, these trends and relationships indicate possible problem areas or opportunities for improvement. For example, a sales manager might brainstorm ways to increase employee time on task. In addition, a corporate trainer may further investigate the relationship between staff training meetings, employee satisfaction, and sales.

In a business world where people are increasingly interested in large-scale data analysis, you will make better sense of millions of numbers as you visualize them. As the great statistician John Tukey (1980) noted, "The picture-examining eye is the best finder we have of the wholly unanticipated" (24). By changing myriad numbers into graphical

pictures, you can leverage your eyes' perceptional ability to complement your brain's analytical and creative capacities.

The following three-part model can also be helpful when analyzing problems:

1. **What?** The first step seeks to understand and describe the problem. This requires careful data gathering from statistical and analytical reports, questionnaires, in-depth interviewing, or other data sources.

2. **So what?** The second step focuses on the importance or impact of the problem. Some problems are so minor in nature or so isolated in frequency that their consequences don't matter much. Some other problems are more serious but require more resources than the solution is worth. Still other problems can't be solved and just have to be endured.

3. **Now what?** The third step seeks to find a solution to the problem, including relevant solution criteria.

Complete problem statements should address all three parts of the model, as shown in the following:

*What?* We have a 60 percent turnover in our sales associates.

*So what?* We are spending too much money and time

recruiting, selecting, and training sales associates. Customer service is lagging because of their limited experience. Morale is also affected because so many people quit after working here for only a short time.

*Now what?* We need to implement a financial-incentive system that rewards good customer service and length of employment.

As you analyze problems, also recall the PAR acronym from Chapter 7. You first have a problem situation that needs an action. The result of the action should be a resolution of the problem. A simple fast-food restaurant example will help illustrate:

**Problem:** ABC Fast Food restaurant seeks to provide food at a competitive price and in a way that provides customer satisfaction. However, sales revenue declined 11 percent in the last six months, and the manager, Harriett Russell, wants to reverse this trend and achieve a 10 percent improvement in the next six months.

**Action:** The manager uses a customer survey to gather data so she can understand the cause of the decline. After using her spreadsheet software to analyze the data, she concludes that (a) limited menu selection and (b) increased advertising by competitors are having the greatest effect on the business. She adds several new menu items and actively advertises the new items.

**Result:** The result for the subsequent six months is a 13-percent increase in customers.

To further assist in your diagnosis, the 5W2H questions (who, what, where, when, why, how, and how much) help to examine the problem from all angles. For each of the following questions, combine *what-is* and *what-is-not* questions. For example, for the question, "What is causing the problem?" also ask, "What is not causing the problem?"

**Who?** Who discovered the problem? Who is affected by the problem? Who might have caused the problem? Who is concerned about the problem? Who has dealt with problems of this nature in the past?

**What?** What is causing the problem? What components of the system failed? What changed recently that might have contributed to the problem? What are the symptoms of the problem? What are the causes of the symptoms? What would have prevented the problem from happening?

**Where?** Where did the problem occur (one location or multiple locations)? Where did it begin? Where can we learn more about the problem?

**When?** When did the problem occur? When did changes occur that might have contributed to the problem? When must the problem be solved?

**Why?** Why did the problem occur? Why does the problem matter? Why did the problem not occur earlier? Why does it happen at some times and not at others? Why did we not prevent the problem?

**How?** How was the problem discovered? How do the various parts of the system interact with each other? How does the system or process work? How serious is the problem? How urgent is the problem?

**How many and how much?** How many people or things are involved? How many people are affected by the problem? How much quantity, volume, distance, or time is involved? How many times has the problem occurred?

Remember the important difference between causes and symptoms. The cause is the origin; the symptom is the outcome. Too many people try to fix the symptoms, only to find that they reappear because the cause is still present. The symptom will only disappear if you fix the cause of the problem. For example, Employee A fails to perform his duties properly. Manager X terminates the employee and hires another, only to find that the problem repeats itself. The real problem is not with the employees but with the manager's failure to train properly. Motivate the manager to train properly (the cause), and the employees' performance problems (the symptom) will largely disappear.

Cause-and-effect analysis (see Figure 8.2) is another useful technique for analyzing problems. It consists of identifying all relevant cause-and-effect relationships. Think of this technique as a tree, with the most obvious effects up on the leaf level. The causes then become the lower, larger branches, ultimately culminating to a main cause serving as the trunk.

To carry out this analysis, identify an effect; then ask what caused the effect. Repeatedly asking "what caused this" or "why did this happen" for every symptom will help uncover additional causes. To discover additional causes, you might focus various cause-effect chains on the 5W2H questions. After you identify each cause, continue creating additional branch links so long as you can identify meaningful causes and effects, ultimately arriving at a root cause

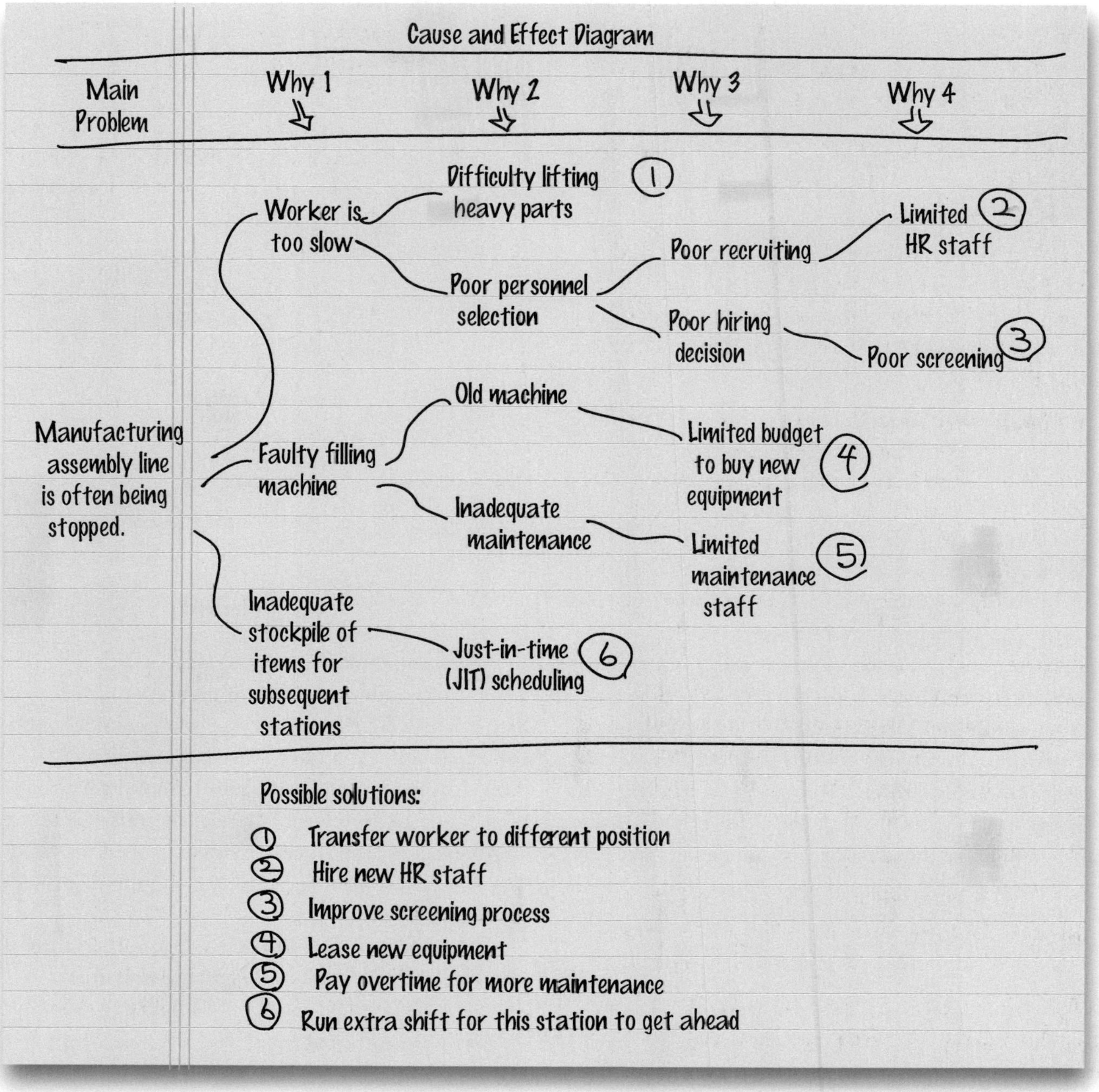

## Cause and Effect Diagram

| Main Problem | Why 1 | Why 2 | Why 3 | Why 4 |

Difficulty lifting heavy parts ①

Worker is too slow

Limited HR staff ②

Poor recruiting

Poor personnel selection

Poor hiring decision

Poor screening ③

Old machine

Faulty filling machine

Limited budget to buy new equipment ④

Inadequate maintenance

Limited maintenance staff ⑤

Manufacturing assembly line is often being stopped.

Inadequate stockpile of items for subsequent stations

Just-in-time (JIT) scheduling ⑥

**Possible solutions:**

① Transfer worker to different position
② Hire new HR staff
③ Improve screening process
④ Lease new equipment
⑤ Pay overtime for more maintenance
⑥ Run extra shift for this station to get ahead

*Figure 8.2  A cause-and-effect diagram can help you understand the causes of a problem and develop different possible solutions.*

of all the effects. With the root cause determined, focus your main problem-solving efforts on that cause. Visualizing this analysis as a mind map (see Figure 8.3) can also be very useful.

Another tool to consider when diagnosing people problems is illustrated in Table 8.2. In this table, you see that most performance problems can be classified into five main categories: ability, training, environmental, motivational, and morale. The table also shows the logical types of solutions that can be implemented to solve the problems. Using this chart will help ensure that you don't misdiagnose

a problem and implement a solution that doesn't fit the situation.

### Develop Alternative Solutions

Once you have analyzed the problem, proceed to work on the solution. Sometimes a solution will be relatively simple. At other times, it may be very complicated, requiring multiple solutions to solve each little piece of a large problem. Each problem is unique and each problem requires at least some creativity to customize an appropriate solution.

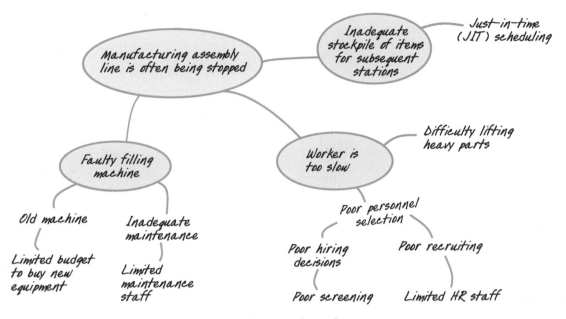

*Figure 8.3  Cause-and-effect analysis can be effectively visualized in a mind map format.*

Effective problem solving requires creative thinking, and brainstorming can help with this process.

Brainstorming can foster creativity and develop potential solutions to a problem. It can be used in countless ways, including identifying problems, designing ways to implement solutions, improving existing products, or creating new services. Brainstorming is the process of thinking of as many different ideas as possible, with little initial concern for the feasibility of the ideas. Brainstorming can force people to think outside the normal way of doing things and to develop different ways of solving problems. The idea behind brainstorming is that quantity will yield quality; in other words, if you come up with enough ideas, at least one or two will likely be good ones.

When brainstorming, don't assume that only one or two possible solutions exist. Sometimes individuals trap themselves in false dilemmas when they consider only two opposing options, without considering the numerous alternatives occupying the middle ground between the two. Usually you can develop a variety of alternative solutions to a problem, and often a combination of ideas proves to be best. Today's problems are complex, and complex solutions are needed to solve them.

Brainstorming can be performed alone (personal brainstorming) or with a group (both oral and written).

## Table 8.2 Personnel Problem Analysis Chart

| Description of Problem | Type of Problem | Solution |
| --- | --- | --- |
| Person cannot physically or mentally perform as desired. | Ability problem | Transfer or terminate the person; assign someone who can perform properly. |
| Person could perform properly but doesn't know how. | Training problem | Give appropriate training and practice. |
| Person knows how and can perform properly, but circumstances are preventing from performing properly. | Environmental problem | Change the environment; eliminate that which is preventing performance. |
| Person knows how and can perform properly, and nothing is preventing proper performance, but the person is not rewarded for proper performance. | Motivational problem | Give appropriate motivation to achieve proper performance. |
| Person knows how and can perform properly, nothing is preventing proper performance, and the person is appropriately rewarded for proper performance, but does not want to perform properly. | Morale problem | Counsel and terminate if performance doesn't improve. |

## Personal Brainstorming

Brainstorming truly creative solutions is often best accomplished by individuals as they consider and ponder a problem for extended periods of time. During this incubation period the human brain exhibits great capacity to engage in divergent thinking, thinking that generates multiple creative solutions. This creative process includes four basic steps:

1. **Understand**: Comprehend the problem and its related issues.

2. **Incubate**: Engage in divergent thinking, pondering endless possibilities, to discover possible solutions.

3. **Develop**: After pondering many possible solutions, settle on one or two potential ideas.

4. **Refine**: Polish and customize the ideas to fit the problem and its related issues.

Creative solutions cannot be forced or rushed; they can take days, weeks, or even months, emerging only after persistently pondering a problem. Creativity can, however, be fostered in a variety of ways. The following suggestions work for many people who rely heavily on creativity in their professional work.

**Thoroughly study the problem.** Fully comprehend the central problem or objective and all its related aspects.

**Enrich your knowledge base.** Read widely. Become exposed to as much of the world as possible—different companies, different industries, different fields, different cultures, and different methodologies. This knowledge increases the data in your mental database so you can increase the number of mental interconnections.

**Eliminate distractions.** Go to a place where you can shut out distractions.

**Set aside large chunks of time to ponder.** Creativity does not happen quickly.

**Arise early.** The morning is usually the time when your mind is most alert and uncluttered. To prepare for waking up early, go to bed early.

**Utilize the Alpha sleep state.** Load your mind with details of the problem the night before, and let your mind work on the problem during the state between deep sleep (Delta sleep) and wide awake (Beta state). This Alpha state can be described as a relaxed-awake state with your eyes closed.

**Keep the problem constantly on your mind.** Many people have found the solution to a problem simply by constantly thinking about it over a long period of time. As they go throughout their normal daily routines, new insights and ideas will often emerge at unpredictable times.

You may choose to follow these suggestions and brainstorm solutions alone when (a) your knowledge of the problem is greater than that of the group, (b) time pressure prohibits getting group input, (c) group members are unaffected by or don't care about the problem or outcome, (d) you prefer to have total control over the outcome, or (e) the group does not work well together. In these cases, the old saying that "two heads are better than one" does not apply.

Additionally, recognize that if you do seek a group's input in such cases, the group expects its opinions to be considered. If you already have a solution in mind that you will be implementing regardless of the group's input, do not seek the group's input. In this way, you can avoid building unnecessary expectations and being viewed as a manager who does not listen.

## Group Brainstorming (Oral)

Involve a group when you need more than your own abilities to solve a problem. Two heads are better than one in these situations! A group brainstorming session can be carried out in four steps.

*Figure 8.4 For more complex problems, involving key personnel is often essential to correctly diagnose and solve the issues.*

1. **Select the group.** The ideal group size is 6 to 12 people. Groups smaller than 6 may lack the necessary diversity to produce the desired results, and groups larger than 12 sometimes break into subgroups or intimidate less assertive members. Group members should have a good knowledge of the problem and its context. They should also feel free to suggest creative

ideas and not be inhibited by organizational politics or other group pressures.

2. **Select a facilitator, or serve as a facilitator yourself.** The facilitator explains the process, coordinates the generation and recording of ideas, and probes for better and deeper thinking.

3. **Select one or two recorders.** People acting as recorders write the group's ideas on a whiteboard or on sticky notes or cards to be taped on a wall or whiteboard. Each written idea should capture a few key words that communicate the essence of the idea. Time is of the essence when ideas are flowing, so the recorders must write quickly, yet neatly and clearly. They should number each item for easy reference later on.

4. **Conduct the brainstorming session.** The facilitator clarifies the group's charge, explaining how the session will be carried out and emphasizing the importance of uninhibited thinking. Group members should be encouraged to be creative, not worrying about feasibility or evaluation criteria. They should have fun, feed off others' ideas, and just let free thinking flow. To stress quantity, the facilitator might say, "Let's try to get 50 new ideas in the next 15 minutes." The group should be encouraged to build on the ideas of others and to look at problem solutions from different points of view.

During the brainstorming, you can allow ideas to come randomly, or you can try a structured go-around. In a structured go-around, each person voices an idea in an orderly way (e.g., from left to right around the room). This process encourages each person to participate, rather than allowing some people to remain silent while others do all the talking. Here are some additional ways to help generate ideas.

**Think of people:** For all types of problems, think of moving people around or utilizing their talents in different ways.

**Think of location:** Think of moving an operation to a different location.

**Think of timing:** Think of moving a task or procedure to an earlier or later time.

**Think opposites:** When one idea is given, think of the exact opposite. For example, if you're trying to solve a financial problem, create solutions that would save money as well as ideas that would generate more money.

**Think of other professions or occupations:** For a human resources problem, think of the way the problem might be solved by the fast food industry, by a farmer, by a clothing manufacturer, or by an airline.

**Add more of the same:** If one person suggests an incentive in a marketing problem, think of adding more incentives.

**Delete an element:** For a marketing problem, think of dropping, rather than adding, a product.

**Think of external factors:** For human problems, think of ways to change the environment as well as people.

**Think specifically:** For general solutions, think of how the solution might be applied to a specific situation.

*Figure 8.5 Group members should be encouraged to be creative in their brainstorming ideas.*

Another approach might be to think of ways to improve in each of the five resources areas:

1. **Manpower:** Reassign, train, fix the environment, motivate, replace

2. **Money:** Add or expand, eliminate, reduce, maintain, control, modify a procedure

3. **Machines:** Repair, replace, upgrade, add, eliminate

4. **Materials:** Improve, reduce, replace, combine, separate

5. **Methods:** Eliminate, mechanize, automate, combine, separate, standardize, formalize, refine, modify, centralize, decentralize

When idea generation starts to slow down, push for deeper thinking, for less obvious ideas, or for creative thinking from a different angle. Brainstorming often occurs in spurts—the ideas flow readily, then slow down, then speed up when someone comes up with a novel idea, and so forth. When it seems that new ideas have stopped completely, explain that other ideas might occur to group members

during the next few hours or days, and provide a way for those ideas to be communicated to the group facilitator.

### Group Brainstorming (Written)

Oral brainstorming with a group has many benefits, but it also has weaknesses. For instance, social inequities within a group may keep some members from participating, and only one person can participate at a time. To solve these problems, you can try gallery writing. Gallery writing generates useful ideas and solves most of the social shortcomings of oral brainstorming. Here is how it works:

- Tape several large sheets of paper on the walls of the meeting room. Space the papers at least several feet apart.
- Invite all members to write their ideas on one of the large sheets.
- Have all members then wander around the room reading other people's ideas and writing additional ideas that are sparked by the ideas they read.

An alternative written approach is the nominal group technique (NGT), where each person writes one or two ideas on a small card. After the ideas are publicly displayed, group members then vote for those they think are best.

Written brainstorming might also take the form of crowdsourcing, a technique that can effectively distribute the opportunity or responsibility for solving a problem from one person to many people. Crowdsourcing frequently occurs in an online setting, such as when an individual poses a question to a social network and requests answers. Keep in mind that crowdsourcing often works best if those contributing solutions have some incentive for par-

ticipating in the problem-solving process. For example, to increase the security of its website, a company might offer a reward to any person who reports and documents a flaw with the site.

### Select a Solution

After generating various solutions to a problem, you must decide which option or options to implement. As Figure 8.6 shows, a different type of thinking is required at this point. Whereas the initial phase of brainstorming needed divergent thinking (diverse thinking), the decision-making phase needs convergent thinking (unified group thinking and moving toward a solution). Further, as you initially analyzed the problem, you looked backward as you mapped effects back to the main cause (effect to cause). When choosing a solution, you look forward, selecting a solution that will cause the effect of a solved problem (cause to effect).

Deciding on a final solution can be accomplished by the manager acting alone, by a smaller group that meets separately, or by the entire brainstorming group. Involving a group achieves two distinct advantages. First, decisions made by a group are, on average, better than decisions made by individuals. Second, people will generally support decisions better when they have participated in the decision-making process.

Regardless of whether you act alone or with a group, consider following this four-step process of decision making.

1. **Organize and refine the list.** Group related ideas from the brainstorming list. Combine overlapping

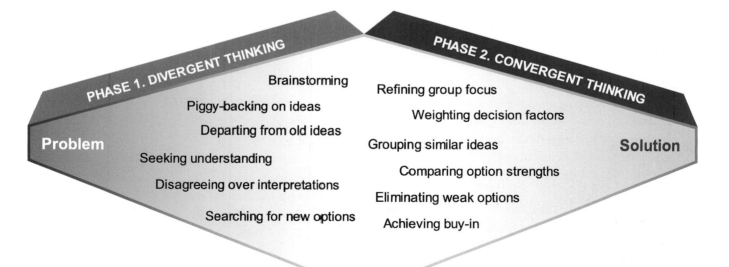

*Figure 8.6  Problem solving moves from divergent to convergent thinking.*

and related ideas. Refine the list so each idea is clear and as mutually exclusive as possible. Any item with one of the following flaws can be dropped from the list, unless it can be modified to eliminate the flaws:

- Doesn't satisfy critical needs
- Poses too much risk
- Is illegal or unethical
- Is contrary to the organization's philosophy or culture
- Is not financially feasible
- Doesn't meet time requirements
- Is technically incompatible with existing systems
- Is unacceptable to affected personnel
- Is too difficult to implement

2. **Establish evaluation criteria.** Evaluation criteria provide a standard for choosing the best option. Most criteria focus on *how well* (such as how well the group will accept an idea) or *how much* (such as how much money an idea will save). Some criteria are quantitative; others are qualitative, as shown in Table 8.3.

### Table 8.3 Quantitative and Qualitative Evaluation Factors

| Quantitative (How Much) | Qualitative (How Well) |
|---|---|
| Financial results | Acceptance by personnel |
| Production speed | Ease of implementation |
| Number of production units | Technical compatibility |
| Percentage of market share | Legal or ethical compliance |
| Number of errors | Compatibility with corporate culture |
| Number of sales | Compatibility with the organization's mission or values |
| Customer retention | |
| Average cost per unit | Risk (financial, technological, environmental, legal) |
| Click-through rate | |

When working with a group, agreeing on the criteria can be a difficult task. Achieving consensus requires your best negotiation skills and can take considerable time. When generating the criteria, write every person's suggestions on the list. Then ask why each criterion is important. Work with the group until you produce a list that everyone can live with, even if everyone does not enthusiastically agree with each criterion.

3. **Weight the criteria.** Not all criteria are equally important; therefore, develop a scale (e.g., from 10 to 1) to indicate the relative importance of each cri-

terion. For example, legal compliance and acceptance by affected personnel might be a 10, ease of implementation might be an 8, and timeliness might be a 5. Be honest with yourself in differentiating between critical *needs* and nice-to-have *wants*.

4. **Select the best ideas from the brainstorm list.** Evaluate each idea according to the weighted evaluation criteria, and choose the idea that most closely adheres with the established criteria. A decision table can be useful in identifying the best options. Decision tables provide a useful visual for making side-by-side comparisons according to how well the alternatives meet the criteria. In Table 8.4, which compares three different potential employees, note that both qualitative and quantitative data are included in the criteria.

### Table 8.4 A Sample Decision Table

| Criteria | Weight | Alternatives | | |
|---|---|---|---|---|
| | | SMX 6600 | PFL 462 | FM 280G |
| Equipment ratings | 10 | 9 | 9 | 8 |
| Price | 9 | 8 | 6 | 7 |
| Compatibility with current line | 9 | 9 | 8 | 7 |
| Reputation of vendor | 8 | 8 | 8 | 7 |
| Training required | 8 | 8 | 8 | 7 |
| Installation time | 6 | 5 | 6 | 6 |
| **Total** | **50** | **47** | **45** | **42** |

If a decision table's numeric totals don't reflect what you hoped for, one of two things has happened. First, bias may be affecting the process. If so, step back, take a broader view of the situation, and do what is *best* for the situation, not just what is preferred for personal reasons. Second, reconsider weighting one or more of the criteria. Perhaps experience, which can't be taught, is more important than technical knowledge, which can be taught. Reconsider every element of the decision table and make changes as necessary.

As mentioned previously, you can decide on a final solution yourself, assign the task to a small group, or involve the entire group, allowing each member to vote. To involve a group, provide each member a certain number of votes to cast. For instance, if 50 ideas have been generated, give each member 5 votes (10 percent of the total). Each member then goes to the chalkboard, wall, or poster papers and votes (using a simple tally mark or sticky dot). After the voting, you can easily see where the group's preferences

lie by noting where the largest clusters of votes have been recorded.

After selecting a solution, remember that you will need to communicate your solution to your audience. As you frame your communication, you must both inform others of the problem and energize them to take action. For instance, the following statements all stem from the same problem, but notice how some focus just on the "what" of the problem, while others attempt to emphasize the larger "so what" or "now what" aspects of the problem.

| | |
|---|---|
| **What:** | One employee is having difficulty keeping up with the assembly line pace. |
| **What:** | The assembly line has been completely shut down three times in the last month. |
| **What:** | Problems with one machine are causing the entire assembly line to stop. |
| **So what:** | The filling-machine station is costing the corporation approximately $12,000 each month. |
| **So what:** | Frequent assembly-line shutdowns are causing frustration throughout the entire organization. |
| **Now what:** | We need to solve the problem of assembly-line shut downs. |
| **Now what:** | We need to stop the filling-machine breakdowns. |

After you experiment with various combinations of framing statements, choose one that will best inform and generate positive and active involvement from the people who will participate in the decision-making process.

## Implement the Solution

When you have authorization to proceed, determine how to implement the solution. This is a critical phase because even a great idea can fail if it is poorly implemented. In addition to *what* you plan to change, remember that *where, when,* and *how* you introduce that change are also important. Remember that people resist change, so the better you anticipate the negative effects of your planned changes, the smoother the implementation phase will be.

Make sure all people who are affected are represented in the implementation plan. Analyze your audience, considering their needs and concerns, and then modify the implementation plan as appropriate. If at all possible, don't force the plan on them. Earn their trust and obtain their cooperation so they will help you make it successful. Remember the old saying: "A man convinced against his will is of the same opinion still."

Lewin's force-field analysis (SkyMark 2012) helps identify the forces working for and against your implementation plans. Draw a large "T" on a page. Across the top of the T, write the goal. On the left side, list the positive forces; on the right side, list the negative forces (see Figure 8.7). Weight each force on a 5–1 scale—with 5 representing a strong force—and total the positive and negative forces to see their overall impact. Your implementation strategy should then work to increase the positive forces and decrease the negative ones. Examples of forces include the following:

- Available resources
- Traditions, culture, personal interests, attitudes, values, desires
- Organizational structures and relationships
- Current policies, procedures, and practices
- Financial costs and benefits

**Goal:** *New Delivery Process*

| + | | | | − |
|---|---|---|---|---|
| Missed deadlines | 4 | 4 | Increased cost | |
| Customer complaints | 5 | 2 | Competing time pressures | |
| Management demands | 5 | 3 | Personnel resistance | |
| | 14 | 9 | | |

*Figure 8.7  A force-field chart helps identify the forces working for and against implementation plans.*

Implementing new programs or procedures can follow one of four plans: pilot, phase-in, parallel, or cold turkey. With a pilot plan, you try out the new program in one segment of your organization, preferably with a group that likes the program and wants it to succeed. After the initial pilot program, you implement throughout the organization, using the knowledge and experience you gained from the pilot.

The phase-in plan involves implementing different phases of the new program at different time periods, such as on January 1, March 1, and May 1. With the parallel plan, you operate both the old and the new systems simultaneously, such as with a new automated system that will replace a manual system. This gives the automation team a chance to identify and fix any problems before completely phasing

out the old and implementing the new. The *cold-turkey* plan is just what the name implies—on a chosen day, the old program or procedure is discontinued, and the new one takes its place.

### Evaluate the Outcome

As part of your implementation plan, include methods for evaluating the outcomes of your solution. Gather before-and-after data to show the impact of the solution. For example, if your solution is intended to increase output on a production line, measure the output before and after implementation so you can see if your solution has worked. If the change is positive, you can continue implementation. If you see no change or negative change, you may need to halt further implementation and perform additional work. Remember that implementing a solution can cause both intended and unintended outcomes, as well as direct and indirect effects, so be sensitive to all types of outcomes when evaluating implemented solutions.

## WRITING PROPOSALS

As you work through the problem-solving process just described, at some point you will likely need to request resources, authorization, assistance, or action from others. Further, as others in your organization solve problems, they may need to request resources from you. A proposal serves as the way you and others make such requests.

Consequently, proposals serve two major purposes. First, with a proposal, you express a need for something from others. If you did not need anything from others, you could proceed to solve the problem without a proposal. Second, with a proposal you also commit to provide something for others. By accepting a proposal, others anticipate certain benefits in return for providing needed resources. In other words, they want to know, "What's in it for me?" (WIIFM).

To increase the likelihood of persuading others to provide your needed resources, remember to complete the PACS planning process, follow an appropriate proposal pattern, and strengthen your proposal's content.

### Plan with PACS

Proposals play vital roles in business, government, and nonprofit organizations. Proposals not only facilitate problem solving in these organizations, but also notably generate significant revenue in the form of grant money, awarded

contracts, and accepted bids. Because of their important roles, proposals should be carefully and strategically written. By analyzing the purpose, audience, and context of your proposal, you can determine an effective strategy to follow.

### Purpose

Proposals can be required at any step in the problem-solving process, so you can think of various types of proposals as researching problems or providing solutions to problems. For example, a client-services manager notices an increase of customer complaints regarding the company website. The manager senses a problem, but the cause of the problem is unknown. The manager therefore proposes a plan requiring resources to define and analyze the problem (a research proposal). Once the manager determines that the problem lies with the company's online-payment application, the manager then proposes another plan requiring additional resources to resolve the problem with the application (a solution proposal).

For either proposal type, you inform your audience of a possible way to research or solve a problem. However, most problems can be researched or solved in multiple ways, so you must not only inform your audience of your proposed way but also persuade them that your way is best. In other words, you must persuade your audience that you correctly understand the problem, that your solution will actually solve the problem, that you can and will implement the solution you propose, and that the solution will bring about outcomes the audience desires.

### Audience

Proposals may focus on both internal and external problems. In other words, you might write proposals to solve problems within your own organization (internal proposals), or you may work for organizations (such as consulting, manufacturing, auditing, or construction companies) that solve problems for other organizations. Employees in these companies write proposals to clients or potential clients (external proposals), proposing to provide fee-based goods or services that solve problems on behalf of the clients' organizations. For these companies, proposals play a vital role in revenue generation. For examples of both internal and external proposals, see Figure 8.12 (internal proposal) and Figures 8.13 and 8.14 (external proposals) at the end of the chapter.

Because you may have easy access to your audience when writing internal proposals, take time to meet with or interview members of your primary audience. Find out

their attitudes and needs in relation to the problem you are proposing to solve, and then tailor your solution and proposal accordingly. Don't forget to consider the needs of secondary and tertiary audiences as well. For example, if you will be proposing a change that affects a team within your company, talk with the team's manager, the individual team members, and anyone else in the company who might be interested in or affected by the change.

While you may have a more difficult time analyzing an audience when you write an external proposal, still do all you can to learn about your audience. For example, call and talk with your primary audience, visit the site where proposed work will be performed, or ask questions via email. Take time to review the audience's website, press releases, or any other media published about the audience's company.

Through this process, you will better understand what your audience values and needs, how your audience will evaluate proposals, and whether other forces exist that will influence whether your audience accepts your proposal. Based on the information you discover, tailor your proposal in a way that shows you have done your research and have the audience's best interest in mind.

Recognize that proposals may be solicited (requested by the organization that has a problem to be solved) or unsolicited (not requested by the organization that has the problem). Even if you are writing an unsolicited proposal, you should usually have a preliminary conversation to prepare your primary audience to receive the proposal. For example, you could talk with the recipient to find out current needs and problems, and then mention that you would like to submit a proposal to help address those needs. A proposal delivered to a prepared audience will generally be accepted more readily.

## Context

In addition to analyzing the audience of your proposal, take time to understand the context of the problem you are seeking to solve. Solicited proposals are often written in response to an external organization's Request for Proposal (RFP), and the RFP can provide valuable contextual information such as background information, evaluation criteria, contact information, the audience's objectives, the submission date, and other important information (see Figure 8.8).

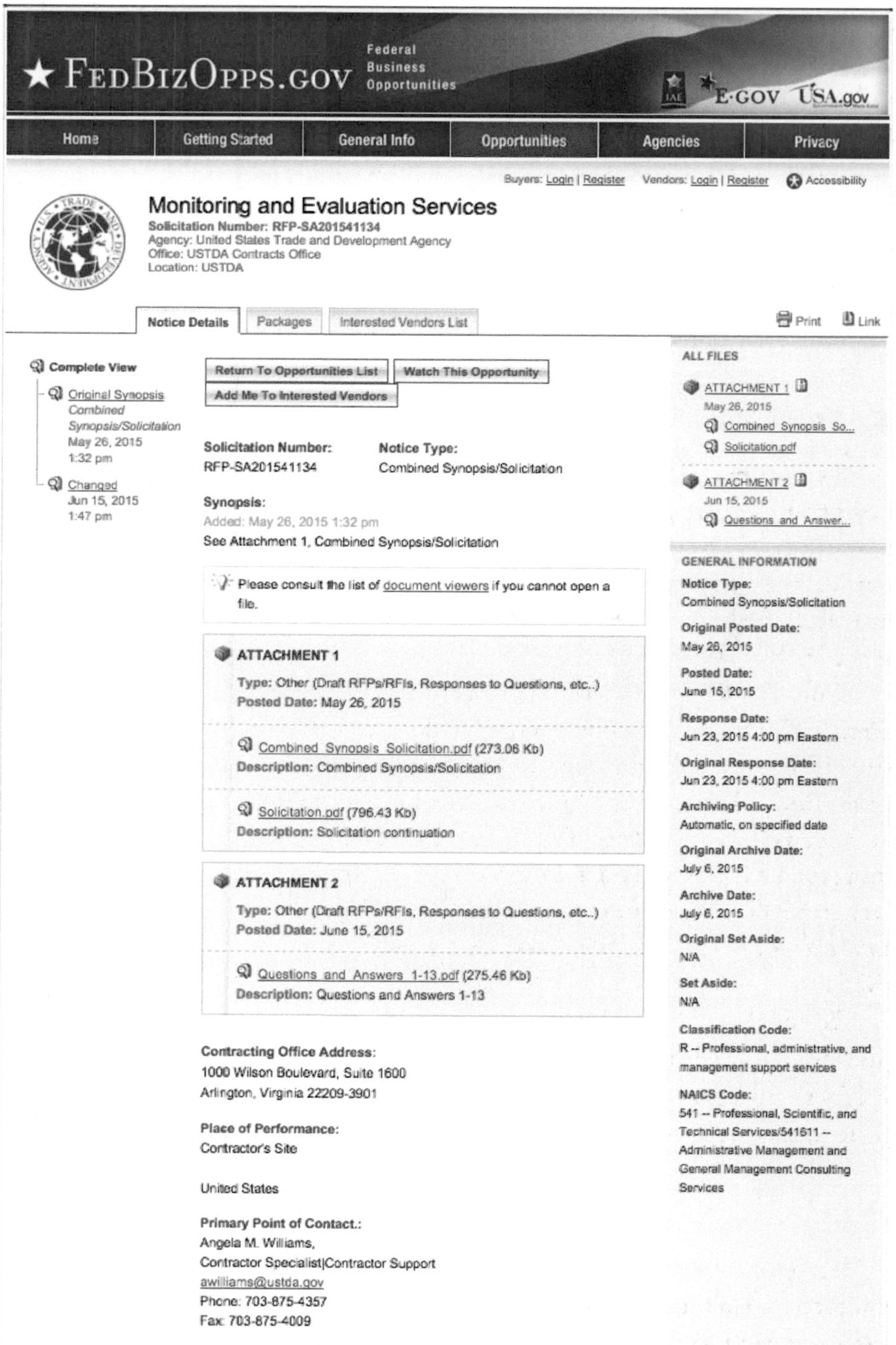

*Figure 8.8  An RFP provides valuable contextual information that can influence your proposal strategy.*

After studying the RFP, research the external and internal factors related to your audience and the RFP's sponsoring organization. External factors such as competitors or industry dynamics can help you better understand why the sponsoring company is experiencing a problem and how you might solve the problem. Further, if you discover that the sponsoring company has been losing money due to competition, then you might assume that cost will be an important evaluation factor for your audience. Internal factors such as the company's mission, organizational structure, and history can also help you recognize themes and vocabulary that will resonate and align with your audience's needs, culture, and values.

By incorporating the contextual information you learn from the RFP and other sources into your proposal, you increase the likelihood that your proposal will be evaluated highly by your audience. Note that proposals submitted in response to an RFP are evaluated in two phases.

**Phase 1.** The requesting organization evaluates the proposals to disqualify any that don't meet RFP criteria. For example, business proposals whose pricing is too high or proposals that don't follow the exact guidelines or structure of the RFP will likely be eliminated during the first phase.

**Phase 2.** The remaining proposals are then evaluated to see which one best meets the RFP criteria and audience needs. For instance, an audit proposal from a CPA firm will be evaluated on the reasonableness of the pricing schedule, expertise of the audit team, timeliness of the proposed work, strength of the firm's reputation, professionalism and readability of the proposal, and so forth.

### Strategy

After analyzing your proposal's purpose, audience, and context, determine an appropriate psychological strategy to follow when creating your proposal. Take a moment to analyze your audience's psychological state—their positive and negative feelings about you, their positive and negative feelings about the topic of your proposal, and their openness to change. Build on their positive emotions (the driving forces to accept your proposal), and seek to address and resolve negative emotions (the restraining forces to reject your proposal). Brainstorm ways that you can build your credibility, increase the logic of the proposal, and prepare your audience to be more open to the solution you will propose.

Consider also which channel would be most appropriate for delivering your proposal. Internal proposals and sales pitches are frequently presented orally as formal stand-up presentations or as less-formal conversation or discussion in meetings. Responses to RFPs are frequently presented through a written channel, such as a memo (see Figure 8.12), report (see Figure 8.13 and Appendix B), or letter format (see Figure 8.14). The internet also enables you to present proposals using a medley of online text, images, and video (for examples of online proposals, explore popular crowdfunding sites such as www.kickstarter.com, www.indiegogo.com, and www.gofundme.com). As you decide which channel to utilize, consider each channel's richness, convenience, speed, permanence, and cost.

### Follow an Appropriate Pattern

While proposals come in many different forms, most business proposals can follow a similar pattern. This pattern anticipates and addresses an audience's questions about your proposal in an organized manner. Building on proposal research (Freed & Roberts 1989), this pattern involves six sections:

1. **Background:** In the background section, describe and define the problem to be solved or researched, providing your audience with enough information that they appreciate and understand the need for the proposal.

2. **Solution:** After providing background on all essential aspects of the problem, propose and define your solution. The solution can be seen as the goal or objective that you need to accomplish in order to research or resolve the problem.

3. **Plan:** With the proposed solution in mind, describe the specific plan, procedures, or methods you will follow to implement the solution. The plan often includes a project timeline and the deliverables you will provide.

4. **Qualifications:** In a proposal, you present a plan that has not yet been implemented; consequently, before your audience will grant you permission or other resources, they must trust that you can and will do what you say you will. The qualifications section therefore details the credentials, education, or experience that evidence your or your organization's abilities to solve the problem and carry out the proposed plan.

5. **Benefits:** This section describes the various benefits of implementing your proposed solution. One main benefit of any proposal should be a better-understood or solved problem.

6. **Costs:** This section details the costs of the proposed solution; in other words, the costs are the resources

(e.g., funding, assistance, authorization, action) that you need from your audience before proceeding to research or solve the problem.

In practice, you might reorder, rename, combine, or break up these sections to meet the needs of your situation and to adapt the proposal to your audience's needs. For example, your proposal can follow a direct approach (solution and plan, followed by the background of the problem) or an indirect approach (the background of the problem, followed by the solution and plan). Depending on your audience's familiarity with the problem and preparation to receive your proposal, you might consider being more indirect with unsolicited proposals.

You will also discover that not all situations, RFPs, or audiences will specifically require some parts of this pattern, but your proposal will be more persuasive if you can somehow answer the questions addressed by the pattern:

- Does the proposal writer understand our problem?
- Does the proposal writer's solution resolve our problem?
- Does the proposal writer's plan lead to the solution?
- Can the proposal writer implement the plan?
- Does the plan lead to our desired benefits?
- Is the cost reasonable for the benefits?

By answering each of these questions in your proposal, you will anticipate your readers' needs, present a more convincing solution, and increase the likelihood of your audience accepting your proposal.

*Figure 8.9 Adapt your proposal approach to your audience's familiarity with the problem and preparation to receive the proposal.*

## Strengthen the Content

Proposals function as persuasive communication—your purpose in writing a proposal is to generate action, action that will enable you and your organization to solve

a problem or take advantage of an opportunity. Chapter 3 outlines five steps you can follow to increase the persuasiveness of your communication, and this section applies those steps to strengthen your proposal's content.

### Frame the Problem

Your audience will judge your proposal partly by how well you understand the problem. A clear understanding and communication of the problem sets up why the proposal is necessary. Once you understand the problem through your research, decide how to frame the problem, considering clarity, causes, and effects.

Clarity encompasses a sharpness of image or a proper focus. Especially for unsolicited proposals, the background section may need to clarify a problem before you give your solution. Only after your audience understands that the problem exists will they understand the need for the solution. For complex problems, the background section also helps isolate the scope, or breadth, of your proposal. If your proposed solution will address only one aspect of a problem, the background section should make that clear.

You might also frame a problem by focusing on its causes or its effects (Johnson-Sheehan 2008). For instance, once you clarify the causes of the problem, you can later show how your solution resolves those causes. Likewise, clarify the effects so you can motivate the audience to take action. People are motivated both by a desire to avoid negative consequences and by a desire to obtain positive results. Thus, you could describe a recent negative situation caused by the problem, and then later show how that outcome would have been different if your solution were accepted.

### Propose the Solution

Once the problem is framed and you establish why the proposal is needed, your audience should be prepared to hear what you recommend to solve the problem. When describing your solution, clearly state the goals you will achieve. Remember that if your proposal is accepted, you will need to implement your solution, so consider writing your goals using the SMART acronym—specific, measurable, assignable, realistic, and time related (Doran 1981). In this way, if your proposal is accepted, you can more easily evaluate and report whether you achieve your goals.

### Support the Solution

Once you have detailed what you recommend to solve the problem, explain in detail how you plan to achieve the solution. As you detail your plan, review the RFP and make

| Tasks | Week 1 | Week 2 | Week 3 | Week 4 | Week 5 | Week 6 | Week 7 |
|---|---|---|---|---|---|---|---|
| On-site visit | ■ | | | | | | |
| Loan & G/L records mapping | ■ | ■ | | | | | |
| Loan & G/L records transferring | | ■ | ■ | | | | |
| On-site employee training | | | | ■ | | | |
| Data conversion | | | | | ■ | | |
| On-site support | | | | | ■ | ■ | |
| Post-conversion debriefing | | | | | | ■ | |
| Off-site support | | | | | | | ■ |

*Figure 8.10 A Gantt chart provides evidence that you can implement your solution within a designated time frame.*

sure the plan meets any criteria listed there. Also think about what you have learned while communicating with your audience, and make sure you have addressed all their needs and concerns.

After solidifying your plan, integrate a timeline or Gantt chart (see Figure 8.10) that shows when you will work on and accomplish each aspect of the plan. Timing may play an important role for some audiences, so schedule sufficient time to accomplish all necessary tasks.

If your plan involves delivering goods or services to your audience, you should also detail their specifications and when they will be delivered. Sometimes RFPs will provide significant detail about the required deliverables, so be sure to pay attention to all details. And even if your proposal focuses on research, remember that your audience will most likely want you to provide a copy of your data or a report of your research findings.

Once you have detailed how you plan to achieve the proposed solution, your audience needs to know whether you can achieve it. Qualifications might take the form of resumes, customer testimonials, employee biographies, company mission statements, descriptions of previous projects, and so forth. By providing this information, you seek to increase your credibility and your company's credibility and to persuade your audience that you can do what you propose to do.

Once your audience knows whether you can achieve the proposed solution, you can discuss the audience's benefits that occur when you implement the solution. These benefits can be found by persuasively turning the features of your proposal into benefits. Features might include an innovative solution, a rigorous timeline, your qualifications, or even low costs. You turn each of these into benefits as you consider what they mean to your audience (see Figure 8.11). For example, your proposal may feature your experienced employees. This experience could mean faster results and better insight for your audience. By detailing these benefits, you offset the costs by answering the audience's WIIFM question.

| Proposal Features | Proposal Benefits |
|---|---|
| On-site visit | Enables better customization of software to meet client's needs |
| Quick record mapping | Completes conversion before busy loan season begins |
| Experienced conversion team | Decreases worry that records will be mistakenly transferred |
| On-site employee training | Reduces employee stress over new software |

*Figure 8.11 Turn a proposal's features into benefits by considering what the features mean to the audience.*

## Resolve Concerns

Anticipate and resolve any concerns that your audience may have about you, your company, or your solution. In many external proposal situations, you will be competing against other individuals or companies. Therefore, identify areas where you might be vulnerable, considering how your competitors' proposals might appear stronger than yours. Emphasize your strengths to compensate, and re-examine your costs, pricing, timeline, procedures, personnel qualifications, and promised benefits; make any possible adjustments toward benefiting the audience.

Audiences may also experience concern when they don't understand the reasoning of your proposal. Whenever possible, seek to anticipate and address the why question. For example, why this solution? Because it solves the problem for these reasons: X, Y, and Z. Why this plan? Because it helps us achieve the solution for these reasons: X, Y, and Z. Why these qualifications? Because they show that we can achieve the plan for these reasons: X, Y, and Z. Seeking to strengthen the reasoning of your proposal will result in a more coherent and logically persuasive proposal.

### Invite Acceptance

As you write or present your proposal, include opportunities for your audience to accept your proposal. For example, in a cover letter accompanying your proposal, include your contact information with an offer to answer any questions. As you close your proposal, conclude with a forward-looking statement such as, "We look forward to hearing from you regarding your decision."

As you improve abilities to solve problems and create proposals, you will increase your power to be a positive influence for change in your organization and to gain greater satisfaction from your professional work.

## CHAPTER SUMMARY

Solving problems involves six general steps: define the problem, analyze the problem, develop alternative solutions, select a solution, implement the solution, and evaluate the outcome. When defining problems, consider the difference between *what is* and *what should* or *could be*. As you analyze the problem, remember the difference between causes and symptoms. The cause is the origin; the symptom is the outcome. Too many people try to fix the symptoms, only to find that they reappear because the cause is still present.

Brainstorming can foster creativity and develop potential solutions to a problem. Brainstorming assumes that quantity will yield quality; in other words, if you come up with enough ideas, at least one or two will likely be good ones. Brainstorming can be performed alone or with a group. Whereas the initial phase of brainstorming fosters divergent thinking, the decision-making phase brings about convergent thinking. A decision table, or decision matrix, can be useful in deciding on the best decision. Seek for a solution everyone can live with.

When you have good buy-in from all stakeholders, decide how to implement the ideas. Make sure all affected people are represented in the implementation plan, and modify the plan as needed to address their concerns. In the plan, be sure to include methods for evaluating outcomes so you can measure whether the solution causes the intended outcomes.

Proposals are a vital part of business, government, and nonprofit organizations, and they play an important role in the problem-solving process. Proposals are written to obtain resources, authorization, assistance, or action from others that enables you to proceed with plans explained in the proposal. In addition, proposals are written to persuade audiences of the benefits of a solution. Persuasive proposals effectively frame the problem, propose and support the solution, resolve concerns, and invite acceptance.

## Works Cited

Doran, G. T. "There's a S.M.A.R.T. Way to Write Management's Goals and Objectives." *Management Review* 70 (1981): 35–36.

Freed, Richard C., and David D. Roberts. "The Nature, Classification, and Generic Structure of Proposals." *Journal of Technical Writing and Communication* 19, no. 4 (1989): 317–351.

Johnson-Sheehan, Richard. *Writing Proposals.* 2nd ed. New York: Pearson Longman, (2008).

SkyMark. "Force Field Analysis." (2012): http://www.skymark.com/resources/tools/force_field_diagram.asp.

Tukey, John. "We Need Both Exploratory and Confirmatory." *The American Statistician* 34 (1980): 23–25.

## CHAPTER QUESTIONS

1. Describe the difference between causes and symptoms.

2. What is a cause-and-effect diagram? How is it used?

3. List three factors a manager should consider in deciding whether to involve the group in making a decision.

4. The idea behind brainstorming is that _____ will yield _____.

5. List three ways to enhance your creativity.

6. What is gallery writing? What are the advantages of gallery writing over traditional brainstorming?

7. What is the difference between divergent thinking and convergent thinking?

8. What is a decision table? Why is it useful in decision making?

9. What are the five categories of personnel performance problems?

10. Describe the role of proposals in problem solving.

11. What is a force-field analysis?

12. What is an RFP?

13. What are the six sections of the pattern that most business proposals can follow?

14. Describe three ways to strengthen the content of a proposal.

# CHAPTER ACTIVITIES

1. Think of a problem in your school or community. Create a cause-and-effect diagram (mind map or other format) to diagnose the problem. Then develop solutions for each of the problem's causes.

2. Using the internet, gather information regarding three comparable products, such as three computers, three cameras, or three cars. Analyze and compare the three alternatives. Develop a decision table to show your comparison.

3. On the internet, find a site that includes complaints filed against a business organization. Analyze some of the complaints, diagnose the main problems, and develop solutions. Create a proposal with the chosen organization as your audience, proposing to solve one of the problems you discovered.

4. Identify a problem within an organization you are a part of. Try out multiple personal brainstorming strategies to come up with solutions. Which strategies worked most effectively for you? Now assemble a small group of colleagues. Try out multiple group brainstorming strategies. Which strategies worked most effectively for the group? Compare your experiences brainstorming individually and as a group. For example, did you or the group come up with more solutions?

5. Examine an RFP on www.grants.gov or www.fedbizopps.gov. Assume you were going to write a proposal in response to the RFP. What information do you learn from the RFP that would influence the way you write your proposal? Now research the primary audience for the proposal. What do you learn that would influence the way you write your proposal?

6. Search the internet for the words "proposal writing," and browse through a few of the sites that you find. Write a brief summary of your findings.

7. Search the internet for the words "sample proposal." Review a few of the proposals, and critique the design, organization, and content of the proposals. For example, in the proposal's content can you find the six sections of the pattern discussed in this chapter? Write a brief summary of your critique.

8. Find a proposal of interest on a crowdfunding site such as www.kickstarter.com, www.indiegogo.com, or www.gofundme.com. Identify examples of the six pattern sections described in this chapter. Are any sections missing? How does an online delivery channel change the way a proposal is presented? What recommendations would you give to the creator to strengthen the content and persuasiveness of the proposal?

To:        Department Managers

From:      Training Department

Date:      May 15, 20XX

Subject:   **CNE Certification Course**

Our CNE Certification Course was developed in 20XX to meet the needs of all units with networks. The company has not charged a registration fee for the course and has paid the participants for the hours spent attending the two-day course and completing the subsequent testing. The participants have been given six weeks to complete the course. If this deadline has not been met, a $25 penalty has been assessed through payroll deduction.

During the past two years, 25 percent of the systems personnel have not completed the course. Non-completion results in heavy resource use without our organization realizing appropriate benefits. The current registration and pay practice does not promote individual commitment or accountability for course completion. Given these problems, the following sections include our proposed solution, followed by sections on benefits, costs, and timing.

**Solution**
To solve these problems, we propose that the registration and pay practice for the CNE Certification Course be changed so each participant's personal financial investment will be linked to course registration and completion. Here are some additional details:

- Employees wanting to register must obtain their department manager's signature on the registration form to indicate competency. As managers become more involved in the process, employee accountability will increase.

- A $100 registration fee will be paid by the participant, increasing individual commitment to the course.

- The unit will pay one-half the number of hours spent in the two-day course at regular hourly wage. Participants will not be paid for testing, once again increasing individual commitment.

- The participants will complete the course within six weeks. If the deadline is met, $50 will be refunded. If the course is not completed within six weeks, the entire registration fee will be forfeited.

**Qualifications and Benefits**
The Training Department implemented similar changes to the CNR course last year, resulting in higher completion rates of that course. In addition to higher completion rates, we anticipate these additional benefits if we implement this solution:

1. Uncommitted employees will likely not register under this proposed arrangement, ensuring that resources invested into the course produce appropriate benefits.

2. This proposal will decrease the cost to the employees' units and help recover course supply costs incurred by the Training Department.

*Figure 8.12  Example of an unsolicited internal proposal in memo format.*

2

### Cost Savings

The following table highlights the major cost differences for the Training Department between the current and proposed practices.

Cost Comparison Between Current and Proposed Practice

| Cost Category | Current Practice | Proposed Practice |
|---|---|---|
| Employee wages (avg. $23 per hr.) | (16 hrs. [course] + 2 hrs. [testing]) x $23 = $414 | (16 hrs. x 1/2) x $23 = $184 |
| IV Supplies | $12 | $12 |
| Handouts | $4 | $4 |
| Refreshments | $4 | $4 |
| **Total Costs** | $434 per participant | $204 per participant |
| **Revenue** | $0 if deadline met or $25 if not | $50 or $100 if not |

The foregoing figures indicate the financial benefits of adopting the new proposal. Our organization's typical cost for a completing employee would drop from $434 under the current practice to $154 ($204 expense minus $50 revenue) with the proposed practice—a per person savings of $280. The proposed procedure clearly makes sound financial sense.

### Time Sequence

We hope to implement this new practice for the next CNE Certification Course, scheduled for August 16 and 19, 20XX. Because the publicity for the course must be available by July 6, allowing time for registration and scheduling of replacement personnel for course participants, we need your decision concerning this proposed change by June 25.

### Conclusion

We feel that the CNE Certification Course proposal is a wise move from both a financial and a personnel standpoint. If you have any questions concerning this proposal, we would be happy to meet with you either prior to or during your May 20 meeting where this proposal will be discussed.

*Figure 8.12 continued.*

# CleanMaster

945 Grey Fox Circle
Brownsville, Texas 956XX
Phone (XXX) 546-12XX

February 5, 20XX

Jose Garcia
Brownsville Medical Plaza
1040 West Jackson
Brownsville, TX 95620

Dear Mr. Garcia:

Here is our proposal for the cleaning process you requested. The proposal contains information about all aspects of our work, including our satisfaction guarantee.

CleanMaster's cleaning processes have been perfected over decades of work in every type of situation imaginable. With CleanMaster, you can be confident that your work will be completed with the best procedures and products available and that the work will cause as little disruption to your business as possible.

As you study our proposal, please feel free to call me if you have any questions or need additional information. We look forward to hearing from you.

Sincerely,

*James A Rogers*

James A. Rogers
Professional Cleaning Specialist

Enclosure: Proposal

*Figure 8.13  Example of a solicited external proposal in report format.*

Proposal to Perform Carpet Cleaning for

## Brownsville Medical Center

1040 West Jackson
Brownsville, Texas

CleanMaster, Inc.
945 GreyFox Circle
Brownsville, Texas 78520
Phone (XXX) 546-1234
Pager (XXX) 546-5678

February 5, 20XX

*Figure 8.13  continued.*

# Proposal to Perform Carpet Cleaning for
# Brownsville Medical Center

Brownsville Medical Center serves the needs of numerous patients year round. Such service results in wear and tear on the Center's carpets, necessitating annual carpet cleaning. To accomplish this cleaning, CleanMaster proposes to perform work for Brownsville Medical Center's labor and delivery unit as follows:

| Area | Number |
|---|---|
| Second-floor hallways | 3 |
| Second-floor Nurses Station | 1 |
| Labor and Delivery Section hallway | 1 |
| Total area to be cleaned | Approximately 4,155 square feet |

## Procedures to be Followed

This project will be performed using CleanMaster's patented carpet cleaning process, which includes the following:

1. Spray carpet with CleanMaster's detergent soil decomposer to break down dirt and residues that accumulate in carpet.
2. Apply special spot removal detergents on darker stains.
3. Scrub carpet with high-performance scrubber to loosen dirt from carpet fiber.
4. Rinse carpet and extract the dirt, pumping it into the CleanMaster cleaning system waste tank.

## Time Line

To disrupt your normal work procedures as little as possible, we propose to perform your work late on a Saturday night, preferably the evening of February 13. Performing the work at this time will enable us to complete the project and have your carpets dried before normal business hours the following day.

## Qualifications of Brownsville CleanMaster

CleanMaster has been doing business in the Brownsville area for 23 years. During this time, we have performed professional work for all types of commercial and healthcare facilities. As part of the nationwide CleanMaster organization, we receive regular training in all the latest techniques to improve the cleaning process and give our customers the level of cleaning service they expect.

Although CleanMaster is a national organization, we and our families live here in the Brownsville area, and we want to earn your trust. Our desire is to have you become a repeat customer, and we know that will happen only if you are satisfied with our work. We will strive very hard to earn your trust and perform to your level of satisfaction.

*Figure 8.13  continued.*

### Benefits

Selecting CleanMaster provides numerous benefits for Brownsville Medical Center, among which are the following:

- Guaranteed clean carpets that are so essential in a medical facility.
- Limited disruption of important work routines as nurses carry out their medical responsibilities.
- Friendly and genuinely concerned CleanMaster employees who are available 24 hours a day.
- Affordable pricing to have limited impact on your budget.
- CleanMaster's Satisfaction Guarantee: "Do it right the first time or do it over—no questions asked."

### Pricing

Based on our initial measurement of your cleaning area, we are prepared to clean approximately 4,155 square feet of carpet. The cost of labor, materials, transportation, and equipment resources applied to this project is $494.45, plus $40.79 tax, making a total of $535.24. This price is valid through May 30, 20XX. If you wish to discuss this pricing structure further, please call me at one of the numbers listed on the cover of this proposal.

### Conclusion

We appreciate the chance to perform cleaning services for Brownsville Medical Center and hope you will consider our proposal carefully. During your decision process, feel free to communicate with us as needed so we can answer your questions and provide any additional information you need.

*Figure 8.13  continued.*

## ABC Consulting, Inc.

*Specialists in Complaint-Management Systems*
5850 Park Lane Road
Commerce, US 84XXX
723.266.21XX ◆ 723.266.23XX

13 March 2008

Mr. Lukas Steiner
FlyHigh Airlines
7500 Airport Drive
Somewhere, US 554XX

Dear Mr. Steiner:

In spite of your best efforts to meet the needs of every customer, sometimes things just don't go quite right and someone has a bad experience with your company. In the past, that customer might complain to a few friends and then let it go. But today, more and more disgruntled customers are using the web to publish their gripes to the whole world. The result is embarrassing publicity and lost business for you. That's where we come in.

### What We Do

We specialize in reducing customer complaints through enhanced complaint management and improved customer service. We have worked with several airline companies and have a superior track record of success. Our team of specialists will work with your organization as follows:
—Analyze customer complaints on all complaint-related websites.
—Develop creative solutions to significantly reduce the most frequently recurring complaints.
—Develop complaint-management methods for effectively working with dissatisfied customers.

### Who We Are

ABC was formed to help reduce customer complaints through improved customer service. Four highly trained specialists, assisted by additional support staff, work on all of our complaints-management projects:

- *Daniel Michalkova*: Co-founder of ABC Consulting, Inc. and a recipient of a Master of Science degree in Statistics from Yale University, Daniel has extensive experience in analyzing data and providing recommendations for many prominent companies.
- *Alene Church:* Customer service specialist for 15 years and a graduate from the MBA program at New York University with an emphasis in Human Resources, Alene has contributed significantly in numerous projects for both enhancing customer service and improving overall business techniques.

*Figure 8.14  An external unsolicited proposal in letter format. Note the Gantt chart on the second page that shows the project timeline.*

- *Christine Taylor:* Upon receiving an MBA degree with an emphasis in Finance from Virginia University, Christine was recruited by Boon Consulting, where she received *Employee of the Year Award* consecutively for three years. Because of her experience in improving companies' efficiency, structure, and profits, she was assigned to a project for Mideast Airlines, which ultimately resulted in a decrease of company complaints by 58 percent.
- *Larry Tryon:* Research specialist and MBA graduate from Harvard University with an emphasis in marketing, Larry is the former Operations Manager of Speedy Airways and has a strong background in the airline industry.

**What You Receive**

FlyHigh Airlines will receive numerous benefits due to ABC Consulting's experience and expertise with complaint management:

*Excellence and Efficiency:* Complaints-analysis projects are conducted in four major phases, with typical duration times as specified in the following chart:

| Project Phases | Week | | | | | | | | | |
|---|---|---|---|---|---|---|---|---|---|---|
| | 1 | 2 | 3 | 4 | 5 | 6 | 7 | 8 | 9 | 10 |
| 1 Gather data | ■ | ■ | | | | | | | | |
| 2 Analyze data | | | ■ | ■ | ■ | | | | | |
| 3 Develop recommendations | | | | | | ■ | ■ | ■ | | |
| 4 Prepare and deliver reports | | | | | | | | | ■ | ■ |

This efficient, 10-week engagement will enable FlyHigh Airlines to quickly address concerns with current customer complaints.

*Information for Improvement:* Upon completion of the project, we will present to the management of FlyHigh Airlines written and oral reports containing key information:

- Detailed analyses of all complaints found on the internet
- Recommendations for significantly reducing the most frequent problems
- Recommendations for establishing an effective complaint-management system to prevent complaints from being posted on the web

*Return on Investment.* ABC Consulting negotiates pricing with each customer, tailoring a cost to meet your needs. Because only a retained customer becomes a return customer, we are confident that your investment will return more customers to FlyHigh airlines.

We would appreciate the opportunity to work with your organization in increasing your customers' satisfaction and helping prevent negative publicity from dissatisfied customers. After you have had a few days to consider our proposal, we will call to request the opportunity to meet for further discussion.

Sincerely,

Daniel Michalkova, Partner

*Figure 8.14 continued.*

## CHAPTER 9

# Conducting Business Research

You live in an exciting world, a world rich with information that provides answers to many questions. Whether you want to learn about stock prices, company histories, product reviews, or market demographics, you can quickly search the internet and other databases to find a wealth of data. Furthermore, you can read books, blogs, news articles, posts, tweets, and other content that provide insight into problems or opportunities that you face in the workplace. With so much information available, you can make better management decisions and help your organization to be more successful.

Given such abundant information, it is hard to imagine that you will tackle problems or opportunities that no person has ever encountered before. Yet in an ever-changing and increasingly personalized business and social environment, you will indeed face situations that are new and unique. In these situations, the knowledge and wisdom of others can take you only so far—you may need to create, collect, and analyze new data to thrive in today's dynamic world.

This chapter discusses research strategies for situations both when you seek to learn from others (secondary research) and when you to create your own data (primary research). After learning the material in this chapter, you should be able to do the following:

- Conduct secondary research using effective search strategies.
- Document secondary research appropriately.
- Conduct primary research using effective data-gathering strategies.

Secondary and primary research constitute the two main types of research conducted in business. Secondary research includes reviewing information that has already been published, such as books, journals, and electronic databases. In other words, secondary research uses existing research. Primary research requires the gathering of original data, using methods such as survey (e.g., sending questionnaires to clients for feedback), observation (e.g., watching consumers' behavior in a retail store), and experimentation (e.g., introducing a new product in one geographic area and not in another and then comparing the results). In other words, primary research creates or gathers new information.

Primary and secondary research include both costs and benefits. Because you create or gather the data in primary research, your data may be crafted to meet your needs more precisely than secondary research. However, gathering primary data can take more time and be more expensive than gathering secondary data. As a general practice, first examine secondary research to see what sources and data are available, and then turn to primary data to find the remaining information you need.

## SECONDARY RESEARCH

In previous decades, secondary research was conducted by slowly searching through printed indexes of journals, books, and reports. With today's databases, you can instantly search millions of records electronically. This section provides guidelines for determining a research topic, searching for information, and documenting research.

## Determining a Research Topic

When conducting secondary research, first determine your topic by thinking through the purpose, audience and context of your research. Sometimes, your purpose will be to inform either yourself or others about previously published information related to your topic. When seeking to inform, try to formulate your research topic into a question, such as, "How can investors effectively manage retirement portfolios?" At other times, your purpose may be to persuade others. For example, you might believe that diversification is the best way to manage portfolios. In this case, formulate a statement or argument to guide your research, such as, "Diversification effectively helps investors manage retirement portfolios." Your question or argument will then guide and motivate you toward information related to your topic.

As you begin finding information, you may find that your topic is made up of many details narrower in scope than your original topic. For example, you might discover that managing a portfolio involves risk and reward, return on investment, cash flow, mutual funds, diversification, or possibly speculation. After learning of this additional detail, you may decide you are most interested in learning about maximizing cash flow. Purposefully narrowing your topic in this way can often result in a more manageable, relevant, or interesting topic for you.

You may also discover information that can guide your selection of a topic as you analyze your audience. For example, if you will be presenting your research at a marketing conference, then your topic should probably relate to marketing. If you will be writing up your research for publication in a journal, magazine, or company newsletter, take time to find out the interests and expectations of those who will be reading your research, and select a topic accordingly.

When you are a student, quite often your audience will be a college professor. Many college professors require an academic proposal before approving students' secondary research topics. To prepare such a proposal, complete some initial secondary research about your possible topic. Then when you write the proposal, describe the topic and its importance, list the research questions you hope to answer, tell how and when your research will be completed, detail the benefits of your research, and request permission to proceed with the research (see Figure 9.1). Based on the resulting feedback from your professor, you can update and refine your topic.

In addition to analyzing your audience, take time to also analyze the context surrounding possible topics. You can think of a topic's context as a conversation. For example, an investor at one company might publish thoughts and experiences related to portfolio management. A researcher at a university might build on the investor's thoughts by conducting a related research study and publishing the results. Finally, an editor might summarize those results in a finance magazine, prompting numerous readers to post critiques and reviews through online comments. As you read these conversations, you will begin to discover ways you can extend others' thoughts, build on others' research, or fill in information missing from the current conversation. These discoveries become excellent research topics since they are guided by a purpose, interesting to an audience, and grounded in the context of the conversation.

## Searching for Information

With your topic settled, next determine the databases and other sources that will likely yield the desired information. Databases can be broad in coverage or more narrowly focused. On the one hand, EBSCO contains articles from thousands of journals in business, finance, management, and accounting. On the other hand, EDGAR is more focused and contains financial reports of publicly traded U.S. corporations.

In addition to selecting the appropriate databases to search, you have four major categories of publications: scholarly journals, trade journals, popular magazines, and newspapers. Any of these publications may be available in print versions, online versions, or both. In general, the information in scholarly journals is more reliable, but is less current; the other three categories contain information that may be less reliable, but is more current.

**Scholarly journals** contain many research-based articles that have been carefully reviewed by the author's professional peers before being cleared for publication. Many have been subjected to a "blind review," which means that the reviewers did not know the identity of the author during the review period, thus allowing the reviewers to be unbiased and objective in their critique. Scholarly journals contain highly reliable information, but they often don't contain information on the latest issues, because of the time it takes to perform the research and conduct peer reviews.

**Trade journals** target a specific market, industry, or profession, such as the beverage industry or the field of human resources management. Although not scholarly in nature, some trade journals are recognized as authoritative within their industry or profession.

To:    Professor Alison Sam
From:  Richard Rawlins
Date:  February 28, 20XX

Re:    **Proposal to Research Affordable Housing in Kansas**

For my public hearing research project, I propose to research the affordable-housing problems in Kansas.

In the United States, housing is generally categorized as affordable when residents spend no more than 30 percent of their income on housing. Affordable housing is essential because it allows individuals and families to contribute to a community in many vital ways. Further, affordable housing enables families to allocate appropriate amounts of resources to other basic needs like food, transportation, and healthcare. Without affordable housing, an area can quickly lose its vital lower-wage workforce, and businesses that depend on lower-wage workers have difficulty filling employment vacancies.

Kansas has two main affordable housing problems. First, minimum-wage earners don't make enough money to afford housing in most areas of the state. For an average two-bedroom rental unit, a minimum-wage earner would need to work more than two full-time jobs. Second, Kansas has an undersupply of affordable housing. Latest figures estimate that Kansas has a 22,000 unit shortage of affordable housing for low-income families.

**RESEARCH OBJECTIVES**
At this stage of my research, I plan to investigate the following questions:

1. To what extent is affordable housing a problem in Kansas?
2. What economic factors are influencing the affordable-housing issue in Kansas?
3. How is the Kansas State government organized to address affordable-housing needs?
4. What can Kansas learn from other states that have successfully addressed affordable-housing issues?

**METHODS OF RESEARCH**
My research will rely heavily on scholarly articles, government statistical data, and agency reports regarding affordable housing. A ProQuest search on this general topic yielded 298 scholarly documents, 29 of which have been published since the beginning of the year, showing that the topic is popular, significant, and timely. After narrowing my search to Kansas, I found 14 articles, some of which are included in the attached bibliography.

**SCHEDULE**
I intend to complete my library research by March 14, 20XX, after which I will begin work on preparing a presentation to be given on March 23, 20XX. For that presentation I will prepare appropriate PowerPoint slides and a handout.

**BENEFITS**
Because I intend to work in real estate development after I graduate, this research will benefit my long-term career while enabling me to apply the secondary research skills taught in this class. When I present my findings, this topic will also benefit any others who are interested in pursuing careers related to real estate, construction, or human services.

**REQUEST FOR APPROVAL**
I ask that you approve my topic, methods, and schedule. Also, please give any suggestions you may have regarding this proposal. Please contact me at rlr@abcuniv.edu if you have any questions about my research ideas and plans.

*Figure 9.1  Academic proposals are used to obtain professors' permission to conduct secondary research.*

*Figure 9.2 Vast electronic databases are available for conducting secondary research.*

**Popular magazines** cover a wide array of current topics and are published for general audiences.

**Newspapers** cover current news for general audiences and include editorial opinions on varied current issues.

You can also search well-known internet sites such as Google or Yahoo. However, remember that when using the internet, you must be cautious about the quality and accuracy of the information you find. Because publishing on the internet is so easy and so accessible to everyone, you will find poorly written, deceptive, and incorrect information along with the good. Here are a few questions and observations to help you determine the quality of a website—or any other information source.

**Currency:** How recently was the content published? How recently was the site updated? How current are the sources and content?

**Authority:** Who is the author? What are the author's credentials? Has the author been cited by other sources on the topic? Can the author be contacted? Is the publisher or site a recognized source of expertise? Is the information well organized and well written? Are there obvious typographical, grammar, spelling, and other writing errors?

**Reliability:** Is the information well organized and well written? Are sources cited? Are they easily traced and verifiable? Are they high-quality sources? Are the conclusions logically supported by the evidence? Does the site have a .com, .org, .edu, or .gov domain? Sites with .com endings are for-profit businesses whose purpose is to make money. Therefore, they have a bias in favor of their own survival and profitability. Most sites with .org endings are owned by non-profit organizations and, depending on their mission, they can be reliable

or not. Sites with .edu endings are owned by either for-profit or non-profit educational institutions, and sites with .gov endings are owned by government entities. For all information gathered from the internet, critically consider the motives of the information's provider.

**Purpose/Point of View:** What is the author's purpose? Is the article written at a popular, professional, or professorial level? Is the author or sponsoring organization motivated by certain values or a mission that might introduce political, cultural, religious, or ideological bias? Or is the author or organization driven by profit? Consider carefully how these motives affect the usefulness of the information source.

To conduct electronic searches, you can search for single words or for phrases. Assume you recently began work at a finance company, and you are seeking to learn more about customers' motivations for taking on unsecured loans. If you use single words, you could search for a word like *debt,* or for a combination of single words like *debt* and *credit.* If you search for a phrase, you search for words that are grouped together, such as *"credit card debt"* (using quotations marks to indicate a phrase). In the first example, the search would find all sources that include the words *debt* and *credit.* However, in the second example, the search would find sources that have only the exact phrase *"credit card debt."*

A variety of search operators may be available, depending on the database or search engine you use. Some operators search for words that are in relative proximity to each other or appear multiple times in a document. Other operators can be used to truncate words (replacing one or more of a word's last letters with an asterisk) or to introduce wild cards (replacing a letter with a question mark). For example, searching for *cred\** would find word variations such as *credit* and *creditor,* but it would also find all occurrences of *credentials, credibility,* and *credenza.* Similarly, searching for *wom?n* would find occurrences of both *woman* and *women.* In addition to these operators, you can limit search results by specifying the document type or date of publication, choosing, for example, to see only scholarly texts published in the past year.

The most common and perhaps most useful search operators are Boolean operators. Effective use of Boolean operators can enable you to narrow your searches to avoid mountains of irrelevant results, or to broaden your searches to avoid empty results pages. The main Boolean operators are AND, OR, and NOT. Here is how they work.

Assume that you are marketing a new ankle brace, so you are trying to find all the articles about women's basket-

ball. If you use just the search term *basketball*, you'll get articles dealing with men's basketball and women's basketball. Thus, you should narrow your search command to include *women's* AND *basketball*. If you want to further narrow your search to include *women's basketball injuries*, just include *injuries* as an additional AND criterion—*basketball* AND *women's* AND *injuries*. Perhaps you want to find articles about either basketball or volleyball. In this case you should broaden your search to include *basketball* OR *volleyball*. If you want to search for college basketball but not professional basketball, you can search for *basketball* AND *college* NOT *professional*. Boolean operators do not necessarily need to be capitalized, but capitalization makes them easy to identify. Figure 9.3 illustrates the narrowing or broadening effect of each additional criterion.

After each search, determine whether the results contain articles of appropriate quality. If the articles are not relevant to your topic, select more precise keywords. Note that different industries or communities of people use the same words in different ways. For example, the word *profit* may mean "revenue minus costs" to an accountant, but it means "revenue minus costs *minus opportunity costs*" to an economist. As you become more familiar with the way your industry or community uses certain terms, you will become more effective in your selection of keywords.

In addition, after each search determine whether the results contain articles of appropriate quantity. Then as appropriate, modify your Boolean operators to be more or less restrictive. As you modify your search, remember the typical tradeoff between quantity of results and their relevance—a more restrictive search will provide fewer results, but those results will be more relevant; a broader search will

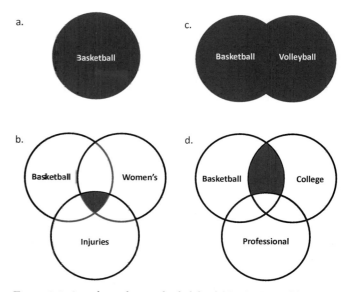

*Figure 9.3  Search results are shaded for (a)* basketball, *(b)* basketball *AND* women's *AND* injuries, *(c)* basketball *OR* volleyball, *and (d)* basketball *AND* college *NOT* professional.

provide more results, but they will include some less relevant items.

To further learn as you go, take time to closely read the content of a few relevant results. This time can yield multiple benefits. For instance, the articles you examine might contain better search terms than the ones you initially thought of. In addition, when you read useful articles, their bibliographies or references will often lead you to other relevant articles.

Figure 9.4 illustrates an advanced search screen from the Library of Congress Online Catalog. As you visit this screen, you enter your keywords in the appropriate blanks, and then indicate whether you want the AND, OR, or NOT Boolean operators to be used. You can then further

| LC Online Catalog | | Browse | Advanced Search | Keyword Search |

Search History | Account Info | Help | LC Authorities

**Advanced Search**

Search

[ ] all of these within Keyword Anywhere (GKEY)
●AND ○OR ○NOT
[ ] all of these within Keyword Anywhere (GKEY)
●AND ○OR ○NOT
[ ] all of these within Keyword Anywhere (GKEY)
➕ Add Limits

Records per page: 25    Clear  Search

*Figure 9.4  The Library of Congress Online Catalog employs Boolean operators to help you focus your information searches.*

tailor your search by specifying that your search terms must be present in the title, in the author's name, or in the keywords tagged to the article. After each search, check to see if your results give you the information you are seeking. If not, change your search fields again to further refine or expand the results. Remember that your librarian can also assist you in identifying relevant databases to use in your research, and assist you in developing effective search strategies.

When you find an article you want to use, select the PDF version if it is available. The PDF version will give you a literal image of the printed pages, including graphics and correct page numbers, whereas the HTML version won't give you accurate pagination. With accurate page numbers included in the PDF, you will have all the information you need to document the location of content you cite from the article.

## Documenting Research

Including information obtained from other people adds credibility to your own writing, but you are required by law to acknowledge that the work came from someone else and to indicate where you found it. The following sections will explain the why, what, and how of documentation.

### Why Document

Documentation is important for at least three reasons: to give credit to the people who created the original work, to tell people how to find the original source, and to comply with copyright law. From a legal standpoint, the owner of an original "expression," or creative work, has the right to determine who can make copies of the work. Just as a patent protects an invention and a trademark protects a name, symbol, or design, a copyright protects music, writing, art, movies, and software. Text that is written by anyone is automatically protected by copyright, even if a formal copyright has not been granted by the United States copyright office.

If you represent other people's unique work as your own, you are being untruthful and are guilty of plagiarism, and the penalties can be serious. For a college student, plagiarism can result in a failing grade for a report, a failing grade for an entire course, or even expulsion from school for extremely serious violations. In a professional setting, plagiarism can result in a tarnished reputation and in disciplinary measures, including dismissal from employment.

Plagiarism can occur in various ways. If you copy someone else's text verbatim (word for word) and you don't give

due credit, you are guilty of plagiarism. If you paraphrase someone else's work and you don't give due credit, you are guilty of plagiarism. If you blend other people's facts or ideas with your own facts or ideas without giving due credit, you are guilty of plagiarism. You can avoid all the problems of plagiarism by knowing what needs to be documented and how to document.

### What to Document

You will generally use three techniques when integrating outside material into your work—quoting, paraphrasing, or summarizing. Regardless of the integration technique you use, you must document the source. Understanding the differences and similarities among these techniques (see Table 9.1) may help you better recognize what must be documented in your own work.

**Quoting**: You quote when you use exact words, sentences, or phrases from others' unique material. Writers generally quote when the exact wording is important. Quotations must always be surrounded by quotation marks, even if you're quoting only a single word. As a rule of thumb, keep direct quotations to a minimum and use more paraphrasing and summarizing.

**Paraphrasing**: Paraphrasing occurs when you substitute your own words for the words used in others' unique material. Writers paraphrase when they want to avoid quoting the original material word for word yet convey the same meaning of the original work. While paraphrases do not need to be surrounded by quotation marks, you still need to document paraphrases so readers know the material comes from an outside source.

### Table 9.1 Three Ways to Integrate Outside Material

| Type | Quotation marks? | Need citation? |
|---|---|---|
| **Quote** <br> *You quote when you use exact words, sentences, and phrases from others' unique material.* | ✓ | ✓ |
| **Paraphrase** <br> *Paraphrases occur when you substitute your own words for the words used in others' unique material.* | ✗ | ✓ |
| **Summary** <br> *Summaries occur when you condense a larger amount of material into its main points.* | ✗ | ✓ |

**Summarizing:** Summarizing occurs when you condense a larger amount of material into its main points. Writers summarize when they want to highlight general ideas or main points, leaving out unnecessary detail. As with paraphrases, summaries do not need quotation marks, but they must be documented so readers know the material comes from another source.

The following examples illustrate the differences between quotations, paraphrases, and summaries (taken from Diana Middleton, "Students Struggle for Words," *Wall Street Journal* [March 3, 2011]: http://on.wsj.com/1w64vtV).

**Quote:**       "While M.B.A. students' quantitative skills are prized by employers, their writing and presentation skills have been a perennial complaint. Employers and writing coaches say business-school graduates tend to ramble, use pretentious vocabulary or pen too-casual emails."

**Paraphrase:**   M.B.A. students' quantitative skills are valued by employers, but the employers say the students' writing and presentation skills are lacking—they ramble, use flowery vocabulary, and write overly informal emails.

**Summary:**     Employers compliment M.B.A. students on their quantitative skills but complain about their writing and speaking skills.

These three integration techniques may be used both individually and in combination with each other. For example, you may summarize a paragraph and quote a few exact words within your summary. Good writers use all three techniques while ensuring that their writing flows coherently and cohesively. For examples of quotes, paraphrases, and summaries, see the example papers at the end of this chapter (Figures 9.11–9.14).

Although this section has stressed the importance of documenting outside material, some information from outside sources does not need to be documented. For instance, information that is considered to be common knowledge does not have to be attributed to anyone. For instance, you could state without documentation that cancer is a major health problem in the United States, because that is common knowledge. But if you state that a study conducted in 2011 found a 15 percent increase in a certain type of cancer, you would have to cite the source of that unique information. If you are ever unsure whether outside information needs to be documented, choose to document just to protect yourself.

## How to Document

Documentation generally consists of two parts: (1) informing your audience with an in-text notation whenever you reference other people's information and (2) providing detailed information about where the original information can be found. The in-text notation serves as a pointer to the more detailed information located in footnotes, endnotes, or a bibliography or reference page.

To standardize the process of documentation, different organizations and groups have developed documentation styles. For example, styles that are widely used by business writers and authors in the social sciences are APA (from the American Psychological Association), MLA (from the Modern Language Association), and Chicago (from the University of Chicago Press). These style guidelines are compiled into hard-copy style guides that writers can use for properly documenting newspaper articles, journal articles, websites, books, and other sources. Additionally, you can find the details of these style guides on your library's website or on the internet by searching for "APA style," "MLA style," "Chicago Style," or simply "style guides." Some databases even include tools that generate citations in the different styles. These auto-generated citations sometimes include errors, but they can greatly speed up your documentation process.

All three documentation styles provide guidelines for in-text citations, meaning that within the body text you insert a brief documentation reference. Then at the end of the document, you provide a complete alphabetized list of all the references. For APA and Chicago, the in-text citations should include the author's last name, year of publication, and page numbers as appropriate. For MLA, the in-text citations should include the author's last name and page reference as appropriate.

*Figure 9.5 Consult print or digital style guides to ensure that your documentation style is appropriate and consistent.*

In addition to the three APA, MLA, and Chicago in-text citation styles, Chicago provides an alternate form—the documentary-note style—that uses footnotes or endnotes. This style includes two parts: numbered superscripts (such as [3]) in the body text and corresponding footnotes (at the bottom of the pages) or endnotes (at the end of the entire document) listed in the sequence in which they occur in the body. For your reference, example articles using these four styles are found at the end of this chapter. (To save space, some conventional vertical spacing standards have not been followed.)

Organizations you work for may have their own style guide, or they may use APA, MLA, or another style guide, such as the AMA Manual of Style published for the medical field. If your organization does not use a specific style guide, just choose a style guide that you like best, and apply it to your work. Regardless of the style you choose for a document, be familiar with that style's guidelines and apply them consistently. Don't let your lack of familiarity with a style guide keep you from documenting! If necessary, you can even develop your own style guide, so long as it complies with the legal requirements of documentation law.

While integrating other people's work and related documentation into your writing, you must still keep a coherent and cohesive flow. Here are three steps that can help you: introduce, insert, and interpret.

1. **Introduce**. When you use the work of others, introduce it. For example, you could state, "In her article on stock portfolios, Smith emphasizes . . ."

2. **Insert**. After introducing outside material, integrate it into your writing using quotes, paraphrases, or summaries. Also, insert appropriate documentation notations both in the text and in the references or bibliography section.

   For notations in the text, place the author and date in parentheses, such as (Smith 20XX). Or include a superscript that refers to a footnote or endnote, such as Smith.[1] (Notice that in the first instance the period comes after the notation, whereas in the second the period comes before.) These signals point to the detailed source information in the references or bibliography section.

   The references or bibliography section includes one entry for each source you reference and is usually located at the end of your material. Each entry gives specific information about the author, title, dates, and other publishing information so the reader can find the original material if needed. When using Chicago documentary-note style, footnotes or endnotes may be adequate without a separate bibliography section.

3. **Interpret**. Clearly indicate the key point you are trying to make with the cited information, such as the following: "Smith's research helps illustrate the seriousness of obesity in our country." An option is to include the interpretation as part of the introduction: "In her article on stock portfolios, Smith (20XX) emphasizes the importance of diversification."

Not all references will fit neatly into the rules of the different documentation styles. Thus, as needed, make appropriate adaptations, applying the spirit of documentation law—give appropriate credit and clearly define the location of the material so the reader can find it.

# PRIMARY RESEARCH

As mentioned previously, primary research involves gathering original data, sometimes using questionnaires, check lists, or interviews, and sometimes using observational research or experimental research methods. Primary research includes three phases: designing the research, gathering data, and analyzing data. This section provides helpful guidelines for each phase. Modify the guidelines as appropriate for the various projects you undertake.

## Designing the Research

Gathering original data can be expensive in both money and time, so carefully designing your research can increase the likelihood that you will receive a good return on your investment. While the work required to design research seems daunting, all it takes is one failed data collection experience for a researcher to realize the importance of investing time upfront to carefully design and plan research. Consider the following guidelines as you design your primary research.

To begin, clearly define your research goals and objectives. Think carefully about what you want to research (e.g., employee dissatisfaction or product defects), and then in a clear, concise statement, write down what problem you are trying to solve or what objective you are trying to accomplish (e.g., determine how employee satisfaction varies by office location). Use this statement as a guide throughout the research process.

Next, review relevant secondary research to determine what others have to say about your research goals and objectives. Through this learning process, you may find existing data that causes you to adjust the scope of your research, or you may find examples of methods that will help you with the next step.

Then, identify the best method for accomplishing your research objective. Among others, you have a number of methods options: interview, focus group, survey, observation, or experimental. Here are some details regarding these methods:

**Interview**: Interviews enable a researcher to gather in-depth, individual perspectives related to a research objective. With that objective in mind, researchers hold structured, semi-structured, or unstructured interviews. In structured interviews, the researcher creates a set of interview questions (an interview protocol) and asks the same questions with little or no deviation to all participants. In semi-structured interviews, a researcher uses an interview protocol, but has more flexibility to ask additional questions that build off of participants' responses. In unstructured interviews, researchers do not follow an interview protocol, but instead let the research objective and the participants' responses guide the questions. Researchers complete interviews either face to face or over the telephone. For example, a manager might hold face-to-face interviews with all employees to determine employee perspectives on morale issues.

**Focus Group**: Focus groups leverage the power of an individual interview and expand it to a group setting, enabling the researcher to gather a large quantity of data in a short amount of time. The researcher gathers a small group of people (6 to 10 individuals) with some common characteristic (e.g., users of a certain product). The researcher acts as moderator and guides the focus group through a series of questions. For each question, the researcher seeks to elicit multiple responses and perspectives from the group. Researchers may organize multiple focus groups to gain insight from more people, but they traditionally hold no more when they stop

*Figure 9.6 Focus groups are assembled to conduct qualitative research about a product or idea.*

hearing unique answers. In a business setting, a marketing team might organize focus groups in a geographic area where the company is planning to roll out a new product; the focus group could provide insight into the perceptions and needs of consumers, enabling the team to assess demand for the product and to develop appropriate marketing materials.

**Survey**: Surveys enable a researcher to gather a potentially large quantity of data to either understand the current status of a population or to explore possible causal relationships between participants' motives and their outcomes. Researchers generally create a questionnaire to mail or email to participants, resulting in standardized answers that can streamline data analysis. In a business setting, a retail-store owner might provide a questionnaire to all customers in order to assess their satisfaction with store employees' level of service.

**Observation**: Observation provides opportunities for researchers to explore behavior within a natural setting. Researchers may observe distantly or may even immerse themselves into the setting. Regardless, the researcher seeks to systematically record behavior in order to achieve the research objective. For example, a small-business owner might count shoppers passing by two potential locations in a mall before deciding which location to lease. Additionally, a sales manager might observe shoppers searching for merchandise in order to more effectively design displays.

**Experimental**: Experiments enable researchers to establish causal relationships between some treatment and an observed outcome. For example, a manager wants to find out whether holding regular performance reviews (treatment) increases team performance (outcome). Researchers establish these causal relationships through various ways: controlling influences outside the treatment that might affect the outcome, comparing the outcomes of groups that receive the treatment (treatment group) and those that do not (control group), randomly assigning participants to both groups, and measuring the outcome in the groups both before the treatment is given and after.

As you consider various methods, always maintain high research standards. Whatever method you use, you must achieve two major standards with your research:

**Validity**. The first research standard is validity; that is, research must measure what it purports to measure. For example, if you are trying to determine whether

an adverse environmental problem in a community is causing cancer, your research must effectively measure environmental problems and cancer rates in the community. Valid research provides truth about the research problem, and its conclusions are based on solid facts and findings. Validity is the highest research standard, and no compromise should be tolerated. Research that is not valid fails at the most basic level and should be disregarded.

**Reliability.** The second standard of research is reliability; that is, research must be repeatable with consistent results. For example, if you conduct research about the viability of a software product in a given marketplace, a subsequent study should yield the same findings as the first. Also, a medical study that finds a correlation between eating disorders and self-esteem should produce the same findings in a subsequent study.

After you select your method, identify the population for your study. For instance, a study of customer satisfaction might include all the citizens living in the city in which a particular store is located. Also, an audit might include all the transactions of a company during the last calendar year.

As you consider your population, always follow appropriate ethical guidelines, especially if you will be collecting data from human subjects. Some guidelines pertain to individuals' decisions and freedom to act, seeking to protect those with diminished decision-making capacity, protecting individuals from harm, maximizing benefits to individuals, and seeking to justly and equally share the costs and benefits of the research (National Commission 1979).

Further, determine whether you can access and analyze the entire population or whether sampling will be required. If sampling is required, consult a reputable statistician, statistics book, or statistics-related website to assist you in determining the needed sample size and in drawing the sample. Three sampling strategies are included here:

**Random**: From a list of the entire population, randomly draw the needed sample of participants.

**Stratified Random**: From a list of the entire population, randomly draw the needed sample, making sure that the sample represents the total population according to certain factors, such as gender, income level, or geographical area. For example, if 20 percent of the population is over 65 years of age, make sure that 20 percent of the sample is over 65 years of age.

**Systematic Random**: From a numbered list of the entire population, randomly draw the first participant and then draw every $n$th sample participant after that until the needed sample size is achieved. For example, if you have a population of 5,000 and you need a sample size of 500, randomly draw a number from 1 to 10. If 7 is chosen, thereafter select number 17, 27, 37, 47, etc. to achieve the goal of 500 participants.

Next, create your data-gathering instrument. Your data-gathering instrument is the tool you use to capture the data created in your primary research. While instruments can take many forms, common instruments include questionnaires, work logs, interview protocols, field notes, or codebooks. This guideline provides examples specific to questionnaires.

Questions on your questionnaire can be constructed in at least seven different formats.

1.  **Closed**: Ask for factual information.

    How many complaints have you received during the past month?
    ○ 0
    ○ 1-5
    ○ 6-10
    ○ Over 10

2.  **Either/Or**: Force respondent to choose one of two options.

    Which of these two sources would you use to purchase a new computer?
    ○ Buy online
    ○ Purchase locally

3.  **Restricted multiple choice**: Choose one of several options.

    Which of the following applies to you? (Choose only one.)
    ○ I feel unhappy in my present job.
    ○ I am generally satisfied with my present job.
    ○ I am excited about my present job.

4.  **Unrestricted multiple choice**: Choose all that apply.

    Which of the following software packages do you use? (Check all that apply.)
    ☐ Word
    ☐ Excel
    ☐ PowerPoint
    ☐ Publisher
    ☐ Other: _____

5.  **Ranking:** Rank each option from high to low. No two items may receive the same ranking.

    Rank the following printer models according to your preference (1 = highest):

    |  | 1 | 2 | 3 |
    |---|---|---|---|
    | ColorPro I | ○ | ○ | ○ |
    | PrintMaster | ○ | ○ | ○ |
    | LaserLine 320 | ○ | ○ | ○ |

6. **Rating**: Evaluate all options on a numeric or semantic differential scale. Different options may receive the same rating. Rating is generally preferred to ranking for three reasons: (1) Ranking is a difficult process; (2) ranking does not allow respondents to give two options the same value, even though the respondent might feel the same about them; and (3) a ranking can be derived from a rating-type question, simply by averaging all the respondents' ratings and sorting them from high to low.

7. **Open**: Ask a question that allows the respondents to pursue whatever avenue of response they desire.

> How do you feel about the new health coverage program offered by our firm?

As you develop questionnaires, apply these additional guidelines to improve your results:

- Give your instrument a clear title and clear instructions (answer all the 5W2H questions). Give examples as needed for clarification.

- Ensure anonymity and confidentiality wherever possible. As appropriate, indicate, "Your identity will not be tied to your answers in any way," or "All information you provide will be kept strictly confidential."

- Keep the main objectives of your questionnaire in mind. Make sure that each question helps you achieve those objectives, and eliminate questions that seek unrelated or unnecessary information.

- Keep the instrument short and simple. If using paper, restrict the questionnaire to one page, front and back. Similarly, if administering a questionnaire online, keep required scrolling and advancing to new pages to a minimum. Regardless of the medium, recognize that long questionnaires discourage people from responding.

- Organize the questions, grouping related questions into the same section of the questionnaire.

- Make questions as easy to answer as possible. For

example, ask for a check mark rather than a complete sentence. Use the same type of question-and-answer format for as many questions as possible, such as a series of multiple-choice questions (a, b, c, d) rather than a combination of multiple-choice, true-false, and fill-in-the-blank.

- Offer some incentive to respond, if necessary and appropriate. Consider giving a small financial reward, a copy of the survey results, or a small gift.

Finally, pilot test your data-gathering instrument with several members of the population being studied. During the pilot test, gather feedback regarding question clarity and length of time required to complete the survey. Use this feedback to polish your instrument and to ensure that you obtain the information you are seeking.

## Gathering the Data

Once you have designed your research, you are ready to collect data. Depending on your method, you may have only one opportunity to gather your data from a particular participant or group of participants, so make sure you arrive early and are well prepared. Make copies, gather necessary equipment, and otherwise prepare well before your data collection is set to begin. Here are a few additional guidelines to keep in mind as you do so.

**Create a script.** To increase the consistency of your data collection, use your research design to create a script to follow as you collect your data. This detailed script could include the step-by-step process you will follow as you interact with participants or otherwise collect your primary data. Scripts serve especially useful functions if you will be collecting data on multiple occasions.

**Ensure that all electronic instruments work properly.** If you will be recording voice or video for interviews or focus groups, ensure that all recording devices are charged and have adequate free storage space. For online questionnaires, ensure that any survey links you will be emailing your population are activated and accessible.

**Follow up appropriately.** Send second or third follow-up communication to get a high response rate. For example, send out a follow-up questionnaire two to three weeks after the initial mailing or email. Similarly, follow up with customers or other participants who agreed to be interviewed, but who have not yet communicated convenient times for them.

*Figure 9.7 Take careful notes throughout your research process to capture important data.*

**Take detailed notes.** The human mind can quickly forget details, so take careful notes about any data that seem important. Remember that you can always discard captured data, but you may never be able to recapture data once you leave a research site or a participant walks out the door.

As you gather your data, take time to reflect on any patterns you are seeing in the data. Reflection is often the first form of data analysis that you complete.

## Analyzing the Data

Many researchers find data analysis the most exciting part of primary research. Through analysis, you achieve the objective or answer the question that first prompted your research design and data collection. Let that objective or question guide your analysis, ensuring that you use correct procedures for analyzing your data. If necessary, consult a reputable researcher, research methods handbook, or relevant website for help with this task. To get started with your analysis, consider these guidelines:

**Standardize your data.** Data can be measured, reported, and stored electronically in many ways, and standardizing your data can make your data analysis much easier. For example, you may need to change a company's quarterly stock price data to annual data in order to make meaningful comparisons with other companies' annual data in your sample. Additionally, you may discover missing or otherwise invalid data, and you will need to choose whether to omit it or fill it in based on trends in the data. Also note that some computer programs you use for your data analysis might require your data to be stored in a particular format; consequently, you may need to change your data

from one storage format (e.g., spreadsheet format) to another (e.g., tab-delimited text format). Take time to get to know your data and standardize it where possible.

**Understand the context of your data.** Data is an abstraction of the real world, and increasing your understanding of what the data actually symbolizes can greatly enhance your ability to analyze it. For example, if you sampled bank teller transactions and noticed a spike in deposits at a certain time each month, you could make much better conclusions about the data by visiting the bank on that day next month, observing customers, and then questioning tellers about the pattern you're seeing in the data. Understanding the context of your data helps you infuse meaning into your analysis.

**Understand your data types.** Much data can be broadly classified as numerical, grouped numerical, and textual. Numerical data might include measures for salary, number of product defects, or customer satisfaction ratings. Numerical data can also be broken down into groups or categories, such as data from part-time versus full-time employees. Textual data might include open-ended responses to questions or transcripts of interviews. Your type of data will influence the way you analyze it.

**Calculate descriptive statistics.** To gain a big-picture view of your numerical data, calculate descriptive statistics as appropriate, including statistics of central tendency (mean, median, mode), frequency (mode), dispersion (range, variance, and standard deviation), and shape (skewness and kurtosis). Note that wildly different data can produce similar descriptive statistics (see Figure 9.8), so don't forget to visualize your data in addition to calculating statistics.

**Visualize your data.** Graphically chart out your numerical data, paying attention to trends, correlations, or outlying data (see Chapter 4 for more information about graphics). For textual data, consider creating word-frequency charts (see Figure 9.9) or word clouds (see Figure 9.10) that emphasize recurring words and textual themes. These patterns and themes alert you to areas for further analysis and help you draw conclusions from the data. Visuals also provide an effective and efficient way to communicate your research to others, condensing large quantities of data into more accessible and refined formats than raw numbers or text.

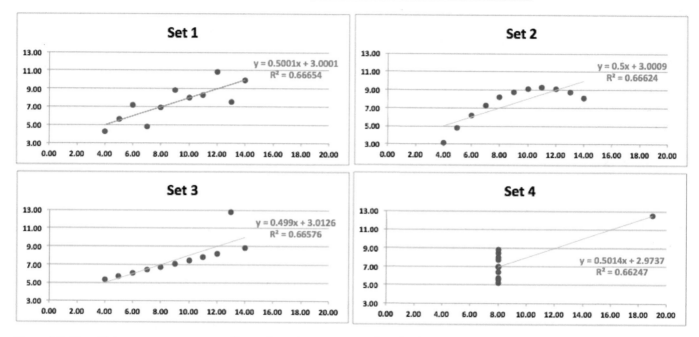

| Datasets | | | | | | | |
|---|---|---|---|---|---|---|---|
| Set 1 | | Set 2 | | Set 3 | | Set 4 | |
| X | Y | X | Y | X | Y | X | Y |
| 10.00 | 8.04 | 10.00 | 9.14 | 10.00 | 7.46 | 8.00 | 6.36 |
| 8.00 | 6.95 | 8.00 | 8.14 | 8.00 | 6.77 | 8.00 | 5.76 |
| 13.00 | 7.58 | 13.00 | 8.74 | 13.00 | 12.74 | 8.00 | 7.71 |
| 9.00 | 8.81 | 9.00 | 8.77 | 9.00 | 7.11 | 8.00 | 8.84 |
| 11.00 | 8.33 | 11.00 | 9.26 | 11.00 | 7.81 | 8.00 | 8.47 |
| 14.00 | 9.96 | 14.00 | 8.10 | 14.00 | 8.84 | 8.00 | 7.04 |
| 6.00 | 7.24 | 6.00 | 6.13 | 6.00 | 6.08 | 8.00 | 5.25 |
| 4.00 | 4.26 | 4.00 | 3.10 | 4.00 | 5.39 | 19.00 | 12.50 |
| 12.00 | 10.84 | 12.00 | 9.13 | 12.00 | 8.15 | 8.00 | 5.56 |
| 7.00 | 4.82 | 7.00 | 7.26 | 7.00 | 6.46 | 8.00 | 7.97 |
| 5.00 | 5.68 | 5.00 | 4.74 | 5.00 | 5.73 | 8.00 | 6.89 |
| Mean | | | | | | | |
| 9.00 | 7.50 | 9.00 | 7.50 | 9.00 | 7.50 | 9.00 | 7.49 |
| Standard Deviation | | | | | | | |
| 3.32 | 2.03 | 3.32 | 2.03 | 3.32 | 2.03 | 3.32 | 2.04 |

*Figure 9.8  Even if datasets appear statistically similar, take time to visualize the data to see trends, correlations, or outlying data. Source: Data from F.J. Anscombe, "Graphics in Statistical Analysis," The American Statistician 27, no. 1 (1973): 17–21.*

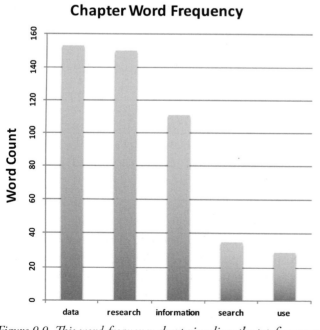

*Figure 9.9  This word-frequency chart visualizes the top five recurring words in this chapter, after removing common words.*

*Figure 9.10  This word cloud visualizes this chapter's text. Because size correlates with frequency, you can sense the themes in the text.*

**Explore differences and similarities.** When your numerical data includes groups, create and compare visualizations and descriptive statistics for each group. You can also run statistical tests to determine differences or similarities in grouped numerical data, including a $t$-test for two groups, an analysis of variance (ANOVA) for three or more groups, and a chi-squared test of independence for two numerical variables broken into groups (e.g., full-time employees satisfied with work, full-time employees not satisfied with work, part-time employees satisfied with work, and part-time employees not satisfied with work). Consult a statistician, statistics book, or statistics-related website for help with these procedures.

**Explore relationships.** To explore relationships between numerical data, visualize and compare the data in a scatterplot or other graphical form. To statistically examine relationships, you can run a Pearson product-moment correlation. If you are interested in prediction, consider looking into various forms of linear regression.

**Explore themes.** One effective way to explore textual data is to analyze themes. To analyze the data, take time to read and become familiar with what is written. As you continue to review the data, note recurring ideas or keywords that you see in the text. Once these recurring themes seem representative of the text as a whole, write them down to create a formal codebook that you can reference. Then review the data again, this time flagging (or coding) examples of themes by copying and pasting examples in a separate document, by color coding or highlighting examples, or by making notes in the margins of the text.

**Analyze content.** Similar to thematic analysis, content analysis enables you to analyze textual data in a meaningful way. To create a codebook, you inductively create coding themes after reviewing the data (similar to thematic analysis), or prior to reviewing the data you deductively create codes based on prior experience, previous research, or the research objective itself. Once your codes are set, you then classify the data based on the presence or absence of the code, analyzing code frequencies. Generally, you should also have at least two researchers code the data, enabling you to calculate an inter-coder reliability score, such as Krippendorf's alpha or Cohen's kappa.

As an illustration of content analysis, imagine that as a product manager, you have noticed numerous cus-

tomer reviews that mention the battery life of your product. After releasing an updated product, you and a colleague classify a sample of customer reviews using two codes you deductively created: "mentions battery life negatively" and "mentions battery life positively." Hopefully, you discover more positive mentions of battery life associated with the new product than with the old!

As you analyze your data, be as objective as possible, ensuring that your methods and analysis adhere to commonly accepted research practices. Biased results occur for many reasons, including sampling improperly, dismissing unexpected results, and analyzing data incorrectly. Avoid common statistical fallacies, such as confusing correlation with causation, mistaking one-time or short-term measures for repeated or long-term patterns, or generalizing findings to all groups within the data. Also, avoid the temptation to embellish the facts or to hide disappointing results.

Finally, after you complete your primary or secondary research, compose a report that clearly describes your research process and communicates the research results. Chapter 10 provides different report formats that you may follow. To make this reporting process easier, write the report during each phase of your research—in other words, write in real time. For example, as you design your research, write out your research objectives, detail your methods, and describe your sampling strategy. Writing as you go will also help you clarify your thinking and provide complete and accurate records that can substantiate claims challenged later on.

## CHAPTER SUMMARY

Secondary and primary research constitute the two main types of research conducted in business. Secondary research involves reviewing information that has already been published, such as books, journals, and magazines. When conducting electronic information searches, you need to know about Boolean operators, which help narrow your searches.

When quoting, paraphrasing, or summarizing the unique work of other people, you are required by law to document—to indicate the source of the original work. To standardize the process of documentation, different organizations and groups have developed documentation styles. Three common styles are APA, MLA, and Chicago.

Primary research involves gathering original data, using interviews, focus groups, or questionnaires. It can also

involve observational research and conducting experiments, with control and treatment groups. Three phases of primary research include designing the research, gathering the data, and analyzing the data.

Designing research involves setting a research objective, reviewing relevant secondary research, choosing an appropriate method, following ethical guidelines, and creating a data-gathering instrument. When conducting research, you must achieve two major standards—validity and reliability. Often you will be required to sample a population, because contacting everyone in the population would be too expensive and take too long. Use your data-gathering instrument to gather your data, and follow up with your research population to achieve a high response rate.

After you gather your data, use appropriate procedures to analyze it. You may need to standardize your data in order to make meaningful comparisons or to analyze it with an appropriate computer program. Take time to understand what your data means, and find out what data types you will be analyzing. These data types can influence the procedures you use to analyze your data for differences, similarities, relationships, and themes.

## Works Cited

National Commission for the Protection of Human Subjects of Biomedical and Behavioral Research. "The Belmont Report." *U.S. Department of Health & Human Services*, (April 18, 1979): http://www.hhs.gov/ohrp/humansubjects/guidance/belmont.html.

## CHAPTER QUESTIONS

1.  What is the difference between primary and secondary research?

2.  List two strategies that can help you determine a secondary research topic.

3.  What factors should you consider when evaluating the quality of a website or other source of information?

4.  What are the three main Boolean operators, and what effect can each have on your searches?

5.  When searching for information, what is the tradeoff between quantity of results and their relevance?

6.  What is plagiarism? Why is documentation important when you quote, paraphrase, or summarize other writers' work?

7.  What are the main differences between the two types of Chicago-style documentation?

8.  What is the difference between validity and reliability? Which is more important?

9.  List five types of research methods.

10. What are the three types of interviews?

11. Describe the three main types of random sampling.

12. What is an unrestricted multiple-choice question?

13. What are the disadvantages of ranking questions?

14. What are the advantages of rating questions?

15. List four ways to improve the response rate of a questionnaire.

16. Discuss three guidelines to follow when gathering primary data.

17. Describe two procedures for analyzing numerical primary data.

18. Describe one procedure for analyzing textual primary data.

## CHAPTER ACTIVITIES

1.  Design a research project to investigate some local problem, such as parking on campus, cost of textbooks, traffic congestion, or campus security and safety. First, find out all you can about the problem using secondary sources. Then, gather additional data using an appropriate method. For example, using Google Docs or other survey software, create and send a questionnaire to fellow students. Finally, analyze and report the results, including in your report two or three graphs that visualize your data.

2.  Download an interesting dataset from the internet, such as a dataset from www.data.gov. Find out all you can about the context of your data and the type of data you downloaded. As appropriate, calculate descriptive statistics for your data. Then, visualize your data, exploring differences, similarities, and relationships within the data set. Write a brief memo reviewing what you found.

3.  Find a Twitter or Facebook page for a company of interest. Gather two samples of tweets or posts: one sample that includes text posted by the company, and the other sample that includes text posted by the company's customers. Explore the two samples for themes, create a codebook for each sample, and formally code each sample. Compare and report the themes you discovered.

4.  Write an academic proposal for your instructor. Clearly explain your topic and conduct a preliminary search for related articles using electronic databases such as EBSCO and ProQuest. Attach or include a

list of at least five articles that will most likely provide the information you need.

5. Conduct a secondary research study of a current business topic related to your professional field. Gather your data from the most current sources (e.g., within the last two years). Create an outline and test it using the structure tests for outlines explained in Chapter 2. As directed by your instructor, create a references page, works-cited page, or bibliography according to APA, MLA, or Chicago documentation style.

6. Conduct secondary research on a business topic of interest. Create a bottom-up outline as described in Chapter 2. For your free list, gather quotes, paraphrases, and summaries from a number of secondary sources. Be sure to appropriately document where you obtained the information. Then, categorize the information by grouping related quotes, paraphrases, and summaries from your free list. Finally, arrange your categories into an appropriate sequence.

7. Using the information you obtained from Chapter Activity 6, write a 2,000–2,500 word article for a business magazine or journal. Using APA, MLA, or Chicago standards, document all of your quotes, paraphrases, and summaries.

**Good News for Bad News**

On six occasions in only four years, three different Yahoo! CEOs faced the unpleasant task of communicating mass layoffs to employees (Associated Press, 2012). Negative consequences of the bad news included decreased employee morale (Efrati, 2011), criticism from investors (Henn, 2012), and mixed responses in stock price (Letzing, 2012; Vascellaro, 2012).

Difficult situations like this are not uncommon—from announcing layoffs to reporting disappointing earnings, most managers occasionally have to deliver bad news. While managers may not be able to prevent all the negative consequences of bad news, an appropriate direct or indirect approach may help.

*Appropriate Approach*

When managers write a message, they follow either a direct or an indirect approach. As one textbook author states, with a direct approach the writer presents the major idea of a message first and then presents supporting ideas. An indirect approach is just the opposite—the writer presents the supporting points first, followed by the central idea (Baker, 2011, p. 24). In the context of bad news, the central idea is the actual bad news, and the supporting points are the reasoning that led to the bad news.

When composing bad-news messages, Baker (2011) suggests that when "conveying bad news . . . consider using an indirect order" (p. 67). Because bad news is often unexpected, an indirect approach helps readers to understand the reasons behind the news before receiving the bad news itself. When managers sense that their audience is not "prepared to receive the message," they should consider an indirect approach (Baker, 2011, p. 24), which has been found to be more persuasive than a direct approach (Frischknect & Baker, 2011). If the bad news is "routine," however, managers may use a direct approach (Baker, 2011, p. 68). Thus, depending on the readiness of the audience, managers should vary their approach.

*Dampened Consequences*

When managers must convey bad news to wide and diverse audiences, they don't have the luxury of customizing a direct or indirect approach for each recipient. Researchers have tried to determine which approach leads general audiences to receive bad news and still favorably view the messenger and the messenger's company. In her experiment with credit-refusal letters, Locker (1999) found that giving a brief explanation before bad news increased readers' acceptance of bad news, but it did not impact how favorably readers viewed the writer. In a later experimental study, Jansen and Janssen (2011) modified Locker's methodology and found that readers not only accepted bad news slightly better with indirect messages, but also viewed the messenger and the messenger's company slightly more favorably.

One scholar has argued against the indirect approach, but his concern seems to focus more on content than on approach. His criticism of using a buffer before giving bad news targets buffers that are unrelated to the bad news (Brent, 1985, p. 6); however, he states that he can "tolerate some delay" when the initial supporting points are related to the main idea and when the indirect structure is appropriate for the message and circumstances (Brent, 1985, p. 8). Given that his criticism focuses on unrelated buffers and not on the indirect approach itself, the prevailing philosophy seems to be the best approach—when conveying bad news to a varied audience, managers' best option is to use the indirect approach.

*Conclusion*

Internal memos from Yahoo! show that when informing employees of pending layoffs, CEOs used both indirect and direct approaches (Carlson, 2008; Swisher, 2012). While we may never know the exact circumstances that led the CEOs to use the different approaches, we do know that the approach used may have made a difference in how employees and stockholders accepted the bad news and subsequently viewed the CEOs and the company. When placed in similar circumstances where bad news must be communicated, managers should consider using an indirect approach to bring about the most positive consequences.

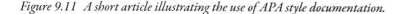

*Figure 9.11  A short article illustrating the use of APA style documentation.*

References

Associated Press. (2012, April 4). Job cuts at Yahoo: 6 rounds of layoffs in 4 years. Retrieved from http://finance.yahoo.com/news/job-cuts-yahoo-6-rounds-181252551.html

Baker, W. (2011). *Writing and speaking for business* (2nd ed.). Provo, UT: BYU Academic Publishing.

Brent, D. (1985). Indirect structure and reader response. *Journal of Business Communication, 22*(2), 5-8. Retrieved from https://www.lib.byu.edu/cgi-bin/remoteauth.pl?url=http://search .ebscohost.com/login.aspx?direct=true&db=ufh&AN=5777777&site=ehost-live&scope=site

Carlson, N. (2008, October 21). Jerry Yang's layoff memo. *BusinessInsider.com.* Retrieved from http://articles.businessinsider.com/2008-10-21/tech/30101126_1_earnings-release-long-term -employees

Efrati, A. (2011, December 5). Yahoo battles brain drain–Internet company braces for wave of exits after holidays. *Wall Street Journal.* Retrieved from http://www.wsj.com

Frischknecht, S. & Baker, W. (2011, October). Enhanced vs. undifferentiated text: A study to assess the effects on readers. In L. Gueldenzoph Snyder (Ed.), *Proceedings of the 76th Annual Convention.* Paper presented at the Association for Business Communication, Montreal, Quebec, Canada. Retrieved from http://businesscommunication.org/conventions/abc-convention -proceedings/2011-annual-convention-proceedings/

Henn, Steve. (Speaker). (2012, April 4). Latest round of Yahoo layoffs the most severe. *NPR: All Things Considered.* [Radio] Steve Henn. NPR.

Jansen, F. & Janssen, D. (2011). Explanations first: A case for presenting explanations before the decision in Dutch bad-news messages. *Journal of Business and Technical Communication 25*(1), 36-67. doi: 10.1177/1050651910380372

Letzing, J. & Efrati. A. (2012, April 4). Yahoo pushes reset. *Wall Street Journal.* Retrieved from http://www.wsj.com

Locker, K. (1999). Factors in reader responses to negative letters. *Journal of Business and Technical Communication 13*(1), 5-48. doi: 10.1177/105065199901300101

Swisher, K. (2010, December 15). Here's Carol Bartz's internal layoff memo to beleagered Yahoo troops. Retrieved from http://allthingsd.com/20101215/heres-carol-bartzs-internal-layoff-memo-to -beleaguered-yahoo-troops/

Vascellaro, J. (2012, February 27). Bartz remakes Yahoo's top ranks. *Wall Street Journal.* Retrieved from http://www.wsj.com

*Figure 9.11 continued.*

**Good News for Bad News**

On six occasions in only four years, three different Yahoo! CEOs faced the unpleasant task of communicating mass layoffs to employees (Associated Press). Negative consequences of the bad news included decreased employee morale (Efrati), criticism from investors ("Latest"), and mixed responses in stock price (Letzing; Vascellaro).

Difficult situations like this are not uncommon—from announcing layoffs to reporting disappointing earnings, most managers occasionally have to deliver bad news. While managers may not be able to prevent all the negative consequences of bad news, an appropriate direct or indirect approach may help.

*Appropriate Approach*

When managers write a message, they follow either a direct or an indirect approach. As one textbook author states, with a direct approach the writer presents the major idea of a message first and then presents supporting ideas. An indirect approach is just the opposite—the writer presents the supporting points first, followed by the central idea (Baker 24). In the context of bad news, the central idea is the actual bad news, and the supporting points are the reasoning that led to the bad news.

When composing bad-news messages, Baker suggests that when "conveying bad news . . . consider using an indirect order . . ." (67). Because bad news is often unexpected, an indirect approach helps readers to understand the reasons behind the news before receiving the bad news itself. When managers sense that their audience is not "prepared to receive the message," they should consider an indirect approach (Baker 24), which has been found to be more persuasive than a direct approach (Frischknecht and Baker). If the bad news is "routine," however, managers may use a direct approach (Baker 68). Thus, depending on the readiness of the audience, managers should vary their approach.

*Dampened Consequences*

When managers must convey bad news to wide and diverse audiences, they don't have the luxury of customizing a direct or indirect approach for each recipient. Researchers have tried to determine which approach leads general audiences to receive bad news and still favorably view the messenger and the messenger's company. In her experiment with credit-refusal letters, Locker found that giving a brief explanation before bad news increased readers' acceptance of bad news, but it did not impact how favorably readers viewed the writer. In a later experimental study, Jansen and Janssen modified Locker's methodology and found that readers not only accepted bad news slightly better with indirect messages, but also viewed the messenger and the messenger's company slightly more favorably.

One scholar has argued against the indirect approach, but his concern seems to focus more on content than on approach. His criticism of using a buffer before giving bad news targets buffers that are unrelated to the bad news (Brent 6); however, he states that he can "tolerate some delay" when the initial supporting points are related to the main idea and when the indirect structure is appropriate for the message and circumstances (Brent 8). Given that his criticism focuses on unrelated buffers and not on the indirect approach itself, the prevailing philosophy seems to be the best approach—when conveying bad news to a varied audience, managers' best option is to use the indirect approach.

*Conclusion*

Internal memos from Yahoo! show that when informing employees of pending layoffs, CEOs used both indirect and direct approaches (Carlson; Swisher). While we may never know the exact circumstances that led the CEOs to use the different approaches, we do know that the approach used may have made a difference in how employees and stockholders accepted the bad news and subsequently viewed the CEOs and the company. When placed in similar circumstances where bad news must be communicated, managers should consider using an indirect approach to bring about the most positive consequences.

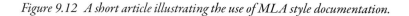

*Figure 9.12  A short article illustrating the use of MLA style documentation.*

Works Cited

Associated Press. "Job Cuts at Yahoo: 6 Rounds of Layoffs in 4 Years." *Yahoo! Finance.* Yahoo! Inc., 4 Apr. 2012. Web. 19 Mar. 2016.

Baker, William H. *Writing and Speaking for Business.* 2nd ed. Provo, UT: BYU Academic Publishing, 2011. Print.

Brent, Douglas. "Indirect Structure and Reader Response." *Journal of Business Communication* 22.2 (1985): 5–8. *EBSCO.* Web. 15 Aug. 2012.

Carlson, Nicholas. "Jerry Yang's Layoff Memo." *Business Insider.* Business Insider, 21 Oct. 2008. Web. 15 Aug. 2012.

Efrati, Amir. "Yahoo Battles Brain Drain—Internet Company Braces for Wave of Exits after Holidays." *Wall Street Journal.* Wall Street Journal, 5 Dec. 2011. Web. 15 Aug. 2012.

Frischknecht, Sierra Sloan, and William H. Baker. "Enhanced vs. Undifferentiated Text: A Study to Assess the Effects on Readers." *Proceedings from the 76th Annual Convention of the Association for Business Communication, Montreal, Quebec, Canada, 19–22 Oct. 2011.* Ed. Lisa Gueldenzoph Snyder. Association for Business Communication, 2011. Web. 8 Sept. 2012.

Jansen, Frank, and Daniël Janssen. "Explanations First: A Case for Presenting Explanations before the Decision in Dutch Bad-News Messages." *Journal of Business and Technical Communication* 25.1 (2011): 36–67. *Business Source Premier.* Web. 8 Sept. 2012.

"Latest Round of Yahoo Layoffs the Most Severe." *NPR: All Things Considered.* Writ. Steve Henn. NPR. 4 Apr. 2012. Radio.

Letzing, John, and Amir Efrati. "Yahoo Pushes Reset." *Wall Street Journal.* Wall Street Journal, 4 Apr. 2012. Web. 8 Sept. 2012.

Locker, Kitty O. "Factors in Reader Responses to Negative Letters." *Journal of Business and Technical Communication* 13.1 (1999): 5–48. *Business Source Premier.* Web. 8 Sept. 2012.

Swisher, Kara. "Here's Carol Bartz's Internal Layoff Memo to Beleaguered Yahoo Troops." *All Things D.* Dow Jones & Company, Inc., 15 Dec. 2010. Web. 15 Aug. 2012.

Vascellaro, Jessica E. "Bartz Remakes Yahoo's Top Ranks." *Wall Street Journal.* Wall Street Journal, 27 Feb. 2012. Web. 8 Sept. 2012.

*Figure 9.12 continued.*

**Good News for Bad News**

On six occasions in only four years, three different Yahoo! CEOs faced the unpleasant task of communicating mass layoffs to employees (AP 2012). Negative consequences of the bad news included decreased employee morale (Efrati 2011), criticism from investors (Henn 2012), and mixed responses in stock price (Letzing 2012; Vascellaro 2012).

Difficult situations like this are not uncommon—from announcing layoffs to reporting disappointing earnings, most managers occasionally have to deliver bad news. While managers may not be able to prevent all the negative consequences of bad news, an appropriate direct or indirect approach may help.

*Appropriate Approach*

When managers write a message, they follow either a direct or an indirect approach. As one textbook author states, with a direct approach the writer presents the major idea of a message first and then presents supporting ideas. An indirect approach is just the opposite—the writer presents the supporting points first, followed by the central idea (Baker 2011, 24). In the context of bad news, the central idea is the actual bad news, and the supporting points are the reasoning that led to the bad news.

When composing bad-news messages, Baker suggests that when "conveying bad news . . . consider using an indirect order. . . ." (2011, 67). Because bad news is often unexpected, an indirect approach helps readers to understand the reasons behind the news before receiving the bad news itself. When managers sense that their audience is not "prepared to receive the message," they should consider an indirect approach (Baker 2011, 24), which has been found to be more persuasive than a direct approach (Frischknecht and Baker 2011). If the bad news is "routine," however, managers may use a direct approach (Baker 2011, 68). Thus, depending on the readiness of the audience, managers should vary their approach.

*Dampened Consequences*

When managers must convey bad news to wide and diverse audiences, they don't have the luxury of customizing a direct or indirect approach for each recipient. Researchers have tried to determine which approach leads general audiences to receive bad news and still favorably view the messenger and the messenger's company. In her experiment with credit-refusal letters, Locker (1999) found that giving a brief explanation before bad news increased readers' acceptance of bad news, but it did not impact how favorably readers viewed the writer. In a later experimental study, Jansen and Janssen (2011) modified Locker's methodology and found that readers not only accepted bad news slightly better with indirect messages, but also viewed the messenger and the messenger's company slightly more favorably.

One scholar has argued against the indirect approach, but his concern seems to focus more on content than on approach. His criticism of using a buffer before giving bad news targets buffers that are unrelated to the bad news (Brent 1985, 6); however, he states that he can "tolerate some delay" when the initial supporting points are related to the main idea and when the indirect structure is appropriate for the message and circumstances (Brent 1985, 8). Given that his criticism focuses on unrelated buffers and not on the indirect approach itself, the prevailing philosophy seems to be the best approach—when conveying bad news to a varied audience, managers' best option is to use the indirect approach.

*Conclusion*

Internal memos from Yahoo! show that when informing employees of pending layoffs, CEOs used both indirect and direct approaches (Carlson 2008; Swisher 2012). While we may never know the exact circumstances that led the CEOs to use the different approaches, we do know that the approach used may have made a difference in how employees and stockholders accepted the bad news and subsequently viewed the CEOs and the company. When placed in similar circumstances where bad news must be communicated, managers should consider using an indirect approach to bring about the most positive consequences.

*Figure 9.13  A short article illustrating the use of Chicago in-text style documentation.*

References

AP (Associated Press). 2012. "Job Cuts at Yahoo: 6 Rounds of Layoffs in 4 Years." *Yahoo! Finance*, April 4. Accessed March 19, 2016. http:// http://finance.yahoo.com/news/job-cuts-yahoo-6-rounds-181252551.html.

Baker, William H. 2011. *Writing and Speaking for Business.* 2nd ed. Provo, UT: BYU Academic Publishing.

Brent, Douglas. 1985. "Indirect Structure and Reader Response." *Journal of Business Communication* 22: 5–8. Accessed August 15, 2012. https://www.lib.byu.edu/cgibin/remoteauth.pl?url=http://search.ebscohost.com/login.aspx?direct=true&db=ufh&AN=5777777&site=ehost-live&scope=site.

Carlson, Nicholas. 2008. "Jerry Yang's Layoff Memo." *Business Insider*, Oct. 21. Accessed August 15, 2012. http://articles.businessinsider.com/2008-10-21/tech/30101126_1_earnings-release-long-term-employees.

Efrati, Amir. 2011. "Yahoo Battles Brain Drain—Internet Company Braces for Wave of Exits after Holidays." *Wall Street Journal.* December 5. Accessed August 15, 2012. http://www.wsj.com/articles/SB10001424052970204083204577078403954893904.

Frischknecht, Sierra Sloan and William H. Baker. 2011. "Enhanced vs. Undifferentiated Text: A Study to Assess the Effects on Readers." In *Proceedings of the 76th Annual Convention of the Association for Business Communication*, edited by Lisa Gueldenzoph Snyder. Montreal, Quebec, Canada: Association for Business Communication. Accessed September 8, 2012. http://businesscommunication.org/conventions/abc-convention-proceedings/2011-annual-convention-proceedings.

Henn, Steve. 2012. "Latest Round of Yahoo Layoffs The Most Severe," by Steve Henn. *NPR: All Things Considered*, NPR, radio, April 4.

Jansen, Frank, and Daniël Janssen. 2011. "Explanations First: A Case for Presenting Explanations before the Decision in Dutch Bad-News Messages." *Journal of Business and Technical Communication* 25: 36–67. Accessed September 8, 2012. http://jbt.sagepub.com/content/25/1/36.

Letzing, John and Amir Efrati. 2012. "Yahoo Pushes Reset." *Wall Street Journal.* April 4. Accessed September 8, 2012. http://www.wsj.com/articles/SB10001424052702303302504577323281769682236.

Locker, Kitty O. 1999. "Factors in Reader Responses to Negative Letters." *Journal of Business and Technical Communication* 13: 5–48. Accessed September 8, 2012. http://jbt.sagepub.com/content/13/1/5.abstract.

Swisher, Kara. 2010. "Here's Carol Bartz's Internal Layoff Memo to Beleaguered Yahoo Troops." *All Things D*, December 15. Accessed August 15, 2012. http://allthingsd.com/20101215/heres-carol-bartzs-internal-layoff-memo-to-beleaguered-yahoo-troops.

Vascellaro, Jessica E. 2012. "Bartz Remakes Yahoo's Top Ranks." *Wall Street Journal.* February 27. Accessed September 8, 2012. http://www.wsj.com/articles/SB123566810152084487.

*Figure 9.13 continued.*

### Good News for Bad News

On six occasions in only four years, three different Yahoo! CEOs faced the unpleasant task of communicating mass layoffs to employees.[1] Negative consequences of the bad news included decreased employee morale,[2] criticism from investors,[3] and mixed responses in stock price.[4]

Difficult situations like this are not uncommon—from announcing layoffs to reporting disappointing earnings, most managers occasionally have to deliver bad news. While managers may not be able to prevent all the negative consequences of bad news, an appropriate direct or indirect approach may help.

#### Appropriate Approach

When managers write a message, they follow either a direct or an indirect approach. As one textbook author states, with a direct approach the writer presents the major idea of a message first and then presents supporting ideas. An indirect approach is just the opposite—the writer presents the supporting points first, followed by the central idea.[5] In the context of bad news, the central idea is the actual bad news, and the supporting points are the reasoning that led to the bad news.

When composing bad-news messages, Baker suggests that when "conveying bad news . . . consider using an indirect order. . . ."[6] Because bad news is often unexpected, an indirect approach helps readers to understand the reasons behind the news before receiving the bad news itself. When managers sense that their audience is not "prepared to receive the message," they should consider an indirect approach,[7] which has been found to be more persuasive than a direct approach.[8] If the bad news is "routine," however, managers may use a direct approach.[9] Thus, depending on the readiness of the audience, managers should vary their approach.

#### Dampened Consequences

When managers must convey bad news to wide and diverse audiences, they don't have the luxury of customizing a direct or indirect approach for each recipient. Researchers have tried to determine which approach leads general audiences to receive bad news and still favorably view the messenger and the messenger's company. In her experiment with credit-refusal letters, Locker found that giving a brief explanation before bad news increased readers' acceptance of bad news, but it did not impact how favorably readers viewed the writer.[10] In a later experimental study, Jansen and Janssen modified Locker's methodology and found that readers not only accepted bad news slightly better with indirect messages, but also viewed the messenger and the messenger's company slightly more favorably.[11]

One scholar has argued against the indirect approach, but his concern seems to focus more on content than on approach. His criticism of using a buffer before giving bad news targets buffers that are unrelated to the bad news; however, he states that he can "tolerate some delay" when the initial supporting points are related to the main idea and when the indirect structure is appropriate for the message and circumstances.[12] Given that his criticism focuses on unrelated buffers and not on the indirect approach itself, the prevailing philosophy seems to be the best approach—when conveying bad news to a varied audience, managers' best option is to use the indirect approach.

#### Conclusion

Internal memos from Yahoo! show that when informing employees of pending layoffs, CEOs used both indirect and direct approaches.[13] While we may never know the exact circumstances that led the CEOs to use the different approaches, we do know that the approach used may have made a difference in how employees and stockholders accepted the bad news and subsequently viewed the CEOs and the company. When placed in similar circumstances where bad news must be communicated, managers should consider using an indirect approach to bring about the most positive consequences.

*Figure 9.14  A short article illustrating the use of Chicago documentary-note style.*

Notes

1. Associated Press, "Job Cuts at Yahoo: 6 Rounds of Layoffs in 4 Years," *Yahoo! Finance*, April 4, 2012, accessed March 19, 2016, http:// http://finance.yahoo.com/news/job-cuts-yahoo-6-rounds-181252551.html.

2. Amir Efrati, "Yahoo Battles Brain Drain—Internet Company Braces for Wave of Exits after Holidays," *Wall Street Journal*, December 5, 2011, accessed August 15, 2011, http://www.wsj.com/articles/SB10001424052970204083204577078403954893904.

3. "Latest Round of Yahoo Layoffs The Most Severe," written by Steve Henn, *NPR: All Things Considered*, NPR, April 4, 2012, radio.

4. Jessica E. Vascellaro, "Bartz Remakes Yahoo's Top Ranks," *Wall Street Journal,* February 27, 2012, accessed September 8, 2012,  http://www.wsj.com/articles/SB123566810152084487; John Letzing and Amir Efrati, "Yahoo Pushes Reset," *Wall Street Journal*, April 4, 2012, accessed September 8, 2012, http://www.wsj.com/articles/SB10001424052702303302504577323281769682236.

5. William H. Baker, *Writing and Speaking for Business*, 2nd ed. (Provo, UT: BYU Academic Publishing, 2011), 24.

6. Ibid., 67.

7. Ibid., 24.

8. Sierra Sloan Frischknecht and William H. Baker, "Enhanced vs. Undifferentiated Text: A Study to Assess the Effects on Readers," in *Proceedings of the 76th Annual Convention of the Association for Business Communication,* ed. Lisa Gueldenzoph Snyder (Montreal, Quebec, Canada: Association for Business Communication, 2011), http://businesscommunication.org /conventions /abc-convention-proceedings/2011-annual-convention-proceedings.

9. Baker, *Writing and Speaking for Business*, 68.

10. Kitty O. Locker, "Factors in Reader Responses to Negative Letters," *Journal of Business and Technical Communication* 13 (1999): 21 accessed September 8, 2012, http://jbt.sagepub.com/content/13/1/5.abstract.

11. Frank Jansen and Daniël Janssen, "Explanations First: A Case for Presenting Explanations before the Decision in Dutch Bad-News Messages," *Journal of Business and Technical Communication* 25 (2011): 56-57 accessed September 8, 2012, http://jbt.sagepub.com/content/25/1/36.

12. Douglas Brent, "Indirect Structure and Reader Response," *Journal of Business Communication* 22 (1985): 8, accessed August 15, 2012, https://www.lib.byu.edu/cgi-bin/remoteauth.pl?url=http://search.ebscohost.com/login.aspx?direct=true&db=ufh&AN=5777777&site=ehost-live&scope=site.

13. Nicholas Carlson, "Jerry Yang's Layoff Memo," *Business Insider*, October 21, 2008, accessed August 15, 2012, http://articles.businessinsider.com/2008-10-21/tech/30101126_1_earnings-release-long-term-employees; Kara Swisher, "Here's Carol Bartz's Internal Layoff Memo to Beleaguered Yahoo Troops," *All Thiings D*, December 15, 2010, accessed August 15, 2012, http://allthingsd.com/20101215/heres-carol-bartzs-internal-layoff-memo-to-beleaguered-yahoo-troops.

*Figure 9.14 continued.*

# CHAPTER 10

# Writing Business Reports

When one of your teachers gives you an assignment to write a report, what goes through your mind? Your thoughts probably include words like *long, difficult, confusing information search, long hours,* and *late nights.* Perhaps you have had enough painful experience with report writing that you dread the thought of ever having to write another one. Yet the need for report writing will continue into your career—although you will be writing about business problems rather than academic subjects.

Report writing is indeed challenging and time-consuming work, but it is important work. Reports are important because they provide information used in making major management decisions. In many cases, the impact of one major report may be greater than the impact of hundreds of short, routine messages. Small decisions may be made without written documentation, but major decisions often involve a written report.

Business reports are documents that explain and ana-

lyze critical facts needed by managers for decision making. For instance, assume that you work for ABC Bakeries, a company that owns numerous bakeries throughout the western region of the United States. Two years ago your company acquired a three-store bakery operation, Tony's Bakeries, in Sacramento, California, and Tony's has been declining in profitability ever since. Your manager assigns you to conduct an in-depth analysis of the Tony's Bakeries to determine what is causing the downward trend.

To complete your assignment, you analyze all the Tony's financial documents before and after the acquisition. You also travel to Sacramento and spend a week gathering more data—interviewing store managers, observing employee-customer communications, surveying customers, and evaluating locations. After gathering and analyzing a large volume of data, your manager wants you to write a report of your findings, including recommendations for improving Tony's operations.

This example represents just one of the thousands of circumstances that call for a business report. Other examples might include a study to determine how to obtain new financing for company expansion, how to use social media to appeal to a particular group of customers, and how to improve assembly-line efficiency in a manufacturing facility. Further, a project manager might need to write a monthly progress report for all the projects she oversees, and a governmental inspector might need to submit a report that explains all safety violations in a chemical plant he has recently visited.

Reports vary in many ways. Some are short, some are long; some are informal, some are formal; some are written with a focus on the future, and some are written to report

*Figure 10.1 Most major decisions involve written reports.*

on the past. Examples of different types of reports are included at the end of this chapter.

Reports can be classified into the following categories:

**Periodic reports** are written on a regular basis, such as monthly or annually. For example, a sales report is generated at the end of each month to give important data for production and marketing decisions. A corporation can produce an annual report for its shareholders. An annual report is a comprehensive report of a company's activities and financial performance for the preceding year. In addition, annual reports typically include a message from the CEO and a statement from the auditor who assures the shareholders that the company is following approved financial practices.

**Progress reports** give an update on the status of an ongoing project. For instance, an analyst writes a report to inform his or her manager about the progress that has been made during the preceding month. Progress reports also usually indicate the goals for the next period. Thus, a progress report looks back at the activities of the preceding time period and looks forward to the activities planned for the next.

**Problem-solving reports** are generally one-time reports that focus on a unique situation, such as the need to fix a major product defect. Problem-solving reports frequently contain a significant amount of quantitative analysis to reveal weaknesses in current practices.

**Compliance reports** indicate whether an organization or group is complying with legal or management policies. Compliance reports are often written by auditors of various kinds. Financial audits are conducted by accountants who examine financial reporting, compliance audits are conducted by auditors who make sure the company is abiding by all applicable laws and regulations, and operational audits are performed by analysts who examine a company's operations to identify problems and inefficiencies that need to be improved.

As with shorter business messages, business reports have two main purposes—to inform and to persuade. Informative reports transmit information and then often conclude with a summary. Persuasive reports transmit information and then wrap up with conclusions and recommendations for future action. As with all messages, reports also give you an opportunity to strengthen your relationship of trust with all who will read your reports. If you do a good

job of report writing, your reputation as an effective problem solver will be strengthened.

This chapter reviews the major steps involved in business research and business report writing, and it describes the differences between short reports, long reports, and slide reports. After learning the material in this chapter, you should be able to do the following:

- Describe the research process.
- Describe the report-writing process.
- Explain the differences between short reports, long reports, and slide reports.
- Demonstrate how to evaluate a written report, using the four DOCS factors.

## BUSINESS RESEARCH PROCESS

The creation of a report comes after you have completed many steps in gathering and analyzing data, as illustrated in the following flow chart. As you can see, the entire process begins with someone identifying a problem or opportunity that needs to be investigated.

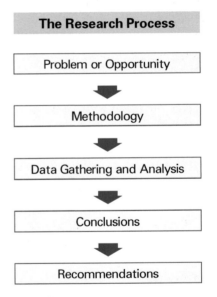

### *Problem or Opportunity*

As explained in Chapter 8, problem solving begins with identifying a problem, which is the difference between what should be and what is, or the difference between what could be and what is. Using the Tony's Bakeries scenario, you might conclude that Tony *should be* better at anticipating product demand, so he could eliminate waste and reduce expenses. Also, you might conclude that he *could be* increasing his income by introducing a new bakery product.

Not all problems need major attention. Some problems

are so minor that they can be ignored without much consequence. Other problems are routine and are resolved very quickly and simply. For example, when Tony starts to run short on sugar or flour, he simply places an order to replenish his supply. But major problems do need major attention, and because solving major problems typically requires expenditures of time and money, a written proposal may be required before the project is authorized.

In this case involving Tony's Bakeries, authorization to expend time and funds has already been given, but you should still develop a written plan to guide your research. Your first step would be to carefully define the research question: *What is causing the two-year decline in profitability?* The research question will serve as a guidepost for the entire research project. Without a clear research question or purpose, researchers might vary from what they should be focusing on.

## Methodology

The research question, or purpose, leads to the next step in the research process: determining *how* to gather and analyze the needed data. As explained in Chapter 9, you can gather two major types of research data—secondary and primary. With secondary research, you learn from reading articles that other people have published about your subject. With primary research, you gather and analyze raw data yourself. For instance, with Tony's Bakeries you would use mostly primary research: review all his financial statements, interview Tony and his employees, survey a representative sample of Tony's customers, and review changes in the local economy to determine what changes might have affected people's purchasing patterns.

After deciding how to gather the data, determine the best way to analyze the data, making sure your analysis will

yield valid answers to your research questions. For example, you might use frequency analyses for quantitative survey data, text analysis for qualitative survey data, and context analysis for local business data—noting that Tony's profitability decline began right after a new Walmart store moved into the neighborhood.

## Data Gathering and Analysis

After you decide on what methods to use for data gathering and analysis, put your plan into action. Obtain and analyze appropriate financial statements, examine appropriate financial ratios that indicate the health of the organization, interview Tony and his employees, obtain survey data from customers, and examine public records to analyze changes in the local economy.

As you gather data, pay attention to detail and be as objective as possible. Make sure questionnaires are clear and free of bias. Be sure your sampling methods represent randomness in selection and that your data is reliable (gets consistent results). In your interviews, avoid leading questions and bias that would cause those you interview to answer the way they think you want them to. Probe answers appropriately to obtain insightful responses.

As you analyze responses to surveys, first make sure the respondent has completed the survey correctly and that the respondent has properly understood the question. As you analyze the data, be sure to use the appropriate statistics. As you perform statistical analyses, the results may or may not be what you expect. If they don't seem logical or reasonable, double check the accuracy of your data or your statistics. However, unless there is a good reason to do otherwise, don't discount, adjust, or misrepresent the data because it doesn't match what you hoped for or expected. After all, you are seeking to find the truth, not to discover data that confirms your preconceived assumptions.

With your secondary research, consult a qualified business librarian to help you obtain the most current and useful information sources. Avoid the temptation to accept whatever you find as being valid. Check information to make sure it meets four important standards:

**Currency:** Is the information current? How recent is the publication, how current are the content and sources, and how recently has the site been updated?

**Authority:** Are the author and publisher credible? Are they recognized experts on the topic?

**Reliability:** Make sure the information comes from

*Figure 10.2 Questionnaires are frequently used in conducting business research.*

a knowledgeable author or organization, and that the information is adequately supported with relevant citations. Are appropriate sources cited, easily traced, and verifiable? Are the conclusions supported by the data?

**Purpose and point of view:** What is the author's purpose and point of view? Is the article written at a popular, professional, or professorial level? Is bias possible because the author or publisher is profit driven?

As stated before, make sure your results are valid and have measured what you intended to measure. Your reputation is at stake, and your results must pass the careful examination of all members of your audience.

## Conclusions and Recommendations

After examining and analyzing the data, you are ready to use your data to benefit your organization. First, you should draw conclusions about what you have learned from the findings. Conclusions are generalized statements that grow out of your findings, and for every significant finding, you should draw one or more conclusions. Next, make appropriate recommendations. Just as conclusions grow out of findings, recommendations grow out of conclusions. Whereas findings and conclusions generally look at what is or what was, recommendations look forward to what *should be* or *could be*. As you move from findings to conclusions to recommendations, you answer the what, so-what, and now-what questions. Table 10.1 illustrates the relationship between findings, conclusions, and recommendations.

The purpose of recommendations, of course, is to generate appropriate managerial action. If you have completed your research and report writing well, chances are good that you will get good results. For example, with the Tony's Bakeries situation referred to earlier, the recommendations you give to management should produce a turnaround in the declining profitability. If they don't, something went wrong with your research, or something went wrong in the action taken to resolve the problem.

In a way, you can analyze your recommendations somewhat like you analyzed symptoms. To determine the cause

of a particular symptom or problem, you asked, "What caused this?" With recommendations, you now ask, "What will this cause?" If all goes well, the implementation of your recommendations will complete the cycle and solve the symptoms and problems that prompted the research in the first place.

## BUSINESS REPORT WRITING PROCESS

As you complete your research, you now have the responsibility to report the results, often including both a written report and an oral presentation. Although this chapter discusses the writing phase after all the research has been conducted, often it is good to complete chunks of the writing process while you are conducting the research. Writing as you go along will prevent you from forgetting valuable insights that come into your mind while you were gathering and analyzing the data.

As with all business communications, complete a PACS plan before you begin. First, clarify the specific purpose of your report so the content stays focused as you compose. Second, analyze all members of the audience so you can tailor the report for their unique perspective and answer their WIIFM questions (what's in it for me?). Consider the demographic, psychographic, and knowledge factors that are relevant in this situation. Third, ponder the context in which the communication occurs. Think of all the relevant external, internal, and situational factors, such as time, financial, operational, and organizational factors. With all these purpose, audience, and context factors in mind, decide on an effective strategy. Carefully select the most appropriate channels and decide on the best psychological approach to achieve your purpose.

Next, take a few minutes to create an outline to guide your writing. With the amount of knowledge you will have of the research subject, you can usually use a top-down outlining procedure—either a traditional outline or a mind map (see Chapter 2). For scientific and academic research, the report follows what is called the IMRAD (introduc-

### Table 10.1 Findings, Conclusions, and Recommendations

| Finding | What? | Our survey revealed that only 32 percent of our supervisors have had management training. |
| Conclusion | So what? | The majority of our supervisors lack management training. |
| Recommendation | Now what? | Our company should provide formal management training for our supervisors. |

tion, methods, results, and discussion) structure. For typical business research, however, the structure usually includes introduction, research methods, analysis of findings, conclusions, and recommendations.

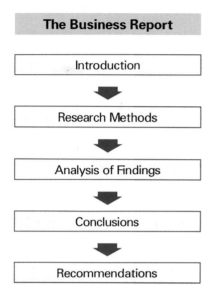

In general, the business report follows the same process as the business research study, with one exception—most managers like to have the recommendations at the beginning. Therefore, a recommendations summary is usually included with the introduction. After managers read the main recommendations, they will read as much of the rest of the report as they feel is important. Managers prefer this approach because time is money, and busy executives usually don't want to take the time to wade through pages of details before they get to the detailed recommendations at the end. Also, in some cases, managers won't feel a need to read all the details about your methodology and findings. They trust that you have followed appropriate procedures and have gathered and analyzed the data in an appropriate manner.

## Writing the Report Sections

The following generic guidelines are provided to guide you as you compose reports. Obviously, different situations will require different approaches, so remember that these are *guidelines*, not *rules*!

### Introduction

Give a brief background, just enough for the reader to understand the context and purpose of the report. Then give the most important conclusions and recommendations.

*For the past two years Tony's Bakeries has been declining in profitability. Therefore, a study was conducted to identify the factors that have caused this slide and*

*to present a strategy for reversing it. Based on the results of this study, the main cause of the profitability decline appears to be . . . Therefore, I recommend the development of a new strategy that includes . . .*

After the preceding paragraph, you could include an agenda that forecasts the rest of the business report, thus using the generic OABC pattern (opening, agenda, body, and closing) introduced in Chapter 3.

*The following report explains the research methods and procedures used, analyzes the data, and presents a comprehensive list of recommendations.*

### Research Methods

After the purpose and agenda, describe the research and analysis methods you used to achieve the purpose. For example, you could describe your survey procedures, your sampling techniques, the number and demographics of people included, and your statistical analyses. If you used a questionnaire, you could include a copy as an attachment or appendix. Following proper data-gathering procedures is critical in achieving research validity.

If you are aware of weaknesses in your research methods, or if you have encountered insurmountable challenges in getting all the data you wanted, be sure to include this as well. Explain what you have done to mitigate those limitations. Of course, including these limitations can weaken your subsequent persuasive efforts, but it is better to be honest.

### Analysis of Findings

The analysis of findings comes next. This section often comprises the largest segment of the report. If your report includes quantitative data analysis, this is where that analysis should be presented. Describe the actual data and your statistical analysis of the data (e.g., averages, percentages, trends, variances, correlations, and predictive variables). Raw numbers and tables of numbers are difficult to process for humans, so consider how you can visually represent the data for easier comprehension. Develop appropriate charts and visuals so the audience can see the shape of the data and understand what it reveals about the area being investigated.

If your analysis included qualitative data, describe that analysis in this section as well. Organize the analysis in a logical manner—compare and contrast, importance (most to least), chronological, spatial, or categorical. Qualitative data can also be presented visually, perhaps with visual timelines, concept maps, or creative infographics, rather than with traditional bar, line, and pie charts.

### Conclusions and Recommendations

The final section of the body of your report includes conclusions and recommendations. Remember that conclusions are generalized statements that are derived from your data analysis, and that for every significant finding you should have one or more conclusions that link to the finding. If you have more than one or two conclusions, present them as a numbered list, so they will be easy to find and easy to refer to (such as conclusion 1, conclusion 2, etc.).

After you write the conclusions, write your recommendations. The same advice given for numbering conclusions applies to recommendations. If you present them as a numbered list, they will be easy to find and easy to refer to in later discussions.

At this point, you should be able to see in your mind the natural progression of research and report writing—you observe a problem, which problem prompts a research question, which question leads you to develop a method for gathering data, which data is then analyzed, which analysis spawns conclusions, which conclusions generate recommendations for action to solve the original problem. The process is both logical and chronological.

## Writing Reports as a Team

Writing short business messages is usually a one-person task, but writing long reports can often be a collaborative effort of the team that performed the research. Team writing can present a number of problems, such as communication breakdowns, unequal work distribution, missed deadlines, personality conflicts, and formatting confusion. With collaboration, pay attention to the writing process as well as the product you are trying to prepare. The following guidelines can help improve the effectiveness and efficiency of writing reports as a team.

**Select an effective team.** Select members who have the knowledge, interest, skills, and time necessary to complete the task.

**Create an overall outline.** Because team members will be completing individual parts of the report, they must understand how their individual work fits in with the overall report.

**Develop a style guide** that standardizes the following writing issues.

- Writing style (e.g., formal vs. informal, writing for target audience, use of jargon)
- Headings (e.g., heading hierarchy and how many heading levels)
- Art and graphics (e.g., use of bullet lists and guidelines for photos, business graphics, and tables)
- Typography (e.g., fonts, font sizes, font style, and alignment for body text and headings)
- Spacing (e.g., margins, line spacing)

**Assign tasks.** Three main types of work are required—writing, editing, and designing. Writers need a good understanding of the content and context and generally good writing ability. Editors also need a good understanding of the content and context, and they need excellent writing skills to make the text correct and appropriate for the audience. Designers need the ability to enhance the content visually, working with headings, art, typography, and spacing.

As you assign writing tasks, you should be aware of three options for collaborative writing. First, the entire group can sit around a computer and compose the text; however, this approach is slow and often frustrating. Second, one person can do all the writing, after which everyone critiques. This approach ensures a consistent writing style, but the unequal workload sometimes causes the writer to feel animosity toward the other group members whose workload is much lighter. A third approach is to assign different parts of the document to different group members, according to their interest, knowledge, ability, and time availability. This approach can produce a report quickly, but because different writing styles are often obvious, a skilled editor is needed to revise the writing as needed so it sounds like one voice.

When members send electronic copies back and forth in a collaborative writing situation, they should identify their changes and suggestions for easy tracking. For example, Microsoft Word has a track-changes fea-

*Figure 10.3 Writing a report with a group can be inefficient and frustrating.*

ture that clearly identifies the changes and suggestions of various individuals. The team leader must also have a clear system for managing different versions of the document, such as custsvc-20XX0403, custsvc-20XX0408, and so forth for 3 April 20XX and 8 April 20XX.

**Establish deadlines and monitor progress.** As the project is launched, establish deadlines for each segment of the project. Then follow up to make sure the deadlines are met. Two tactics are helpful in project tracking. First, hold regular reporting meetings. Because of competing work assignments, people often delay work until just before the reporting meetings, and then they work extra hard to meet the deadline. Therefore, hold frequent meetings so the team will be motivated to perform ongoing work in a timely manner. Second, develop a project-tracking mechanism to record all progress. For example, a simple spreadsheet can show the various writing assignments, people assigned to each assignment, deadlines, and completion dates.

Throughout the project, ensure open, supportive communication and maintain a positive outlook on the project. Give positive reinforcement and express confidence in all team members, making sure your praise is sincere and specific, rather than manipulative and general.

# DIFFERENCES IN SHORT, LONG, AND SLIDE REPORTS

The creation of reports varies from one company to another and from one type of situation to another within a company. The following information highlights the major differences between short, informal reports; long, formal reports; and slide reports. (Figures 10.8, 10.9, and 10.10 at the end of this chapter provide examples of these types of reports.)

## Short Reports

Many report-writing assignments involve short reports, often written in memo format (see Figure 10.4). The following guidelines walk you through the process of writing a short decision report, which is a problem-solving report that evaluates multiple options.

1. Give adequate background information regarding the context of the problem. State the central problem you're trying to solve or the central objective of the report.

2. In most cases, use a direct approach. At or near the beginning, state your recommendation: "We recommend that XYZ company . . ." Then indicate, "The following analysis gives support for this recommendation." (If you were to use an *indirect* approach, you would delay your recommendation until after the analysis.)

3. Identify the critical factors considered in solving the problem (e.g., cost, personnel acceptance, ease of implementation, ease of maintenance, and customer service) and defend your choice of these factors. In other words, tell what the factors are and why those factors were chosen. Determine the relative importance of each factor in quantifiable terms. Additional criteria may be included, such as "The selected option must cost no more than $22,500" or "The selected alternative must be implemented by the end of this calendar year."

4. Define and introduce the options, or alternative solutions to the problem, arranged in an appropriate sequence (e.g., most to least preferred). Follow this same sequence in subsequent sections that evaluate the options.

5. Evaluate the alternatives, using a factor-by-alternative or an alternative-by-factor sequence. As appropriate, you may include a comprehensive evaluation of all the factors or just provide coverage where the greatest and most significant differences occur.

*Factor-by-alternative sequence:*

   I. Cost
      A. Alternative A cost
      B. Alternative B cost
      C. Alternative C cost
  II. Quality
      A. Alternative A quality
      B. Alternative B quality
      C. Alternative C quality
 III. Ease of Implementation, etc.

*Alternative-by-factor sequence:*

   I. Alternative A
      A. Cost of Alternative A
      B. Quality of Alternative A
      C. Ease of Implementation of Alternative A
  II. Alternative B
      A. Cost of Alternative B
      B. Quality of Alternative B
      C. Ease of Implementation of Alternative B
 III. Alternative C, etc.

| To: | Laurie Peterson, Director of Administrative Services |
|---|---|
| From: | Joseph Bigler, Purchasing Agent |
| Date: | March 4, 20XX |
| Subject: | **RECOMMENDED NEW CAR PURCHASE FOR SALES FLEET** |

In your February 21 Automobile Replacement memo, you asked for information about several vehicles that might be acceptable replacements for the oldest car in our sales fleet. This memo contains the information you requested. The vehicles and models chosen for evaluation include the following:

- **Mazda Model X**
- **Ford Model Y**
- **GM Model Z**

After evaluating the three alternatives, I recommend the Mazda Model X. The Model X equals or surpasses all the vehicles analyzed in all the evaluation categories.

The following text includes (a) a list of the critical factors used in the evaluation and (b) a comparison of the three vehicles.

### Critical Factors

Four factors were used in choosing the best alternative. Each factor was weighted according to its importance in the car-selection process. The total weighting of the factors equals 100.

- **Price and Depreciation**—the purchase price and three-year resale price. (Weighting = 30)
- **Safety**—safety features, including anti-lock brakes and air bags. (Weighting = 30)
- **Fuel Efficiency**—miles per gallon (mpg) of gasoline. (Weighting = 25)
- **Overall Performance**—Consumer Reports, May 20XX. (Weighting = 15)

### Comparative Evaluation

Each of the three cars was evaluated according to the four selection factors. The following paragraphs discuss these evaluations.

**Price and Depreciation.** The figure at right compares the purchase price and depreciation prices of all three cars over a three-year period, assuming an annual driving distance of 12,000 miles. As the figure illustrates, the Ford has the highest new price, but the lowest resale price after three years. The Mazda, although being only $896 less than the Ford initially, has a three-year resale value that exceeds that of the Ford by $4,675. The slower annual depreciation decline of the Mazda makes it a much more appealing vehicle from a financial standpoint.

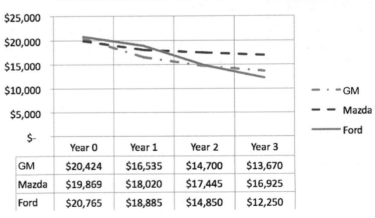

**COMPARISON OF DEPRECIATION**

| | Year 0 | Year 1 | Year 2 | Year 3 |
|---|---|---|---|---|
| GM | $20,424 | $16,535 | $14,700 | $13,670 |
| Mazda | $19,869 | $18,020 | $17,445 | $16,925 |
| Ford | $20,765 | $18,885 | $14,850 | $12,250 |

*Figure 10.4  Short decision report written in memo format.*

**Safety.** No comparable crash statistics are available for the three vehicles, but given the safety features of each car, the highest marks go to the Mazda Model X. The Model X has antilock brakes and driver/passenger air bags. The Model Z and Model Y have antilock brakes, but they have air bags only on the driver's side.

**Fuel Efficiency.** The most fuel efficient car is the Mazda Model X. The Model X averages 21 mpg, one mile per gallon better than both the Model Z and the Model Y. Obviously, the fuel efficiency will vary according to the type of driving involved.

**Overall Performance.** As rated by *Consumer Reports,* the GM Model Z is rated highest, with Ford Model Y and Mazda Model X scoring slightly lower in overall performance. Our conclusion, however, is that any of the three vehicles would give satisfactory performance.

The following table displays the four critical factors and the ratings of all three vehicles. The total line of this table indicates a fairly wide performance spread amongst the three vehicles, with the Mazda Model X being 105 points ahead of the lowest-rated vehicle, the Model Y.

### CUMULATIVE EVALUATION OF AUTOMOBILES*

| Factors | Weight | Alternatives | | |
| --- | --- | --- | --- | --- |
| | | Model X | Model Y | Model Z |
| Price and Depreciation | 30 | 9 = 270 | 8 = 240 | 7 = 210 |
| Safety | 30 | 7 = 210 | 6 = 180 | 6 = 180 |
| Fuel Efficiency | 25 | 8 = 200 | 7 = 175 | 7 = 175 |
| Overall Performance | 15 | 6 = 85 | 6 = 100 | 5 = 95 |
| **Total Scores** | **100** | **765** | **695** | **660** |

*Rating: 10–1, with 10 being high; scores are Weight **x** Rating.

### Conclusion and Recommendation

In light of the foregoing evaluation, I conclude that the Mazda Model X is the best alternative. The Model X equals or surpasses the other vehicles in almost all evaluation categories. Therefore, I recommend that Lakeview City purchase a new 20XX Mazda Model X for our sales fleet.

2

*Figure 10.4  continued.*

6. Include a decision table showing the results of your evaluation. Arrange the weighting factors and the alternatives in a high-to-low sequence for easier reading. Be sure to introduce the table before it occurs, and identify the important parts of the table that you want the reader to notice.

7. Close the report by drawing the best conclusions and giving specific recommendations. For many long, formal reports, the recommendations may be the last part of the report. For shorter reports, recommendations are usually followed by a cordial closing that invites questions and reinforces the recommendations. For example, "We are confident that our recommendations will help you achieve your objectives in the best way possible. Please call us if you have questions or if you would like us to help implement these recommendations."

8. As appropriate, attach any useful appendixes, such as technical specification sheets, illustrations, or research reports.

## Long Reports

Long reports are required to report the findings of in-depth investigations and complex studies (see sample reports at the end of the chapter, as well as report formatting guidelines in Appendix B). Some studies may run for many months or even years. As a result, the volume of information they generate is huge, and the size of the resulting reports is extensive. Some reports will be several hundred pages long. A long, formal report is organized into three sections: front matter, report, and back matter (see Figure 10.6). The front-matter pages are numbered with lowercase Roman numerals, with page numbers omitted from the cover letter and title page. The rest of the report is numbered consecutively with Arabic numerals.

*Figure 10.5 Some reports are the result of months or several years of work and can be hundreds of pages long.*

## Front Matter

### Cover Letter

The cover letter is a short message that officially conveys the report to the person who requested the report or who needs the report. It usually begins with, "Here is the report you asked us to provide . . ." or "Here is a report about . . ." The letter generally does not summarize the report findings or recommendations, but it may tell what sections the reader will find in the report, such as analyses, conclusions, and recommendations for action. It often closes with a statement inviting the recipient to contact the report writer for additional information or needed clarifications.

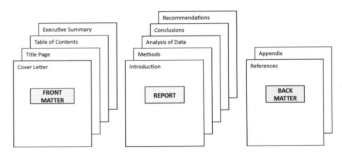

*Figure 10.6 Long, formal reports contain many parts and sections.*

### Title Page

The title page usually contains four main items of information, all centered horizontally on the page: title of the report, name of the person or organization for whom the report was written, name and organizational position of the writer or writers, and date. If multiple authors have contributed to the report, alphabetize them by their last name, except for the team leader or lead author, who should be listed first.

### Table of Contents

A table of contents is important for longer documents for two reasons: it gives an overview of the report structure and gives the page numbers where various report sections begin. Depending on how you write the report headings, it can also preview recommendations.

### Executive Summary

The executive summary is a mini-report that contains all the critical information needed by managers if they don't have time to read the full report. It gives a brief overview of critical background information (the need for the report and the purpose of the report), a concise description of the methods used to gather and analyze needed data, and a

summary listing of the major conclusions and recommendations. As with all summaries, the writing should have the following attributes:

- It should be clear and complete. Make sure the reader gets a clear presentation of the main points contained in the full version.
- It should be concise. Be stingy with your words, and pack as much information as possible into the words you use.
- It should be coherent. Make sure the summary flows logically from beginning to end—here is why we conducted this research, here is what we sought to accomplish, and here is how we gathered and analyzed the information, and here is what we conclude and recommend as a result of our study.
- It should be quick to read. Create bite-size information chunks, and use headings and bulleted or numbered lists to make the information easy and quick to read.

### Report

The main report contains a full introduction (such as background, problem, and purpose), a detailed description of methodologies used in gathering and analyzing the data, a detailed analysis of findings, a list of conclusions, and a list of recommendations. For example, you might be asked to analyze the customers' complaints about a retail establishment. The following sections could be included:

- Introduction, including background information, problem description, and purpose of the study.
- Methods used to gather data (such as questionnaires completed in the store, a telephone survey, text analysis of complaints filed online, or individual interviews) and analyze the data.
- Analysis of the data, including appropriate tables and charts that reveal important findings.
- Conclusions and recommendations to solve the problems.

### Back Matter

#### References

Include a references or bibliography section whenever secondary research is involved. Most business research includes only primary research, so a references section is not included. However, as appropriate, references could be included to strengthen your recommendations and to add credibility to your report.

#### Appendix

As needed, include one or more appendixes to supplement information given in the body. The appended pages include supplemental information, such as detailed tables and graphics. Appendixes (or *appendices*) are individually noted as Appendix A, Appendix B, and so forth. Further, all appendixes should be referenced in the body of the report, such as, "Appendix A includes additional data related to . . ."

## Slide Reports

Computers have had a significant impact on people's reading habits. Instead of wanting to read long reports filled with long paragraphs and long sentences, today's readers want information presented in smaller chunks and enhanced with visuals, enabling quick reading and quick referencing. In some organizations this new reading preference is spawning a new type of report—the slide report. Slide reports are, as the name implies, reports presented electronically on slides, rather than on paper (although each slide can be printed on paper, if needed). Each slide in a slide report is considered to be a page of the report.

Slide reports offer at least five advantages over traditional paper reports:

- Slide reports encourage chunking of information, forcing the writer to create well-defined units of information for clear communication.
- People would rather read information on slides than information presented as running text, because slides present information in more reader-friendly, bite-size chunks, rather than in long difficult-to-read paragraphs.
- Slide reports convey critical information more effectively and efficiently than traditional reports. Ideas are easy to find and easy to understand. Critical information is not buried in the middle of a page of text.
- Because the information is chunked and modular, slides can be easily copied and shared with others. You could, for instance, copy slides 5–9 from a slide report and send them to a colleague.
- Slide reports can contain hyperlinks for easy navigation. On the table of contents slide, for instance, the reader could click on one table of contents item and be instantly taken to the appropriate slide.

In essence, a slide report is a hybrid type of report that brings together the best of text documents and the best of slideshows. From text documents, they allow opportunity for full paragraphs of analysis and discussion, each page allowing for more information than a slide in a typical slide-

show. From slideshows, they are well suited for enhanced layout, design, and visualization of information. Slide reports are an especially good option for reports that contain significant numbers of visuals. Traditional reports may be a better option where there is a need for greater amounts of discussion and analysis.

Slide reports are not intended to be projected on a screen for a large audience, but to be read on a person's individual computer. This has great implications for layout and design. Regarding the layout, slide orientation can be either landscape or portrait. Further, all slides should follow a formal grid pattern of visual organization to ensure consistency of appearance across all the slides. For instance, you could present text in two columns, which would allow for a shorter line length that is easier to read.

Regarding design, you should develop a style guide to standardize the layout, color, typography, and visuals of all slides. Each slide should have a distinct front door and path. Textual information should be presented in a way that enables easy reading—as short paragraphs, bullet lists, callouts, and so forth. Further, the information should be presented visually as much as possible for quick comprehension. Slides should also have a generous amount of white space to make them visually inviting.

From an information-architecture perspective, try to make each slide a complete self-contained unit of information. This might not always be possible when you have to convey complex information, but it is a standard to work toward. Regardless of how you present the information chunks, make sure the overall flow reflects a smooth coherence from one slide to the next. Further, number the slides as you would regular pages so they have the feel of a traditional report and can be referenced easily.

Slide reports should contain all the parts of a traditional report, including an introduction, methods, analysis, conclusions, and so forth. A slide report might consist of the following segments:

*Slide 1—Title (title, author, and date)*

*Slide 2—Table of Contents*

*Slide 3—Introduction and Purpose*

*Slide 4—Methodology*

*Slide 5–8—Data Analysis*

*Slide 9—Conclusions and Recommendations*

*Slide 10–13—Appendix and Supplementary Information (if needed)*

Chapter 11 discusses how to create effective slides for slideshows. The Chapter 11 guidelines can be followed for creating slide reports as well, with the exception that slide reports usually contain more text on each slide than would be the case for traditional slideshows. For more information on creating well-designed slide documents, visit www.duarte.com.

## REVIEW AND REVISION OF REPORTS

After you compose a report, give it a comprehensive review, using DOCS as the rubric (see DOCS explanation in Chapter 5). For best results, review the report for each of the four DOCS elements individually, rather than attempting to check for all the elements while going through the report only once. These guidelines can apply to both traditional paper reports and slide reports, although some adaptations will be necessary for slide reports. Because slide reports are relatively new, few design and organization standards have been established.

### *Design*

Start by checking the entire report for design and visual aspects, including the format of the report and the appropriate use of HATS.

**Headings**: Check the headings—include an appropriate number of headings to serve as guideposts for reading and skimming. (Figure 10.7 provides examples of different heading levels.)

**Art**: Check for appropriate art and graphic elements, especially for quantitative data. For explaining numeric data, tables are better than text, but graphs are often best of all. The human brain is limited in its ability to process large amounts of quantitative data. Therefore, see if line charts, bar charts, maps, and other graphics have been used wherever they can be helpful. Figures should be numbered Figure 1, Figure 2, etc., and tables should be numbered Table 1, Table 2, etc. If only one table or only one figure is included, however, it does not need to be numbered.

**Typography**: Evaluate the typography of the body text, headings, captions, and special words. For body text in paper reports, an 11-point serif font is a good choice, and a sans serif larger font is useful for headings. For various heading levels, be sure that the font type, font

### TITLE

Headings serve several important functions in business and professional writing.

#### FIRST-LEVEL HEADING

First, they serve as signposts, revealing the content of the subsequent text. Without headings, readers have to read each sentence to know what information is contained in the text.

#### Second-Level Heading

Second, headings and their accompanying spacing serve a visual function. Without headings, a page of text would look uninviting and difficult to read. With headings, text looks more inviting and readable.

#### Third-Level Heading

Third, headings reveal the architecture of the information.

*Paragraph Heading.* Fourth, headings help writers focus their composition, preventing them from meandering into unrelated content. Professional writers should learn to use headings effectively.

*Figure 10.7 Different heading levels are indicated by varying placement, size, capitalization, and font.*

size, alignment, and font style (bold or italics) create an easily recognizable hierarchy. For text used with charts and graphics, be sure the type is large enough to be read easily. Throughout the report, check text alignment for consistency (left alignment is usually preferred for most text).

**Spacing**: Finally, review the use of white space. Check margins and ensure that the information does not look crowded on the page. Break up long paragraphs that look difficult and uninviting to read.

## Organization

Check two main aspects of organization. First, the report should include an agenda to forecast the overall structure of the report, as well as agendas needed to fore-cast the structure of report sections. Second, as mentioned previously, see if a direct approach has been used, with the main conclusions and recommendations at or near the beginning. For long reports, the conclusions and recommendations will be in the executive summary, which comes before the main report.

## Content

After checking the organization, read the report in detail to make sure the information is clear, complete, correct, considerate, and convincing. Make sure sections logically build on each other—the introduction gives enough context for the problem, the methods detail how the problem is researched, the findings flow from methods, the conclusions build on findings, and the recommendations flow from conclusions. Check all body paragraphs for compliance with CLOUD (coherence, length, organization, unity, and development). Consider testing the effectiveness of the report by asking other people to read it give you feedback. Ask them to tell you whether they think it will accomplish its intended purpose.

## Sentences

As the final part of this phase, review each sentence for SPELL compliance.

- Evaluate the structure. Be sure there is a clear flow between subject, verb, and complement. Make sure subjects and verbs are close together, and ensure that verbs are in the active voice. Check also for correct parallelism.

- Proofread for correct punctuation. Check for correct comma usage, hyphenations with compound adjectives, and other frequently occurring punctuation errors.

- Check for grammar errors. Make sure all rules have been followed with regard to case, agreement, tense, numbers, and capitalization.

- Check sentence language. Make sure appropriate words have been used. Evaluate both word formality and word precision.

- Check sentence length. Omit unnecessary words and ensure that sentences are written as concisely as possible.

Depending on the length, complexity, and significance of the report, you may want to have several people complete a DOCS review. Remember that the longer and more complex the report, the more opportunity there is for errors. Therefore, be thorough as you review long reports.

# CHAPTER SUMMARY

Reports constitute an important part of business writing for most managers and professionals. Business reports are documents that explain and analyze critical facts needed by managers for decision making. Four general categories of reports include periodic reports, progress reports, problem-solving reports, and compliance reports. As with shorter business messages, business reports have three general purposes—to inform, persuade, and build trust. Informative reports transmit information and then often conclude with a summary. Persuasive reports transmit information and then wrap up with conclusions and recommendations for future action. All reports should build trust.

Many written business reports are a collaborative effort involving various members of the writing team. Three approaches can be taken to collaborative writing. First, the entire group can sit around a computer and compose the text. Second, one person can do all the writing, after which everyone critiques. Third, different parts of the document can be assigned to different group members.

The creation of a report comes both during and after you have gathered and analyzed your data. Many business reports consist of an introduction, an explanation of research methods, a discussion of the findings, and a section containing conclusions and recommendations. Report formats vary according to whether they are short reports, long reports, or slide reports. All report types can be evaluated and revised according to four main factors: design, organization, content, and sentences (DOCS).

# CHAPTER QUESTIONS

1. What is a business report?

2. What are the three major purposes of business reports?

3. List three different categories of business reports.

4. What are the major steps in conducting business research?

5. What is the first step in problem solving?

6. List the elements included on the title page of a formal report.

7. What is an executive summary? Discuss its importance in primary reports.

8. Explain why most reports should employ a direct approach.

9. What does the term "methodology" refer to?

10. Describe a decision table and tell how it helps with decision making.

11. What is the difference between a factor and an alternative?

12. Why is high-to-low sequencing important in decision tables?

13. Describe the difference in using a factor-by-alternative and an alternative-by-factor approach. Discuss the advantages and disadvantages of each as applied in decision reports.

14. What is the difference between a finding, a conclusion, and a recommendation?

15. What should be included in report appendixes?

16. Compare and contrast short reports, long reports, and slide reports.

17. What are the advantages of slide reports?

18. What four major factors should be examined in revising reports?

# CHAPTER ACTIVITIES

1. Visit the website of the U.S. Government Accountability Office (http://www.gao.gov). Analyze two of the reports you find there, and write a half-page description of each of the reports. Explain the topic of the reports, list the total number of pages, and describe the sections included in each report. Also, describe the visuals included in the reports.

2. Visit the website of the U.S. Government Accountability Office (http://www.gao.gov). Create a slide report for one of the reports you find.

3. Using the information you obtained from Chapter Activity 2 in Chapter 8, write your results in a decision report.

4. Using the information you obtained from Chapter Activity 3 in Chapter 8, write a recommendation report.

5. For this project, choose ads for two competing products of your choice, such as two toothpaste ads, two automobile ads, or two cell phone ads. The ads may be either online or in print. Evaluate the two ads according to their creativity, clarity, likability, memorability, and effectiveness. After your evaluation, write a report that compares the two ads, and make a final recommendation based on your evaluation. The report should contain the following sections, presented in this order: introduction, statement of purpose, recommendation, methodology and criteria, analysis,

conclusions, and recommendation section. Include a decision table near the end of the report.

6.  You have been assigned to conduct an advertising research study to determine the effectiveness of an ad created by your advertising agency. You may choose the ad. Select an advertisement on YouTube. Select an audience of 10 people. Have the 10 people view the ad and answer the questions below. Analyze the data and then write a report explaining your results.

- *Creativity*: How creative it is?
- *Clarity*: How clear is the message about the product?
- *Likability*: How much do you like the ad?
- *Memorability*: How well will you remember the ad?
- *Effectiveness*: How much does the ad make you want to buy?

To:     Kristin Oliver
        Executive Vice President—Walmart U.S. People

From:   Matthew B. Johns
        Chair—Quality Improvement Committee

Date:   December 20, 2014

Re:     RECOMMENDATION FOR WALMART'S ORGANIZATIONAL NARRATIVES

Here is the report of the organizational research you asked us to perform for Walmart. This document, which we have entitled "Walmart's Organizational Narrative: Redefining the Story," describes our research procedures and gives our recommendations to address your concerns about employee morale.

The study compared differences between Walmart's internal organizational narratives and external employee narratives. The purpose of the study was to discover opportunities for improvement and change in Walmart's current story-telling efforts. Our recommendations address each point of dissonance in these two narratives, and we are confident that the recommendations will be welcomed by your employees.

Thank you for the opportunity to perform this research. We hope our efforts will be of value to you. If you have any questions about this report, we would be happy to meet with you for further discussion.

Sincerely,

Matthew B. Johns

*Figure 10.8  Sample short report with text analysis.*

# Walmart's Organizational Narrative: Redefining the Story

Walmart is a gigantic organization. Started in 1972 by founder Sam Walton, Walmart is now the world's largest company in terms of gross revenue, as well as the world's largest employer. Yet in the past decade, Walmart has faced allegations that it treats its employees unfairly and unethically. For example, in 2003, reporters noted that Walmart employees took home an average of $13,861 per year, while the federal poverty line for families of three was $14,630[1]. Others accused Walmart of gender discrimination[2], of failing to pay employees overtime and allowing them to take rest and lunch breaks[3], of inadequate benefits for employees[4], and of unjustified termination[5].

Most recently, in November of this year, Walmart employees in six states announced strikes ahead of upcoming Black Friday, perhaps the most important shopping day of the year. The reasons given by employees included a desire for "more respect" from Walmart management, for wage increases, for "consistent, full-time hours," and for an end to employee reprimand for "speaking out"[6].

These criticisms fail to include the positive actions taken by Walmart in recent years. For example, in 2006, Walmart began raising wages by 6 percent in one-third of its U.S. stores; in addition, the same year, Walmart rolled out new benefit plans with premiums as low as $11 per month. Walmart had also created roughly 240,000 jobs for the economy, providing employment and benefits to a significant portion of the United States workforce[7]. In fact, in total, Walmart currently employs 1.3 million Americans in over 5,000 stores throughout the nation, and last year the store promoted 170,000 members of its workforce to positions of greater responsibility and higher pay[8].

Walmart has obviously been making positive changes in terms of wages, benefits, and promotions, but for some reason many current Walmart employees and many outside entities still are not recognizing Walmart's efforts. Walmart, therefore, requested that our internal Quality Improvement Committee assess Walmart's organizational narratives and determine whether they need to be updated and improved.

**Purpose of the Study**

After analyzing Walmart's current situation, we decided to compare online messages being published by Walmart against online messages being written by current and former Walmart employees. Our goal was to identify the variance between the two and then develop recommendations to bring the two more in line with each other.

---

[1] Anthony Bianco and Wendy Zellner, "Is Walmart Too Powerful?" *Bloomberg Businessweek* (October 5, 2003): http://www.businessweek.com/stories/2003-10-05/is-wal-mart-too-powerful.
[2] Jeff M. Sellers, "Woman Against Wal-Mart," *Christianity Today* (April 22, 2005): http://www.christianitytoday.com/ct/2005/aprilweb-only/52.0b.html.
[3] The Associated Press, "Wal-Mart to Face Employee Suit in Missouri," *USA Today* (November 2, 2005): http://usatoday30.usatoday.com/money/companies/management/2005-11-02-walmart-employees_x.htm.
[4] Aaron Berstein, "A Stepped-Up Assault on Wal-Mart," *Bloomberg Businessweek* (October 19, 2005): http://www.businessweek.com/stories/2005-10-19/a-stepped-up-assault-on-wal-mart.
[5] Andrew Adams, "4 Walmart Employees Fired after Disarming Gunman Caught Shoplifting," *KSL.com* (February 9, 2011): http://www.ksl.com/?nid=148&sid=14319284.
[6] Dave Jamieson, "Walmart Workers Launch Black Friday Strike," *Huffington Post* (November 26, 2014): http://www.huffingtonpost.com/2014/11/26/walmart-workers-protest_n_6225034.html.
[7] The Associated Press, "Wal-Mart Increases Starting Pay, Adds Wage Caps," *USA Today* (August 7, 2006): http://usatoday30.usatoday.com/money/industries/retail/2006-08-07-walmart-pay_x.htm.
[8] Walmart.com, *"Our Locations,"* (December 19, 2014): http://corporate.walmart.com/our-story/locations/united-states.

2

*Figure 10.8  Short report continued.*

## Methodology

Our initial challenge was to gather all the textual data needed for analysis. First, we examined corporate employee narratives found on the corporate website http://careers.walmart.com/our-people/testimonials/. This site is intended to give potential employees a glimpse into the working life of Walmart employees, and we analyzed eight randomly selected narratives from this site. We read each narrative and coded the main points of each one. We then reviewed all coded narratives and classified them into appropriate categories. This analysis enabled us to determine the current organizational themes being publicized by Walmart.

Second, we similarly reviewed, analyzed, and classified narratives written by Walmart employees on the website www.glassdoor.com. This site enables employees to post reviews and tell stories about their experiences within a company. This site provided a source of data rich with stories of how Walmart's current employees really feel about their work experience inside this gigantic organization.

Third, we compared and analyzed the themes from these two groups to discover any areas of disharmony. After our analysis, we brainstormed to create potential solutions. Keeping the objectives of Walmart in mind, we then refined the most promising solutions in hopes of achieving the desired harmony between Walmart management and employees.

## Results

Our data analysis consisted of two parts, the first including the narratives of Walmart corporate careers website and the second including the narratives of Walmart employees.

### Part 1: Management's Message

Our Walmart narratives came from Walmart's corporate careers website. Three major themes were uncovered in these narratives:

- **Opportunity.** Multiple narratives discussed the great opportunities employees experience at work. For example, one employee noted, "I was offered a game-changing opportunity to help lead the thought-leadership and development of Walmart's social insights capability for Global Customer Insights & Analytics." Employees discussed their satisfaction with working on large-scale projects, working with Walmart's eCommerce technology, and opportunities for volunteering in the community.

- **Customer Focus.** Customers look to Walmart for a wide range of products offered at low prices, and this focus came through in these employee narratives. As one employee noted, "I deliver an endless aisle for our global customers and have fun fulfilling our customer promise." In light of Walmart's current situation, however, not one of the employees mentioned any effort by Walmart to deliver excellence to its employees.

- **Management.** Because this website stems from the main Walmart.com domain, we expected that Walmart frontline associates would be represented in these narratives. However, that was not the case—all the narratives we sampled were written by management-level employees. One narrative told about starting out as a stocker and eventually moving up to management, but no other narratives came from or mentioned the numerous associates working as hourly employees in Walmart stores throughout the country.

3

*Figure 10.8  Short report continued.*

**Part 2: Employees' Message**

Our employee narratives came from glassdoor.com, most of which were written by current Walmart employees. Here are a few of the themes uncovered from these narratives:

- **Wages, Benefits, Training, and Flexibility.** Mostly positive comments were made about Walmart's wages, benefits, training, and flexibility. Three mentioned wages as being just fine, while two mentioned them as being low or increased infrequently. Benefits were mentioned four times in a positive light, and only once negatively. Employees seemed especially to appreciate volunteer, scholarship, and health benefits. Two employees also complimented Walmart's training as a great opportunity to obtain skills needed for future promotions.

- **Opportunity.** Narratives commented on the opportunity for growth and promotion within Walmart. One associate noted, "Walmart promotes its people to higher positions in as little as 6 months. . . ." However, another associate commented that this rapid promotion to management may produce negative consequences: ". . . management can constantly be changing, [and] sometimes promotions feel like set ups for failure." Likewise, another associate stated that leadership sometimes seemed scattered, with different people giving different directions. One employee also cautioned management about assuming that every employee wants to be promoted—some just want a basic job without the added worries that come with promotion. One person wrote, "Don't be quite so concerned about corporate as you are about your 'good' employees." In other words, focus less on pushing people up the corporate ladder and more on retaining good employees.

- **Employee Focus.** The most critical employee comments focused on their desire for managers to listen to their employees, including "back up your employees," "listen to your people," "talk to your people," and "get to know your employees" since "they are on the front lines for you." Although the majority of these people were hourly associates, the one narrative from a first-level manager made a similar comment: "[It is] difficult to get upper management to have your back when dealing with difficult employees . . . stop making it so difficult for your 1st level managers and they will get more from everyone down." Notably, most employee narratives focused on employees—no one mentioned importance of customers.

- **Management.** As noted above, almost all of those narratives reviewed on this site seemed to be hourly associates or non-management employees.

## Conclusions

The stories we analyzed enabled us to assess where Walmart's organizational narratives were not in harmony with the image perceived by employees. Four conclusions grew out of our assessment.

1. **Wages, Benefits, Training, and Flexibility.** Overall, associates seem to view wages, benefits, training, and flexibility very favorably. Walmart's efforts to portray their employee relations in a positive light is consistent with this employee sentiment.

2. **Opportunity.** Corporate-level associates see their jobs as full of opportunity. Hourly associates also see opportunity for advancement within the company. The advancement opportunities are viewed with mixed feelings, however, because rapid movement into management often presents confusion and responsibilities they are not fully prepared to assume.

3. **Customer and Employee Focus.** Corporate-level narratives tell how Walmart places customers as its highest priority, yet these narratives fail to discuss any priority given to employees within

4

*Figure 10.8  Short report continued.*

Walmart's corporate culture. This is consistent with the customer-focused Walmart mission statement: "We save people money so they can live better." Employees are noticeably absent from Walmart's mission statement. In contrast to the customer-oriented corporate narratives, the narratives of the hourly associates reflect unmet needs, recommending improved listening to employees, getting to know employees, and "having employees' backs."

4. **Management.** All entries from Walmart's organizational narrative were produced by employees in highlighted corporate-level positions, while all but one glassdoor.com narratives came from non-management employees. This is problematic because it tells the story of only a fraction of the Walmart community.

## Recommendations

Given the conclusions drawn above, we recommend the following changes to Walmart's current organizational narrative:

1. **Place More Emphasis on Training and Flexibility.** Because of associates' positive comments about Walmart training and workplace flexibility, Walmart should tell more organizational stories about these two benefits. This is a success story already happening, and Walmart should exploit the benefits it can produce.

2. **Expand the scope of the corporate narrative.** We recommend that Walmart expand its narrative to include caring for customers *and* employees, and to put that expanded narrative into action. Founder Sam Walton once stated, "Appreciate everything your associates do for the business. Nothing else can quite substitute for a few well-chosen, well-timed, sincere words of praise. They're absolutely free and worth a fortune"[9]. Walton expected a balance between focus on customers and employees, and the narratives we examined suggest the need for correcting the current imbalance, both in the corporate voice and in company-wide management practice.

3. **Redefine employee success.** Instead of defining success by working toward future promotion, Walmart needs to include success by performing well into today's position. Helping employees feel success today is critical for successful day-to-day business operations, as well as for employee morale and self-esteem. This emphasis is especially important for associates who are not ready for or interested in promotion.

4. **Include Narratives from Hourly Employees.** We recommend that Walmart include stories from front-line employees, because none of our sampled narratives came from this group. A more balanced voice will add greater diversity, as well as greater credibility, to the corporate message.

These four recommendations focus on modifying Walmart's corporate narrative, but we also recommend a change in training Walmart managers. The need for concentrated, frequent training in caring for front-line employees is obvious from employees' online comments, and the sooner this training can begin, the better.

As the foregoing recommendations are implemented, we are confident that the number of online complaints filed by employees will decrease, reflecting a greater sense of workplace satisfaction. We are also confident that the overall corporate culture will improve as employees feel more valued and appreciated for the vital work they perform.

---

[9] Ben Brinkopf, "Ten Rules of Success from Sam Walton," *The Leadership Institute at Harvard College* (January 25, 2011): https://harvardleadership.wordpress.com/2011/01/25/ten-rules-of-success-from-sam-walton/.

5

*Figure 10.8 Short report continued.*

## Neel Consulting Group, LLC

614 East Pleasant Hill Road, Des Moines, Iowa 50317  ▪  515.385.26XX

April 3, 20XX

Mr. Patrick Tobin, Contracting Officer
Grace & Bannock
700 Sumac Street, 16th Floor
Des Moines, IA 50309

Dear Mr. Tobin:

Neel Consulting is pleased to present to Grace & Bannock our "New Directions for Sales"
report. The purpose of this report is to provide you with the results of our sales department
analysis and recommendations.

We appreciate the cooperation of everyone at Grace & Bannock as we gathered data and
performed our analysis. We believe our recommendations will help guide Grace & Bannock in
its future development and growth.

If you have any questions as you review this document, please do not hesitate to give me a call
(317-555-55XX).

Sincerely,

Lisa T. Adams
Managing Partner

*Figure 10.9  Sample long formal report with front matter and back matter. (Adapted from report written by Katelyn Drapeau,* Report of
Findings and Recommendations, *April 2015.)*

# GRACE & BANNOCK:
# NEW DIRECTIONS FOR SALES

Prepared for

Patrick Tobin
Contracting Officer
Grace & Bannock

Prepared by

Neel Consulting, LLC
Lisa T. Adams, Managing Partner
Leslie Salgado, Team Leader
Melissa Baxter
Jameson Brown
Jennifer Paxton

April 3, 20XX

*Figure 10.9  Long report continued.*

# Table of Contents

*Figure 10.9  Long report continued.*

# Executive Summary

Since its creation, Grace & Bannock has pursued an aggressive plan to increase its market share. Through rapid growth and high sales quotas, this approach was relatively successful. Recently, however, G&B's sales department is severely underperforming. The purpose of our research was as follows:

- Improve employee sales performance
- Improve employee morale
- Provide appropriate support for clients

After gathering data from company metrics, employee surveys, and interviews, we performed both quantitative and qualitative analysis and arrived at the following conclusions and recommendations.

### Conclusions

1. **Work output is dependent on time on task.** As expected, our analysis revealed high positive correlation between employee time on task and employee work output. This finding gives G&B managers justification for implementing stricter workplace practices and procedures.

2. **Sales department employees are dissatisfied with their work.** This dissatisfaction has three main causes. First, management rewards team metrics, ignoring superior individual performance. Second, to achieve team goals, some employees are having to do the work of others and are not getting credit for it—sometimes preventing them from completing their own work. Third, poorly performing employees are not being held accountable.

3. **Customer needs are not being met.** Some sales employees are sharing clients, causing confusion as to who is their point of contact with Grace & Bannock. Also, face-to-face meetings are becoming increasingly rare, being replaced by less-effective phone calls. This problem is more prevalent among newer sales employees.

### Recommendations

1. **Monitor time on task.** Implement procedures to gather time-on-task data and review this data in quarterly performance interviews. This may include individuals logging the time they spend helping other employees, automatically tracking time spent on all types of phone calls, and time spent on unauthorized websites. Holding individuals more accountable for their personal performance will most surely communicate the importance of individual accountability

2. **Provide individual incentives.** The emphasis here needs to be on giving acknowledgement to those employees who consistently perform well. Incentives can come in many forms, such as financial bonuses, recognition awards, and simple statements of thanks or acknowledgement when superior performance is achieved.

3. **Improve and monitor customer service.** Develop appropriate policies and procedures, along with regular training and accountability, to ensure that sales employees understand the G&B way of treating clients. Stress regular face-to-face meetings and no sharing of clients as critical parts of this effort to improve client satisfaction.

*Figure 10.9  Long report continued.*

# Grace & Bannock:
# New Directions for Sales

Neel Consulting Group has prepared this report of findings for Grace & Bannock (G&B) as a result of the acceptance of our previously submitted proposal. This report includes a review of the current problem within the sales department, the objectives of our research, the methods used to obtain data, our analysis of the data, and appropriate conclusions and recommendations growing out of our analysis.

Since its creation, G&B has pursued an aggressive plan to increase its market share. Through rapid growth and high sales quotas, this approach was relatively successful. Recently, however, it appears that the plan may have backfired, and G&B is now dealing with a sales department that is severely underperforming.

## Problems and Objectives

As a byproduct of high consumer demand and rapid company growth, the Sales Department of Grace & Bannock has experienced increasing difficulty in fulfilling its mission. The following problems are symptomatic of this difficulty:

- Missed sales quotas
- Unmet needs of clients
- Loss of contracts
- Low employee morale

The purpose of our research was to determine the cause of these symptoms and develop viable solutions. Three general objectives were defined for this study:

1. Improve employee sales performance
2. Improve employee morale
3. Provide appropriate support for clients

## Methodology

To assist in meeting our project objectives, we sought answers to the following four questions:

1. Is the work volume expected of the sales staff reasonable?
2. How severe and pervasive is the low morale problem?
3. Are employees appropriately focused during their working hours?
4. How well are individual employees meeting their goals?

Our consultancy methodologies were broken into two phases—data gathering and data analysis.

**Data Gathering Methods**
To gather the data needed to understand the causes of the performance problems, Neel Consulting gathered data in three primary ways:

1

*Figure 10.9  Long report continued.*

- *Obtained company records of work performance for the past three months.* Grace & Bannock's internal performance metrics were used to generate the work output of individual sales representatives. Eight sales representatives were evaluated based on their time on task and its correlation with expected output, results of which can be statistically analyzed to assess daily contribution.

- *Administered a questionnaire to all employees in the Sales Department.* Short surveys and interviews were conducted to attain employee insight and measure employee satisfaction. The anonymous, online surveys provided data that assessed employee satisfaction. The results of the surveys were obtained using a Likert Scale with numbers 1-4 designating level of agreement.

- *Conducted interviews with employees in the Sales Department.* Personal interviews were held with sales department employees to gain insight about what they are experiencing on a day-to-day basis and to hear their perceptions about the causes of the department's low performance.

**Data Analysis Methods**

After the data-gathering phase, members of our team carefully analyzed the data using appropriate descriptive and textual statistics. First, all data was examined to ensure that it had been recorded accurately. Second, the statistical analyses were completed. Third, the data was converted into visual form to help give it meaning. Finally, the team members discussed all data and its implications, drawing appropriate conclusions on which solid recommendations could be made.

## Data Analysis

The results of our analysis are presented for the four major types of data we gathered: Company work-performance records, questionnaires, interviews, and use of equipment.

**Work Performance**

Figure 1 shows the work-performance data obtained from Grace & Bannock's internal metrics. This scatter-plot graph reveals the high correlation between time on task and work output, which would be expected. One example of residual is denoted on the graph. This residual (deviation of a given data point from the best fit line) is somewhat significant by itself, but all the other residuals have a value of less than five units.

This figure shows a high degree of variance among the sales department employees, with two individuals spending only 50 percent of their time on task. Spending time on unauthorized websites, taking personal phone calls, waiting for time on computers, and dealing with other types of interruptions are among the causes of this problem.

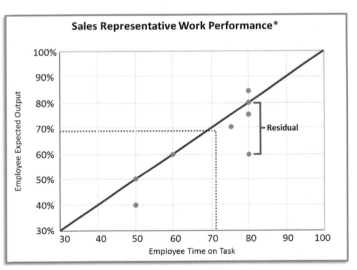

*Figure 1. Work-performance data reveals a high correlation between employee expected output and time on task.*

2

*Figure 10.9  Long report continued.*

The dashed lines in Figure 1 identify the average percentages of time on task and work output. The average percentage of time spent on task is 68 percent and the average work output is 72 percent. Notice

The last survey question was open ended and asked for any additional inp  each respondent wanted to give about working in the sales department. Textual analysis of the responses to this question yielded the following data:

| Theme of Response | Times Mentioned |
|---|---|
| Picking up slack of others | 3 |
| Not enough time | 2 |
| Metrics | 2 |
| Structure of operations | 2 |

While it is commendable that certain employees are willing to "pick up the slack of others," they obviously realize that such assistance interferes with their own work. It seems that what they would prefer is for everyone to do his or her work and to be held individually accountable. Along with other causes, this work aspect adds yet another reason for low morale.

## Interviews

The one-on-one interviews of Grace & Bannock's employees were conducted over a three-day period, and the audio recordings of these interviews were subsequently transcribed. Our analysts then performed a textual analysis of keywords in the interviews to identify common themes. Four themes took precedence over the others:

- Poor customer service
- Unbalanced workload among employees
- Excessively high focus on team metrics
- Equipment shortage

Figure 5 provides a visualization of the impact of these themes based on how many times they were mentioned in the interviews. The top, right, and bottom diamond points all point to a concern over how employees are spending their time—not enough with customers and too much on the work of others.

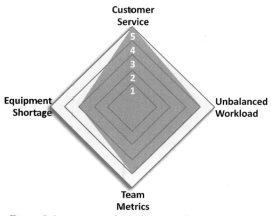

*Figure 5. Interview analysis shows employees' consistent concerns about team metrics and unbalanced workloads.*

The root cause of these concerns seems to be (a) the department policy of emphasizing team goals over individual goals and (b) the absence of policies and procedures to reward individuals and to hold them accountable for their personal performance. (Selected interview comments are listed in Appendix B.)

7

*Figure 10.9  Long report continued.*

## Conclusions

In light of the foregoing data analysis, we draw the following conclusions.

1. **Work output is dependent on time on task**. Through analysis of the work performance data, it can be concluded that overall employee work output is positively correlated with employee time on task. Although this result is intuitive, it gives the managers of Grace & Bannock justification for implementing stricter workplace practices and procedures.

2. **Sales department employees are dissatisfied with their work**. There is widespread dissatisfaction among sales department employees, with the majority of employees being dissatisfied with multiple aspects of their work environment. First, management stresses team metrics more than individual metrics, and this may be causing low morale within the office. Second, to achieve team goals, some employees are having to pick up the slack for others and are not getting credit for it—sometimes preventing them from completing their own work. Third, poorly performing employees are not being reprimanded or held accountable.

3. **Customer needs are not being met**. This problem was mentioned more than any other in the one-on-one interviews. First, some sales employees are sharing clients, causing confusion as to who is their point of contact with Grace & Bannock. Second, face-to-face meetings are becoming increasingly rare, being replaced by less-effective phone calls. This problem is more prevalent among newer sales employees. This lack of attention to client needs could be a major contributing factor behind loss of clients.

## Recommendations

To address the problems explained in our major conclusions, we recommend three actions.

1. **Monitor time on task.** Implement procedures to gather time-on-task data and review this data in quarterly performance interviews. This may include individuals logging the time they spend helping other employees, automatically tracking time spent on all types of phone calls, and time spent on unauthorized websites. Holding individuals more accountable for their personal performance will most surely communicate the importance of individual accountability.

2. **Provide individual incentives.** The emphasis here needs to be on giving acknowledgement to those employees who consistently perform well. Incentives can come in many forms, such as financial bonuses, recognition awards, and simple statements of thanks or acknowledgement when superior performance is achieved.

3. **Improve customer service.** Develop appropriate policies and procedures, along with regular training, to ensure that sales employees understand the G&B way of working with clients. Stress regular face-to-face meetings and no sharing of clients as critical parts of this effort to improve client satisfaction.

We are confident that these actions will address the major problems now being experienced in the sales department. However, the actions will obviously cause a stir in the sales department and may cause an increase of dissatisfaction among some poor performers. Thus, we recommend that the actions be implemented with a positive spin—to help all employees become the best they can be, to reward top performers appropriately, and to help the company grow by taking better care of clients.

*Figure 10.9  Long report continued.*

# Appendix A
## Raw Survey Data

**Employee comments regarding completing their work tasks: "Why or why not?"**

- I do what I'm asked to do with no problems.
- I do what I'm asked to do. What more is there to it? Sometimes I'm done early.
- My performance metrics are clear to me, and I meet them.
- My team seems to be doing all right. Only a few of the team members seem to be kind of off task.
- I need more support for all I have to accomplish.
- Too much required for so little time.
- Too much required for the time we are given.
- I have to do the work of my colleagues sometimes because they don't seem to get it done.
- I have to pick up the slack from my colleagues.
- Some of my colleagues don't meet their metrics, and it affects our team reviews. I end up doing the work.
- We don't seem to have a good infrastructure to get all our work done. Too many phone calls.
- The performance metrics are too steep for one team like this. No overtime pay? Why not?

*Figure 10.9 Long report continued.*

## Appendix B

## Selected Raw Interview Comments

### Team Metrics

- The metrics themselves are not that much per person. I know I can meet my individual metrics, but the team's metrics are harder to meet. I think I sometimes end up taking other people's clients because I can sense they're not getting what they need. I do sometimes feel that it's affecting my ability to meet my own clients' needs, but then the team's metrics seem to be emphasized over the individual's. So maybe that's causing some stress. The emphasis on team can get under your skin.
- . . . the review is always for the team. So we're missing something. I guess they know who is not doing what individually, but we don't.
- Well, like I said the team has to meet a certain sales metrics, but then we also have to meet individual numbers, so maybe I try to help the team more than myself.
- . . . leadership really only wants the team numbers. They could care less how John Smith is doing. Our support staff keeps track of metrics on a more weekly and individual level, though. They put it all together into a quarterly report to me, and I usually put that into context for Grace & Bannock's leadership.
- Grace & Bannock's leadership is only interested in quarterly stuff.
- Well I wouldn't be a manager if I didn't [notice if team members are off task], but usually I save the reprimands until after a few repeated offenses.
- But you know with this team metrics thing, I never have much time to keep that good of track of people. I mean I have to meet my metrics, too.

### Working with Clients

- I usually work with [Employee A]. We tend to share clients. Whatever one doesn't get to, the other will help.
- . . . I know the client might like one face and voice to the deal, but we can't help it sometimes. . . . wouldn't you just want the same guy when you are trying to do business? I mean I would. Well, we can't because there's so much going on.
- I usually schedule meetings if the sales rep requests it. But that happens only occasionally.
- [Only some sales reps meet face-to-face with clients,] especially the ones that have been around longer. I don't recall a new member requesting a meeting this year, but I do it all the time for the older ones. At least three a week.

### Individual Accountability

- . . . the thing is if one member doesn't do their part the team metrics won't be met, makes sense? But no one seems to be hammering the ones that don't.
- But you know that's a bit of a cop-out. I do have to let a few individuals know if I notice them doing something off task with their computers, which, let me tell you, is actually kinda' common. I mean don't some companies have software to block websites not related to work stuff? Well, we don't, so I have to make do.

*Figure 10.9  Long report continued.*

# Grace & Bannock
## Recommendations for Sales Department

Neel Consulting Group, LLC
May 20XX

## Table of Contents

2

*Figure 10.10  Sample slide report.*

# Background and Purpose of the Study

Grace & Bannock, once a small civil engineering consulting firm, has grown to employ nearly 100 professional staff, mostly in the engineering and business administration departments. This growth has occurred because of increased market demand, fueled by an ASCE (American Society of Civil Engineers) report on deteriorating U.S. infrastructure.

Unfortunately, the sales department was not granted a staff increase, and the current sales associates are suffering as a result.

We believe the root cause of the problem in sales is G&B's pursuit to meet increased market demand. G&B has tried to grow too fast, and the following symptoms have resulted:

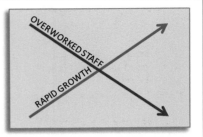

- Unmet sales quotas
- Numerous outstanding projects
- Dissatisfied clients
- Loss of contracts
- Overworked employees
- Low employee morale

After submitting a proposal to G&B, Neel Consulting was authorized to perform the following actions:

- Gather additional data.
- Analyze data to determine causes of problems.
- Make appropriate recommendations.

3

# Research Methodology

We gathered the relevant data needed for this research from three different data sources:
- Work performance data that is captured on a regular basis inside G&B
- Personal interviews with employees
- Online surveys sent to employees

These sources helped us answer four main research questions, as shown in the figure on the right. This combination of data sources helped us understand the most pressing problems in the G&B organization.

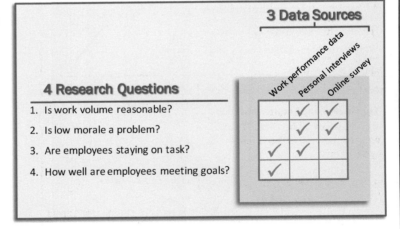

4

*Figure 10.10  Slide report continued.*

# Work Performance Data

G&B's internal performance metrics were used to generate the work output of individual sales representatives. Time on task vs. expected output was analyzed for eight sales representatives to assess daily contribution.

This figure shows that time on task is highly correlated with work output, as would be expected.

The dashed lines identify the average percentages of time on task and work output. The average percentage of time spent on task is 68% and the average work output is 72%. Thus, if you know an employee's percentage of time spent on task, you could assume that their work output percentage will be similar.

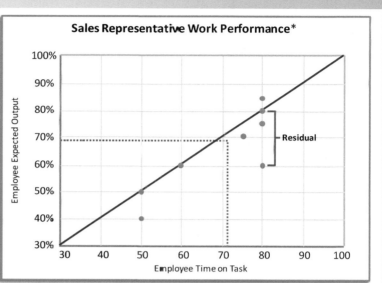

*One example of residual is noted on the graph. This residual (deviation of a given data point from the best fit line) is somewhat significant by itself, but all the other residuals have a value of less than 10 units.

5

# Online Survey Data

Short surveys were conducted to obtain employee insight and measure their satisfaction.

The anonymous online surveys provided data that measured employee satisfaction.

The results of the surveys were obtained using a Likert scale, with numbers 1-4 designating level of agreement.

The accompanying figures show that the majority of the staff is dissatisfied with the work environment. Some indicated that they cannot keep up with their work, mainly because of excess work and making up for less-productive colleagues.

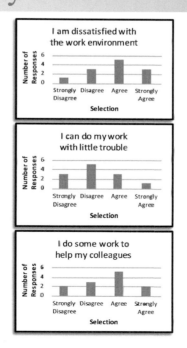

6

*Figure 10.10  Slide report continued.*

## Personal Interview Data

We conducted interviews to gain additional employee insight. Interviews were audio-recorded and transcribed.

We analyzed the interview transcripts and performed a textual analysis to identify dominant themes. Four main topics emerged:

- Customer service
- Workload among associates
- Team metrics
- Equipment availability

The figure on the right gives frequency data. Poor customer service, unbalanced workload, and excessive focus on team metrics appear to be the most troublesome problems.

The personal interview feedback suggests the following:

1. **Poor customer service is a real issue in this department, including limited time for face-to-face meetings with clients.**
2. **The sales staff is unhappy with the unbalanced workload.**
3. **Employees feel that team sales success is more important than individual success.**

"I can meet my individual metrics, but the team's metrics are harder to meet. I sometimes end up taking other people's clients because . . . they're not getting what they need. I feel that it's affecting my ability to meet my own clients' needs, but then the team's metrics seem to be emphasized over the individual's."

7

## Conclusions

1. **Work output and time on task are positively correlated—an increase of time on task yields an increase in work output.**

2. **Employee dissatisfaction is a major problem, largely because team performance is emphasized over individual performance.**

3. **In general, the department is not providing good customer service.**

## Recommendations

1. **Monitor time on task, and review this metric in quarterly performance interviews.**

2. **Provide individual incentives, and place more emphasis on individual performance, not just team performance.**

3. **Improve and monitor customer-service performance, and review this metric in quarterly performance interviews.**

8

*Figure 10.10  Slide report continued.*

# Designing Visual Aids

Can you remember a time when a teacher or presenter showed slides that included text too small to read easily? As you concentrated on trying to read the text, did your attention wander from what was being said? Now think of a time when a presenter's slides were well designed and complemented the spoken message of the presenter. Were you able to stay focused on the speaker's message, while still understanding the visuals? Visual aids should be an important part of your business presentations. They will help your audience members learn with their eyes and their ears. Nevertheless, they must be created and used effectively, or else they can work against you.

Because humans are primarily visual thinkers and learners, visual aids are effective in many different settings and with many different types of presentations. The human brain works most efficiently as an image processor; it has a harder time processing conceptual, textual, and quantitative information, as shown in the following table.

| Image | Mental Processing Required |
|---|---|
| Photograph | Easy |
| Bar chart | Fairly easy |
| Table with some complexity | Somewhat difficult |
| Text with embedded quantitative data | Difficult |

As you work with information that is more difficult to process, think of visual ways to communicate that information. For example, to visualize the process of reaching company goals, you might use a mountain peak to represent the

goal, a backpack to represent the methods and techniques of preparation, and the trail to represent the time required to reach the peak.

This chapter will help you learn effective processes, principles, and patterns in developing visual aids, with primary emphasis on slideshows, handouts, and videos. In today's marketplace, you can find a variety of software packages for creating various media, each with its own advantages and disadvantages. This chapter will not focus on software-specific content, but rather on universal principles of layout and design that remain constant even as software tools change. In addition to the content in this chapter, you can find numerous resources on the internet to help you learn principles of effective design.

After learning the content of this chapter, you should be able to do the following:

- Create effective slideshows, applying principles of layout and design.
- Create effective handouts.
- Create effective videos.

## SLIDESHOWS

As with all communication situations, complete a PACS plan before creating your slides. Understand your purpose in creating the slideshow, analyze the audience and context, and develop an appropriate strategy. If your audience is a group within your own company and you will be speaking while showing the slides, the slides can be a bit less detailed because you will give those orally. If you will be posting your slides online at www.slideshare.net, how-

ever, anyone in the world will be able to view your slides and you will not be giving any oral message. With such a diverse audience, your slides will need to be more detailed. For this chapter, the assumption is that your slides will be used primarily as visual aids to your oral presentations.

Slides can perform several important functions in meetings. First, as you create slides to explain and illustrate your thinking, the slide-creation process forces you to formalize and clarify your ideas—it helps you transform a hazy idea into something more real, visible, and tangible. Second, slides provide a common document that all can see and share simultaneously. Third, slides help people stay more focused on the issues. Without slides, discussion is more likely to wander.

Different types of presentations call for different slide designs, as shown in the following list.

**Informative presentations**: Clear informative content should be accompanied by clear and effective slide design that enhances learning and information retention.

**Persuasive presentations**: The content must appeal to the logical, emotional, and ethical concerns of the audience. Therefore, thoughtful reasoning, appeals to strongly held beliefs and emotions, and sincere concern for the needs of the audience should be evident in your slide design, thus enhancing the credibility of both you, the messenger, and your message.

## Create a Storyboard

When you are required to create a presentation with slides, avoid the temptation to create the slides first. Trying to create good slides first is inefficient and can waste a lot of time because you get bogged down in details before deciding on the overall plan. Therefore, first think strategically about the purpose of the presentation, the audience and context, and the strategy you have chosen, and then proceed to create a storyboard, a small-scale sketch of the slides.

As you create the storyboard, draw a thumbnail sketch of each slide. Keep the sketches simple and don't worry about small details at this time. Using stick figures, shapes (such as rectangles), or squiggly lines to represent text elements can help you focus on the larger visual organization and the overall idea you want to get across. Think creatively and try multiple ideas for a given slide before selecting the final one. For example, if you are trying to illustrate the rapid growth of smartphones, sketch several different ideas

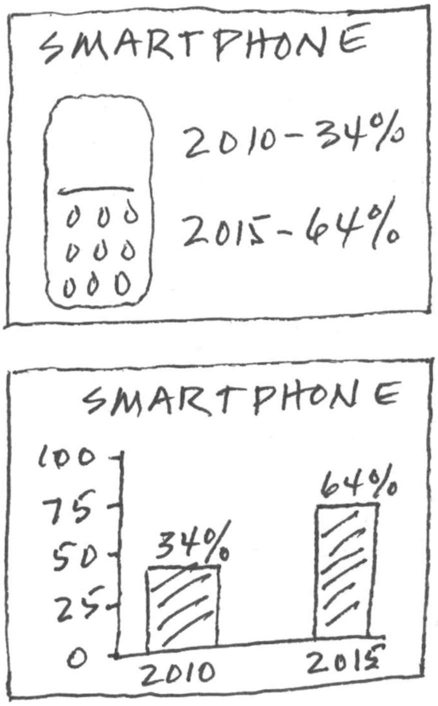

*Figure 11.1 Storyboard slides are simple sketches that show the essence of the slide content.*

and then pick the one you like best. Figure 11.1 shows two different thumbnail sketches of how this slide could be designed.

You can sketch the slides in small rectangles drawn on standard-size paper, but using small sticky notes is perhaps a better idea. With each sticky note representing a slide, you can easily create, modify, and discard slides, as well as move them around to decide on the best sequence. Their small size also forces you to keep your sketches simple.

Mind mapping also works well as an aid in clarifying your ideas and organizing your storyboard. A mind map helps capture important content, but it also reveals logical hierarchies and important relationships that should be included as you create the slideshow (see Chapter 2 for a review of mind mapping).

Use brainstorming to determine what graphics could make your content more visual and impactful. Consider tables, business graphs, photographs, line drawings, concept maps, and original creations to help the audience see and understand your message. Become familiar with commonly used information representations, such as fishbone diagrams, cause-and-effect diagrams, force-field analysis charts, decision trees, Venn diagrams, flow-process charts, mind maps, organization charts, scatterplot diagrams, and bar, line, and pie charts (see Chapter 4 for a review of these visuals).

## Create the Layout and Design

When your storyboard is completed, create your slide layout and design. This is a creative effort fostered by free-flowing thinking and new ideas. However, as you make layout and design decisions, exercise appropriate constraint and don't become so creative that your design becomes excessive. Remember, you are designing—not decorating! Therefore, make sure the layout and design are appropriate for the purpose, audience, and context of the presentation.

The layout and design guidelines in this chapter are intended for most informative and persuasive presentations in a business context. However, if an audience is more diverse and the context is more social in nature, you might need to take a less structured and more entertaining approach. For example, if you are asked to speak to a civic group as an after-dinner speaker, your presentation will need to be both informative and entertaining—sometimes classified as infotainment. Thus, in preparing an infotainment slideshow, you can be more creative and design your slides in a more cinematic style, with less text, a less structured layout, and more use of photographs and creative text and typography.

### Layout

Layout refers to the way you arrange your text and graphic elements on the screen. Obviously, you want the arrangement to look clean and well organized, rather than chaotic and cluttered. PowerPoint, Keynote, and other slideshow software provide a variety of templates for you, but don't assume that you have to use their predesigned layouts. They tend to foster the creation of boring slides with too many bullet lists. Instead, you can easily create your own layout. Here are a few suggestions.

#### Grids

An important key to creating a good layout is to use a grid, consisting of columns and rows. For example, Figure 11.2 shows a five-by-six grid (five columns and six rows). With this grid, you can then develop a three-part template that includes a slide-title row, an agenda column, and a four-by-five area for the slide body. You could just as easily create a six-by-six grid and move the agenda to the bottom row, giving you a six-by-four area (six columns and four rows) for the slide body. The important idea is to develop a grid that works for you and to use it consistently for all the slides. Using a grid achieves good visual organization and makes your slides look well organized and professional.

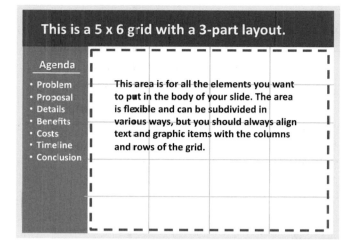

*Figure 11.2  A grid will help you create a good layout for your slides.*

#### Running Agendas

Consider including a presentation agenda along the side or bottom of your slides. This is especially appropriate for informative presentations, such as training or briefing presentations. The agenda provides two benefits—it shows the overall structure of your presentation, and it shows where you are in that overall structure. When you use an agenda, include a pointer or other visual element to indicate where you are in the presentation. For instance, while you are talking about "Benefits" in your presentation, change the color of "Benefits" in the agenda or place a small arrow beside it. When you move from the "Benefits" section to the "Costs" section, change the color of "Benefits" back to the normal color and change the color of "Costs," or move the arrow from "Benefits" to "Costs."

#### Front Door

As you arrange information on a slide, remember two additional guidelines—make sure each slide has an obvious front door and a clear pathway. The front door is a visually dominant object or text item that you want your audience to notice first. Because readers' eyes naturally enter messages at the top of a page or slide, generally place your front-door item in that area. For many slides, your front-door item will be the title of the slide, displayed in a large font. For example, the title of a slide could be made highly visible by using a 44-point, red, bolded Arial font, with all other text on the slide in a smaller, less visually emphatic font. The large title would therefore catch the immediate attention of the audience and serve as the entry point (front door) of the slide. For other slides, the front door could be a large photograph or other eye-catching visual.

*Pathway*

After entering at the front door, the reader should see a clear and obvious pathway through the remainder of the slide, generally following a natural reading trail—from top to bottom and left to right (except for languages written from right to left). As an example, for a two-column layout, this path might be from top to bottom on the left side of the screen and then top to bottom on the right side of the screen. Regardless of the specific pattern on a given slide, the path should be visually obvious to the reader. As needed, you can include numbers or arrows to make sure the pathway is clear. For instance, if you have four text boxes arranged in a two-by-two pattern, use arrows or numbers (1, 2, 3, 4) to designate whether to read the boxes in top-to-bottom-left-to-right or left-to-right-top-to-bottom sequence (see Figure 11.3).

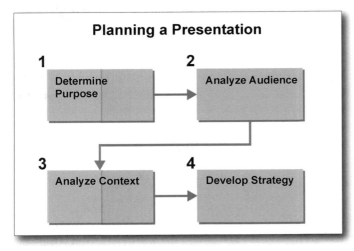

*Figure 11.3  Numbers or arrows can be used to make a slide's pathway clear.*

You may also place a slide number at the bottom of each slide if you would like, in either the left or right corner. Numbering slides is helpful when you want to go to a specific slide directly. For instance, an audience member might say, "I'd like to go back to slide 12 and ask you a question."

## Design

Compared to layout, which focuses on an orderly visual structure, design is more creative and less structured. Nevertheless, it is governed by principles to help ensure that your creativity looks pleasing to the eye. To make sure your design looks professional and harmonious, first decide on the color, typography, and graphic patterns you will use in creating your slides. Then create a design style guide that includes a color palette and guidelines for typography and graphics based on those patterns.

Developing design style guides will yield two significant benefits. First, they enable you to produce slides that have visual consistency. Second, they save time, preventing you from having to make design choices time and time again. The following sections give design guidelines for color, typography, and graphics.

## Color

For your slideshows, identify four or five colors that go well together. You might use one of the colors as the slide background, another for slide titles, another for body text, and another for graphic borders.

Color is a powerful attribute of design, and it can be introduced as text color, graphic color, or background color. Because of the dramatic impact color can have on communication design, it is essential to have a basic understanding of color properties and how different colors interact with each other.

**Hue:** The human eye is estimated to be able to perceive about 10 million different colors or hues. Rather than naming each one, however, various systems have been developed to identify and differentiate these colors. These systems, often referred to as "color spaces" are usually based on a "color model" that combines a small set of primary colors in varying amounts to produce secondary hues. Color spaces vary in size (how many distinct colors they identify) depending on how they are organized and the color model they use.

Two of the most common color models are RGB and CMYK, named from the primary colors they use. RGB is often used with TVs, computer screens, and other electronic devices that combine Red, Green, and Blue light in varying amounts to create different colors. CMYK is used in laser printers and large printing presses where Cyan, Magenta, Yellow, and Key inks or toners are combined. ("Key" is the printer's term for the color that adds detail to a picture, which is usually black).

Figure 11.4 illustrates how various hues are made from mixing different amounts of a color model's primary colors. Figure 11.5 contains a much simpler and familiar color model—a color wheel. In this space the primary colors are the familiar red, yellow, and blue, and the secondary hues are shown in between the primaries used to create them. The color wheel is also helpful in understanding other properties of color.

**Value:** Color value is yet another attribute to be aware of. Value refers to a color's relative darkness or lightness. Notice in Figure 11.5 how each hue gets lighter

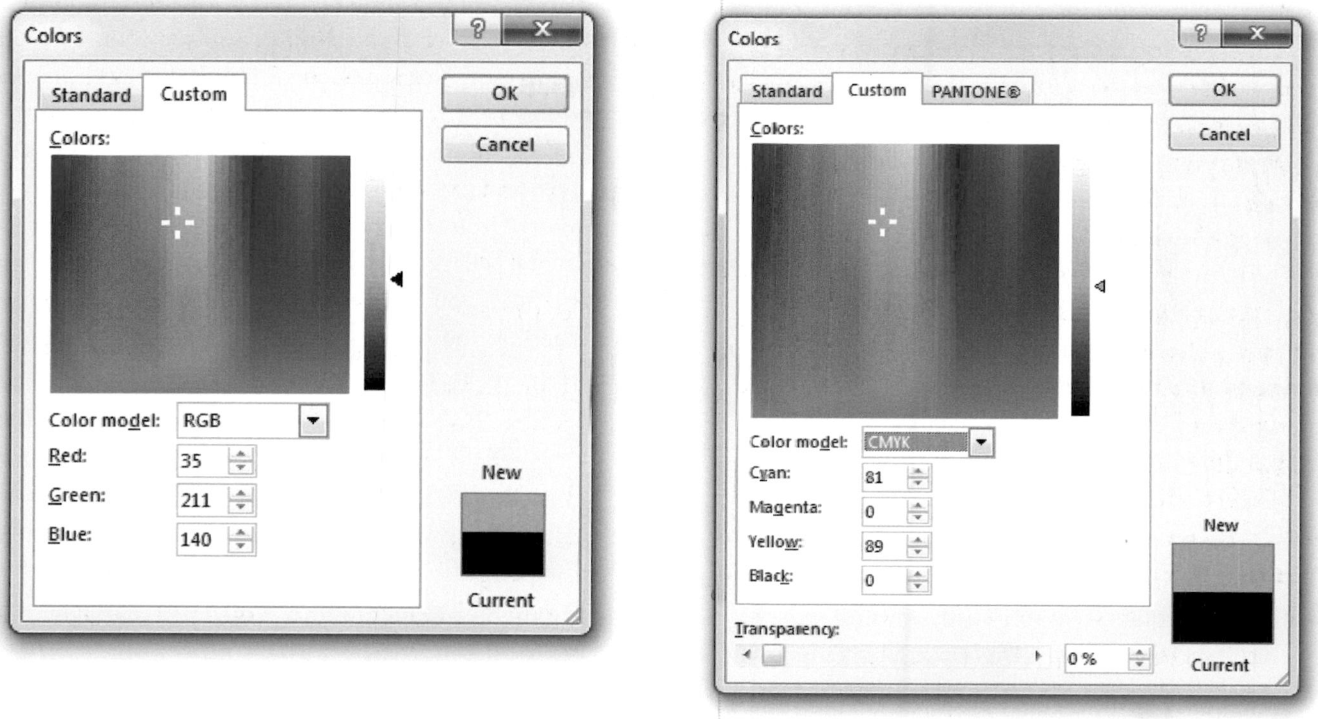

Figure 11.4 *Software color palettes give precise control over color used in graphics. The color field allows hue and vibrancy selection while the slide bar at its right permits shading and tinting. The palette on the left shows an RGB color model, while the palette on the right shows the same color using a CMYK color model.*

towards the center of the wheel, and darker at the outer edge. Adding black to a color creates a shade; adding white to a color creates a tint (although black and white themselves are not considered colors).

When deciding on the text color and background color for a slideshow or website, use highly contrasting values. For example, you can't easily read black text on a shaded blue background or tinted yellow text on a white background, because of the low value contrast. Light yellow text on a dark blue background, however, is very readable because of the high value contrast. Depending on the colors you choose, you may need to adjust tint and shade in order to create enough value contrast. Alternately, you may use simple black and white for slides, with either black text on a white background or white text on a black background. Both approaches provide high contrast and good readability. Figure 11.6 illustrates a variety of both effective and ineffective foreground-background color combinations.

**Temperature:** Colors are also classified as having a temperature—some colors are warmer, and others are cooler. Generally, red, yellow, and orange are considered warmer colors than blue, purple, and green. However, tinting a color will also make it cooler, and it is possible to have both warm and cool versions of any

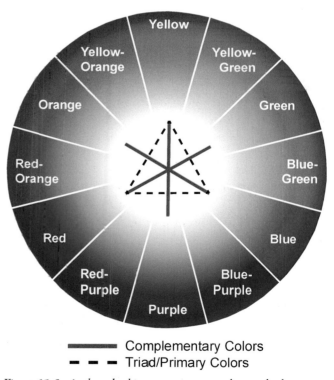

## The Color Wheel

Figure 11.5 *A color wheel is a great way to understand color properties. This color wheel uses three primary colors (red, yellow, and blue) to create a color model of twelve hues. Each color is also shown as a scale of tinting and shading. Each color's complement lies directly across the color wheel.*

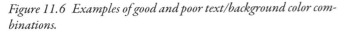

| Background Color | Recommended Foregrounds | Foregrounds to Avoid |
|---|---|---|
| White | Black, dark blue, red | Yellow, light blue, light gray |
| Blue | White, yellow | Green, red |
| Light Gray | Black, dark blue | Green, yellow |
| Dark Gray | White, yellow | Brown, gray |
| Black | White, light blue, yellow | Dark red, dark blue |
| Dark Blue | Yellow, white | Dark green, black |
| Brown | Yellow, white | Red, pink |
| Dark Green | White, Yellow | Dark blue, dark red |

*Figure 11.6 Examples of good and poor text/background color combinations.*

hue. Color temperature is important to keep in mind because when warm and cool colors are used together, the warm colors seem to visually advance, and the cool colors seem to recede. Therefore, you generally want warmer colors for more important elements such as text and cooler colors for elements like backgrounds. Placing a cool color of text (such as blue) over a yellow background can cause the background to compete with the text visually. Figure 11.7 demonstrates this problem and how it can be fixed by highly tinting the background to make it cooler.

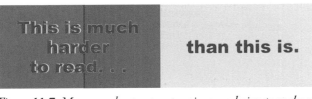

*Figure 11.7 Manage color temperature in your design to make sure it communicates effectively.*

**Complement:** Each color also has a complementary color, and each color's complement is the color directly opposite on a standard color wheel (see Figure 11.5 ). Complementary colors represent the greatest amount of visual contrast possible in hue.

**Vibrancy:** The vibrancy of a color refers to its purity and brightness. The more a color is mixed with its complement, the less vibrant and more gray it becomes. The color palettes in Figure 11.4 illustrate a scale of vibrancy from top to bottom. Gray is said to be color neutral, and because it is neutral, it can be used effectively with all other colors. The more a color is modified toward gray, the more it becomes color neutral and harmonizes with other colors.

Which colors should you use in your slideshow or on a handout? Rather than selecting random colors, develop a strong color theme based on your purpose, audience, and context.

For instance, if your purpose is to advertise a Christmas party, red and green may be a better theme than red, white, and blue. If your audience is scholars and administrators from a local college, the school's colors may be an appropriate theme. And if you are presenting in the context of a corporate meeting, you may want a theme based on the colors of the company's logo.

In selecting a color theme, it may helpful to consider the following four types of color combinations. These combinations all appear harmonious to the human eye, and choosing one of them as a framework for your color theme can help you avoid color chaos.

**Monochromatic** combinations consist of different values of the same color. Various tints or shades of blue would be considered monochromatic. These combinations are simple and unifying, may save on printing costs, and may copy nicely to black and white.

**Analogous** combinations consist of two colors adjacent on the color wheel, such as blue and blue green. These are great for adding just a bit more color variation but without a lot of contrast.

**Complementary** combinations use both a color and its complement, such as yellow and purple or red and green. Complementary combinations represent the highest degree of color contrast. If you want a color or colored object to be noticed, place it beside its complement. (An interesting thing about complementary colors is that if you stare at a colorful object for 30 seconds and then close your eyes, you will see the colors' complements as a visual after-effect, as in Figure 11.8).

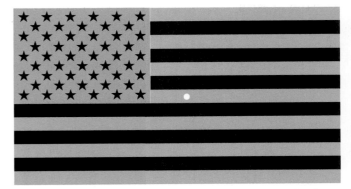

*Figure 11.8 Stare at the white dot in the middle of the flag for 30 seconds. Then close your eyes and see what image remains with your eyes closed.*

**Triad** combinations consist of colors that lie at the points of a triangle on a color wheel. Red, yellow, and blue represent a triad combination. Triads allow for greater color variation while maintaining harmony.

As you make color decisions, don't get carried away. Keep in mind that color plays a supporting role in helping to communicate your message. You do not want a color theme that draws attention to itself, overpowers the content, or distracts from the message. No matter how simple or complex, how dull or vibrant your color theme is, if the audience will remember it instead of the content of your message, you should choose a different theme.

To help you choose effective color combinations and themes, examine theme colors suggested by your computer software or consult various websites devoted to color (e.g., color.adobe.com, paletton.com, colormatters.com, and www.colorcombos.com).

### Typography

Typography is another important element of design. Most typographic experts recommend two contrasting, but complementary, typefaces for each document. In other words, the two faces should be noticeably different in shape, but they should look good together. After choosing the two typefaces, use those faces throughout your documents and slides. For the printed page, experts recommend one serif and one sans serif. For electronic displays with lower resolution, however, the tiny serifs of some typefaces might not display well. Therefore, you could use two contrasting, but complementary, sans serif fonts, or use a sans serif font and a serif font with bolder serifs, such as Georgia.

After selecting the two typefaces, use size and style variations of those typefaces to designate headings, body text, and emphasized text. For instance, if you choose a sans serif and serif combination, you could use large, bolded Calibri (sans serif) for headings and smaller Georgia (serif) for body text (see Figure 11.9). Alternately, if you choose two sans serif faces, you could use a large, bolded Helvetica font for headings and a smaller Calibri font for body text. For slides, remember to keep the text large enough to be seen easily anywhere in the room. Also, avoid excessive typographic creativity. Don't go overboard with italics, bold, color, size, or font variations.

As mentioned in the preceding section on color, ensure high contrast between text and its background, either with color or with value (value is the relative lightness or darkness of an object or text). If you use a colored font and colored background, generally use a warm color for the text and a cool, highly contrasting color for the background.

Regarding typographic color, be consistent throughout your slideshow or document (e.g., all bullets in blue or all main headings in red). For typographic emphasis, use color on just a few words on a slide. Adding color to more words reduces the amount of emphasis each colored word gets; therefore, more is less and less is more.

As you create headings, break multi-line titles at logical places. Avoid dangling title fragments. Notice the difference in the line breaks of the two following examples:

No:

Analysis and Evaluation of ABC's International Cash
Transactions

Yes:

Analysis and Evaluation of
ABC's International Cash Transactions

### Graphics

You can include a variety of graphics to enhance message clarity and slideshow effectiveness, including photographs and business graphics. Many slideshows also use vector shapes, such as arrows, connecting lines, or boxes that serve as backgrounds for text. As you plan a slideshow, choose the shapes and shape attributes to use throughout the slideshow. For instance, you could decide to use rounded rectangles for your text boxes, with a tan fill color (a mix of 234 red, 218 green, and 192 blue), and a lower-left drop shadow for those boxes (see Figure 11.9).

**Sans Serif Heading: Bolded Calibri**
Serif body text: Georgia

**Sans Serif Heading: Bolded Helvetica**
Sans serif body text: Calibri

*Figure 11.9 Sample rounded rectangle, with drop shadow, text box.*

One type of graphic not widely used is a watermark—a faded graphic that appears behind the main text and graphics on the slide. Watermarks can help create a mood or tone for the slideshow, but they can also be distracting and make text harder to read. Therefore, use watermarks only when they will contribute to the message and not interfere with the other material on the slide.

When you include business graphics, all the information must be visible and clear. Make sure all the typography is large enough to read easily. Also, as shown in Figure

**Quarterly Audit Violations Report**
20XX Calendar Year

| Branch | 1st Quarter Missing Invoices | 2nd Quarter Missing Invoices | 3rd Quarter Missing Invoices | 4th Quarter Missing Invoices | Total Missing Invoices |
|---|---|---|---|---|---|
| 116 | 2 | 1 | 0 | 0 | 3 |
| 124 | 0 | 0 | 1 | 0 | 1 |
| 157 | 0 | 0 | 0 | 0 | 0 |
| 187 | 2 | 4 | 4 | 5 | 15 |
| 213 | 0 | 0 | 0 | 1 | 1 |
| 224 | 1 | 1 | 0 | 1 | 3 |
| 264 | 1 | 1 | 0 | 1 | 3 |
| 287 | 0 | 1 | 0 | 0 | 1 |
| 356 | 1 | 1 | 0 | 0 | 2 |

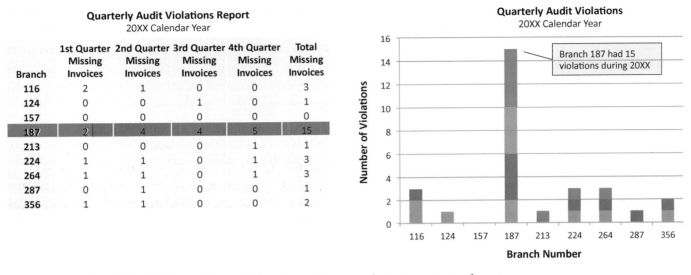

*Figure 11.10  Use highlighted cells in tables and callouts in graphics to emphasize important information.*

11.10, you should use color highlights, arrows, callouts, and other techniques to make sure the message of each graphic is clear.

As you work with graphics, be aware of the following four important attributes.

**Direction.** The attribute of direction refers to where an object directs the reader's eyes. For instance, the text you are reading moves your eyes from left to right and from top to bottom. A vertical bar chart moves your eyes upward to the top of the bars. A photo of a man walking will draw your eyes in the direction he is going. A horizontal or vertical line will move your eyes in the direction of the line. As a general guideline, make sure directional elements don't send the reader's eyes off the slide. Instead, place elements so they move the reader's eyes toward the middle of the slide or toward another element that you want to be noticed (see Figure 11.11).

**Number.** Graphic elements can be used alone or with a group, but remember that the more items you have in a group, the less each one will be noticed—the human brain can process only a few things at a time. Therefore, if you want to highlight one or two items, exclude or visually diminish the competing items. For instance, avoid having too many lines on a line chart or too many items in a list. If you have numerous items to present, such as 13 items in a bullet list, create three or four categories and place those items in the appropriate categories. Try to avoid more than four or five parallel elements to make human processing easier.

**Shape.** All visual elements have a shape, and the human eye instantly recognizes common shapes, such as rectangles, circles, stars, bicycles, trees, people, and thousands of others. Therefore, use bold shapes to attract and hold attention and to communicate your ideas. For example, if you include a close-up photograph of a person, the viewers' attention will be drawn to the person's eyes. Shapes are also important in working with text and typography, because each alphabetic letter and each word has a unique shape. Remember that words in lower-case type are easier to read than words with letters in all upper case—typography vs. TYPOGRAPHY. You may type a heading in all capital letters, but avoid using all capitals for body text because it is extremely difficult to read.

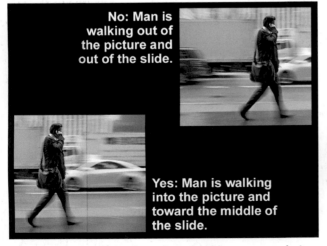

*Figure 11.11  Directional graphics should move a reader's eyes toward the middle of the photo or slide. Note the white text on the black background.*

**Size.** Pictures, text, and other elements can be small or large. Generally, larger text is noticed before smaller

text, and larger pictures are noticed before smaller pictures. Further, large items are usually assumed to be of greater importance than small items. Therefore, increase the size of text and graphics when you want them to be noticed and to be perceived as more important.

## Assemble Information

When your design style guide is finalized, assemble all the text and graphics needed to create the slideshow. Some of the information you will need to create yourself. Other information you may be able to obtain from colleagues, the internet, or other sources. For example, you can obtain photographs, sound files, and videos from shutterstock.com, www.istockphoto.com, www.dollarphotoclub.com, www.loc.gov, www.fotolia.com, videohive.net, www.videoblocks.com, www.123rf.com, gettyimages.com, and www.pond5.com. Adhere to all copyright laws as you use text and graphics from various sources.

To be well organized, place all the text, graphics, audio, and video files together in one electronic location so they can be quickly and easily pulled into the slides as they are needed. Name each element meaningfully, such as *WomanBeingInterviewed*.

## Create the Slides

In the slide-creation phase, you bring your storyboard slides to life. Create a slide for each storyboard slide, following your layout grid and using the design colors, fonts, and shapes you chose earlier. For every slide, ask, "How can I present this information in the most brain-friendly and visually interesting way?" Figure 11.12 illustrates a bland slide with information presented as a bullet list, followed by two slides that present the same information in more visually appealing and brain-friendly ways—one as a table and the other as a visual timeline.

As you assemble and organize the chunks of content on each slide or page, apply the following five principles of layout and design—contrast, alignment, repetition, balance, and spacing. Remember these principles with the acronym CARBS.

### Contrast

Contrast is the key to attracting attention. Contrast can be achieved in countless ways, such as using a different size, color, number, or direction. To use contrast effectively, decide what textual or graphic elements you want to draw attention to, and then make them different from everything around them. For instance, make the font larger, bolder, or more colorful, or include an eye-catching photograph that contrasts with the text that surrounds it. Experiment with different contrasting methods, and then select those that best achieve your objectives. Make sure to use contrast with the main element—the front door—so readers' eyes will be drawn to that place first.

### Alignment

Every item on a page or slide should align with something. For instance, text in paragraphs should be left aligned—that is, aligned on the left margin. For a more formal look, you may fully justify the text (have both left and right line endings aligned on the left and right margins). Headings are usually either left aligned or centered, but occasionally you might want a heading to be fully justified, extending from the left margin to the right. Columns of numbers should be right aligned or aligned by decimals, if decimals are used.

Graphic elements should also be aligned with other elements on the page. For example, align the left edge of a picture with the left edge of text that precedes or follows the picture, or align the middle of a picture with the middle of a column of text that follows it. An alternate form of alignment is curvilinear. For example, if you are designing a slide to advertise a new car, you could insert a picture of the car and then align the left edge of text to follow the curved

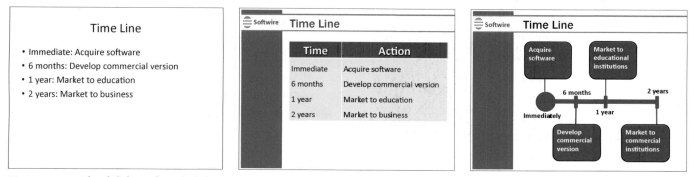

*Figure 11.12 Bland slides such as the left one above can be visually enhanced with tables or graphics like those to the right.*

body of the car. With a finished page of text and graphics, you should be able to see that every element on the page is appropriately aligned with something else on the page. Elements that are not aligned with anything appear to float aimlessly on the page, as if without a visual anchor.

## Repetition

Slides and other graphically rich documents should have a visual theme, and the theme is established mainly by repeating one or more elements or attributes throughout the slides or documents. You can develop a theme with a variety of textual or graphic attributes (see Table 11.1). For example, if you are creating a slideshow about your company's soccer team whose jerseys are red, you could choose a soccer ball and the color red as two elements of the theme. Small soccer balls could be used as bullets for lists, and red could be used for headings and all horizontal or vertical lines. You can also create a company brand by carrying a theme throughout all of your company's slides and web documents, making all publications instantly recognizable.

### Table 11.1 Examples of Repeating Elements

| Repeating Element | Example |
|---|---|
| Type | Arial Rounded MT Bold, 20 point, bold headings |
| Color | Red borders |
| Object | Soccer ball |
| Shape | Circle |
| Arrangement | Photograph at the top of each text column |

## Balance

All the text and visuals on a slide or page should be visually balanced either symmetrically or asymmetrically. Symmetrical balance produces a page that looks evenly balanced, with the left and right sides being mirror images of each other. With asymmetrical balance, the left and right sides are not visually the same. Nevertheless, in some cases there may still be balance, such as two small items on the right to counter-balance one large item on the left. To the human eye, symmetrical layout looks more formal, but less interesting; asymmetrical layout looks less formal, but more interesting (see Figure 11.13).

*Figure 11.13 Visually intensive documents should be created with either symmetrical or asymmetrical balance.*

## Spacing

As you organize the various textual and visual chunks on a slide or page, decrease space between items within chunks (such as between lines of a paragraph) and increase space between chunks (such as between a photograph and a neighboring paragraph). The space around each chunk serves as a frame or border, dividing one chunk from another. If you want an especially strong separator between items, you can put an actual line; but often the extra white space will suffice. To check your slide for chunking, subject it to a squint test. While looking at a slide, close your eyes almost shut until you cannot read the text but can still see fuzzy images of the various visual and textual chunks. With your eyes squinted, see how many visual chunks you can see (each chunk has extra white space around it). Generally avoid more than four or five chunks per slide.

As you apply the various design principles, remember the principle of simplicity. As mentioned previously, you are designing, not decorating. Know when enough is enough. A slide that has too much text, too many elements, too many treatments, or too much of anything will appear cluttered and busy. Some people apply what is called a six-by-six text standard: a maximum of six lines of text and six words per line. This is not a strict standard, but it helps emphasize the principle of simplicity. As you design slides, handouts, and similar documents, think of the main idea you want to get across. Then remove elements that don't add to the message and simplify everything that remains.

Further, make sure all the elements and treatments harmonize well with each other and help achieve the purpose of the message. For instance, a brightly colored, friendly type font, with a photograph of people in a party setting, would complement one another and work well for a flyer announcing a company party. The same treatments, however, would not work for a handout accompanying a

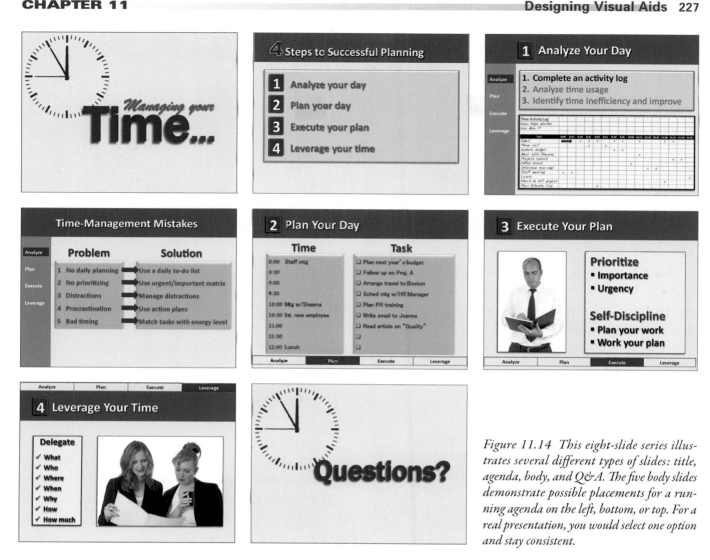

*Figure 11.14  This eight-slide series illustrates several different types of slides: title, agenda, body, and Q&A. The five body slides demonstrate possible placements for a running agenda on the left, bottom, or top. For a real presentation, you would select one option and stay consistent.*

slideshow focusing on a bank's financial problems. In that situation, darker tones, conservative fonts, and business graphics revealing the major causes of the bank's problems would be more in order.

Figure 11.14 contains an example of slides that contain a variety of information. In spite of the varying types of information, the slides all conform to the same layout and design styles.

In addition to applying the preceding design principles, remember the following three slideshow creation tips. First, consider integrating the beginning and ending slides of a presentation. For instance, develop the opening slide around the opening hook, such as highlighting a problem commonly encountered by the audience. At the end of the presentation, display a similar slide and revisit the opening hook, suggesting that applying the solution given in the presentation will help solve the problem.

Second, use slide transitions, animations, and builds purposefully.

Transitions refer to the way a new slide is first brought onto the screen (e.g., moved in from left to right). Use a consistent transition throughout the slideshow, rather than using a mix of different transitions, which can be distracting.

Animations move individual slide objects onto, off of, or around on the screen. Use animations only when they complement, not compete with, the clarity and effectiveness of the message. For example, making text fly onto the slide from various directions serves no useful purpose and can be distracting.

Builds add various details of an entity one by one, eventually revealing the entire entity. For instance, showing a nationwide marketing network layer by layer may be more understandable than showing the entire network at once (Figure 11.15). If you decide to use animations and builds, be aware that PDF copies and hard copies of the slides will not print accurately. Therefore, you'll have to remove animations and builds if you want to print copies to distribute.

Third, develop backup slides to use during the question-and-answer period. Try to anticipate questions the audience might ask in response to your presentation, and

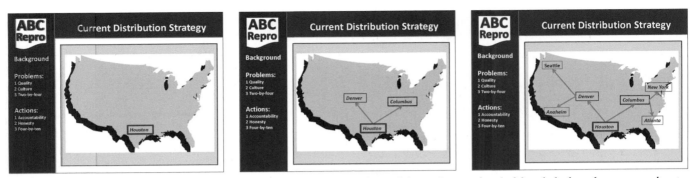

*Figure 11.15 The slides above demonstrate a build as each slide (moving left to right) reveals more detail of the whole than the ones preceding it.*

develop slides to answer those questions. Major questions, of course, should be answered in the main presentation; but the audience might think of additional questions as you present.

### Strengthen the Slideshow

After creating your slideshow, review the following questions and identify any areas where the slides could be improved.

*Layout and Design*

- ❑ Do slides look professional? Do they adhere to all CARBS principles and reflect a simple and clutter-free design?
- ❑ Are relationships made visually clear between related items?
- ❑ Does an appropriate visual theme run throughout the slideshow?
- ❑ Is each slide and graphic clear and easy to process?
- ❑ Are all animations and transitions meaningful?
- ❑ Are animations and builds used purposefully?

*Typography and Text*

- ❑ Are appropriate font sizes used to show textual hierarchy?
- ❑ Does the slideshow use appropriate typefaces and fonts?
- ❑ Is all typography large enough to be read easily?
- ❑ Is there enough color contrast between the text and background?
- ❑ Is all text easy to comprehend?
- ❑ Are slides free from too much text?
- ❑ Is related information on each slide visually chunked?
- ❑ Is text free of grammatical, spelling, and typographical errors?

*Graphics*

- ❑ Are visuals used to complement or replace text?
- ❑ Is the message of each visual clear?
- ❑ Are callouts, color, and other labeling devices used to enhance the clarity of visuals?
- ❑ Is the data in tables and business graphs arranged in logical sequence?
- ❑ Are photographs and visuals appropriately documented and cleared for use?

*Space*

- ❑ Are all visuals and text chunks surrounded by appropriate white space?
- ❑ Do slides contain enough external and internal white space?
- ❑ Does each slide pass the squint test?

*Overall*

- ❑ Are slides arranged in an appropriate and logical sequence?
- ❑ Are beginning and ending slides integrated?
- ❑ Does the slideshow accomplish what it is intended to accomplish?

## HANDOUTS

You can enhance the effectiveness of many presentations by providing a handout for the audience. For each handout, you will need to decide what content to include, how to design it, and how to integrate it into the presentation. Figure 11.16 shows a handout with a creative layout and design, giving it a professional appearance and good visual appeal.

Word processing, page layout, or even slideshow software can be used for creating handouts. If you use slideshow software, such as PowerPoint or Keynote, just switch from landscape mode to portrait mode, and create one slide for a

one-page handout or multiple slides for a multipage handout. Then print full-page slides and make additional copies for each member of your audience.

Most of the design guidelines previously discussed in this chapter also apply to handout creation. A few important guidelines deserve additional emphasis.

1. Use the same basic design for the handout that you used for the slideshow, so the two will reflect a close visual relationship. Match fonts, colors, typography, and graphic style as closely as possible.

2. Regarding the content, create the handout as a stand-alone document, because it may be read by others who did not see your slideshow or attend your presentation. Include all necessary text to ensure that the content is clear. Include a suitable title, the purpose or objective, and adequate content to achieve your objective. Also, include your contact information if you want people to be able to reach you by phone, email, or other means.

3. Use graphics that help clarify and strengthen the main purpose of the handout. Line, bar, and pie graphs; flow-process charts; concept maps; and other visual images can add impact to your text message.

4. Use appropriate typography. Tastefully mix serif and

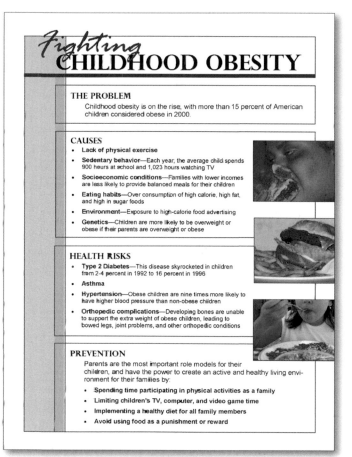

*Figure 11.16 Effective visual design greatly enhances information included in handouts. (Courtesy of Marilyn Pike)*

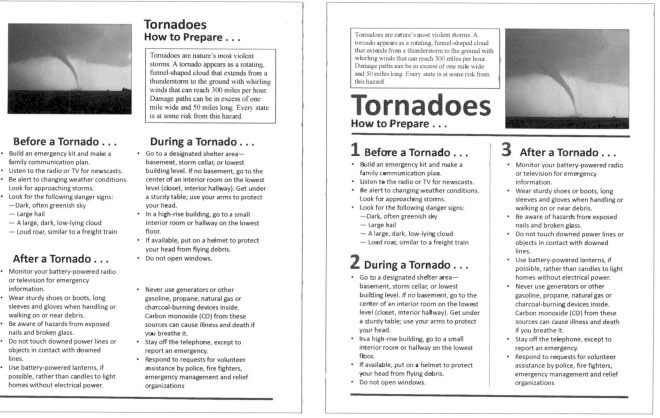

*Figure 11.17 The handout on the left is confusing and disorganized. The handout on the right has been redesigned to have a distinct front door and clear pathway.*

sans serif fonts, and use various font sizes to show hierarchy and text importance.

5. Arrange the layout with an obvious front door and a clear pathway through the document. Numbers or arrows can help define the reading pathway. Figure 11.17 shows a poorly organized handout on the left with its clearly organized counterpart on the right.

6. Apply the same CARBS principles you applied in the slideshow—contrast, alignment, repetition, balance, and spacing. Use contrast to draw attention to the front door and to other important elements. Arrange all elements so they align properly with other related elements. Repeat a color or graphic attribute to tie everything together visually. Use appropriate symmetrical or asymmetrical balance. Leave adequate white space between information and graphic elements.

7. Decide when to distribute the handout. If the audience will refer to the handout during your presentation, distribute it at the beginning or at the point it is needed. Otherwise, distribute it at the end.

As a student you might be asked to create a poster and give a poster presentation. To create a poster, you can follow the same layout and design principles that govern the creation of slides and handouts. However, you will be working with a much larger document (such as 36 by 48 inches), so you will have much more room for content. You will also be working with larger font sizes, in some cases larger than 100 points. Further, you will be printing much larger photos, so you will need high-resolution images to prevent problems with pixelation. Even with these larger elements, however, you can still create poster-size pages with your slideshow software. Once your poster document is created, have it printed according to your size specifications on a large-format printer.

As you learn and apply the visual-design principles presented in this chapter, your slideshows and handouts will help strengthen your presentations. However, you might experience some frustration as you try to apply the principles of this chapter. Remember that learning effective visual design takes time, so don't expect to become an expert overnight. Continue to examine visual design everywhere you go—look at billboards, websites, flyers, business cards, periodicals, books, magazines, and ads. For each visual design, analyze what works well and why it works. Then try to apply what you learn.

*Figure 11.18 Videos are effective in extending the reach of your presentations to distant locations.*

## VIDEOS

Sometimes a video is a good way to convey the information you want to present. A video can be used either as a visual aid to a live presentation, or it can replace the live presentation. For example, you might want to provide a training video for hundreds of employees in 15 branch offices across the country. To fly a presenter from your home office to all of these branches would be logistically difficult, time consuming, and expensive. In this situation a video can be a viable option.

As you prepare to create a video, complete the four standard PACS planning steps. First, clarify your purpose and objectives. For instance, if you are preparing a training video, you will need to present informative content and persuade them to apply the training in their personal operations.

Next, consider the audience. Decide who should receive the video, and then put yourself in their shoes—imagine being in their offices and locations. Think of what challenges you would face, how you would perform their daily functions, and how you would feel about a request to watch a training video. Think of the driving and restraining forces—what would make you want to watch and apply the training video versus what would make you not want to watch and apply.

After analyzing the audience, consider all contextual factors, including technical concerns. Consider what equipment your audience will use to watch your video, as well as what software platforms are used by the audience. Also think of your own video-production resources—cameras, lights, microphones, video-production resources of your company, video-editing software, and so forth. Consider also the timing of the video—when would be the best time to distribute the material. Your strategy might even include

creating different videos for different subsections of the audience, based on different needs, different functions, and different skill levels. The length of the video is also an important factor, including whether to produce one longer video or several shorter segments.

After analyzing the audience and context, develop an overall strategy for creating the video. To create videos, you have three basic options: hire an outside firm, work with your in-house video-production department, or do it yourself. Obviously, expertise, cost, time, and equipment are the main factors that will guide this decision.

Regardless of the production option, develop a storyboard, as explained earlier in this chapter. As you develop the storyboard, keep the message simple, straightforward, and focused. Avoid distractions that compete with the central message. In addition to creating a storyboard, you will need to write the actual word-for-word script. Writing script takes time—time to create, time to review, time to revise, and time to polish. Every word has to be carefully chosen and spoken in producing videos.

If you decide to produce the video yourself, you can gain experience by using your slideshow software and capturing your voice as accompaniment to the slides. Also, you can also use your own webcam to capture your voice and video. Afterward, post the video on your website or on a video-hosting site, send an email to your audience with a link to the location of the video, and provide instructions on how to view the video and how to use it in their workplace.

As you gain more experience, you may decide to pursue a more advanced alternative, investing in video-production technology. The basic steps in the video-production process described above also apply to creating more advanced videos; only the technology is different. Obviously, a video camera and microphone are essential. Sound is crucial to your video's success, so purchase a good microphone. You will also need appropriate lighting, perhaps a green screen for projecting images behind a speaker, and special video-editing software, such as Adobe Premier or Final Cut. As you edit the video, eliminate parts that don't contribute to the purpose. Keep the video concise and focused. Also, avoid video enhancements that distract from the message.

With so much video-production technology available in today's marketplace, you can create good video materials that enhance your presentation to a local audience or that can be transmitted online to distant audiences in many locations.

## CHAPTER SUMMARY

Visual aids are effective in many different settings and with informative and persuasive presentations, because humans are primarily visual thinkers and learners. As you prepare your presentations, brainstorm to identify visual ways to communicate that information. Slideshows, handouts, and videos are three common aids to presentations.

To create a slideshow, first create a storyboard. Mind mapping also works well as an aid in clarifying your ideas and organizing your storyboard. Before creating a storyboard, think strategically about the purpose of the presentation, the audience and context, and the strategy you have chosen. When your storyboard is completed, create the layout and design of your slides.

Layout refers to the way you arrange your text and graphic elements on the screen. The key to creating a good layout is to use a grid, consisting of columns and rows. Compared to layout, design is more creative and less structured. It is governed by five CARBS principles (contrast, alignment, repetition, balance, and spacing). Also remember the principle of simplicity.

To make sure your design looks professional and harmonious, first decide on the color, typography, and graphic patterns you will use in creating your slides. When your design is finalized, assemble all the text and graphics you need, and then create a final slide for each storyboard slide, implementing the layout and design plans you made earlier.

For many presentations you give, you can enhance your effectiveness by providing a handout for the audience. Apply the same CARBS principles you applied in the slideshow. Decide when to distribute the handout, whether before, during, or after your presentation.

Sometimes a video recording is a good way to convey the information you want to present to your audience. A video can be used either as a visual aid to a presentation, or it can actually replace a live presentation. To create videos, you have three basic options: hire an outside firm, work with your in-house video-production department, or do it yourself. With so much video-production technology available in today's marketplace, you can create good video materials that enhance your presentation to a local audience or that can be transmitted online to distant audiences in many locations.

## CHAPTER QUESTIONS

1. Why should you not place large amounts of text in all capitals?

2. What are primary colors? What are the primary colors of computer screens?

3. What is a shade? A tint?

4. How can you determine the complement of a color?

5. What is color value? Why does color value matter in creating slides?

6. Describe two ways to achieve good contrast between the color of text and the background color.

7. What is the difference between symmetrical and asymmetrical balance?

8. What design principle is the key to attracting attention?

9. What alignment option is generally preferred for body text?

10. What is the more-is-less, less-is-more principle?

11. Should a handout be distributed before, during, or after a presentation? Why?

12. What is a storyboard?

13. What is a layout grid?

14. Regarding slide layout, what is meant by the terms "front door" and "path"?

15. What do the initials RGB and CMYK have to do with color?

16. What colors does gray go well with?

17. What is a watermark? What part does it play in slideshow design?

18. What is a callout and how is it used in slideshows?

19. What is the difference between symmetrical and asymmetrical balance?

20. What is a squint test?

21. What does the acronym CARBS stand for?

22. What part do the following principles play in design: contrast, alignments, repetition, balance, and spacing?

# CHAPTER ACTIVITIES

1. Create a flyer to sell something that belongs to you (e.g., car, computer, textbook, or bicycle). Take a well-composed photo of the object with a digital camera and include the photo in the flyer. After creating the flyer, explain how you applied the attributes of contrast, alignment, repetition, balance, and spacing.

2. Go to the website usa.gov and find information about a topic of interest to you (such as consumer safety, emergency planning, health and nutrition, or money and taxes). Create a slideshow that will effectively teach others about the topic. Follow all the slide design guidelines given in this chapter.

3. Create a basic bullet slide on a topic or chapter from one of your textbooks. Then redesign the slide, demonstrating your ability to apply the effective use of visuals and visual-design principles.

4. Using content from this book, create a slide that demonstrates a meaningful animation or build.

5. Create a one-page handout for one of the chapters in this textbook. Apply all the design principles taught in this chapter, and use color effectively.

6. Using the technology of your choice, create a three-minute video that teaches a process or principle from this textbook.

7. Using your slideshow software, create a three-minute narrated slideshow that teaches a process or principle from this textbook.

8. Create a slide with black text on a white background. Then create a reverse of the same slide, with white text on a black background. Insert a colored photograph in one corner of each slide. Compare the two slides. Which do you prefer and why?

## CHAPTER 12

# Giving Business Presentations

Stop for a minute and look around you. Notice everything in your context that has been created by humans. Think of the clothes you wear, the car you drive, the computer and phone you use, and the personal products you use. All of these items first originated in someone's mind, and those original creators had to convince others that those products were worthwhile. Think of the thousands of persuasive presentations that preceded all of these products, and think of the thousands of presentations going on every business day as engineers, designers, entrepreneurs, programmers, marketers, and countless others present new ideas in hopes of gaining support.

Presentations are a critical part of business success. Some presentations are short; some are long. Some presentations are given while seated at a conference room table; some are given while standing and using a slideshow for visual support. Some presentations are given in large convention center rooms to audiences that include people from many organizations; some are given to a small group of colleagues. Regardless of the situation, as a professional you are expected to give presentations clearly, confidently, and effectively.

To become an effective presenter, make the study of effective presentations a lifelong pursuit. Listen to others give presentations, consider their overall approach to their topic, analyze their message structure, list the different ways they support their key points, notice how they begin and end, and observe how they connect with the audience. After each presentation, think about what went well and why it went well. Then learn from it. Strive to develop a deep understanding of what it takes to be a good presenter.

TED Talks (ted.com) is a good online source of quality presentations. On this site you can watch an almost endless number of presentations on all kinds of topics. As you watch and listen to the presenters, pay attention to the structure of their content, notice how they begin and end,

*Figure 12.1 Business professionals have to give many presentations, some while seated at a conference room table and some while standing.*

consider how they develop their theme, and observe their nonverbal communication—eyes, face, hands, and body. List the things you like and incorporate them into your own presentations.

After reading and applying the material in this chapter, you should be able to do the following:

- Create effective content for business presentations.
- Use media effectively in presentations.
- Demonstrate effective delivery skills when presenting to a business audience.

The success of business presentations depends mostly on two major elements—the message and the messenger. Add the media element that often accompanies presentations, and you have a three-M model for creating, presenting, and evaluating business presentations.

## PREPARING THE MESSAGE

Just as you plan before you create written messages, so should you plan before you create spoken messages. With effective planning you can craft messages that will be informative, interesting, and influential.

### Plan with PACS

Before you begin creating a presentation, remember to complete the four important PACS planning steps.

### Purpose

First, clarify your purpose. Know why you are presenting and what you want to accomplish with your presentation, including what you want the audience to know, do, and feel as a result of your presentation. Remember that the three main purposes of business communications are to inform, to persuade, and to build relationships of trust.

After clarifying the purpose, create a good working title. Often one of the 5W2H words works well as the opening word, such as "How to Implement the New Process of Handling Customer Complaints" or "Why We Should Develop a Working Relationship with ABC Company." Later you might develop a more catchy title, such as "Winning Back Our Customers—How to Handle Customer Complaints." Keep the purpose of the presentation uppermost in your mind throughout the entire planning phase and throughout your actual presentation. Make sure each element of your presentation supports the central purpose, and develop your presentation so it answers all what, so-what, and now-what questions.

### Audience

Next, analyze the audience. Find out who will be attending (their organizational affiliation, knowledge of the topic, and needs) and who will speak before and after you. If someone is speaking after you, be sure to finish on time. Few things are more annoying than speakers who go overtime and thereby rob time from the following speaker.

Consider the positions and responsibilities of everyone in the audience. Try to understand the pressures they feel and their needs that are unmet. Learn who the decision makers are and how to best approach them. Identify the parts of your message they will likely agree with and the parts they might oppose. List those positive and negative items on a T chart so you can see the influences working for you and against you.

Look at the presentation through the eyes of your audience. Think of what most people like and dislike about presentations.

| Like | Dislike |
|---|---|
| A clear, relevant message | A disorganized, irrelevant message |
| An interesting, engaging message | A boring, irrelevant message |
| A concise presentation | A long presentation |
| A credible presenter | An unqualified presenter |
| An enthusiastic presenter | An unenthusiastic presenter |
| A presenter who understands the audience and values their feelings | A presenter who doesn't understand the audience and doesn't value their feelings |

### Context

After analyzing the audience, analyze the contextual factors. Ask appropriate 5W2H questions so you understand all relevant who, what, where, when, why, and how much information.

**Who** will be attending, who are the power people, who will be speaking before and after you, who is your contact person for the event, who is the technical support person?

**What** is the topic, what is the occasion, what is the expected dress standard, what technology will be available (computer projector, screen, and whiteboard)?

**Where** will the meeting be held (in person or remote as a webinar or podcast), where are the projector and screen located in the room?

**When** will you present, when should you finish your presentation, when can you set up the room and the technology?

**Why** is the meeting being held, why have you been asked to present?

**How** big is the room, how will the room be laid out, how much natural light is in the room?

### Strategy

After clarifying the purpose of the message and analyzing the audience and context, develop an overall strategy for the presentation, considering the following options.

- Direct or indirect approach
- Individual or team presentation
- Handout or no handouts
- Visual aids or no visual aids
- Audience involvement or no audience involvement
- In person or video or audio

For informative presentations, you could use a direct approach with handouts and visual aids to ensure good understanding, and include audience involvement so they can learn by doing. For persuasive presentations, you could use the standard five-step persuasion model from Chapter 3, with handouts and visual aids, and with audience involvement so you can assess how your presentation is being received. You would also identify the situational aspects that help or hinder your cause, and develop a strategy to strengthen the positive influences and weaken the opposing influences.

Deciding on a strategy must also include choosing a type of delivery:

**Memorized**—the presentation is written in full text form and is memorized word for word. This type of presentation is rarely used in management presentations. A danger of memorized presentations is that presenters focus more on remembering the words than on thinking about the ideas they want to communicate. If you have to give a memorized presentation, decide on a strategy for remembering your key points. For example, you might think of walking into your home or apartment, with the first point representing the front door to your house. Then, as you walk in the front room, somehow associate that room with your second point, and so forth throughout the house.

**Manuscript**—the presentation is written in full text but is read verbatim. This type of presentation is used most frequently when exact wording is critical, as in the case of a crisis-management presentation. It is also sometimes used when addressing large audiences in formal settings. With a manuscript presentation, print your manuscript in large type for easy reading. As you give your presentation, maintain eye contact. Move your hand along each line as you read so you can look up and then find your place when you look back down at your manuscript.

**Extemporaneous**—an outline is created in advance, and the presenter follows the outline while spontaneously choosing the wording of the message. This is the most frequent type of management presentation. For extemporaneous presentations, prepare an outline and memorize the outline as much as possible. Then rehearse the presentation so you feel comfortable giving it with minimal use of notes.

**Impromptu**—almost no time is given for preparation. This type of presentation occurs often in meetings, such as when a manager says, "Alexandra, I'd like you to take a minute and bring us up to date on the ABC project." For these presentations, think clearly and don't panic. Think of the one or two key points you want to make, and then organize them in a simple OABC structure: "Yes, I'd be happy to give an update on our ABC project. Two things are most important to mention. First, …" After the two points are given, provide an appropriate closing statement: "Overall, I would say that we're on target and that things are moving along well."

Business presentations are often a combination of these four delivery types. For instance, the opening and closing might be somewhat memorized, an important statement might be read verbatim, a short segment you think of during the actual delivery might be given impromptu, and the bulk of the body may be given extemporaneously.

As you work on the message, you may change your mind about the strategy. Because message creation is a learning process, keep an open mind and make modifications as you gain new insights and discover new ideas.

## Create the Message

Armed with the knowledge you gained from your PACS planning, you are ready to prepare the content of your message.

## Gather the Content

Deciding what to include in your presentation is guided by the purpose of the presentation and influenced by the audience and context. For informative presentations, consider what the audience already knows, and then add to that knowledge. For persuasive presentations, blend reason and emotion so you reach the mind and heart of the listeners. In both informative and persuasive situations, you take the audience from where they are to where you want them to be—and you strengthen your relationship with them along the way.

Coming up with the right content is a creative process, so take time to brainstorm, by yourself and with others. Ask yourself, "How can I capture the audience members' attention and then inform them or persuade them so I achieve the purpose of my message?"

Mind mapping and bottom-up outlining can help identify and create content ideas. To create a mind map, draw a circle in the middle of a blank page, and write the working title inside that circle. Then write the presentation parts inside secondary circles surrounding the main circle. Then draw lines outward from the secondary circles as you think of additional information and ideas that could be included (see Figure 2.6).

Bottom-up outlining begins by listing all the ideas that pop into your brain as you think or read about your presentation topic. The more ideas you have, the better. As you make the list, don't worry about information structure. After you create the list, arrange the information that you want to include. Decide on the categories into which you could place each item on the list. Generally, restrict the number of categories to five or fewer.

As you develop your presentation, think of three "in" words—informative, interesting, and influential. All three words help answer the WIIFM question asked by all audiences: "What's in it for me?"

**Informative**: Your presentation should inform people, giving them useful knowledge they can use to improve their circumstances—new ideas, new information, and new methods or products that will make their lives better.

**Interesting**: Your presentation should be interesting and hold the attention of the audience. Fascinating facts, unusual ideas, and stories usually have high interest value.

**Influential**: Your presentation should influence and persuade the audience to accept your way of thinking—reinforcing their beliefs that support your ideas and addressing their concerns that oppose your ideas.

## Develop the Presentation Structure

With the body content broken into presentation parts, decide on the sequence of the parts. Information typically falls into one of two sequencing categories: chronological or non-chronological. Chronological is appropriate for explaining processes, sharing experiences, and telling stories. Non-chronological is better for prioritizing problems, reasons, and benefits.

For instance, if you are attempting to persuade your company to adopt an employee wellness program, you could follow the five-step persuasion process. Discuss the problem of poor employee fitness, present your proposed solution, describe how the solution can be implemented (in chronological sequence), list the benefits (in most-important-to-least-important sequence), resolve concerns (in most-important-to-least-important sequence), and close with a call for action.

You could also follow the generic OABC pattern, which might look like the following:

*Opening:* Provide background information, a statement of purpose, and your proposal.

*Agenda:* As appropriate, insert an agenda to forecast the body of the presentation.

*Body:* Present the body content, including an implementation plan, benefits, costs, and concerns. Each content element seeks to strengthen the proposal or minimize resistance to the proposal.

*Closing:* Summarize the problem, proposal, and benefits, and close with a call for positive action, followed by a question-and-answer time.

The basic OABC pattern can be modified in a variety of ways to meet the unique needs of each situation. Figure 12.2 (opposite page) provides nine sample outlines for different types of presentations.

The OABC structure for oral presentations can be envisioned as an arrow, as shown in Figure 12.3. As the shape of the arrow suggests, the bulk of a presentation's time

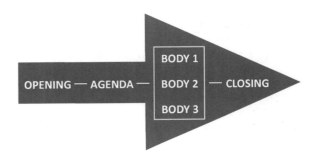

*Figure 12.3 The OABC pattern works well for many different types of business presentations.*

## *Presentation Outlines*

Because each presentation situation is unique, you must tailor your approach accordingly. Presentations can vary greatly in how they are organized depending on their purpose and content. As a resource for preparing different types of presentations, rough outlines and tips for nine common presentation types are included below. Use them as a guide and starting point, but remember that no one specific way is right for all situations. Take time to analyze each situation, and develop your presentation to fit that situation.

### Introducing a Speaker

**Opening** (direct approach): Welcome the speaker.

> *Part 1:* Give speaker's professional credentials.
>
> *Part 2:* Give any other appropriate human-interest information.
>
> *Part 3:* Tell what the speaker is going to speak about.

**Closing:** Transition to the speaker—"We'll now be happy to hear from XXXXXX."

*Tips:* Make it sincere—don't give false praise or give too much praise. Keep it interesting, but keep it short—the audience came to hear the speaker, not you.

### Giving a Briefing

**Opening** (direct approach): Explain the topic and purpose of the presentation; give an opening hook.

**Agenda:** Cite the main presentation parts.

> *Part 1:* Explain the first main point, along with supporting information.
>
> *Part 2:* Explain the second main point, along with supporting information.
>
> *Part 3:* Explain the third main point, along with supporting information.

**Closing:** Revisit the opening

**Q&A:** Take questions for an appropriate amount of time, and then give another brief closing.

*Tips:* Briefings can be about various topics, from boring technical issues to highly charged societal issues. Maintain interest so you don't put people to sleep. A briefing is a mostly informative presentation, so make it well organized and clear. Use clear transitions from one point to the next so the audience can follow. Sometimes audience members may have strong feelings about a topic, so maintain your composure if emotions become involved. Use effective visuals, such as a slideshow, a handout, or both.

### Presenting a Project Report

**Opening** (usually a direct approach mixed with a chronological sequence): Quickly explain the topic and purpose of the presentation. Give the main outcome in general terms.

**Agenda:** List the main parts of the presentation.

> *Part 1:* Provide background; tell why the project was undertaken.
>
> *Part 2:* Explain the procedures you followed to complete the project.
>
> *Part 3:* Report main findings and key points of the data analysis.

**Closing:** Cite the main conclusions drawn from the project. Recommend what action should be taken as a result of the project.

**Q&A:** Answer any questions and then give another brief closing.

*Tips:* Don't spend too much time on the earlier parts of the presentation. Avoid long boring stretches of data analysis. Use clear transitions from one point to the next so the audience can follow. Move relatively quickly to the conclusions and recommendations. Keep the recommendations clear and straightforward. This is what the audience is mainly interested in. Use effective visuals, such as a slideshow, a handout, or both.

### Training

**Opening** (direct approach): Give an opening hook, and then explain the topic and purpose of the training

**Agenda:** List the main segments of the training.

> *Part 1:* Refer to the current procedure (what they know), and then explain and demonstrate the new procedure (what they don't know).
>
> *Part 2:* Have the audience practice the new procedure.
>
> *Part 3:* Ask the audience to respond or give their reaction to the new procedure.
>
> *Part 4:* Give appropriate feedback to the audience comments.
>
> *Part 5:* Explain implementation process and timeline (how and when the new procedure will happen).

**Closing:** Close with a forward-looking statement.

*Tips:* Take a brief moment at the beginning to establish a distinct need for the new procedure, then move to the training. Provide clear demonstrations of the new procedures (show, don't just tell). Get everyone involved. Be somewhat flexible in time management, making sure that you achieve the purpose of the training. Allow the audience to ask questions and give input at any time throughout the meeting. Sometimes people resist change, so be prepared to address emotional and procedural concerns in a calm manner. Follow up afterward to make sure the training procedures are effectively implemented. Use effective visuals, such as a slideshow, a handout, or both.

### Presenting a Proposal
*(to adopt a new idea or to change a procedure)*

**Opening** (indirect approach): Welcome and thank the audience for coming. Give a general statement about the purpose of your presentation (e.g., "to address an issue that has become an important concern").

**Agenda:** Probably skip the agenda, or else give just a general statement about how the presentation will proceed.

> *Part 1:* Explain the current situation.
>
> *Part 2:* Describe the problem and the negative consequences it is causing.
>
> *Part 3:* Describe the solution—the new idea or procedure. Provide all appropriate five-W-two-H information.
>
> *Part 4:* Highlight benefits and cover (but de-emphasize) costs.
>
> *Part 5:* Provide plausible implementation timeline.
>
> *Part 6:* Provide time for Q&A.

cont. →

*Figure 12.2  When preparing a presentation, review these outlines to see if one can be used as a basic framework.*

**Closing:** Summarize and close with a forward-looking statement.

***Tips:*** Be enthusiastic and confident. Be prepared with all necessary content. Keep things moving along; avoid spending too much time on potentially boring sections. Be somewhat flexible in moving through the presentation, taking time to answer all relevant questions at any time and to deal with negative emotions calmly. Pay attention to the concerns of the decision makers and be sure to address those concerns. If the audience is considering other ideas, emphasize the strengths and downplay the weaknesses of your proposal; then do the opposite with the alternate proposals. Use effective visuals, such as a slideshow, a handout, or both. Don't be disappointed if you don't close the deal; situations like this sometimes take months to finalize.

### Seeking Funding for a New Venture

**Opening** (mostly direct approach, mixed with a problem-solution sequence): Welcome and thank the audience for coming. Give a general statement about the purpose of your presentation.

**Agenda:** Probably skip the agenda, or give just a general statement about how the presentation will proceed.

*Part 1:* Quickly describe the funding opportunity.

*Part 2:* Describe the need (the current problem to be solved and its significance).

*Part 3:* Describe the solution—how the problem will be solved.

*Part 4:* List all benefits and discuss costs.

*Part 5:* Provide an implementation timeline.

*Part 6:* Highlight the qualifications of you and your organization.

**Q&A:** Transition to a Q&A segment.

**Closing:** Proceed to an action ending.

***Tips:*** Be positive and upbeat throughout the presentation. Don't go into too much detail with your analysis; stick with the few key points and keep the presentation moving along. Clearly establish a need and provide a crystal-clear description of the solution, along with your qualifications to wisely and carefully administer the funding. Focus on appropriate values, and seek to stir the audience members' emotions. Be prepared also to answer a wide variety of questions in a calm and confident manner. Use effective visuals, such as a slideshow, a handout, or both. Be prepared to follow up numerous times after the meeting, because people don't make decisions like this in a hurry.

### Selling a Product or Service

**Opening** (mostly direct approach, mixed with a problem-solution sequence): Welcome and thank the audience for the opportunity to meet. Give a general statement about the purpose of your presentation.

**Agenda:** Probably skip the agenda, or give just a general statement about how the presentation will proceed.

*Part 1:* Quickly describe the product or service.

*Part 2:* Discover and discuss the customer's needs.

*Part 3:* Tell how the product or service will solve the customer's problem. Tell stories of others who have purchased the product or service.

*Part 4:* Cite benefits and emphasize why your product is superior to others.

*Part 5:* Discuss costs.

*Part 6:* Emphasize the credibility of your organization.

**Closing:** Proceed to an action ending, attempting to close the sale.

***Tips:*** You must clearly establish a need so the customer will feel a need to act. Emphasize the benefits of the new product, perhaps also lightly covering the consequences of not taking action. Be a good listener and seek for input throughout the presentation. Focus on the values held by the customer, not on your desire to make a sale. Be prepared also to answer a wide variety of questions in a calm and confident manner. Use effective visuals and product models.

### Defending an Unpopular Policy or Decision

**Opening** (mostly direct approach): Welcome and thank the audience for the opportunity to meet. Give a general statement about the purpose of the meeting.

**Agenda:** Explain the procedure to be followed—probably a brief statement from you, followed by questions from the audience.

*Part 1:* An appropriate segment by you, explaining justification for the policy or decision.

*Part 2:* Questions from the audience and answers by you (or others who may be accompanying you)

**Closing:** At an appropriate time, or when questions cease, thank the audience for their questions. Then express your hope that your answers have provided useful information to help the audience better understand the rationale behind the policy or decision.

***Tips:*** When going before a "firing line" like this, prepare yourself both logically and emotionally. Have a well-prepared opening statement that highlights your key talking points. Throughout the rest of the session, refer back to those talking points again and again. Know your positive points, and emphasize them. Be aware of your vulnerabilities, and address them. Focus on important values, such as fairness, honesty, integrity, and concern for people's well being. Avoid the appearance of being rigid and unbending. Tell brief stories to support your key points. Emphasize the negative consequences of taking alternative courses of action. Answer questions clearly, but concisely, and then move on. Don't get bogged down with one person or one issue, and never at any time become impatient or angry.

### Giving a Keynote or Special Event Speech

**Opening** (depends on the content): Thank for the opportunity to speak. Acknowledge leaders and audience members. Give positive comments about the event or occasion.

**Agenda:** List the key topics you will cover.

*Part 1:* State the topic and give supporting content.

*Part 2:* State the topic and give supporting content.

*Part 3:* State the topic and give supporting content.

**Closing:** Give a summary statement and a wish for success to the audience.

***Tips:*** Because this type of presentation often involves a more general audience, keep the content relatively general and light. Use informative, interesting, and inspiring stories to develop the key points and to keep the audience involved. Perhaps the most important tip is—keep it short!

*Figure 12.2 continued.*

is spent on the body, but the opening, agenda, and closing are vital in achieving the overall purpose of the presentation, whether to inform or to persuade. If everything works together, the arrow hits the intended target and the presentation is a success.

The following sections provide additional information on how to use an OABC pattern for presentations, including a question-and-answer (Q&A) segment.

### Opening

At the opening of your presentation, each of your audience members will be thinking about something different. Therefore, your first priority is to hook their attention and pull them into your presentation. Just as a fisher uses an attractive lure on the end of the line to attract and hook a fish, you use a creative opening to attract and hook the audience. Consider using one of the following approaches:

- A shocking statistic or trend. For instance, "Only 10 percent of today's young people believe they will be financially able to retire at age 65!"

- A rhetorical question (a question used to prod the audience to think but not to actually answer aloud). For example, "If our company were to convert to solar energy, how much money do you think we would save on our monthly utility bills?"

- Humor that is appropriate for the audience and the topic. The humor should be in good taste, should generate at least a smile, if not laughter, and should relate to the presentation topic.

- An attention-grabbing object or visual. For instance, training on business writing could begin with a visual of a poorly written letter, filled with writing flaws and grammatical errors.

- A short, memorable saying or quotation. An example in a presentation on the need for product innovation

could be, "You've heard that if it ain't broke, don't fix it, but I say if it ain't broke, let's break it!"

- An interesting story. Select short stories that capture attention and emotion and that clearly drive home your key point. Stories hold audience members' attention because they want to know how the stories end.

- An example related to the topic. Examples can be about something good or something bad, depending on which one best illustrates the point.

- A problem frequently encountered by the audience. For a group of marketing managers, talk about the challenge of getting the right product message to the right people at the right time.

- A captivating video clip. Many clips are available on YouTube and can be easily downloaded for showing in a presentation.

Make sure the opening hook relates to your topic and helps establish the theme of the presentation. Because repetition is a vital part of learning, refer back to the hook or theme a few times during the presentation. Each repetition will make the theme more and more dominant in the mind of the audience.

Make sure the hook also helps set the tone of the presentation (e.g., serious, humorous, or urgent) and helps you connect with the audience. The importance of connecting with the audience cannot be overemphasized. First, you must connect as a likable, genuine human being—someone they can feel comfortable with. Second, you must connect as a credible authority on the topic. Third, you must connect with the needs and interests of the audience. Thus, make sure your opening helps establish you as a likable, credible, audience-oriented presenter.

In most cases, transition to the main message right after your hook. Because most managers prefer a direct approach in presentations, this is the best time to give your key point. For persuasive presentation you might say, "Today I'm recommending that we implement a formal employee wellness program." For an informative presentation you might say, "Today I'm going to announce upcoming changes in our call center and tell how these changes will help us be more sensitive to customers' needs."

### Agenda

After the opening, create the agenda. When a person is giving a presentation and says, "Here are three things you should know," what happens inside your mind? First, the statement creates anticipation—you want to know what those three things are. Second, the statement causes your brain to create three empty mental buckets for storing the

*Figure 12.4 Humor can play an effective role in business presentations if it is used properly.*

three things. That is the power of an agenda—it generates anticipation and gives the audience a structure for receiving the message.

An agenda forecasts what will follow in the body of your presentation. The agenda can tell the number of body segments, identify the segments, or announce the structure of the segments. Examples of these three agenda types are as follows:

*I believe we'll achieve three major benefits from moving to solar energy.*

*Let me explain how such a program can reduce absenteeism, improve morale, and improve our bottom line.*

*Our survey has identified our customers' most troublesome complaints, which I'll cover in order of frequency.*

An agenda can also combine any of the three preceding types:

*We can achieve significant benefits in the three areas of absenteeism reduction, morale improvement, and bottom-line improvement. I will explain each of those, in order of greatest impact.*

### Body

The body supports the main message of the presentation and develops the ideas introduced in the agenda. Explanations, examples, and other useful information help the audience understand what you want them to know.

For informative presentations, the body develops the various parts of the overall topic. These should, of course, be sequenced in a brain-friendly, logical pattern for easy comprehension. Each part should ensure that the audience has a clear understanding of the topic. Stories are especially helpful in conveying information in a way that it is understood and remembered. People love stories!

For persuasive presentations, the body provides support, or evidence, for your recommendation. Each body segment has a role to play. Like different witnesses in a court of law, each part provides convincing evidence in support of the recommendation. For example, each segment could show how life will be better for the audience if they accept and adopt your idea. A typical before-and-after approach works well: "Today we have 56 lost work days per month; with an employee-wellness program, I'm optimistic that we could reduce that number by 15 percent to 47." As you move from one segment to the next, your presentation can follow a cyclical pattern of what is vs. what could be, what is vs. what could be, and so forth.

Be aware that several forces are at work when you attempt to persuade an audience. Graber (2003, 182) has identified four factors that affect your ability to persuade and influence others.

1. You must have relevant information
2. You must have good persuasion skills
3. You must have internal capital (respect and credibility)
4. The audience must be open to persuasion

The degree to which your audience is open to persuasion will vary. They will usually have both driving and opposing forces competing in their minds. Of course they want lower absenteeism, they want to achieve greater morale, and they want to achieve greater profitability. However, they also wonder if a wellness program will be a distraction to the real work of the company and if the added expense of the program will really be cost effective. In your presentation, reinforce the driving forces and provide evidence to eliminate or reduce the opposing forces.

You have numerous options for developing each of the body segments:

**Explanations:** definitions, descriptions, statistics, details, and logical analyses

**Illustrations:** examples (both good and bad), metaphors, and stories

**Evaluations:** qualitative and quantitative comparisons (compare and contrast) and testimonials

**Applications:** where an idea has been tried before and how it could be applied in the future

**Visuals:** business graphics, concept maps, illustrations, and photos

As you persuade management to implement a company wellness program, for instance, you could develop your points as follows:

- Display a line graph to show the percentage of Americans who are out of shape.
- Cite statistics showing that your company employees would welcome a fitness program.
- Display another line chart that tracks the growth of wellness programs in the last 10 years.
- Tell the story of two companies that implemented a wellness program.

- Quote a well-known leader who stresses the importance of physical fitness.
- Explain how a wellness program would function in this company.
- Explain the increase in employee motivation that accompanies wellness programs.
- Show pictures of fitness center equipment that could be part of a wellness program.

Many persuasive presentations include a process of choosing one of several alternatives. Displaying a decision table enables the audience to see your evaluations and to summarize the process in one simple visual (see Figure 4.3). Depending on the mindset of the audience, you can give a detailed description of just the option you recommend or give details about all the options and highlight the strengths of your recommended option against the others.

As you work on the body of a presentation, keep it interesting. Remember that the body of a presentation can be boring, especially when it involves long segments of data analysis! Therefore, insert a few interesting tidbits throughout the body to keep the audience engaged. The list of hooks given earlier in this chapter can be helpful in keeping the audience engaged during the body of the presentation.

### Closing

As with other parts of the presentation, the closing will be different for an informative presentation than for a persuasive presentation. For informative presentations, the closing provides an opportunity to summarize the most important parts of the presentation, thus enhancing retention.

For persuasive presentations, the closing should be a call to action! For instance, you can give an overall picture of "what is" versus "what could be," and then encourage the audience to adopt your recommendation. You can also revisit the opening hook, which describes a problem, and then restate how your proposal will solve the problem. For example, "At the beginning I showed you the disappointing stress-test results for our employees. With the employee wellness program I have described today, you can play a major role in helping our employees enjoy better physical fitness, so you'll never have to see statistics like this again."

### Questions and Answers (Q&A)

As you give a well prepared presentation, you have control over the content and sequence of your material. When you get to the question-and-answer segment of a presen-

tation, however, you have to deal with whatever questions are asked and in whatever sequence they arise. Thus, you need principles and guidelines to help in dealing with this unpredictable part of your presentation. Those given in the following paragraphs can be applied in a variety of presentations, including public hearings when audience emotions can be a potential problem.

For some presentations, you will invite questions during the presentation, but for others you will want to reserve questions until the end. The advantage of taking questions throughout the presentation is that you'll know how the audience is feeling, and you can address people's concerns as you go along. Audience members will also appreciate the opportunity to ask questions when they think about them, rather than having to wait.

However, questions during the presentation can derail your presentation, causing you to present your information in a different sequence and in a different way than you had planned. Therefore, if you invite questions during your presentation, retain control. To do so, you might have to delay some questions with a comment like, "That's a good question; we'll answer that in just a few minutes."

To introduce the Q&A portion of the presentation, make your closing comments and then say, "I will now be happy to answer any questions you might have." You may also prepare a special "Q&A" slide to show at this point (see Figure 12.5).

What do you do if no one asks a question! One option is to close with a comment like, "If there are no questions, then let me again emphasize the importance of this proposal. . . ." Alternately, you could pose an open question to the audience about something in your presentation, such as, "In my presentation, I mentioned the possibility of creating a training video. What do you think about this idea?"

Treat the Q&A segment of your presentation as seri-

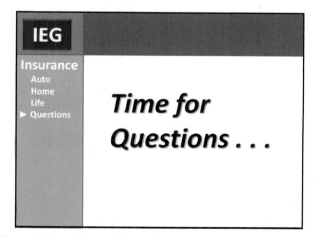

*Figure 12.5 A Q&A slide can be used during the question-and-answer segment of your presentation.*

ously as you do the main presentation. Try to anticipate the 5W2H questions that might arise:

**Who** will be affected by this change? Who will implement and manage the change?

**What** impact will this have on our expenses, our income, our bottom line?

**Where** will changes be made? Where will funding come from?

**When** should we implement the new program? When will we see the desired results?

**Why** should we adopt your idea and not another? Why do we even need to make a change?

**How** would this program be managed? How will you deal with problems that arise? How will we know it is achieving the results we want?

**How much** risk does this idea present for us?

Be prepared to answer all the questions you can think of, especially the tough questions that pose the greatest opposition to your presentation success. Rehearse your answers to these questions, and include any previously shown slides or backup slides that will help strengthen your answers.

When a question is asked, make sure everyone has heard the question. If they haven't, repeat it so all can hear. Also, make sure you understand the question. If you're unsure, ask the person to restate the question ("Could you restate the question, please?"), or paraphrase the question as you understand it ("So you're wondering about the impact of the new program on your part-time employees, is that correct?").

*Figure 12.6 Q&A time gives an opportunity for good two-way communication.*

When you answer a question, involve everyone in your answer. Look at the person who asked the question for the first few seconds of your response, and then speak to the rest of the audience. You can also invite other members of the audience to respond to the question, as appropriate. This conveys an attitude of openness on your part, and it gives others a chance to share their insights.

Here are a few additional guidelines for answering questions:

- Answer each question clearly and concisely. Avoid overly long answers. Give the answer and then move on to the next question.

- If you are unsure whether you adequately answered the question, ask, "Did that answer your question?"

- If you don't know an answer, don't guess. Admit that you don't know, and offer to get an answer and provide it to the questioner later. Be sure to get the person's contact information so you can fulfill your promise.

- If someone asks a question that you have already answered, politely answer it again so you don't embarrass the person. The audience will be impressed with your patience. Don't say, "I already answered that question." Also, if someone asks an irrelevant question, answer it briefly and politely and move on.

- If someone begins to dominate the time with self-promoting mini-speeches of their own or with multiple questions not of interest to others, you might need to be a bit assertive to regain control. If necessary, politely cut in and state something like, "Thanks for your comments; let's take a few more questions." Then look away from the person and take a question from someone else. Always retain control.

- If someone challenges you in anger or frustration, respond in a calm, considerate manner, regardless of the emotional state of the person or audience. Remember that whenever you sense anger, resistance, or any other negative emotion, remain calm, cool, and collected—NO MATTER WHAT! If you cave in to their negative emotion, you stand to lose your credibility, your reputation, and your chance to have your ideas accepted by the group.

When you sense that enough time has been taken for questions, state something like, "Thank you for your questions. We probably should close now, but I'll be happy to take individual questions afterward, either right now or by phone or email back at my office." Then take 10–20 seconds to give a few final words of support for your presentation and sit down.

# PREPARING THE MEDIA

This section of Chapter 12 focuses on preparing media used in conjunction with an oral presentation. However, you should be aware that you may occasionally work with media that captures your entire presentation for transmission on the internet. For instance, you could video record your entire presentation and upload it to YouTube (www.youtube.com) for later viewing by either a general or specific audience. You could also audio record your presentation and make it available as a podcast on your website. Further, you might be asked to give a live presentation to a remote audience as a webinar. Such presentations lack the personal interaction that is possible in a face-to-face setting, and you can't read the body language of the audience to know how they are reacting to your presentation. Thus, you have to do your best to give an engaging presentation that is interesting, as well as informative, so you can capture and keep their attention.

As you prepare media to augment your oral presentation, remember that people learn in a variety of ways, including (a) auditory, (b) visual, and (c) kinesthetic or experiential learning. Auditory learning occurs by listening, visual learning occurs by watching, and kinesthetic learning occurs by doing. To enhance all types of learning, try to incorporate a full mix of auditory, visual, and kinesthetic elements in your presentations. For instance, with your voice you help auditory learning, with visual aids you help visual learning, and with audience-involvement activities you help with experiential learning.

Slideshows are the most common form of visual aid used in business, but you might also use whiteboards and flip charts, especially for department and team meetings. The following paragraphs give a few tips for using these three types of media.

## Slideshows

Chapter 11 covers the creation of slideshows; the following section explains how to integrate slideshows in your presentation.

Before the meeting, decide how you want the room arranged. If working with a facilities management department, describe how you want the room to be set up. If you are giving a training presentation, a wider arrangement with fewer rows of chairs may be better than a deeper layout with more rows (see Figure 12.7). If possible, locate the projection screen so it is not directly behind you as you stand in the front center of the room. Also, make sure not to stand

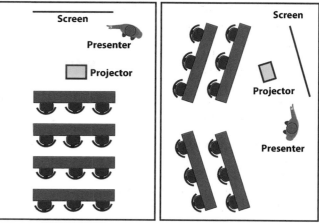

*Figure 12.7 Ineffective and effective room arrangements.*

between the projector and the screen, causing the slide images to project on your face.

Whenever you use technology in your presentation, go early to the presentation room and make sure everything works. Technology does fail and often at the worst possible times! Therefore, have backups in case of equipment failure. For example, if the computer projector fails, arrange for another projector or have handouts as a backup. Also, take a backup copy of the slideshow in case one copy becomes unusable.

As you give your presentation, integrate your slides into your presentation effectively. However, don't assume that you are required to show slides throughout your entire presentation. As appropriate, you may blank the projector and talk without the slides. Sometimes it is easier to connect with the audience that way.

As you are showing your slides, you may turn briefly toward the screen and point to the important items you want the audience to notice. Then immediately turn again toward the audience and discuss the information. Avoid

*Figure 12.8 As needed, point to an item on a slide, but turn immediately back toward the audience to talk about it.*

looking at the screen too often or too long, because it interrupts your eye contact and engagement with the audience. It also suggests that you are not prepared and are using your slides as notes.

Finally, be prepared with backup slides to use during the Q&A time. As you anticipate the questions you might be asked, create backup slides to accompany your answers. Having backup slides will help communicate the message, "I'm prepared!"

## Whiteboards and Flip Charts

To write on whiteboards and flip charts, use strong colors such as black, blue, green, and red. Use red mainly for points that you want to emphasize. Write in the style that is most legible for you, whether print or cursive, upper or lower case. Make letters large enough to be seen from anywhere in the room. A final word of warning—before the meeting, check to make sure the markers have not dried up. Arrange for appropriate backups.

In addition to written text, use graphics wherever appropriate. You don't have to be a great artist, so stick figures are just fine. Arrows, straight and curved lines, rectangles, circles, stars, triangles, and other common shapes can also be used. You may also draw simple business graphics such as mind maps, bar and line charts, flowcharts, organizational charts, and so forth.

Capture and save your information for appropriate follow up. Interactive whiteboards automatically save electronic copies, as do virtual meeting whiteboards. For standard whiteboards and flip charts, just take a digital photo of the information, and transmit it to yourself by email.

*Figure 12.9 Whiteboards are useful in interactive meetings.*

## PREPARING THE MESSENGER

Once you have the message and media developed, it is time to prepare yourself, the messenger. When giving presentations, one of your most important tasks is to connect with the audience. To connect with an audience and to deliver your message with confidence and competence, pay attention to three important elements:

Verbal—what you say.

Voice—how you say it.

Nonverbal—what you communicate with your eyes and face, your gestures, your appearance, and your movement.

## The Verbal

The verbal part of your presentation is the actual words you use. Because words have the major responsibility to convey your message, choose your words carefully. Select words that are appropriate for the audience. When speaking to accountants, use the language of accountants; when speaking to engineers, use the language of engineers. To a general audience, the technical jargon of accountants and engineers would be inappropriate, so use words that the audience understands. Also, use language that is socially appropriate, neither too formal nor too casual.

As you speak, remember the factors of pronunciation and enunciation. First, pronounce words properly.

| Don't say | Do say |
|---|---|
| Aks | Ask |
| Asterix | Asterisk |
| Excape | Escape |
| Excetera | Etcetera |
| Exspecially | Especially |
| Irregardless | Regardless |
| Probly | Probably |
| Pronounciation | Pronunciation |
| Relitor | Realtor |
| Reoccur | Recur |
| Revelant | Relevant |
| Supposably | Supposedly |
| Ta | To |
| Upmost | Utmost |

Second, pay attention to enunciation, which refers to how distinctly you say the syllables in each word. Avoid mumbling or slurring words. For instance, say "incidentally," not "incidently," and say "sales," not "sells." Also, remember "ing" endings, and avoid the casual forms of speakin' and talkin'. Several online dictionary sources can help you with both definitions and proper pronunciation (e.g., m-w.com and dictionary.com).

When you discover that you misuse or mispronounce

words or fail to enunciate clearly, work to improve. The way people speak is very habitual. Speaking habits are hard to break, but you can change if you have a desire to change and if you persevere. Therefore, make a list of the language habits you want to change and work hard to establish the new habits. Use recording technology to help with this process, and invite others to remind you when you forget.

## The Voice

How you use your voice is important in connecting with an audience and in delivering your message effectively. Your voice quality is affected by the pitch (high or low frequency), rate (speed at which you speak), volume (how loudly you speak), and tone (your cumulative vocal attributes). No one pitch, rate, volume, or tone is right. However, a lower pitch is generally preferred to a high pitch, as is a rich tone from the throat, instead of a nasal tone.

Voice energy is critical in your presentations. No one likes to listen to a monotone voice. Increase your voice volume for emphasis, slow down for articulation, and raise the pitch at the end of a question (e.g., "Are you sure?"). Record yourself reading a passage of text, and then listen to your voice. Is it too slow or too fast, too soft or too loud, or too monotone? Make changes to ensure that your voice conveys energy, sincerity, and conviction.

In considering the use of your voice, don't forget to think about silence—the absence of voice. Silence is one of the punctuation marks of oral communication. Just as a rise in the tone of voice can indicate a question, a pause can indicate a comma, a period, or a dash.

## The Nonverbal

Your nonverbal communication is critical in connecting with an audience and delivering a successful presentation. The most important factors include maintaining good eye contact, gesturing with energy, dressing appropriately, and using the floor space effectively.

### Face and Eyes

When people look at one another, they instinctively focus on the eyes and face. Thus, maintain good eye contact with the audience. Carry on a series of three-second conversations with individual audience members throughout the room, including those in the extreme left and right corners. Looking at people individually will help them feel engaged in your presentation. Not looking at people individually does just the opposite.

Also, make sure your face projects positive expressions, such as happiness, enthusiasm, and optimism. Smile when it is appropriate; let your personality show through. Avoid negative expressions of frustration, impatience, or anger, unless you are telling a story where those expressions are appropriate.

### Gestures

Arm and hand gestures should accompany the content spoken by your voice. However, many speakers are unsure about what to do with their hands. As a result, they clasp their hands in front of their body, fold their arms, put their hands in their pockets, put their fingertips together in a prayer-like fashion, or nervously play with their rings or other jewelry. The following suggestions will help you become more comfortable with your gestures:

- Match your gestures with your content. An improvement in sales could be accompanied by an upward sweep of the hand; a series of three items could be accompanied by one, two, and three fingers; reference to a personal experience might be accompanied by a brief touch to the upper chest. During your practice sessions, perhaps exaggerate the gestures a bit to get yourself to relax and to be more animated. Your gestures might seem awkward and forced at first, but practice will make them more spontaneous and natural.
- When you gesture, bring your hands above your waistline so they convey more energy and can be seen.
- When your hands are not being used for gesturing, drop them to your sides (the neutral position) or return

*Figure 12.10 Use effective gestures during your presentation.*

one hand to the waist area (middle of the abdomen) and drop the other hand to the side. In a very informal setting, you may put one hand in a pocket.

- When you are speaking to an international audience, avoid hand and finger gestures that might be offensive. Gesturing with the open palm of your hand is acceptable in all cultures.

## Dress and Appearance

Find out what the dress standard is for the occasion where you will be speaking. Then dress at least to the level of the audience, if not a step above. Avoid faddish clothing, jewelry, and hair styles that would draw attention to themselves. The way you appear should never attract detract from your message or damage your ethos. Check your personal hygiene and grooming. Carry a handkerchief or tissue in case you need it for some unexpected emergency. Always strive to look the part, as well as be the part.

## Floor Space

Use your presentation floor space effectively. Remember two key points. First, close the distance between you and the audience. Unless you are speaking from a podium, move toward the audience so you don't appear aloof and distant. Standing close to the audience will help your presentation be more conversational and will help you connect with the audience.

Second, if not speaking from a podium, move purposefully during your presentation. For example, at a major transition point, you might move a few feet to the left or right as you say, "Now, let's move on to the third reason for recommending this change." Regarding the use of floor space, remember these three words: walk, stop, talk! As you move from one point to another, generally take only three or four steps. Don't pace aimlessly back and forth, and don't rock back and forth from one foot to the other as you present.

## The Unexpected

Unexpected things happen often during presentations, and you have to deal with them instantly when they do. For example, you might say a wrong word or make some other small mistake. What do you do? Just fix the problem and move on. Stay focused on your presentation. If you don't make a big issue of it, neither will the audience. Unless the problem is a major one, they will quickly forget it.

Another unexpected factor might be that you have people from another country in the audience. Even if the internationals speak English, you should modify your language—especially avoid figurative speech and unfamiliar metaphors. For instance, phrases like "bottom line" or "hit a home run" may not be understood in other cultures. Also, remember to enunciate clearly and speak more slowly.

You might also encounter technology problems caused by equipment malfunction or unexpected time limitations caused by previous speakers taking too long. To deal with technology problems, have a backup whenever possible. To deal with unexpected time limitations, plan in advance what content you will eliminate, while still achieving your purpose.

Problems can also occur because of your audience. As you present, watch the audience, noting signs of misunderstanding, boredom, or fatigue. When these problems arise, modify the content, the presentation style, the length, or other aspects of the presentation as needed. Suggestions for dealing with various types of problems are given in Table 12.1.

## The Rehearsal

Just as polished writing requires good reviewing and revising (as discussed in Chapter 5), good presentations require rehearsing and improving. Rehearsing helps polish a presentation and helps reduce stage fright. Even question-and-answer sessions should be rehearsed.

Rehearsing is not merely talking through a presentation while sitting at your work station; it is literally giving the presentation, complete with gestures and visuals, as though you were giving it to the real audience. Rehearsing produces significant results—it helps you stay within time constraints, it helps ensure that your slides work properly, and it helps you practice your gestures. Rehearse at least three times to achieve the best results.

You can rehearse by yourself while talking to an imaginary audience, but rehearsing in front of a practice audience is especially helpful for formal presentations. Early in the presentation development process you can conduct a structured walk-through, explaining the overall format and asking reviewers for feedback. Later you can rehearse your actual presentation, followed by audience feedback. Some organizations use pink teams and red teams for rehearsal—pink teams act as friendly audiences; red teams act as hostile audiences.

Another approach is to video record yourself, using real-time feedback technology that enables you to see and hear yourself and that enables others to give detailed feedback during your rehearsal. For example, with GoReact technology (see goreact.com) the audience can give you

## Rubric for Evaluating Oral Presentations

Presenter_____  Topic_____

Evaluator_____

| Rating (10-1) | **Evaluation Factors**<br>Circle ⟨strengths⟩ <u>underline</u> weaknesses, add +/- comments |
|---|---|
| **Message** | —*Content:* clear and coherent, complete and well developed, correct, convincing, creative, concise (within time limit)<br>—*Strategy:* appropriate for purpose, audience, and context<br>—*Organization:* distinct opening, agenda, body, closing, and Q&A<br>*Comments:* |
| **Messenger** | —*Ethos:* confidence, competence/preparedness, professionalism, integrity, connection with audience<br>—*Voice:* volume, energy, pronunciation, enunciation<br>—*Nonverbal:* eye contact, gestures, energy, dress/appearance, use of floor space<br>*Comments:* |
| **Media** | —*Slides, handouts, etc.:* professional layout, design, graphics, typography, animations<br>—*Clear, relevant information:* easy-to-comprehend, effective in achieving objectives<br>—*Integrated into presentation*<br>*Comments:* |
| _____/30 Total | |

# APPENDIX A

# Sentence Basics

Appendix A covers the basic unit of all writing—the sentence. You must be able to compose good sentences to create good business documents, whether emails, blogs, websites, proposals, or business reports. Poorly written sentences can transmit incorrect meaning, and poorly composed sentences negatively affect your credibility. If you can't write good sentences, your colleagues and managers will not have confidence in you to communicate in writing with clients. As a result, your career opportunities might be damaged, even if you have major strengths in other areas.

This appendix will help you learn five major elements of sentences represented by the acronym SPELL: Structure, Punctuation, Errors, Language, and Length.

## STRUCTURE

Sentences are groups of words organized together to express meaningful ideas. The following sections discuss sentence parts, sentence types, and sentence-composition guidelines. Before delving into sentence parts, however, make sure you understand the role of individual words in sentences.

Words are the basic building blocks of language. They are classified into eight categories called *parts of speech*. Word classification depends on how the word is used in a sentence; therefore, the same word may be classified differently, depending on how it is used.

Example: Emily was *running* along the path by the river. [Running is a *verb*.]

Example: *Running* is my favorite type of exercise. [Running is a *noun*.]

Example: The *running* water is interrupting my concentration. [Running is an *adjective*.]

The eight parts of speech are described in Table A.1.

### Sentence Parts

The main parts of sentences can be broken into two categories: (1) subjects, verbs, and complements and (2) phrases and clauses, as explained in the following sections.

#### Subjects, Verbs, and Complements

A sentence is a group of words expressing an *idea*. Most ideas have three main *elements*:

- Subject—the thing that is *doing* something or *being* something
- Verb—what the subject is *doing* or *being*.
- Complement—the *completion* of the idea started by the subject and verb

Consider the following sentence: **Roger** <u>drove</u> *to St. Louis.*

**Subject:** Roger (the thing that did something)

<u>Verb:</u> drove (the action)

*Complement:* to St. Louis (the rest of the idea started by the subject and verb)

### Table A.1 Parts of Speech

| Name | Definition | Examples |
|---|---|---|
| Noun | A word that names a person, place, or thing. | *Jill, dog, vacation, Boston*<br>*Jill* took her *dog* with her when she went on a *vacation* to *Boston*. [These nouns are persons, places, or things.]<br>*Patience* is a *virtue*. [These two nouns describe human attributes.] |
| Pronoun | A word used in place of a noun. | *I, you, she, it, they, who, him*<br>*She* gave the report to *him*. [*She* and *him* are pronouns that replace nouns, such as *Tiffany* and *Andrew*.] |
| Verb | A word or word group that describes the action or state of being of the sentence subject. | *Ran, tried, thought, felt, was, is, are*<br>Chris *saved* the file on his hard drive. [*Action* verb.]<br>Shannon *is* the new manager. [*Being* verb.] |
| Adjective | A word that modifies or describes a noun or pronoun. | *Red, new, poor, warm, tall*<br>Rick fixed the *leaky* pipe. [*Leaky* modifies, or describes, the noun *pipe*.]<br>She is *qualified* for the job. [*Qualified* modifies or describes the pronoun *she*.] |
| Adverb | A word that modifies or describes a verb, adjective, or other adverb | *Really, very, extremely*<br>Rachel walked *slowly* back to the car. [*Slowly* modifies the verb *walked*.]<br>Jeannie is a *very* effective manager. [*Very* modifies the adjective *effective*.]<br>Lon sang *exceptionally* well today. [*Exceptionally* modifies the adverb *well*.] |
| Preposition | A word that relates a noun or pronoun to some other word in the sentence. The preposition and its following related words constitute a prepositional phrase. | *In, on, into, for, to, beside, at*<br>The employees *in* the training program will become supervisors. [*In* relates the *employees* to the *training program*.]<br>The book is *on* the desk. [*On* is the preposition; *on the desk* is a prepositional phrase.] |
| Conjunction | A word used to join or connect words, phrases, or clauses. | *And, or, but*<br>Joshua *and* Ryan play golf. [*And* joins two words: *Joshua* and *Ryan*.]<br>We'll have our meeting *and* then we'll break for lunch. [*And* joins two clauses.] |
| Interjection | A word used to express emotion or surprise. | *Oh, ouch, wow*<br>*Oh*, I hadn't thought of it that way before. [*Oh* expresses surprise.] |

When you have more than one subject or verb, it is called a compound subject or compound verb:

>   Compound subject: **Roger** and **Alene** drove to St. Louis.

>   Compound verb: Roger <u>drove</u> to St. Louis and then <u>flew</u> to Miami.

## Phrases and Clauses

Words in sentences are organized into word groupings called phrases and clauses. This section discusses the differences between phrases and clauses, discusses the different types of conjunctions that are used, and illustrates how basic sentences can be expanded. The terms phrase and clause are defined as follows:

>   **Phrase:**   A group of related words without a subject and verb.

>   **Clause:**   A group of related words with a subject and a verb.

Let's add a phrase to the basic sentence just discussed:

>   [After passing Kansas City,] **Roger** <u>drove</u> *to St. Louis.*

"After passing Kansas City" is a prepositional phrase. It is a phrase because it does not have a subject; it is a prepositional phrase because it begins with the preposition "after." "To St. Louis," the complement identified earlier, is a prepositional phrase. It is a phrase because it contains no verb; it is a prepositional phrase because it begins with the preposition "to." "Roger drove to St. Louis" is a clause. It is a clause because it contains a subject (**Roger**) and a verb (<u>drove</u>).

Clauses are of three types: independent, dependent, and embedded, as shown in the following table.

**Independent clause:**   A clause that conveys a complete idea and that can stand alone.

**Dependent clause:**   An idea that cannot stand alone; it *depends* on an independent clause to complete its meaning.

**Embedded clause:**   A minor clause used within an independent or dependent clause.

Let's add a dependent clause to our earlier sentence:

>   [After **he** <u>made</u> *the final decision,*] [**Roger** <u>drove</u> *to St. Louis.*]

This sentence has two clauses, the first being a dependent clause and the second being an independent clause.

You can see that each clause has a subject, a verb, and a complement. If you encountered "After he made the final decision" as a sentence by itself, you probably would ask, "What happened after he made the final decision?" This is a dependent clause because it depends on the second clause (the independent clause) to answer that question.

Independent clauses are called *main* clauses, and dependent clauses are called *subordinate* clauses. A sentence may have more than one main clause and more than one subordinate clause.

>   After **he** <u>made</u> *the final decision,* | **Roger** <u>drove</u> *to St. Louis.*
>      **Subordinate clause**                    **Main clause**

An embedded clause is a clause within a clause. It is a minor clause attached to either an independent or a dependent clause, such as, "I noticed that you were at the meeting," or, "Although I noticed you were at the meeting, I decided to stay." In both cases, "you were at the meeting" is the embedded clause because it is the complement of the clause "I noticed."

Let's add an embedded clause to our sample sentence:

>   [After **he** <u>made</u> *the final decision,*] [**Roger** <u>drove</u> *to St. Louis,* **which** <u>is</u> *east of Kansas City.*]

Notice how the embedded clause in this example is part of the independent clause, describing the complement "St. Louis." Although embedded clauses are important in sentence construction, they are *not* important in determining basic sentence type, as you will see later on.

### *Conjunctions*

Multiple clauses in a sentence are often connected by a conjunction. These conjunctions can be classified as (a) coordinating conjunctions or (b) subordinating conjunctions.

1.  **Coordinating conjunctions** connect clauses of equal strength. The seven coordinating conjunctions are for, and, nor, but, or, yet, and so—remember these with the acronym FANBOYS.

2.  **Subordinating conjunctions** connect clauses of unequal strength—they place the main emphasis on one clause and secondary emphasis on the other. Examples of subordinating conjunctions are if, as, unless, although, when, after, and because.

Subordinating conjunctions generally fall into one of five categories:

| Category | Example |
|----------|---------|
| Cause | *Because* |
| Concession | *Although, even though* |
| Condition | *If, unless* |
| Place | *Where, wherever* |
| Time | *After, before, since, then, when, while, until* |

The following sentences are examples of clauses separated by conjunctions:

- I will work for you on Saturday, *and* you work for me next Tuesday. [Two main clauses joined by the coordinating conjunction *and.*]
- I will invite Kristy to the game, *or* you can invite Ashley. [Two main clauses joined by the coordinating conjunction *or.*]
- I attended his game *because* I hadn't seen him play before. [One main clause joined by the subordinating conjunction *because.*]
- I am majoring in accounting, *although* I don't plan to be an accountant for the rest of my life. [One main clause joined by the subordinating conjunction *although.*]
- She will be able to go on the trip *if* she meets all the academic requirements. [One main clause joined by the subordinating conjunction *if.*]
- We will be happy to talk with you *wherever* you'd like to meet. [One main clause joined by the subordinating conjunction *wherever.*]
- He will call to arrange an appointment *after* you submit your forms. [One main clause joined by the subordinating conjunction *after.*]

The sequence of two clauses in a sentence can be reversed. If a coordinating conjunction is involved, in most cases it remains between the clauses as follows:

- I will work for you on Saturday, *and* you can work for me next Tuesday.
- You can work for me next Tuesday, *and* I will work for you on Saturday.

If a subordinating conjunction is involved, the conjunction is moved with the subordinate clause.

- I am majoring in accounting, *although* I don't plan to be an accountant for the rest of my life.
- *Although* I don't plan to be an accountant for the rest of my life, I am majoring in accounting.
- He will call to arrange an appointment *after* you submit your forms.

- *After* you submit your forms, he will call to arrange an appointment.

## Sentence Types

Most sentences can be classified as one of four types. This classification is based on the number and types of *clauses* in a sentence, not on *phrases*. The number or location of phrases in a sentence does not influence the sentence classification, nor does the presence of embedded clauses.

1. *Simple*—Contains one independent clause and no dependent clauses:

   Example: After last week's events, [**nothing** <u>surprises</u> me].

   Example: [**I** <u>will take</u> her to the airport this morning.]

2. *Compound*—Contains two independent clauses and no dependent clauses:

   Example: [**I** <u>will compose</u> the text] and [**you** <u>create</u> the graphics].

   Example: [**I** <u>will take</u> her to the airport this morning,] and [**you** <u>pick</u> her up on Friday.]

3. *Complex*—Contains one independent clause and one or more dependent clauses:

   Example: [When the **copier** <u>arrives</u>,] [**you** <u>complete</u> the warranty paperwork].

   Example: [If **you** <u>will take</u> her to the airport this morning,] [**I** <u>will pick</u> her up next Friday.]

4. *Compound-complex*—Contains a minimum of two independent clauses and one dependent clause.

   Example: [After the **meeting** <u>starts</u>,] [**I** <u>will present</u> the report] and [**you** <u>answer</u> the questions].

   Example: [**You** <u>take</u> her to the airport this morning;] [when **she** <u>returns</u>,] [**I** <u>will pick</u> her up.]

The following examples show how a simple one-clause sentence can be expanded by adding another clause; the following examples show how a clause can be expanded by adding words or phrases within the clause. These examples all build on the basic two-word main clause, "*Gary reads.*" Remember that adding words and phrases like the following does not change the sentence type. Only the addition of clauses can change the sentence type.

| Expand the subject | *Our technical specialist,* Gary, reads computer manuals. [Added adjectives before the subject] |
| | Gary and *Brian* read computer manuals. [Two subjects become a compound subject] |
| Expand the verb | Gary reads *slowly* and *carefully.* [Two adverbs more completely describe the verb] |
| | Gary *reads manuals* and *watches training videos.* [Two verb phrases become a compound verb] |
| Expand the complement | Gary reads *technical manuals.* [Noun complement (manuals) with a modifier (technical)] |
| | Gary reads *manuals at work and science fiction books at home.* [Compound complement phrases] |
| Add an introductory phrase | *Before downloading new software,* Gary reads computer manuals. |
| Add an interrupting phrase | Gary, *before downloading new software,* reads computer manuals. |
| Add a concluding phrase | Gary reads computer manuals *before downloading new software.* |

When the addition of more words results in long sentences, make sure the main sentence structure remains clear and obvious. Read the following two sentence examples. In the first sentence, notice how difficult it is to find the main message and understand the sentence structure. The sentence has 37 words and is cluttered and disorganized. In the second sentence, the main sentence structure is clearer—the secondary information is gathered together in an introductory phrase and the primary information is placed in the main clause. The sentence is also much more concise (only 22 words).

No:    Over 60 percent of the 1,086 respondents in this nationwide study agree to the fact that the implementation of Regulation 605 in their organizations has improved controls in two major areas of mine safety and health protection.

Yes:    Of the 1,086 respondents in this nationwide study, over 60 percent agree that Regulation 605 has improved their miners' safety and health.

As you work to ensure clear structure, also keep in mind the importance of introducing variety among your sentences. Readers get tired of seeing the same sentence type over and over again. In the following paragraph, notice that all six sentences lack variety—all are structured as single clauses of about the same length.

No:    Starting a business requires that you develop a business plan. A business plan includes a description of the business. The description covers marketing, competition, operating procedures, and personnel. A business plan also includes financial data. The financial data section includes a balance sheet, sources of funding, pro-forma income projections, and cash flows. A business plan must also include any other relevant supporting documents.

In contrast, the four sentences in the following paragraph vary in structure and length. Sentence 1 is a 16-word complex sentence (one dependent and one independent clause). Sentence 2 is a 19-word simple sentence (one independent clause), with a concluding segment containing four items in a series. Sentence 3 contains 26 words structured as an introductory phrase, a main clause, and a four-part series. Sentence 4 is a 16-word sentence in a simple-sentence construction (one independent clause).

Yes:    If you decide to start your own company, a business plan can be of great assistance. Most business plans start with a description of the business, with subsections on marketing, competition, operating procedures, and personnel. Following the description of the business, business plans need a financial section, usually containing a balance sheet, sources of funding, pro-forma income projections, and cash flows. Finally, business plans may include any other sections or supporting documents that the writer considers relevant.

## *Sentence Composition Guidelines*

To make your sentences structurally sound, as well as clear and effective, remember the letters S, V, and C (representing subject, verb, complement). Also remember a few simple writing guidelines pertaining to S, V, and C.

1.  **Subject**—use Strong Subjects.
2.  **Verb**—place verbs in the Vicinity of subjects, and use active Voice.
3.  **Complement**—keep sentence complements Clear and unCluttered.

The following guidelines elaborate more on sentence-construction guidelines that will help you write sentences that are clear and easy to follow.

## Subjects

Subjects are the actors of sentences. Subjects may be nouns (e.g., athlete), pronouns (e.g., they), or even verb forms (e.g., thinking) or other parts of speech acting as nouns. For example, the word "and" is usually a conjunction, but here it can be used as a noun subject as follows: "*And* is an interesting word."

1.  Use strong, clear subjects in preference to vague "*It is*" and "*There are*" structures. Also, avoid complex nominalizations as subjects (*nominalizations* are nouns made from verbs).

    No:   There will be no meeting held on Friday.

    **Yes:**   No meeting will be held on Friday.

    No:   It is imperative that we reduce our expenses.

    **Yes:**   We must reduce our expenses.

    **Yes:**   The new computer has arrived. It will be installed tomorrow. [It is acceptable because it has a clear antecedent: computer.]

    No:   Consideration of the new hiring policy was the committee's first subject of discussion. [Consideration is a nominalization.]

    **Yes:**   The committee first considered the new hiring policy.

## Verbs

Verbs indicate two things about subjects. First, verbs can indicate *action* being taken by the subject, such as, "The applicant *described* her experience." Second, verbs can indicate the *state* or *condition* of the subject, such as, "The applicant *is* ill today." ("*Is*" indicates the state of the person; it is a *state-of-being* verb).

2.  Place verbs in the vicinity of their subjects. Sentences with subjects and verbs placed far apart can be hard to follow.

    No:   The purpose of this report on the causes and effects of global warming is to educate the public.

    **Yes:**   The purpose of this report is to educate the public about the causes and effects of global warming.

3.  In most cases, prefer the use of active-voice verbs.

    *Active voice*—a clause in which the actor is the subject of the sentence. Example: Julie drove the car.

*Passive voice*—a clause in which the object of the action is the subject of the sentence. Example: The car was driven by Julie. (Note: Passive voice always requires an extra verb: e.g., was driven.)

Only clauses with transitive verbs can be written in passive voice—clauses with state-of-being verbs or with intransitive verbs cannot. A transitive verb requires a direct object that receives the action of the verb. An intransitive verb does not require a direct object.

*Transitive verb:* The supervisor *fired* the disobedient employee. [*Fired* is a transitive verb; *employee* is the object of that firing. This sentence can be rewritten in passive voice as "The disobedient employee was fired by the supervisor."]

*Intransitive verb:* Today I've been *running* around in circles. [Running is an intransitive verb; it requires no object. The sentence cannot be written in passive voice.]

Both active and passive voice are grammatically correct, but active voice is preferred in most situations—especially when you want to emphasize the actor or de-emphasize the action. Use passive voice in situations when you want to de-emphasize the actor or emphasize the action.

*Active:*   Our secretary *purchased* an airline ticket. [The secretary is the actor and is the subject of the clause.]

*Passive:*   An airline ticket *was purchased* by our secretary. [The airline ticket is the object of the action, but here it is used as the subject of the clause.]

*Passive:*   An airline ticket *was purchased*. [This passive clause omits the actor.]

*Neither:*   Whitney *is* our secretary. [No action is involved with this state-of-being verb.]

No:   A new proposal was submitted by ABC Corporation. [Writer wants to emphasize ABC Corporation.]

**Yes:**   ABC Corporation submitted a new proposal.

No:   Michael overlooked several important details. [Writer wants to emphasize the overlooked details.]

**Yes:**   Several important details were overlooked by Michael.

**Yes:**   Several important details were overlooked. [This option completely omits mention of the guilty person.]

No:   The neighbor called the police about the child-

abuse problem. [Writer wants to emphasize the police.]

**Yes:** The police were notified about the child-abuse problem. [Properly emphasizes the police.]

**No:** I have decided to put you on disciplinary probation because of your behavior last week. [Writer does not want to tell who made the decision.]

**Yes:** You are being put on disciplinary probation because of your behavior last week. [Hides the person who made the decision.]

## Complements

After you write the subject and verb of a sentence, complete the sentence by writing the complement. As you do so, remember parallelism and modification guidelines.

The principle of *parallelism* requires that sentence parts that are structurally parallel also be grammatically parallel.

4. Use words of the same part of speech after parallel connectives. (Connectives link sentence branches to the main trunk of the sentence.) Four examples of parallel connectives (connective *twins*) are as follows:

- Not only/but also
- Both/and
- Either/or
- Neither/nor

**No:** Liz is going not only to Chicago but also New York. ["To" is a preposition; "New York" is a noun. The structurally parallel parts are not grammatically parallel.]

**Yes:** Liz is going not only to Chicago but also to New York.

For long parallel elements, consider repeating the connecting word as necessary to ensure clarity. Another option to ensure clarity is to mark the parallel items with letters, numbers, or bullets.

**No:** Effective systems analysis requires that we study and identify the major problems to be solved and describe our solutions in an understandable manner. [Confusing!]

**Yes:** Effective systems analysis requires that we study and identify the major problems to be solved and that we describe our solutions in an understandable manner. [Better.]

**Yes:** Effective systems analysis requires that we (a) study and identify the major problems to be solved and (b) describe our solutions in an understandable manner. [Clearer.]

**Yes:** Effective systems analysis requires two major steps:

1. Study and identify the major problems to be solved.

2. Describe our solutions in an understandable manner. [Clearest of all!]

5. Use parallel parts of speech for words in a series.

**No:** Before you give your speech, make sure to consider the context, analyze the audience, and then your strategy should be developed. [Two of the three ideas in the series begin with verbs (consider and analyze); the last one begins with a pronoun (your). Thus, the three parallel ideas do not use parallel grammar.]

**Yes:** Before you give your speech, make sure to consider the context, analyze the audience, and develop your strategy. [The three parallel ideas also have parallel construction—they all begin with a verb—consider, analyze, and develop.]

Adjectives and adverbs are known as *modifiers*; they describe other words. The two major classes of modifiers are adjectives and adverbs:

**Adjectives** limit, describe, qualify, or make more exact the meaning of any noun, pronoun, or subject of a clause.

**Examples:** *The real* winners are *the* employees. [*Winners* is described by *The real; employees* is described by *the.*]

*This business* report needs *some careful* proofreading. [*Report* is described by *This business; proofreading* is described by *some careful.*]

**Adverbs** limit, describe, qualify, or make more exact the meaning of any verb, adjective, or other adverb.

**Examples:** He walked *very slowly* back to his office. [*Walked* is modified by *very slowly.*]

I am *really* happy you came. [*Happy* is modified by *really.*]

He doesn't feel *very well.* [*Feel* is modified by *very well.*]

6. Use adjectives and adverbs correctly.

**No:** I did good in my presentation today.

**Yes:** I did well in my presentation today.

**No:** You're doing a real good job.

**Yes:** You're doing a really good job. [Remember the necessary *ly* ending for certain adverbs.]

No:   I'm sure happy you're on our team.

**Yes:** I'm surely happy you're on our team.

7.   Place modifying words and phrases close to the words they modify.

No:   I'm giving the computer to the young employee with a dead battery.

**Yes:** I'm giving the computer with a dead battery to the young employee.

No:   I'll only ask for $10,000. [Only ask?]

**Yes:** I'll ask for only $10,000. [Only $10,000.]

No:   Daniel asked her to introduce herself hesitantly.

**Yes:** Daniel hesitantly asked her to introduce herself.

8.   Avoid *dangling* (ambiguous) *modifiers.* The most common type of dangling modifier consists of (a) an introductory verbal phrase that tells of an action, followed by (b) a main clause whose subject does not tell who performed the action. Introductory verbal phrases can be gerunds (an "ing" form of a verb used as a noun) or infinitives (a "to" form of a verb used as a noun).

No:   Still perspiring from playing the last 18 holes, the company president awarded the first-place golfing trophy to Landon's team. ["Perspiring" is a gerund. The introductory phrase does not tell who was perspiring, so the reader incorrectly assumes it is the subject of the subsequent clause—the president.]

**Yes:** Still perspiring from playing the last 18 holes, Landon's team was awarded the first-place golfing trophy by the company president. [This structure clarifies that Landon's team was still perspiring, not the president.]

No:   As an authority on data security, I am sure you will be a very interesting speaker. [I am not the authority.]

**Yes:** As an authority on data security, you will be a very interesting speaker.

**Yes:** Because you are an authority on data security, I am sure you will be a very interesting speaker. [Introductory phrase is changed to an introductory clause, clearly showing who is the data-security authority.]

No:   To succeed in this company, I suggest that you enroll in our advanced training courses. [I am

not the one who is concerned about succeeding in the company.]

**Yes:** To succeed in this company, you should enroll in our advanced training courses. [You are the one who wants to succeed in this company.]

## PUNCTUATION

With a good understanding of sentence structure, you are now prepared to study punctuation. Punctuation has a very close tie to the structure of sentences, because commas, semicolons, dashes, periods, and other punctuation marks usually occur at logical breaks in sentence structure. Combined with good sentence structure, punctuation marks segment sentences into meaningful units so readers can more clearly understand the intended message.

The English language contains over a dozen punctuation marks. The following section covers the punctuation marks most frequently encountered in business writing.

### Comma [,]

The comma is a punctuation mark used for two basic functions: (1) to divide and (2) to replace.

To divide:   Before I attended college, I worked at a fast-food restaurant. [The comma *divides* the dependent clause from the main clause.]

To replace:   I flew to Seattle; Brian, to Portland. [The comma in the second clause *replaces* the word "flew."]

Few problems occur with the replacement function. Therefore, the following rules will highlight the most frequent problems encountered with the dividing function.

1.   Use a comma to divide main clauses joined by a coordinating conjunction (for, and, nor, but, or, yet, so).

**Yes:** I will send you my report next week, and you can give me feedback when we meet next month. [The comma divides two independent clauses joined by *and.*]

Note: If the first clause in a compound sentence is very short (five or fewer words), you may omit the comma. However, use commas whenever you want to *force* a pause in the reading.

**Yes:** I'll turn off the lights and you lock the doors.

**Yes:** He heard my message, but he didn't respond. [Writer wants to force a pause after message.]

Note: A clause with two verb phrases generally does not require commas to divide the verb phrases.

**No:** We'll launch the new marketing plan on January 1, and expect to see improved sales within two weeks. [This sentence includes one independent clause with two verb phrases beginning with launch and expect.]

**Yes:** We'll launch the new marketing plan on January 1 and expect to see improved sales within two weeks. [No comma is required between the two verb phrases.]

**Yes:** We'll launch the new marketing plan on January 1, and we'll expect to see improved sales within two weeks. [Here the sentence is changed from one independent clause with two verb phrases to two independent clauses, thus requiring a dividing comma before the word and.]

2. Place a comma after many *introductory* elements, such as dependent clauses, introductory phrases, and transitional words, and wherever confusion might occur without a comma. Commas may be optional after some brief prepositional phrases.

**Yes:** Before you try to fix the electrical switch, be sure to turn off the power. [A dependent clause.]

**Yes:** After working with that group for more than a year, I think I understand where they're headed. [A long introductory phrase.]

**Yes:** Nevertheless, I think she is the best person for the management position. [An introductory transition word.]

**Yes:** Before shooting, the hunter looked beyond his target to make sure no people would be injured. [Confusion would occur without the comma.]

**Yes:** In the meeting he presented our goals for next year. [No comma is needed after the brief prepositional phrase.]

3. Use a comma to divide *all* items in a series.

**No:** I asked for markers, erasers and flip charts. [A comma is missing after erasers.]

**Yes:** I asked for markers, erasers, and flip charts. [DO use a comma before the conjunction preceding the last item in a series.]

**No:** For this class you'll need a textbook, a computer and printer and pencils and notepads. [Confusing!]

**Yes:** For this class you'll need a textbook, a computer and printer, and pencils and notepads. [Much better.]

4. Use a comma to divide adjacent adjectives that could be divided with the word *and* or that could be reversed without changing the meaning.

**No:** The lengthy detailed report was finished last night.

**Yes:** The lengthy, detailed report was finished last night. ["The lengthy and detailed report" or "the detailed, lengthy report . . ."]

5. Use a comma to divide nonessential, or interrupting, sentence elements from essential sentence elements.

**Yes:** He was, however, flawless in the way he presented the material. [However interrupts the main sentence flow.]

**Yes:** Pick up the annual report, assuming it is completed, and take it to the printer. [Assuming it is completed interrupts the main sentence flow.]

**Yes:** Let's use red for the company logo, not blue. [Not blue gives additional, or nonessential, information.]

**Yes:** I'd like you to meet Ken, my next-door neighbor, who will be traveling with us. [My next-door neighbor is not essential to the meaning of the sentence.]

**Yes:** My neighbor Ken is the person you'll meet this morning. [Ken is an essential appositive. Without the word Ken, the sentence would not be clear.]

6. Insert commas before and after the year when the month, day, and year are given. Don't use a comma with a partial date or a date written in day-month-year format.

**Yes:** The meeting on July 23, 20XX, will be held in Dallas.

**Yes:** The September 20XX deadline cannot be adjusted.

**Yes:** The report was first issued on 16 September 20XX.

7. Use commas to divide elements of an address. Place commas before and after the last element, except when a ZIP code is the last element.

**Yes:** We'll be moving our corporate office to Chicago, Illinois, next year.

**Yes:** He lives at 460 North Oakcrest Lane, Denver, CO 80123, but he'll be moving soon.

8. Use commas where they are needed for clarification.

**Yes:** Tess, we must take action now. [Use a comma in directly addressing a person.]

**Yes:** He remarked, "I have lived here for less than a year." [Insert a comma before a full-sentence direct quotation.]

**Yes:** She said the article reported "hundreds of lay-offs during the economic downturn." [A comma is not needed for partial-sentence quotations.]

## Semicolon [;]

Think of a semicolon as a *super-comma,* a divider more powerful than the lowly comma.

1. Use a semicolon to divide two independent clauses not joined by a coordinating conjunction.

**No:** Last year was our worst since 2009, next year will be much better. [This is an example of a comma splice.]

**Yes:** Last year was our worst since 2009; next year will be much better. [No conjunction is used; therefore, a semicolon is required.]

**Yes:** Last year was our worst since 2009, but next year will be much better. [A comma is acceptable because a conjunction is used.]

**Yes:** Last year was our worst since 2009. Next year will be much better. [Two simple sentences.]

2. Use a semicolon before a conjunctive adverb that joins two independent clauses. Examples of conjunctive adverbs are however, nevertheless, thus, and hence.

**Yes:** The shipment arrived on schedule; however, the chemicals were not included. [However is a conjunctive adverb joining the two independent clauses.]

**Yes:** The shipment did, however, arrive on schedule. [Here the word however is not used between two independent clauses; therefore, it is not preceded by a semicolon.]

3. If necessary to prevent confusion, a semicolon may be inserted to divide parallel sentence elements that have internal commas.

**Yes:** I can't attend the executive meeting this month; but I'll send Steve, the assistant store manager, who will present our status report. [The second clause has internal commas. Therefore, the two clauses are divided by the more powerful semicolon, showing that the main sentence division occurs where the semicolon occurs, not where the commas occur.]

**Yes:** Attending this meeting will be Steve, Assistant Store Manager; Avery, Director of Purchasing; and Natalie, Director of Advertising. [Semicolons are used between items in this series; commas are used within the three items in the series.]

4. Use a semicolon before *e.g.* (meaning *for example*) and *i.e.* (meaning *that is*) when no other punctuation is used to set off the e.g. or i.e.

**Yes:** Let's also involve several other media; e.g., brochure, blog, website, and billboard.

**Yes:** Let's also involve several other media (e.g., brochure, blog, website, and billboard).

**Yes:** We should work hardest on our most pressing problem; i.e., lack of proper training.

**Yes:** We should work hardest on our most pressing problem (i.e., lack of proper training).

## Colon [:]

Use the colon to introduce. Leave only one space after a colon, and do not begin the following word with a capital letter unless it is a proper noun or begins a direct quotation or complete sentence.

1. Make sure the colon is preceded by a full independent clause that introduces.

**No:** I bought presents for: Bridget and Kyle. ["I bought presents for" is not a full independent clause.]

**Yes:** I bought presents for Bridget and Kyle.

**Yes:** I bought presents for two people: Bridget and Kyle.

Note: When items in a series follow a colon, they may be arranged in one of several ways, depending on how much emphasis is desired.

**Yes:** The following three shipments arrived on schedule: January 15, March 1, and May 30. [Low emphasis.]

**Yes:** I'll be responsible for three of the tasks: (a) scheduling the building, (b) sending out flyers, and (c) welcoming the guests. [Moderate emphasis.]

**Yes:** I'll bring the following items:

1. Hamburgers
2. Soft drinks
3. Dessert

[Heavy emphasis. Notice that no comma is required after *"Hamburgers"* or *"Soft drinks,"* and no period is required after *"Dessert."*]

2. Use a colon after the salutation in formal business letters.

**No:** Dear Mr. Gentry, [A comma may be used in informal letters, such as "Dear Mom,"]

**Yes:** Dear Mr. Gentry:

## Dash [—]

A dash may be used to set off sentence interrupters, to emphasize, or to introduce.

1. Use a dash to set off interrupters or to emphasize.

**Yes:** He implied—although he didn't exactly say it—that our plant might be the next one to shut down.

**Yes:** Plan to attend Friday's training session—it will be very worthwhile.

**Yes:** We're holding a party Friday evening to socialize—and to highlight our record-setting sales.

2. Use a dash to introduce (in place of a colon).

**Yes:** He had only one message for her—find a new job!

Note: A dash is longer than a hyphen. If you don't use a real dash (the one in your word processor's special character set), use two hyphens. As a general rule, do not leave any space before or after the dash.

## Hyphen [-]

A hyphen is used to connect prefixes and word pairs.

1. Use a hyphen in the following situations:

- The prefix ends with the same letter that begins the main word; e.g., anti-inflammatory.
- The word might be mistaken for another word; e.g., reform vs. re-form.
- The prefix is *self;* e.g., self-assured. [But not selfless or selfish.]
- The word may be mispronounced; e.g., coworker vs. co-worker. [Dictionaries disagree on this.]

- The base word is capitalized; e.g., non-American.
- The base is a number; e.g., pre-1990.

2. Hyphenate compound adjectives when they *precede* a noun or pronoun. A compound adjective is two or more modifiers that act *jointly* as one modifier.

**No:** Send me an up to date report. [Not an up report, a to report, or a date report, but an up-to-date report.]

**Yes:** Send me an up-to-date report.

**No:** Is this report up-to-date?

**Yes:** Is this report up to date? [The modifier follows the noun; therefore, no hyphens are needed.]

**No:** The small business managers will meet next month in St. Louis. [This means small managers.]

**Yes:** The small-business managers will meet next month in St. Louis. [The businesses are small, not the managers.]

**No:** We used the six and eight-foot commercial ladders last year.

**Yes:** We used the six- and eight-foot commercial ladders last year. [A floating hyphen is needed to show the connection between six and foot.]

Note: Hyphens aren't needed after adverbs with *ly* endings, because the *ly* ending adequately indicates that the adverb modifies the subsequent word.

**No:** That was a carefully-calculated strategy.

**Yes:** That was a carefully calculated strategy.

3. Usually do not use hyphens with the following prefixes: re, pre, sub, mis, or semi.

**No:** You will be required to take a pre-test before the training begins.

**Yes:** You will be required to take a pretest before the training begins.

Note: To enhance the readability of text, try to avoid hyphenating words at the end of a line or page.

**No:** Riverside School has introduced a reading program that enables parents to participate as volunteers. Although this program has been successful, it has not been without an accompanying set of problems.

**Yes:** Riverside School has introduced a program that enables parents to participate as volunteers. Although this program has been successful, it

has not been without an accompanying set of problems.

## Parentheses [( )]

1. Use parentheses to set off incidental comments, to introduce abbreviations that will be used later in the document, or to enclose enumerations.

   **Yes:** Use red and green (Christmas colors) for the December ads.

   **Yes:** I attended Central Michigan University (CMU) for two years.

   **No:** I have attended three schools: 1) Arizona State University, 2) University of Arizona, and 3) Central Michigan University.

   **Yes:** I have attended three schools: (1) Arizona State University, (2) University of Arizona, and (3) Central Michigan University. [Both left and right parentheses are preferred.]

## Apostrophe [']

1. Use the apostrophe for three main purposes in English:

   • To indicate the omission of one or more letters when two words are combined to form a contraction.

   • To indicate the plural form of some letters and abbreviations when omitting the apostrophe would result in confusion.

   • To indicate the possessive form of a noun or pronoun (e.g., "Nancy's apartment," instead of "the apartment of Nancy").

   **Yes:** I am sure he does not know the address.

   **Yes:** I'm sure he doesn't know the address. [Does and not combine to form the doesn't contraction.]

   **No:** Two Ph.D.s attended the event.

   **Yes:** Two Ph.D.'s attended the event.

   **No:** He earned three As and two Bs last semester.

   **Yes:** He earned three A's and two B's last semester.

**Note:** The apostrophe rules governing possession are given in the Possessive Case section of this appendix.

## Quotation Marks [" "]

Quotation marks indicate just what their name implies: They surround *verbatim* statements quoted (spoken or writ-

ten) by someone else. They may also be used to surround some titles or words used in a special way.

1. Use quotation marks for direct quotations but not for paraphrases.

   **Yes:** Christine said, "I'll accept your proposal." [Direct quotation.]

   **No:** Christine said she "would accept his proposal. [A paraphrase—not a direct quotation.]

   **Yes:** Christine said she would accept his proposal.

2. Use quotation marks properly with other forms of punctuation.

   **No:** Christine said, "I'll accept your proposal".

   **Yes:** Christine said, "I'll accept your proposal." [For American English, commas and periods at the end of a quotation always go inside the quotation marks.]

   **Yes:** He has a good understanding of the "underground movement"; therefore, he should be a member of the special-investigation team. [Colons and semicolons at the end of a quotation nearly always go outside the quotation marks.]

   **Yes:** Jesse asked, "What have we here?" [Place question marks and exclamation points inside the quotation marks when they apply only to the quoted material.]

   **Yes:** Jacob said, "I'd like to quote my father: 'Never underestimate the power of determination.'" [A quotation within a quotation requires single quotation marks.]

## Ellipsis [ . . . ]

An ellipsis is three periods usually used to indicate an omission in a quotation. If you type the periods separately, space before and after each period. If you use your computer's special-character set, the ellipsis will be set as one character. (In informal writing, the ellipsis may be used to indicate an omission or a pause.)

1. Leave a space before and after an ellipsis.

   **No:** "Our goal is to be the best. . .in the industry." [The ellipsis replaces "Ohio-based firm."]

   **Yes:** "Our goal is to be the best . . . in the industry."

   **Yes:** "Our goal is to be the best ... in the industry." [Ellipsis provided by a special character set.]

2. Use the ellipsis to indicate omitted text, retaining the

same punctuation marks (e.g., commas or periods) that would occur with full text.

Yes: "Before we build . . . , we will have to increase sales by 200 percent." [Omitted from the first clause is "a new building."]

Yes: "Before we build, . . . we will have to increase sales by 200 percent." [Omitted from the second clause is "the budget director says."]

Yes: "This policy will produce a major snowball effect. . . ." [In an unfinished but grammatically complete sentence, the first dot is the period; the last three dots are the ellipsis.]

Yes: "This policy will produce . . ." [In an unfinished and incomplete sentence, there is no terminal punctuation.]

## Period [ . ]

1.  Use periods with the following abbreviations. Do not use periods with acronyms (initials pronounced as a word).

    Yes:  Dr.    Jr.     Mr.    Ms.    C. W. Smith
          Ave.   Corp.   Inc.   Ltd.   a.m. (or AM)
          et al.  etc.    e.g.   i.e.   No. (Nos. = plural)

    No:  The rocket was launched this morning by N.A.S.A. [An acronym pronounced as "nasa."]

    Yes: The rocket was launched this morning by NASA.

2.  Avoid commas or semicolons at the end of incomplete sentences in a bulleted list. Generally, use periods only at the end of complete sentences. Use consistent punctuation for all items in a list.

    No:  • 20 reams of paper.
         • 8 boxes of pencils.
         • 3 staplers.

    Yes: • 20 reams of paper
         • 8 boxes of pencils
         • 3 staplers

    Yes: • Close the Dallas office.
         • Combine the two Canadian offices.
         • Hire a new manager for the Portland office.

3.  Use a period with a polite request that asks for an action rather than for a yes or no response.

    No:  Will you please send me your email address?

Yes:  Will you please send me your email address. [Requests action.]

## ERRORS

Grammatical errors in your writing can severely undermine your credibility; they present an image of ignorance or laziness, that you don't know or you don't care. This section will help you understand and apply proper rules of case, agreement and reference, tense, numbers, and capitalization.

### Case

Case encompasses the three different types of nouns and pronouns: (1) subjective (or nominative), (2) objective, and (3) possessive. Deciding which of the three "cases" is appropriate depends on how nouns and pronouns are used in each sentence.

**Subjective case** (as the *subject* in a clause)

**Objective case** (as the *object* of some action)

**Possessive case** (as the *owner* of something)

| *She* | gave *me* | a copy of *her* book. |
|---|---|---|
| **Subjective case** (she) | **Objective case** (me) | **Possessive case** (her) |

Table A.2 and A.3 show the different case types for first-, second-, and third-person situations and illustrate how the different cases can be used in a simple sentence.

#### Subjective Case

1.  Always use the subjective case for the subject of a clause.

    No:  Me and him have been there many times.

    Yes: He and I have been there many times. [With two subjects or two objects, one of which is you, always put yourself last. Do not say, "I and he have been there many times."]

    Note: Use the subjective case for the subject of a clause, even when the subject is also the object of a previous clause.

    No:  Give the package to whomever is there.

    Yes: Give the package to whoever is there. [Whoever is the subject of is there, but whoever is also the object of Give the package to. In this situation,

### Table A.2 Case Chart

| Case | 1st Person Singular Pronoun | 1st Person Plural Pronouns | 2nd Person Singular and Plural Pronouns | 3rd Person Singular Pronouns | 3rd Person Plural Pronouns | Relative Pronouns |
|------|------|------|------|------|------|------|
| Subjective | I | we | you | he, she, it | they | who, which, that, what, whatever, whoever |
| Objective | me | us | you | him, her, it | them | whom, whomever, which, whichever |
| Possessive | my, mine | our, ours | your, yours | his, her, hers, its | their, theirs | whose |

### Table A.3 Using Cases in a Simple Sentence

| Subjective Case | | Objective Case | | Possessive Case | |
|------|------|------|------|------|------|
| I | gave | me | a copy of | my | book. |
| We | | us | | our | |
| You | | you | | your | |
| He | | him | | his | |
| Who | | whom | | whose | |
| She | | her | | her | |
| It | | it | | its | |
| They | | them | | their | |

the subjective case takes precedence over the objective case.]

2. Use the subjective case for a noun or pronoun that completes the meaning of a being verb (am, is, are, was, were, will be, has been, etc.).

No: It was her who answered the phone.

**Yes:** It was she who answered the phone. [Think of a being verb (e.g., is, are, was) as an equal sign: "It is she" is the same as "It = she."]

## Objective Case

1. Use the objective case for all objects.

No: Send your replies to Richard or myself.

**Yes:** Send your replies to Richard or me.

Note: The word *myself* may be used for intensive or reflexive situations.

*Intensive:* I myself will be there.

*Reflexive:* I hit myself with the racquet.

No: Julia asked she and I to give the report.

No: Julia asked her and I to give the report.

**Yes:** Julia asked her and me to give the report. [To decide which case is appropriate with com-

pound pronouns, think of each pronoun alone; e.g., "Julia asked her to give the report" and "Julia asked me to give the report."]

No: The technical support representative showed we sales representatives how to use the new program.

**Yes:** The technical support representative showed us sales representatives how to use the new program.

No: You gave the message to who?

**Yes:** You gave the message to whom? [In who/whom situations, think of who as being he and of whom as being him. For example, think of "You gave the message to whom?" as "You gave the message to him?"]

## Possessive Case

The possessive case enables nouns and pronouns to show ownership. Instead of saying "the home of the man," we can say, "the man's home." Many possessive-case applications require using the apostrophe ['].

1. For a singular noun or pronoun, show possession by adding an apostrophe and an *s*.

No: The cashiers purse got stolen.

**Yes:** The cashier's purse got stolen.

Yes:  The company's stock price has fallen dramatically during the past eight months.

Yes:  Give the gift to Jennifer's sister's friend Carol.

2.  To show possession by more than one person, place the apostrophe after the plural form of the word. First form the plural and then apply the apostrophe.

| Singular Form | Plural Form | Plural Possessive Form |
|---|---|---|
| manager | managers | managers' handbook |
| Mr. and Mrs. Jackson | the Jacksons | Jacksons' new house |
| man | men | men's clothing store |
| child | children | children's toys |
| boy | boys | boys' bikes |

No:  The cashier's purses got stolen. [Two or more cashiers' purses.]

Yes:  The cashiers' purses got stolen. [Two or more cashiers' purses.]

No:  The childrens' teacher contacted our company. [More than one child.]

Yes:  The children's teacher contacted our company. [More than one child.]

Note: Usually you should apply Rules 1 and 2 for possessive words ending in an *s* or *z* sound; but it is also common to add the apostrophe without an extra *s*, especially if the word sounds better without the extra *s*.

No:  General Motors's first-quarter earnings were up by 3 percent.

Yes:  General Motors' first-quarter earnings were up by 3 percent.

No:  Bill Gates's influence has been immense.

Yes:  Bill Gates' influence has been immense.

Yes:  Jose Gonzalez' house is on fire! [Acceptable.]

Yes:  Jose Gonzalez's house is on fire!

Yes:  The Gonzalez' house is on fire! [Acceptable.]

Yes:  The Gonzalezes' house is on fire!

3.  Do not add an apostrophe for personal possessive pronouns such as hers, his, its, ours, theirs, or yours. Add an apostrophe with indefinite possessive pronouns, such as everyone's, no one's, and anybody's. Also, add an apostrophe for inanimate objects.

No:  That report had it's cover torn. [Because "it's" is

a contraction for "it is," this sentence is saying, "That report had it is cover torn."]

Yes:  That report had its cover torn.

No:  Wednesdays meeting will be short. [Add an apostrophe for inanimate objects in possessive form.]

Yes:  Wednesday's meeting will be short.

No:  The new products entry into the marketplace had an immediate impact on everyones bottom line.

Yes:  The new product's entry into the marketplace had an immediate impact on everyone's bottom line.

4.  For multiple owners of an item, place an apostrophe only with the last owner. For individual ownership, place an apostrophe with each owner.

No:  Joan's and Brent's cars were sold a month ago. [Joan and Brent jointly owned the cars.]

Yes:  Joan and Brent's cars were sold a month ago.

No:  Joan and Brent's passports were renewed a month ago. [Passports are individually owned.]

Yes:  Joan's and Brent's passports were renewed a month ago.

5.  Whenever a noun or pronoun occurs before the "ing" form of a verb, use the possessive case if the emphasis is on the action. Use the objective case if the emphasis is on the performer of the action. (Note: The possessive case is appropriate in most situations with this type of sentence construction.)

No:  Maria questioning every decision is annoying.

Yes:  Maria's questioning every decision is annoying. [Emphasis is on the gerund questioning, not on Maria.]

No:  I can't imagine his being late.

Yes:  I can't imagine him being late. [Emphasis is on him, not on the gerund being.]

## Agreement and Reference

Agreement refers to consistency among the various parts of a sentence. Sentence elements must agree in three major ways: (1) number—singular or plural, (2) person—first, second, or third, and (3) gender—masculine, feminine, or neuter (neither). In each of your messages, be sure to maintain a consistent point of view within each of these three writing aspects.

*Number:*

> Singular—one person or thing; e.g., "*Ken is* my brother."
>
> Plural—more than one person or thing; e.g., "*We are* competing on Saturday."

*Person:*

> First—the writer or speaker; e.g., "*I am* the speaker."
>
> Second—the person to whom the message is being written or spoken; e.g., "*You are* going to like this movie."
>
> Third—someone or something else; e.g., "*She is* going to call me back."

Note: When writing business messages, maintain a consistent point of view with regard to *person.* Writing in first person is usually preferable, except in very formal situations where third person is appropriate.

> First person: *We* recommend that you sell this property. [Less formal]
>
> Third person: *The analysts* recommend that the property be sold. [More formal]

*Gender:*

> Masculine—male; e.g., "*He* cannot keep *his* appointment."
>
> Feminine—female; e.g., "*She* hurt *her* ankle."
>
> Neuter—neither/either male or female; e.g., "The *dollar* found *its* way back into my wallet."

To help achieve sentence agreement, follow a two-step process:

1. Find the true subject(s) of the clause.
2. Make the rest of the clause agree with the subject(s).

Follow a similar two-step formula to make pronouns and their antecedents (the words to which they have reference) agree:

1. Find the true antecedent of the pronoun.
2. Make the pronoun agree with the antecedent.

The following rules will help you comply with all agreement and reference standards.

1. When a subject and verb are separated by a prepositional phrase ending with a plural word, make the verb agree with the subject, not with the plural word in the prepositional phrase.

No: One of our owners are planning to retire next year.

Yes: One of our owners is planning to retire next year. [One is the subject, not owners.]

No: One of the women who is running for mayor is dropping out.

Yes: One of the women who are running for mayor is dropping out. [This sentence actually has a minor clause nested within the main clause. It could be rewritten as, "Of the women who are running for mayor, one is dropping out."]

Note: Treat company names as singular.

No: Robert Jensen & Associates were omitted from our list.

Yes: Robert Jensen & Associates was omitted from our list.

2. Use plural verbs with all compound subjects (two or more subjects) joined by *and.*

No: The computer and printer is on sale.

Yes: The computer and printer are on sale.

No: Planning the conference and the party are very taxing.

Yes: Planning the conference and the party is very taxing. [This clause has only one subject: Planning.]

3. If two subjects are joined by *either-or, neither-nor,* or *not only-but also* conjunctions, the latter subject governs the verb form. If a singular and a plural subject are used, place the plural subject nearer the verb to avoid awkward-sounding construction.

No: Either Logan or Brooks are up for promotion.

Yes: Either Logan or Brooks is up for promotion.

Yes: Either is capable of being a good manager.

No: Neither Logan nor Brooks are up for promotion.

Yes: Neither Logan nor Brooks is up for promotion.

Yes: Neither is up for promotion.

No: Roger Anderson or the Browns is going to host the meeting.

No: The Browns or Roger Anderson are going to host the meeting.

Yes: The Browns or Roger Anderson is going to

host the meeting. [Grammatically correct, but awkward sounding.]

**Yes:** Roger Anderson or the Browns are going to host the meeting. [Best.]

4. Treat collective words as singular or plural, depending on how they're used in the sentence; e.g., all, any, more, most, none, some, who, that, and which.

**Yes:** Some of the candy is left.

**Yes:** Some of the flowers are dying.

**Yes:** All of the employees are leaving the building.

**Yes:** All of the morning is left for free time.

Note: The following words are always singular—anybody, each, everybody, everyone, much, no one, nobody, and one.

5. Be consistent in using singular or plural forms.

**No:** Each member told of their experiences with Michael.

**Yes:** Each member told of his or her experiences with Michael. [Grammatically correct but wordy.]

**Yes:** All members told of their experiences with Michael. [Best.]

6. Use relative pronouns (who, that, and which) properly.

**Who**     Refers to people.
            Introduces essential and nonessential clauses.

**That**    Refers to things or to groups.
            Generally introduces essential clauses.

**Which**   Refers to things or to groups.
            Generally introduces nonessential clauses.

**No:** He's the one that will be hired.

**Yes:** He's the one who will be hired. [That refers to things. Who refers to people.]

**No:** The team who wins will be honored next week.

**Yes:** The team that wins will be honored next week. [The team is a group.]

**No:** The memo which came from Spencer is critical.

**Yes:** The memo that came from Spencer is critical. [That came from Spencer is essential to the meaning of the sentence.]

**No:** This delivery van, that I dearly love, has over 300,000 miles on it and must be sold.

**Yes:** This delivery van, which I dearly love, has over 300,000 miles on it and must be sold. [Which I dearly love is not essential to the meaning of the sentence.]

7. Avoid inappropriate gender references.

**No:** Each manager should make sure he stays within budget guidelines. [Not all managers are male.]

**Yes:** Each manager should make sure he or she stays within budget guidelines. [Better than the first, but wordy.]

**Yes:** Managers should make sure they stay within budget guidelines. [Best.]

8. Avoid ambiguous antecedents and references.

**No:** If the key won't fit in the lock, have it replaced by our maintenance staff. [What is it, the key or the lock?]

**Yes:** If the key won't fit in the lock, have the key replaced by our maintenance staff.

**No:** Jed told me that he forgot to schedule a room for our next meeting. This is what I feared might happen. [Does this refer to Jed's forgetfulness or to not having a room to meet?]

**Yes:** Jed told me that he forgot to schedule a room for our next meeting. This lack of follow through is what I feared might happen.

**No:** When Kristen talked with Amy, she said her mother was feeling better. [Unclear she!]

**Yes:** When Amy talked with Kristen, Amy said, "My mother is feeling better."

**Yes:** Amy told Kristen that her (Amy's) mother was feeling better.

## Tense

Tense refers to *when* some action occurred or *when* some condition existed, whether in the past, present, or future. As a writer, you are responsible for placing your words in accurate time sequences. The key is to decide the precise time from which you are writing. Then write everything that occurred prior to that time in past tense, everything that is happening at that time in present tense, and everything that will happen after that time in future tense.

For example, if I were sitting in a meeting on January 13 at 1:30 p.m., I might write the following: "I didn't feel well [past] before I came to the meeting; therefore, I think [present] I will leave [future] early." There you have all three

### Table A.4 Tense Chart

| Verb Form | Past Tense | Past-Perfect Tense | Present Tense | Present-Perfect Tense | Future Tense | Future-Perfect Tense |
|---|---|---|---|---|---|---|
| **Being verb** | I was | I had been | I am | I have been | I will be | I will have been |
| **Irregular action verb** | I wrote | I had written | I write | I have written | I will write | I will have written |
| **Regular action verb** | We hired | We had hired | We hire | We have hired | We will hire | We will have hired |
| **Progressive form** | I was writing | I had been writing | I am writing | I have been writing | I will be writing | I will have been writing |

tenses in one sentence, and they are correct because they are consistent with your particular "time" point of view.

The accompanying tense chart will help you understand different conjugations of verb tenses.

Using proper tense is quite intuitive, and most writers have little difficulty with tense in their writing. However, five rules will help where problems seem to occur most frequently.

Remember the following guidelines about tense.

1.  Maintain a consistent point of time. Decide the exact time point on which your document's tense will be based, and then adjust the tense of all verbs accordingly. (This rule is most frequently violated in spoken communication.)

### Table A.5 Irregular Verb Tense Examples

| Base Form | Past | Past Perfect |
|---|---|---|
| begin | began | had begun |
| buy | bought | had bought |
| cling | clung | had clung |
| come | came | had come |
| do | did | had done |
| go | went | had gone |
| hang (suspend) | hung | had hung |
| hang (execute) | hanged | had hanged |
| lay (put) | laid | had laid |
| lead | led | had led |
| lie (recline) | lay | had lain |
| prove | proved | had proved/en |
| see | saw | had seen |
| shrink | shrank/shrunk | had shrunk/en |
| sing | sang | had sung |
| sit | sat | had sat |
| swim | swam | had swum |
| swing | swung | had swung |
| take | took | had taken |
| write | wrote | had written |

No:  We were chatting in the hall when suddenly everyone starts running for the exit.

Yes:  We were chatting in the hall when suddenly everyone started running for the exit. [All happened in the past.]

2.  Use the present tense to describe a relatively permanent truth or condition.

No:  In her recent magazine article, Gabriella described the challenges of a virtual team.

Yes:  In her recent magazine article, Gabriella describes the challenges of a virtual team. [The article still exists.]

No:  He remembered that I liked chocolate-covered nuts.

Yes:  He remembered that I like chocolate-covered nuts. [I still do.]

Note: You may also use the present tense for text that you want the reader to assume is happening in the present.

Yes:  In the year 20XX, I see us expanding into more international markets.

Yes:  "President of XYZ Corporation Dies in Tragic Plane Crash" [Newspaper headline.]

3.  When an infinitive (the word *to* followed by a verb) follows a verb in the past or past-perfect tense, shift the infinitive verb to the present tense.

No:  I wanted to have attended the product launch, but I couldn't.

Yes:  I wanted to attend the product launch, but I couldn't. [To have attended is shifted to the present tense to attend.]

No:  We would have liked to have spent more time in Germany, but we had to get back home.

Yes:  We would have liked to spend more time in Germany, but we had to get back home.

4. For irregular verbs, use the correct form for all "perfect" tenses, as shown in the accompanying chart.

No:  Grace hadn't went to get the supplies when I last talked with her.

Yes:  Grace hadn't gone to get the supplies when I last talked with her.

5. Use the appropriate verb tense for subjunctive mood. Sentences can be constructed in one of three moods: indicative, imperative, and subjunctive.

*Indicative* mood is used to make a statement of fact. Most management writing is in indicative mood.

Example:  Entrepreneurs should create a detailed business plan.

Example:  We will likely receive three benefits.

*Imperative* mood is used to give a command or make a direct request. It always involves the implied second-person subject "you." Imperative mood is concise and direct and is useful in giving commands or explaining procedures. If it seems too strong, add softening words before the main verb; e.g., "*Please* schedule the conference room for our 4 p.m. meeting."

Example:  Get Annabelle to cover for you in today's meeting. [Understood as "*You* get Annabelle..."]

Example:  Turn the power switch to the "on" position. [Understood as "*You* turn..."]

*Subjunctive* mood is used to express a supposition, an indirect command or request, or a condition that is not true or not likely to be true.

Example:  Suppose all entrepreneurs were to create a business plan. [A supposition.]

Example:  I suggest that you create a thorough business plan. [An indirect command.]

Example:  If all entrepreneurs created thorough business plans, more startup companies would be successful. [An untrue condition—all entrepreneurs don't create thorough business plans.]

No:  I suggest that you should apply for the opening in finance.

Yes:  I suggest that you apply for the opening in finance.

No:  I recommend that the two departments should be combined.

Yes:  I recommend that the two departments be combined.

No:  It is important that new employees are trained.

Yes:  It is important that new employees be trained.

No:  If that statement was true, I would take a different action.

Yes:  If that statement were true, I would take a different action. [Present tense, subjunctive mood.]

No:  I wish Tara was here to conduct this meeting.

Yes:  I wish Tara were here to conduct this meeting. [Present tense, subjunctive mood.]

Yes:  I wish Tara had been at the meeting. [Past tense, subjunctive mood.]

Yes:  I wish Tara were going to be at the meeting. [Future tense, subjunctive mood.]

## Numbers

The major concern about numbers is whether to write them as numerals (1, 2, 3) or as text (one, two, three). The following number rules will cover most situations you'll encounter. But because number rules have so many exceptions, you'll occasionally have to consult a major style guide for additional answers.

1. In general, spell out single-digit numbers (one through nine); write as numerals everything larger than nine. All other rules are exceptions to this basic rule. (Some standards vary from this basic rule.)

No:  Our company is 3 years old.

Yes:  Our company is three years old.

No:  Bring me fifteen widgets.

Yes:  Bring me 15 widgets.

2. Always spell out numbers that begin sentences.

No:  11 violations of this policy have occurred since February.

Yes:  Eleven violations of this policy have occurred since February.

3. Use numerals in dates, addresses, percentages, and page references.

No:  I'll call you on March 3rd.

Yes:  I'll call you on the 3rd of March. [Use the "rd" ending only when the day precedes the month.]

**Yes:** I'll call you on March 3. [You would normally read this aloud as "March third."]

**Yes:** I live at 135 North Maple Drive.

**Yes:** This year's net income represents a 3.5 percent increase. [Spell out percent, rather than using %.]

**Yes:** Turn to page 5.

4. Use numerals to express time when a.m. or p.m. is used (use a colon to separate the hour figure from the minute figure). Don't use the colon and zeros with full hours unless the full hour is in the same text with a partial hour. Spell the hour in full when *o'clock* is used (e.g., eight o'clock).

   **No:** Joe will come at eight; Eliza will come at 8:30; and London will come at 9. [Two full hours and one partial hour.]

   **Yes:** Joe will come at 8:00 p.m., Eliza will come at 8:30 p.m., and London will come at 9:00 p.m.

   **No:** Joe will come at 8:00 p.m., and London will come at 9:00 p.m. [Two full hours.]

   **Yes:** Joe will come at 8 p.m., and London will come at 9 p.m.

5. Use numbers consistently for mixed numbers in the same category. If the largest number is more than 10, express all numbers in the group as numerals. Spell out the smaller number when numbers of two categories occur side by side.

   **No:** The group consisted of one major, three lieutenants, and 26 enlisted personnel.

   **Yes:** The group consisted of 1 major, 3 lieutenants, and 26 enlisted personnel. [All are military offices.]

   **Yes:** The 11-person delegation visited six European countries. [People and countries are not in the same category.]

   **No:** I printed 100 30-page booklets.

   **Yes:** I printed 100 thirty-page booklets.

6. Except in legal documents, write money amounts as numerals. Express even sums of money without the decimal and zeros, unless the sums are in a group of money amounts that includes both even and uneven figures.

   **No:** Send the eighty-three dollars you owe me.

   **Yes:** Send the $83 you owe me.

   **No:** I received checks for $28, $36.42, and $73.50.

   **Yes:** I received checks for $28.00, $36.42, and $73.50.

7. For large numbers, use a combination of words and numerals.

   **No:** Their net profit for last year was seven point two million dollars.

   **Yes:** Their net profit for last year was $7.2 million. [Read this out loud as "seven point two million dollars."]

8. Use numerals to express decimals and whole numbers with fractions; spell out and hyphenate fractions that stand alone.

   **Yes:** That time period shows a jump of 1.89 points.

   **Yes:** Increase the material by 8 2/3 inches.

   **No:** I took 1/2 of the week off for sick leave.

   **Yes:** I took one-half of the week off for sick leave.

   **No:** I set aside 1/10 of my income for savings.

   **Yes:** I set aside one-tenth of my income for savings.

9. Form the plural of numbers as with other nouns.

   **Yes:** We found several sixes and sevens among the low scores.

   **No:** We found several six's and seven's among the low scores.

   **Yes:** The use of email expanded during the 1990s.

   **No:** The use of email expanded during the 1990's.

## Capitalization

Alphabetic characters should be capitalized according to established standards. Using capital letters calls attention to certain words. Capital letters indicate proper nouns and mark the beginning of sentences. Capital letters can also affect the meaning of words, such as march or March and china or China.

Nonstandard and inconsistent use of capital letters slows reading and inhibits understanding. Equally inappropriate is the practice of writing in all lowercase or all capital letters. For example, writing an email message in all caps suggests that you are shouting at the reader.

The following capitalization rules will cover most situations you'll encounter. But because capitalization rules have so many exceptions, you may occasionally have to consult a major style guide for additional answers.

1. Capitalize the first word of every sentence, question,

command, or expression that has terminal punctuation (period, question mark, or exclamation point).

No:    What would most people change in their lives if they could? their physical appearance? their job? their income?

Yes:   What would most people change in their lives if they could? Their physical appearance? Their job? Their income? [Capitalize each segment that has terminal punctuation.]

2.   Capitalize the first word of a quoted complete sentence.

No:    The international office has stated that the company will hire only translators who are "Native speakers of the language." [Quotation is not a complete sentence.]

Yes:   The international office has stated that the company will hire only translators who are "native speakers of the language."

Yes:   According to the international office, "We will hire only translators who are native speakers of the language." [Quotation is a complete sentence.]

Yes:   "Integrity," says my supervisor, "is essential for someone in that position."

3.   Capitalize proper nouns (nouns naming a specific person, place, or thing) and adjectives created from proper nouns. Do not capitalize seasons (spring, summer, fall, winter).

Yes:   When did you go to England? [Proper noun]

Yes:   I enjoy English literature. [Proper adjective]

No:    I'm taking math, german, and physics.

Yes:   I'm taking math, German, and physics.

No:    My findings are presented in exhibit a.

Yes:   My findings are presented in Exhibit A.

No:    I bought a new xerox copier.

Yes:   I bought a new Xerox copier. [Xerox is the name of a company; copier is a generic term.]

4.   Capitalize business and professional titles when they immediately precede names and when they appear in addresses.

No:    He briefly introduced president James Martin.

Yes:   He briefly introduced President James Martin. [President immediately precedes the name.]

Yes:   The president of our company will attend the celebration.

Yes:   Mr. James Martin, President
1500 North Maple
Anywhere, US 642XX
[Address in a business letter]

5.   Capitalize the beginning and ending words and all the principal words in titles of organizations, reports, books, magazines, journals, and newspapers; but do not capitalize prepositions of four or fewer letters unless they begin or end the title. Also, do not capitalize articles (the, a, or an) unless they begin a title or are officially part of the proper noun.

No:    An Analysis Of Central California's Challenges With Water Pollution

Yes:   An Analysis of Central California's Challenges with Water Pollution

6.   Capitalize directions when they refer to a specific area or to people from a specific area.

No:    In the south, you'll find people to be very friendly.

Yes:   In the South, you'll find people to be very friendly. [This South is an area of the USA.]

No:    Drive South until you come to Highway 6. [This south is a direction, not a location.]

Yes:   Drive south until you come to Highway 6.

No:    You'll find that southerners are a warm and friendly people.

Yes:   You'll find that Southerners are a warm and friendly people.

7.   Capitalize the first letter of items in a vertical list:

Yes:   The shipment delay was caused by the following factors:

- Bad weather
- Poor scheduling
- Equipment failure

8.   Capitalize specific academic degrees.

Yes:   I'll be getting my Bachelor of Science degree next April. [Not Bachelor's of Science.]

Yes:   I'll be getting my bachelor's degree next April. [Does not identify the specific degree.]

## LANGUAGE

The previous appendix sections focus on the mechanics of sentences—structure, punctuation, and grammar rules. This section concentrates on the style aspect of sentences—choosing appropriate words. For a writer, the choice of words (diction) is as critical as the choice of paint colors for an artist. If you choose the wrong words, you convey the wrong message.

The words you use must be clear, complete, correct, and considerate.

### Clear—Words that Are Understood

Some writers use uncommon or esoteric words in an attempt to impress, often resulting in obfuscation! Most people will be more impressed by your ability to communicate clearly than by your use of fancy language. Choose words that will be understood by your audience. The following list gives examples of uncommon words that should be used with caution, as well as more widely understood words that may be used in their place.

| Uncommon Word | | Preferred Word |
|---|---|---|
| eschew | ➔ | avoid |
| exacerbate | ➔ | worsen or make worse |
| exasperate | ➔ | annoy |
| remuneration | ➔ | payment |

Be careful using jargon words. Jargon refers to technical terminology used in a unique situation or context. For instance, insurance personnel use unique insurance terminology, marketing specialists use unique marketing terminology, and computer technicians use unique computer terminology. Using such terminology is appropriate when the audience understands, but not otherwise.

No: I see greater risk exposure because of the company's high ceded reinsurance leverage. [Unacceptable if the reader does not understand insurance jargon.]

Yes: I see greater risk exposure because of the company's high ceded reinsurance leverage. [Acceptable if the reader understands insurance jargon.]

### Complete—Words that Give the Right Amount of Precision

Different words have different levels of precision—some words are general and others are specific. Choose words that give the level of precision appropriate for the situation. The table below shows a spectrum of words from general to specific.

| More general | vehicle |
|---|---|
| | ⬇ |
| | truck |
| | ⬇ |
| | pickup |
| | ⬇ |
| More specific | blue 20XX 4WD Dodge Ram |

For a report on traffic patterns, you may want to use the term *vehicle,* because the word covers all the different automobile types involved in traffic. However, when you advertise your vehicle for sale, you will want to use more specific terms like make, model, year, or trim line. In each instance, the selected words are appropriately precise because they convey the level of information needed.

No: We need to hire a new employee.

Yes: We need to hire a new data analyst.

No: We'll meet again in a few days.

Yes: We'll meet again on Friday at 3 p.m.

No: I won't be coming to work today because I'm vomiting. [Too specific.]

Yes: I won't be coming to work today because I'm ill.

### Correct—Words that Are Correct in Spelling, Usage, and Meaning

Make sure the words you use are correct in spelling, usage, and meaning. Today's software will catch most spelling errors, but not all. Therefore, don't let tight deadlines pressure you to skip your duty to proofread for spelling. Be particularly mindful of words with troublesome spelling, such as the following 25.

| | | |
|---|---|---|
| accommodate | leisure | pronunciation |
| acquire | liaison | questionnaire |
| congratulations | license | relevant |
| equipment | maintenance | restaurant |
| embarrass | misspell | separate |
| gauge | occurrence | supersede |
| grammar | perseverance | weird |
| grateful | personnel | |
| dependent | precede | |

Remember also that a word may be spelled correctly and yet have the wrong usage. For instance, a person might

write "then" for "than," "past" for "passed," or "sell" for "sale." Such words likely will be missed by spellchecking software. To catch errors in word meaning, watch for homonyms (a word with the same pronunciation as another but with a different meaning, such as *compliment* and *complement*) and with other related word pairs that have different meanings. The words in Table A.6 are frequently misused.

Finally, make sure the words you use convey the correct message. Never attempt to deceive or distort the true meaning by using "weasel words." Weasel words are vague words that give an untrue positive impression but that also give the writer a way to "weasel" out of responsibility for deception. Always be ethical and honest in your communications.

| Weasel Words | Challenges for Weasel Words |
|---|---|
| Research shows that . . . | What research? Who conducted the research? |
| Experts have found that . . . | What experts? Experts in what? |
| This doctor-tested product . . . | What doctor? A Ph.D. or an M.D.? |
| Make up to $20,000 in a single summer . . . | That means I might make only $5. |
| A special offer of just $49.95 . . . | What is the regular offer, $39.99? |
| This product will give you a better night's sleep. | Better than what? |
| Our prices are lower. | Lower than what? |

## Table A.6 Frequently Misused Words

| Words | Examples |
|---|---|
| *Appraise* is a verb meaning to determine the value, quantity, or amount of something. *Apprise* is a verb meaning to inform. | I'll *appraise* the Albertson property and then keep you *apprised* on the progress of our project. |
| *Affect* as a verb means to influence. *Effect* as a noun is the consequence or result of something; *effect* as a verb means to cause or implement. | Next month our company will *effect* a modified retirement policy for new employees; however, the policy will not *affect* current employees, nor will it have any *effect* on people who have already retired. |
| *Allow* gives permission. *Enable* empowers. | Karen will *allow* us to visit her company Friday morning, *enabling* us to gather the data we need. |
| *Compliment* is a nice comment. *Complement* means to complete. | I gave her a nice *compliment* on how her experience *complements* her education. |
| *Counsel* refers to advice itself or to the process of giving advice. *Council* refers to a group of people. | The student *council* will *counsel* the president. The president requested the *counsel*. |
| The abbreviation *e.g.* means "for example." The abbreviation *i.e.* means "that is." | They manufacture products in all major sports lines; *e.g.,* soccer, basketball, and football.<br>I think his announcement is a decoy; *i.e.,* they are covering up their product-defect problems. |
| *Ensure* means to guarantee. *Insure* refers to insurance. | Because you are properly *insured*, your spouse's financial welfare is *ensured*. |
| *Farther* refers to distance. *Further* indicates degree. | Let's discuss this matter *further* as we walk *farther* along this jogging trail. |
| *Fewer* refers to individual items. *Less* refers to uncountable bulk or quality. | We can order *less* pancake flour since we expect *fewer* people coming to our restaurant this week. |
| *Its* is the possessive form of *it*. *It's* is the contraction of *it is*. | *It's* up to the committee to determine *its* mission. |
| *Lay* means to put or place. *Lie* means to rest. | I'm going to *lay* this book down while I go *lie* down for a nap. |
| *Principal* refers to money, the CEO of a school, and the main element. *Principle* refers to a belief or concept. | The *principal* reason for our meeting is to discuss the *principal's* delinquent payment on the *principal* and interest of the loan. He has apparently forgotten the *principle* of honesty. |
| *Stationary* means not moving. *Stationery* refers to paper. | The *stationary* box of *stationery* is collecting dust. |
| *Your* refers to something you possess. *You're* means "you are." | *You're* invited to a birthday party at *your* sister's house. |
| *Lose* is the opposite of win. *Loose* means not tight. | If I *lose* 20 pounds, my clothes will be *loose*. |

## Considerate—Words that Reflect Social Sensitivity

In all your communication with others, be sensitive to the needs of the audience. Then make sure your messages to the audience are considerate and reflect this concern. Applying a *"you attitude"* will build trust and strengthen your relationship with the audience. Applying a *"me attitude"* says to the reader that you are mostly interested in serving yourself, which destroys your credibility.

As you show consideration for the audience, make sure your words have the necessary level of formality and the appropriate tone.

### Formality

Formality varies according to the social closeness of people in a communication relationship. It also is dictated by the social setting. For example, you would not address your supervisor in the same way you would address your golfing partner. In addition, if your golfing partner is also your supervisor, you would probably address him differently while in a board meeting than on the golf course.

Formal communication style employs respectful words and language. For instance, you might use the word "father" in a more formal setting, but use the word "dad" for informal situations. Formal writing avoids the use of casual speech and sometimes uses more passive voice.

Informal style employs more conversational wording and a more casual writing style. The context and the people involved in the situation dictate the level of formality to be reflected in the writing. The following examples illustrate when to use formal and informal language.

*Use more formal language for . . .*

- An invitation to an awards banquet
- A request for an interview with the CEO
- A written proposal to a client
- An office policy regarding dress standards

*Use less formal language for . . .*

- An email announcing a department meeting
- A flyer announcing an office party
- An email to a long-time friend
- A text to a friend

Slang is very casual language used in some settings but considered to be substandard and undignified in most. It often substitutes novel meanings for existing words, such as using "cool" to mean "very good." It may also use initials, such as LOL, for texting between people who know each other well. Using slang in your writing can have a powerful negative effect on the formality of the document, so avoid its use in nearly all communications. The following list shows slang words on the left and the preferred words on the right.

| Slang Word | | Preferred Word |
|---|---|---|
| grouse | → | complain |
| nab | → | catch |
| smooth | → | clever |
| snow job | → | deception |

### Tone

Many words carry an emotional element in addition to their basic dictionary meaning. The dictionary definition of a word is referred to as its *denotation*. Ideas or feelings associated with a word are called its *connotation*. The connotations of the words you choose will create the tone of your communication. Always select terms that are appropriate for the purpose, audience, and context, giving preference to words and expressions that are positive and considerate of people's feelings.

Compare the tone of the following two examples that deliver bad news. The first is considerate and delivers the bad news with social sensitivity; the second one does not.

**Positive***:*

Thank you for your request to return the shipment of books you purchased from us. After receiving your request, we checked the shipment date and found that the books were purchased four months ago, which is one month past the three-month return deadline. If the books had been returned a month earlier, we would have been happy to give a full refund.

**Negative***:*

We received your request to return the shipment of books you purchased from us. Unfortunately, you didn't return the books by the three-month deadline. Therefore, your request is denied. Next time you have books to return, remember the deadline.

Be aware that the connotations of words may change over time. For example, words that tie gender to job titles (*mailman*) have become less appropriate than gender-neutral terms (*mail carrier*). Euphemisms that replace socially unacceptable words or expressions (*pass away* vs. *die*) may also change. Use appropriate terms and euphemisms, and when in doubt, always err on the side of more formal language.

No: We had the same stewardess on our flight last week. [Socially insensitive.]

Yes: We had the same flight attendant on our flight last week. [Socially sensitive.]

No: We are cognizant of the magnitude of your current engagements. [This sentence sounds stuffy and pompous.]

Yes: We are aware of your current project commitments.

For all of your writing, check the wording of sentences to ensure that the tone is appropriate. Generally, use words that are positive, cordial, conversational (yet professional), and reader oriented—customized to the reader's vocabulary and circumstances.

No: We can't ship your parts until March 1. [Wording is negative; focuses on what you can't do.]

Yes: We will ship your parts promptly on March 1. [Words focus on the positive—states what you can or will do.]

No: We got your order today. It will be shipped as soon as we can get to it. [Words are mechanical and uncaring.]

Yes: Thank you for your order. It will be shipped to you within the next 24 hours. [Words are warm and friendly.]

No: Per your request that we scrutinize the various purported ethical violations suggested in the management audit report, we hereby submit the attached. [Words are pompous and arrogant—not conversational.]

Yes: Here is our analysis of the three ethics violations described in the management audit report. [Words reflect conversational language.]

## LENGTH

Sentences may be structurally sound, with proper punctuation and grammar, and have appropriate language, yet still be too long and wordy. This circumlocution problem can be overcome by being concise. Concise writing is not short, choppy writing with just the minimal content included. Rather, concise writing contains complete content, but reflects carefully crafted sentences with no unnecessary words. In other words, every word should be necessary and make a useful contribution to the sentence. As you review sentences for conciseness, constantly ask yourself, "How can I convey the needed information with as few words as possible, while maintaining an appropriate style?" Read the following sentence:

Much of the writing currently done in business today contains an excessive number of words, and this excessive wordiness makes it necessary for each and every reader of a message to spend much more time reading than he or she would have to do if the message were more concise."

The foregoing sentence is wordy (51 words) and is cluttered. What is the problem? First, it contains seven prepositional phrases: of the writing, in business, of words, for each, of a message, to spend, and to do. Second, it contains redundant wording. Redundancies are two or more words that mean the same thing:

*each and every* (use each or every, but not both)

*currently* and *today* (use currently or today, but not both)

Third, the sentence contains several wordy passages that could be shortened without sacrificing any content, such as the following:

*Much of the writing currently done in business today . . .* [Could be stated as, "Much of today's business writing . . ."]

*contains an excessive number of words . . .* [Could be stated as, ". . . is wordy."]

You could rewrite the 51-word sentence as follows:

Much of today's business writing is wordy, unnecessarily increasing the time required for reading.

The sentence is now 14 words long, reflecting a 37-word reduction, yet it still conveys the essential information and has a clear, readable style.

Long, wordy sentences can be shortened in four simple ways:

1. Omit useless words.

No: Before the interview, review the company's past history. [Past is redundant.]

Yes: Before the interview, review the company's history.

No: The product list created by the designers in the advertising department contained several pricing errors. [Created by the designers in the advertising department is useless information.]

Yes: The product list contained several pricing errors.

No: Where are you at? You need to hurry up! ["At" and "up" are useless words.]

**Yes:** Where are you? You need to hurry.

2. Replace passive-voice writing with active-voice writing.

   **No:** The report was written by Mandy. (Write in active voice, rather than passive.)

   **Yes:** Mandy wrote the report.

3. Condense wordy passages of text.

   **No:** Expenses that come from the unnecessary color copies could be reduced. [Eliminate unnecessary embedded clauses.]

   **Yes:** Expenses from unnecessary color copies could be reduced.

   **No:** We have a need for the hiring of two new employees. [Condense wordy verb phrases.]

   **Yes:** We need to hire two new employees.

   **No:** Due to the fact that last month's payment was skipped, he owes two payments for this month. [Eliminate wordiness throughout the sentence.]

   **Yes:** Because he skipped last month's payment, he now owes two payments.

4. Divide long sentences.

   **No:** Our employee turnover rate is among the lowest in this region, enabling our staff to develop long-term relationships with our clients.

   **Yes:** Our employee turnover rate is among the lowest in this region. This low rate enables our staff to develop long-term relationships with our clients.

Today's mobile technology has created a level of conciseness that sacrifices traditional writing style for brevity. For instance, an email might contain the following:

> Angie, can you join Alisha, Katie, Tesla, and me for lunch today at noon? We're meeting at Ivy's Place on Pine Ridge Road. Please let me know by 11 a.m. so I can make appropriate reservations.

However, a text message may be shortened to something like the following:

> Lunch today at noon? Ivy's Place on Pine Ridge Road. RSVP me by 11.

While this condensed style may be appropriate for texting or for informal, close relationships, it is not appropriate for other situations. Always be sure your style is appropriately formal for the situation. If you are not sure how formal you should be, choose to be *more* formal.

# APPENDIX QUIZZES

## Sentence Structure Quiz

For questions 1–10, mark A for simple sentences, B for compound sentences, C for complex sentences, and D for compound-complex sentences.

1. A B C D  After selling one of the smaller presses, the company acquired two new ones.

2. A B C D  Even though she arrived before the doors opened, she still was unable to get a ticket.

3. A B C D  We moved from St. Louis to Chicago, feeling the need to be closer to my parents.

4. A B C D  After a brief introduction, we watched an interesting video and then we walked through the flower gardens.

5. A B C D  The new policy manual, developed last year, is much clearer than the old one.

6. A B C D  After I purchased my new bike in Miami, I shipped it to Atlanta and then rode it in the 25-mile race.

7. A B C D  Although I couldn't attend this year's conference, I enjoyed reading the proceedings and I plan to attend next year's meetings.

8. A B C D  I have some good news for you—you have been cleared to receive the loan.

9. A B C D  The conference rooms on the first and second floors are occupied, but the third-floor conference room is available.

10. A B C D  I'd like to play racquetball with you, although I don't have a good racquet.

For questions 11–15, mark A for phrases, B for dependent clauses, and C for independent clauses.

11. A B C  Although the group voted in favor of this proposal

12. A B C  In spite of his excellent score on the test

13. A B C  To find your way to the library

14. A B C  A new freeway entrance is being constructed

15. A B C  Think about it

For questions 16–26, select the best option (a, b, c, or d).

16. Which of the following sentences includes a coordinating conjunction?

    a. Sale items may not be returned under any circumstances.

    b. If we want to prevent a decline in employee morale, we must implement a pay increase.

    c. After the nurse completes the training, she will be given a completion certificate.

    d. Our temporary employees feel undervalued, and their motivation suffers as a result.

17. Which of the following is a subordinating conjunction?

    a. but
    b. nor
    c. if
    d. yet

18. Which of the following sentences includes the best subject?

    a. There will be a special orientation meeting for new employees every Thursday at 10 a.m.
    b. Financial specialists will be available to answer questions after the meeting.
    c. Anticipation of the weekend sale caused great excitement among the college students.
    d. It is important for you to gain two years of business experience before you apply for the MBA program.

19. "A formal cross-training program for the compensation and benefits employees is proposed." The foregoing sentence suffers from all but which one of the following?

    a. The subject and verb are too far apart.
    b. Passive voice is used.
    c. A prepositional phrase is in the wrong place, given the voice used in the sentence.
    d. A transitive verb is misplaced.

20. Which of the following is written in active voice?

    a. The charges were filed last November.
    b. The charges were filed by the attorney last November.
    c. The new music will be performed during next week's symphony.
    d. Brooks McCallister will direct the training and will expect everyone to attend.

21. Which of the following is an adverb?

    a. carefully
    b. slow
    c. high-pitched
    d. diligent

22. Which of the following is a transitive verb?

    a. think
    b. sit
    c. throw
    d. run

23. Which of the following is an adjective?

    a. extremely
    b. slow
    c. very
    d. beauty

24. Which of the following does not contain a parallelism error?

    a. I suggest that we stay an extra day (unless you object) and visit the home office of American Family Insurance.
    b. The strengths she offers are that (a) she has related work experience, (b) a strong educational background, and (c) a great personality.
    c. Once everything is set up, we can train the employees and then the customers can be notified.
    d. Fifty-two of the participants said their accommodations were comfortable and would recommend the hotel to others.

25. Which item is correct?

    a. Go get the report from the filing cabinet that analyzes the impact of social media.
    b. To do well in this department, lots of creativity is needed.
    c. I'm going to have only a vegetable pizza and a diet drink for lunch.
    d. I'm sure excited that their team will be playing on Friday night.

26. Which of the following sentences does not contain a modifier error?

    a. The on-line system enables all employees to make investment changes at their convenience.
    b. Please bring me a cold glass of water.
    c. Taking the earliest flight that morning, his noon-time arrival surprised Katie who expected him at 3:30.
    d. She said she thought I did real well in my presentation last week.

## Punctuation Quiz

For each of the following quiz questions, select the best option (a, b, c, or d).

1. Which of the following is punctuated correctly?

    a. Andrew was introduced to Glen, the sales representative, Chad, the marketing manager, and Ben, the development manager.
    b. This job requires long, tiring hours of work, but you will have great people to work with.
    c. I'm going to call: Allison, Diana, Carol (our newest agent), and Staci.
    d. We rode our mountain bikes to the top of the hill, we then turned around and came back.

2. Which of the following is punctuated correctly?

    a. You call Sam and I'll call Ryan—then we can relax.
    b. Eilley said her experience with this low budget airline company has been great, so she said she is going to "recommend it without hesitation . . ."
    c. Coming down the home stretch the leader stalled, and came in second place.

d. Jesse, my new boss said he is planning some major changes but he declined to say what they will be.

3. Which of the following is punctuated correctly?

   a. I didn't really like the main course, however, the dessert was great.

   b. Frank's birthday party, which will be at noon on Friday; will be held at Roberto's Restaurant.

   c. His stubborn minded attitude about the change made life difficult for everyone on the sixth-floor.

   d. Be sure to bring your (a) procedure manual, (b) smartphone, and (c) project idea.

4. Which of the following is punctuated correctly?

   a. She said the terrorism threat: "would continue to pose a threat throughout the summer."

   b. We'll have lunch at El Rio Cafe, and then go shopping at several hardware stores, e.g., Home Aid, Long's, and Anderson Home Center.

   c. Matt asked Linden, "When can you meet on Friday"?

   d. We have several seven- and ten-passenger vans in our motor pool.

5. Which of the following is punctuated correctly?

   a. His pace was slow and erratic, nevertheless, he finished the course on time.

   b. He's a plodder but he always does top-notch work.

   c. You'll find; however, that you get ahead only when you speak up.

   d. Sharon is taking her son, Matt, on her trip to Boston. [Sharon has two sons.]

6. Which of the following is punctuated correctly?

   a. We'll return on February 27, 20XX and will be available to meet within a few days after that.

   b. Jacob said he could meet on 3 March 20XX or on 17 March 20XX.

   c. He says he'll accept nothing but a full-apology for her negative comment.

   d. Erin said, "Karen, I think you should be in charge of that activity".

7. Which of the following is punctuated correctly?

   a. The first is obvious, provide more healthy lunch options for our employees.

   b. On August 13, 2009 their group filed a class action lawsuit against the company.

   c. She lives at 178 Elkhorn Drive, Denver, CO 80209.

   d. He lacks self discipline and should not be trusted with this account.

## Case Quiz

For each of the following quiz questions, select the best option (a, b, c, or d).

1. In the sentence, "I am sorry you missed yesterday's meeting," what case is represented with "I"?

   a. Subjective

   b. Possessive

   c. Objective

   d. Declarative

2. Which of the following represents "third-person singular objective" case?

   a. Mine

   b. Him

   c. They

   d. Who

3. Which item is correct?

   a. I sent the laser pointer to Dan and Jake; I assume it is their's.

   b. Dan and me will be in charge of the activities.

   c. Dan and I will be in charge of Friday's activities.

   d. Dan and myself will take charge of the activities.

4. Which item is correct?

   a. Katherine and myself are going to sponsor next months tennis tournament.

   b. Katherine asked if you and me would help with the publicity.

   c. Call Jennifer Larkin and see if it is she who wants to work with the new PR program.

   d. If Jennifer isn't in, talk with whomever answers the phone.

5. Which item is correct?

   a. She and I visited the school to recruit any volunteers whom would like to participate.

   b. After our work on the December project, he gave the new design assignment to Heather and I.

   c. When you're finished, give the completed document to the receptionist or myself.

   d. They encouraged us sales representatives to revisit all our old accounts.

6. Which item is correct?

   a. Tyler's wife's friend came to spend the weekend.

   b. Tylers wife's friend came to spend the weekend.

   c. Tylers' wife's friend came for the weekend.

   d. Tyler's wifes' friend came for the weekend.

7. Which item is correct?

   a. Lets drive to Tucson and see the Hansen's new house.

   b. Let's drive to Tucson and see the Hansens' new house.

    c.   Let's drive to Tucson and see the Hansen's new house.

    d.   Lets drive to Tucson and see the Hansens' new house.

8.   Which item is correct?

    a.   Terry and Ben's personnel records have not been updated.

    b.   Terry's and Ben's personnel records have not been updated.

    c.   Terry's and Ben's new product design is four inches long.

    d.   Terry and Ben waited for three days while their new product finish it's testing.

9.   Which item is correct?

    a.   The Rodriguez's reputation was tarnished by their employee's bad behavior. [One employee]

    b.   Martin's memories of our company include many interesting stories.

    c.   The mens' department is upstairs.

    d.   My childrens' teacher said she will be retiring in two more years. [Two children]

10.   Which item is correct?

    a.   I get tired of him jumping to conclusions before we have a chance to present our whole story. [Emphasis is on the person, not on the action "jumping."]

    b.   I get tired of his jumping to conclusions before we have a chance to present our whole story. [Emphasis is on the person.]

    c.   Whom do you think will win the sales competition?

    d.   I told the counselor that we would work with whomever needed the most help.

## Agreement and Reference Quiz

For each of the following quiz questions, select the best option (a, b, c, or d).

1.   Which item is correct?

    a.   The road to three of the most famous canyons are not passable after heavy rainstorms.

    b.   The person that you have to talk with won't be available until next Tuesday.

    c.   One of the people who are being evaluated is my neighbor.

    d.   Two of the job candidates, which I believe are the strongest, are cousins.

2.   Which item is correct?

    a.   Each new employee tries to surpass his personal best.

    b.   Every fireman will participate in the nationwide food drive next Thursday.

    c.   Each flight attendant must be thoroughly trained in first aid before she can fly.

    d.   One of my grandparents is coming for a visit this weekend.

3.   Which item is preferable?

    a.   Either Alisha or her colleagues are responsible for the system backup.

    b.   Either her colleagues or Alisha is/are responsible for the system backup.

    c.   Either Alisha or her colleagues is responsible for the system backup.

    d.   Either her colleagues or Alisha are responsible for the system backup.

4.   Which item is correct?

    a.   Each of the workers are planning to attend the Christmas party next Friday night.

    b.   I think she is the one that should be put in charge of the San Francisco office.

    c.   The legislation which governs PM10 standards has been particularly important in this area.

    d.   The researchers discovered that their hard drive had crashed and that all their data had been destroyed.

5.   Which item is correct?

    a.   This old printer, which we've had for over five years, is ready for retirement.

    b.   Neither the bad economy nor our competitors is having a significant effect on our progress.

    c.   Cole's aide said he needs more time to complete the project.

    d.   One of the agents who is competing in the sales competition is experiencing new health problems.

6.   Which item is correct?

    a.   If the managers haven't picked up their new recruits by 10:30 a.m., have them go to Room 266.

    b.   Fred Jepson & Sons is a reliable plumbing company.

    c.   Fred Jepson & Sons are a reliable plumbing company.

    d.   The new employees and their manager is to attend the orientation meeting on Saturday.

7.   Which item is correct?

    a.   Either Andrew or Benson are being considered for a promotion.

    b.   One of the ads we placed in Sunday's newspapers is printed upside down.

    c.   If the trainers don't explain the new procedures well enough for the employees to understand, work with them as needed to make sure this problem is solved.

    d.   The students will visit our branch office and talk with employees on Project Youth Day; this will have a positive influence on their education.

## Tense Quiz

For each of the following quiz questions, select the best option (a, b, c, or d).

1.   Which item is not correct?

a. He was reading the training manual when he heard a loud crash.

b. He was slow during the first part of the competition, but he is catching up and will likely finish in the top three.

c. Are you sure he was the one who called you for an interview last Saturday?

d. In five years, I see him becoming a partner in our firm.

2. Which item is correct?

a. We would have liked to have stayed for all nine innings, but I had to leave for a meeting.

b. She usually buys treats from the bakery, but yesterday she decides to bring treats from home.

c. After I asked her what her maiden name was, I realized that we were cousins.

d. Jill told me that she doesn't see any point in our continuing negotiations with Robert.

3. Which of the following is a regular verb?

a. try

b. go

c. write

d. tell

4. Which of the following is written in past-perfect tense?

a. By the time the Olympics came, he had run over 10,000 miles.

b. I thought about running for the legislature.

c. Have you considered working for private industry instead of for a CPA firm?

d. I have eaten at all the Wendy's restaurants in Chicago.

5. Which of the following statements is written in imperative mood?

a. I wish we were able to purchase the office building on Maple Street.

b. Everything seemed to be going well until the accident happened.

c. Just to be sure, take her to the emergency room.

d. The paramedic says he thinks she will need stitches in her forehead.

6. Which of the following statements is not correct?

a. I want to major in accounting or management information systems.

b. If I were interested in plants, I would major in horticulture.

c. After graduation, I plan to work for a major CPA firm.

d. I suggest that you should attend the important kickoff meeting this Friday.

7. Which of the following statements is correct?

a. I was driving down 100 South when I suddenly see two vehicles obviously involved in a road-rage incident.

b. I think what the Bible was trying to say is that we shouldn't condemn, not that we shouldn't judge.

c. When I heard of his minor theft, I tried to convince him that honesty was the best policy to follow.

d. I would have liked to attend your meeting, but I was out of town attending my uncle's funeral.

8. Which of the following statements is correct?

a. First, his brother was in a car accident; then his mother dies suddenly.

b. If today's weather was better, I would be happy to take you to the airport.

c. If he had went to the training meeting like he should have, the accident wouldn't have happened.

d. Even though I couldn't attend yesterday, I'll be there for sure tomorrow.

9. Which of the following is written in indicative mood?

a. It is not my responsibility to follow up; you need to have more self-discipline.

b. Before the weather turns colder, arrange for appropriate snow removal in the parking lot.

c. I suggest that she be nominated as next year's co-chair.

d. Please submit your monthly report before you go to Portland.

10. Which of the following is an example of past-perfect tense?

a. I was

b. I had written

c. We have hired

d. I will be writing

## Numbers Quiz

For each of the following quiz questions, select the best option (a, b, c, or d).

1. Which item is correct?

a. On August 18th, I'll call to confirm my reservation.

b. I called at 7:00 a.m. and again at 7:30 p.m., but he must have slept through both of my calls.

c. Only six percent of the voters turned out for this election.

d. Our company showed a profit of $1,200,000 for the fourth quarter of 2015.

2. Which item is correct?

a. 10 percent of our clients are enrolled in all three programs.

b. Although he owed me $506.60, I accepted $500 to settle the debt.

c. In the months since December, our complaint calls have dropped from 16 to 10 to 6.

d. He pays 1/10 of his income to his church.

3. Which item is correct?
   a. Our branch office is about twenty miles west of our home office.
   b. 11 of our accountants will be transferred next month.
   c. Our customer research disclosed that 9 percent of our customers are generating over half of our revenue.
   d. We'll leave for Europe on May 15th and return home on June 3rd.

4. Which item is correct?
   a. The remainder of the discussion is on page eight.
   b. The meeting will run from 8:00 p.m. until 10:00 p.m., but we'll take a 5-minute break at 9 p.m.
   c. Please send $150 for next month's payment, and then send the remaining $150.58 the following month.
   d. Our firm's assets were only $2.5 million in the 1990s.

5. Which item is correct?
   a. When the merger is completed, we'll have to lay off about 1/3 of our assembly-line employees.
   b. I'm happy to report that the company made a $3,800,000 after-tax profit.
   c. Five of the 12 passengers were killed in the crash.
   d. I covered only three of the six guidelines in my training session last Friday.

6. Which item is correct?
   a. She is 11 years old and lives at 13990 South 1850 East.
   b. The class consisted of eight boys and 13 girls.
   c. I sold 5 six-volume sets of the author's personal history.
   d. We received checks for $56, $21.88, and $28.75.

## Capitalization Quiz

For each of the following quiz questions, select the best option (a, b, c, or d).

1. Which item is correct?
   a. Mr. Green said he is "Being tried without any solid evidence to convict."
   b. The coroner's report is included in appendix G.
   c. The Samsons moved to the northwest where Justin got a job with Boeing.
   d. Because I'm on Susy Slim's low-cholesterol diet, I avoid French pastries.

2. Which item is correct?
   a. When he was in the Middle East, he learned much about Jewish culture.
   b. The Bookkeeper was blamed for the error.
   c. I plan to get my Master's degree at the University of North Carolina.

   d. A Study Of Water-Pollution Causes In The State of Texas [Report Title]

3. Which item is not correct?
   a. Brynn told us to bring our "Detailed goals for the new year."
   b. We're going to move to the East when I graduate from college.
   c. I'll be receiving my bachelor's degree next April.
   d. I think I'll take classes in physics, astronomy, and German literature.

4. Which item is correct?
   a. His speech highlighted general christian history but avoided specific mention of church doctrines.
   b. Congratulations on receiving your mba degree.
   c. I'm going to be visiting his father this weekend, so I'll ask about Robby then.
   d. Wesley asked, "will you be going to the service project this Saturday?"

5. Which item is correct?
   a. I know several Russian people, but I don't much about russian literature.
   b. The senior mechanic told me my Mazda was fixed and ready to go.
   c. I just bought a new canon digital camera at the bookstore.
   d. Sample documents are included in appendix A.

6. Assuming the following is a title, which item is correct?
   a. Working With Teens And Young Single Adults—A Discussion About Drug Intervention Programs
   b. Working With Teens and Young Single Adults—A Discussion About Drug Intervention Programs
   c. Working with Teens and Young Single Adults—A Discussion about Drug Intervention Programs
   d. Working with Teens and Young Single Adults—A Discussion About Drug Intervention Programs

## Language Quiz

For each of the following quiz questions, select the best option (a, b, c, or d).

1. Which of the following is most socially acceptable?
   a. mail carrier
   b. stewardess
   c. fireman
   d. woman attorney

2. Which of the following words is misspelled?
   a. accommodate
   b. judgment
   c. principle (referring to money)
   d. receive

3. Which of the following words is used correctly?
   a. complement (a nice comment)
   b. council (to give advice)
   c. i.e. (for example)
   d. ensure (to make sure)
4. Which of the following sentences has no words that are misused?
   a. After driving further down the road, he finally found the stationery store.
   b. He gave me counsel not to let her bad attitude effect my performance.
   c. After laying down for a nap, I noticed that the magazine had its cover torn off in the mail.
   d. The new insurance coverage will ensure that we are protected against that type of loss.
5. Which of the following are homonyms?
   a. near and close
   b. compliment and complement
   c. hot and cold
   d. farther and further

### Length Quiz

1. Which of the following does not contain a redundancy?
   a. If you sign the contract today, you'll get an added bonus.
   b. Just bring the basic necessities on our hike today.
   c. The large room contained nothing but empty space.
   d. It's your turn to write the monthly newsletter article.
2. Which of the following is most concise?
   a. It is my intention to hire him by July 1.
   b. The book that was on my desk is missing.
   c. I would like to take a moment to introduce you to my friend Ashley.
   d. The red spot on the left side of my car was for sure caused by a paint ball.
3. Which sentence best employs concise writing?
   a. His main argument is that the manager should have included the group in the decision.
   b. You should be sure to plan in advance for the emergency drill.
   c. A great many writers fail to adequately and appropriately proofread their written emails.
   d. The three triplets will keep their two parents very busy.
4. Which sentence best employs concise writing?
   a. I believe his overall approach to fixing the troublesome problem is appropriate, but I think he has overlooked some small details.
   b. In order to implement the new training, we must first get prior approval from Brian's manager.
   c. To succeed in business, you must write and speak well.
   d. The key to the car is hanging on the key rack.
5. Which sentence best employs concise writing?
   a. In the event that Jill does not attend the committee meeting, we will not discuss the proposed change in benefits.
   b. The reason for his failure was due to the fact that he couldn't get all of his employees to support his plan.
   c. After Marianne edits the manuscript, Liam will complete the layout and design work.
   d. The fact that he is the only prospective candidate to follow up after the employment interview improves his chance of being hired.

## ANSWERS TO QUIZ QUESTIONS

*Structure*

1. A
2. C
3. A
4. B
5. A
6. C
7. D
8. B
9. B
10. C
11. B
12. A
13. A
14. C
15. C
16. D
17. C
18. B
19. D
20. D
21. A
22. C
23. B
24. A
25. C
26. A

*Punctuation*

1. B
2. A
3. D
4. D
5. B
6. B
7. C

*Case*

1. A
2. B
3. C
4. C
5. D
6. A
7. B
8. B
9. B
10. A

*Agreement/Reference*

1. C
2. D
3. A
4. D
5. A
6. B
7. B

*Tense*

1. C
2. D
3. A
4. A
5. C
6. D
7. D
8. D
9. A
10. B

*Numbers*

1. B
2. C
3. C
4. D
5. D
6. A

*Capitals*

1. D
2. A
3. A
4. C
5. B
6. D

*Language*

1. A
2. C
3. D
4. D
5. B

*Length*

1. D
2. B
3. A
4. C
5. C

# APPENDIX B

# Document Formats

## EMAIL

## LETTERS

## MEMOS

## REPORTS AND PROPOSALS

## DOCUMENT EXAMPLES

## Email

The general format for writing emails is governed by the software you use, with specific spaces allotted for sender, receivers, subject line, and so forth. You may send copies to other recipients with a CC or BCC (carbon copy or blind carbon copy). The email address of everyone who receives a CC copy is visible to the main recipient, all CC recipients, and the sender; the email address of anyone who receives a BCC copy is not visible to anyone except the sender. Be aware, however, that if a BCC recipient replies to your email with "Reply to All," his or her email will be sent to everyone on the original email list. To prevent this accident from happening, the best practice is not to use BCC, but rather to "Forward" the email.

As you compose emails, follow five guidelines. First, remember that your content may be forwarded to others. Therefore, don't assume that email messages are private. Second, avoid becoming too lax in your writing. Always use correct grammar, spelling, and punctuation. Third, to enhance the visual aspect of emails, consider using OABC and HATS, especially for longer messages. Even if you have limited font options, you can capitalize the headings and use dashes or small o's for bullets. Fourth, proofread emails carefully by reading them slowly out loud. Fifth, before clicking "send," check the "To" field to make sure the right recipients are receiving the email, and check for any necessary attachments.

---

Recipient's email address →

| To | sstaylor@email.com |
| BCC | jtstewart@email.com ← |

Be cautious about using BCC.

| Sent | 23 June 20XX; 4:26 p.m. |

Sender's email address →

| From | mlj100@email.com |
| Subject | Request for Feedback on Training Schedule ← |

Write a descriptive subject line.

| Attached: | Training Schedule.doc ← |

Remember to attach needed documents.

Hi Sandi, ←

Use a cordial, friendly salutation.

Refer to previous email as needed. →

In response to your question about this year's training meetings, xxxx xxx x xxxxx. Xxx xxxxx xx xxxx xxxxxxxx xxxx xxx xxxxx. Xxx xxxxxx xx xxxx xxx xxx xxxxxxxx xxxxx xxxxxxx xxx x. Xxxxx xxxxx xxxx xxxxxx xx x xxxxx xxxxx xxx xxxxx xx. Here are our preliminary plans for Tuesday and Wednesday. ←

Agenda

1 blank space between paragraphs →

TUESDAY ←

Use headings as appropriate.

Two hyphens can serve as a bullet. →

— Xxxx xxx x xxxxx xx xxxxxx xx xxxx xxx xxx xxxxxxxx xxxxx xxxxxxxx xxx x. xxxxx xxxxx xxxx xxxxx xx x xxxxx xxxxx xxx xxxxx xx.

— Xx xxx xxxxxx x xxx xxxxxxxxx xx xxxxx xxxx xxxxx x xx xxxxx xxx x xxxxxxx xx xxxxx xx xxxx xxxxxxxx xxx.

Type headings in all caps to make them stand out. →

WEDNESDAY

— Xxxxxxxxxxx xxxxxxxxxxx xxx x xxxxxx.

— Xxxx x xxxxx xx xxxxx xx xxxx xxx xxx xxxxxxx xxxxx xxxxxxx xxx x. xxxxx xxxxx xxxx xxxxx xx x xxxxx xxxxx xxx xxxxx xx.

The attached document gives additional xxxx xxxxx xx x xxxxxxxxxx xxx xx. Please call me if you have any questions. ←

Make an appropriate closing comment.

1 blank space →

Thanks,

1 blank space →

Mark ←

Include your name so the receiver knows this is the end.

## Full Block Letter

A letter is a paper document sent to someone outside the organization. Almost all business letters follow a full-block style, with every line of text beginning at the left margin. The letter should have one-inch left and right margins. A one-page letter should be vertically centered. If a letter is more than one page long, leave a one-inch top, bottom, left, and right margin. After page 1, every succeeding page should begin with the name of the recipient, the page number, and the date.

**ABC, Inc.**
1234 Service Way
Fun City, US 62390

*Variable space—add more for short letters; less space for long letters.*

April 14, 20XX

*Company letterhead is used for page 1. Blank stationery is used for all subsequent pages.*

*The date may also be written as 14 April 20XX.*

*1-3 blank spaces*
*Address block of recipient*

Ms. Sandi S. Taylor, CFO
Qwerty Manufacturing, Inc.
4321 Corporate Road
Somewhere, US 38243

*1 blank space*
*Salutation*
*1 blank space*

Dear Ms. Taylor:

*Or "Dear Sandi:" if you are on a first-name basis. Use a colon (:) to end the salutation.*

Body text xxxx xxx x xxxxx xx xxxxxx xx xxxx xxx xxx xxxxxxxx xxxxx xxxxxxxx xxx x. xxxxx xxxxx xxxx xxxxxx xx x xxxxx xxxxx xxx xxxxx xx.

*1 blank space between paragraphs*

Body text xxxx xxx x xxxxx xx xxxxxx, xx xxxx xxx xxx xxxxxxxx xxxxx xxxxxxxx xxx x. Xxxxx xxxxx xxxx xxxxxx xx x xxxxx xxxxx xxx xxxxx xx. Xx xxx xxxxxx x xxx xxxxxxxxxx xx xxxxx xxxx, xxxxxx x xx xxxxx xxx x xxxxxxxx xx xxxxx xx xxxx xxxxxxxxx xxx.

Body text xxxx xxx x xxxxx xx xxxxxx xx xxxx xxx xxx xxxxxxxx xxxxx xxxxxxxx xxx x. xxxxx xxxxx xxxx xxxxxx xx x xxxxx xxxxx xxx xxxxx xx.

*1 blank space*
*Complimentary close*

Sincerely,

*3-4 blank spaces*

Mark L. Jones
CEO

*The author's name and title may also be on the same line: Mark L. Jones, CEO.*

*1 blank space*

Enclosure
cc:  Cambri Ellison
       Keith Blake

*Enclosure and CC notations are added as needed.*

*1" top margin*

*Horizontal format*

Ms. Sandi S. Taylor                    Page 2                         14 April 2011

OR

*Vertical format*

Ms. Sandi S. Taylor
Page 2
14 April 2011

*2 blank spaces*

xxxxx x xxxxxxxx xxx xx xxxxx xxxxxx xxx

*Blank stationery, with no letterhead, is used for all pages after page 1.*

*The recipient's name, page number, and current date should be repeated on all pages after the first page. Either horizontal or vertical format is acceptable.*

## Full Block Letter with No Letterhead

Sometimes you will write a personal letter and have no company letterhead. You may either create a letterhead for yourself or type your return address at the top of the letter.

1 blank space

1-3 blank spaces (variable)
Address block of recipient

1 blank space
Salutation
1 blank space

1 blank space
between paragraphs.

1 blank space
Complimentary close

3-4 blank spaces

2876 Oakcrest Lane
Neighborville, US 398XX

April 16, 20XX

Ms. Sierra R. Topham
4321 Corporate Road
Somewhere, US 38243

Dear Sierra:

Body text xxxx xxx x xxxxx xx xxxxxx xx xxxx xxx xxx xxxxxxxx xxxxx xxxxxxxx
xxx x. xxxxx xxxxx xxxx xxxxx xx x xxxxx xxxxx xxx xxxxx xx.

Xxxx xxt xxxx xxx x xxxxx xx xxxxxx xx xxxx xxx xxx xxxxxxxx xxxxx xxxxxxxx
xxx x. xxxxx xxxxx xxxx xxxxx xx x xxxxx xxxxx xxx xxxxx xx. Xx xxx xxxxx x
xxx xxxxxxxxx xx xxxxx xxxx xxxxx x xx xxxxx xxx x xxx.

Xxx xxxx xxx xxx x xxxxxxx xxxx xx xxxxx
xxxxx xxxxx xxx x xxxxx xx xxxx

Body text xxxx xxx x xxxxx xx xxxxxx xx xxxx xxx xxx xxxxxxxx xxxxx xxxxxxxx
xxx x. xxxxx xxxxx xxxx xxxxx xx x xxxxx xxxxx xxx xxxxx xx. Xx xxx xxxxx x
xxx xxxxxxxxx xx xxxxx xxxx xxxxx x xx xxxxx xxx x xxxxxxx xx xxxxx xx

Sincerely,

*Diane Faris*

Diane Faris

*Return address (typed in this position when you are not using company letterhead).*

*Or "Dear Ms. Topham:" if you are not on a first-name basis. Use a colon (:) to end the salutation.*

*No title is needed when you are writing a personal letter.*

## *Simplified Letter*

A simplified-format letter differs from a full-block format in three ways. First, the salutation is replaced by a subject line in all capitals. Second, the complimentary close beneath the body of the letter is omitted. Third, the name and position of the writer is typed in all capitals on one line. All other formatting is the same as full block (see page 49).

**ABC, Inc.**
1234 Service Way
Fun City, US 62390

*Company letterhead is used for page 1. Blank stationery is used for all subsequent pages.*

*Current date* → April 14, 20XX

*1-3 blank spaces*

*Address block of recipient* → Chris M. Tomlinson
4321 Corporate Road
Somewhere, US 38243

*1-2 blank spaces*
*Subject line, all caps* → REQUEST FOR XXXXX XXX XXXXX:
*1-2 blank spaces*

Body text xxxx xxx x xxxxx xx xxxxxx xx xxxx xxx xxx xxxxxxxx xxxxx xxxxxxxx xxx x. xxxxx xxxxx xxxx xxxxxx xx x xxxxx xxxxx xxx xxxxx xx.

*1 blank space between paragraphs*

Xxxx xxxxx xxxx xxx x xxxxx xx xxxxxx xx xxxx xxx xxx xxxxxxxx xxxxx xxxxxxxx xxx x. xxxxx xxxxx xxxx xxxxxx xx x xxxxx xxxxx xxx xxxxx xx. Xx xxx xxxxxx x xxx xxxxxxxxxx xx xxxxx xxxx xxxxxx x xx xxxxx xxx x xxxxxxxx xx xxxxx xx xxxx xxxxxxxxx xxx.

Xxxx xx xxxxx xxxxx xxx x xxxxx xx xxxxxx xx xxxx xxx xxx xxxxxxxx xxxxx xxxxxxxx xxx x. xxxxx xxxxx xxxx xxxxxx xx x xxxxx xxxxx xxx xxxxx xx.

*3-4 blank spaces*  [signature: Mark L. Jones]

MARK L. JONES—CEO

*The author's name and title are typed on the same line in all caps.*

*1 blank space*

Enclosures (2)

*Indicate the number of attachments if more than one.*

## Envelopes

Two common envelope sizes are used in business. The #10 envelope is about 4 x 9 1/2 inches; the #6 3/4 envelope is about 3 1/2 x 6 3/4 inches. Most business envelopes will have the sender's address preprinted in the upper left corner. For the receiver's address, the United States Postal Service (USPS) recommends all uppercase type, with no punctuation, to enhance the efficiency of postal scanning equipment. Standard business stationery must be folded as shown below to fit in both envelope sizes.

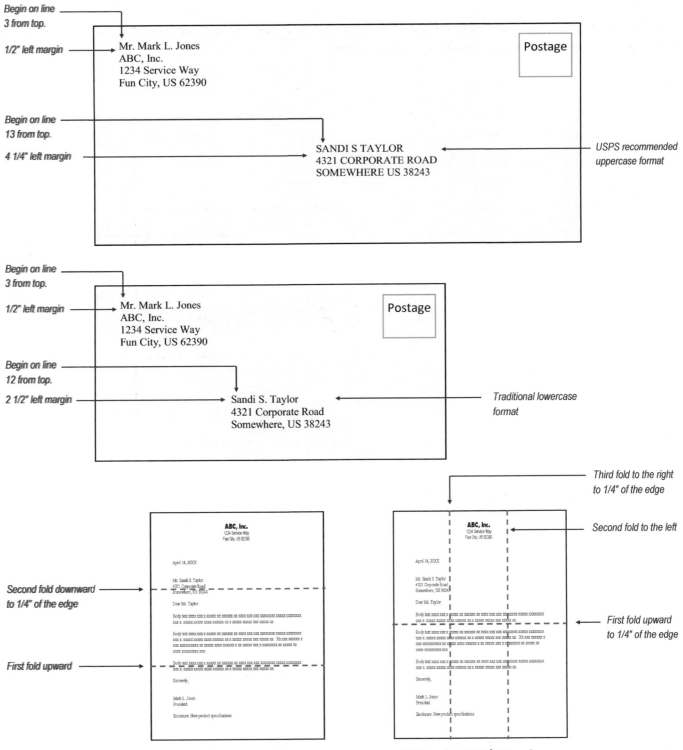

**Folding for #10 Envelopes**      **Folding for #6 3/4 Envelopes**

## *Memo*

A memo is a paper message sent within an organization, although paper memos have largely been replaced by email. Memos are used to transmit a wide variety of information, from short, informal messages to long, multipage memo reports. The language style and tone vary according to the topic and the audience.

Some organizations provide printed memo stationery, and some organizations sequence the standard heading information differently. Nevertheless, the following example will provide an acceptable format to follow whenever you need to prepare a paper form. Use a block format, with no indentation for the first line of paragraphs. Insert appropriate to, from, date, and subject (or "Regarding") information at the top (may be either single or double spaced, as shown below). Leave a one-inch top, bottom, left, and right margin. To sign a memo, you may put your initials beside your name in the heading lines, or you may sign at the bottom left after the last line of text.

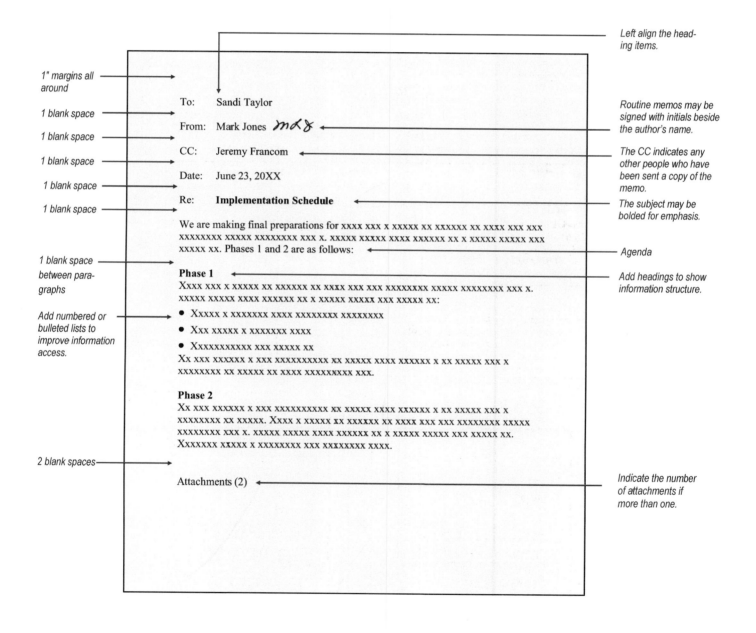

## *Memo with Two Pages*

For memos that are longer than one page, put a page number at the bottom of page 1 and at the top or bottom of all following pages. The page numbers may be centered or placed at the right margin.

*1" margins all around*

*1 blank space*

*1 blank space*

*1 blank space*

*1 blank space*

*1 blank space between paragraphs.*

*Add headings to show message structure.*

*1" margins*

To:     Sandi Taylor
        Richard Marshall
        Seth Olsen

From:   Mark Jones

Date:   17 July 20XX

Re:     REPORT OF XXXXXXX XXXXX

For the past month, our management auditing team has been xxxx xxx x xxxxx xx xxxxxx xx xxxx xxx xxx xxxxxxxx xxxxx xxxxxxxx xxx x. xxxxx xxxxx xxxx xxxxx xx x xxxxx xxxxx xxx xxxxx xx. Xxxx xxx x xxxxx xx xxxxx xx xxxx xxx xxx xxxxxxxx xxxxx xxxxxxx xxx xxxx. xxxxx xxxxx xxxx xxxxx xx x xxxxx xxxxx xxx xxxxx xx.

Xxxx xxx x xxxxx xx xxxxx xxx xxxx xxx xxx xxxxxxxx xxxxx xxxxxxxx xxx x. xxxxx xxxxx xxxx xxxxx xx x xxxxx xxxxx xxx xxxxx xx. Xxxxxxxx xxx x. xxxxx xxxxx xxxx xxxxx xx x xxxxx xxxxx xxx xxxxx xx. Xx xxx xxxxx x xxx xxxxxxxxx xx xxxxx xxxxx xxx x xxxxx xxx x xxxxxxx xxx xxxxx xx xxxx xxxxxxxxx xxx.

**Heading**
Xxxx xxx x xxxxx xx xxxxx xx xxxx xxxx xxx xxxxxx xxxxx xxxxxxx xxx. xxxxx xxxxx xxxx xxxxx xx x xxxxx xxxxx xxx xxxxx xx. Xxxxxxxx xxx x. xxxxx xxxxx xxxx xxxxx xx x xxxxx xxxxx xxx xxxxx xx.

Xx xxx xxxxx x xxx xxxxxxxxx xx xxxxx xxxx xxxxx xx xx xxxxx xxx x xxxxxxxx xx xxxxx xxx xxxx xxxxxx xxxx xxx. Xxxxxxxx xxx x. xxxxx xxx xxxx xxx xxxxx xx x xxxxx xxxxx xxx xxxxx xx. Xxxxxxxx xxx x. xxxxx xxxxx xxxx xxxxx xx x xxxxx xxxxx xxx xxxxx xx. Xx xxx xxxxx x xxx xxxxxxxxx xx xxxx xxxxx xxxx x xxxx xx xxxx xxxxx xxxxxxxx xxx.

**Xxx 1. Xxx xxx x xxxxxx**

1

*List vertically all who are receiving the memo.*

*You may also use July 17, 20XX.*

*You may use uppercase characters for emphasis.*

*Leave at least one line of space before and after visuals.*

*Leave at least one line of space before and after visuals.*

*Sign formal memos at the bottom.*

2

Xx xxx xxxxxx x xxx xxxxxxxxx xx xxxxx xxxx xxxxx x xx xxxx xxx x xxxxxxxx xx xxxxx xx xxxx xxxxxxxx xxx. Xx xxx xxxxx x xxx xxxxxxxxx xx xxxxx xxxx xxxxx x xx xxxx xxx x xxxxxxx xx xxxxx xx xxxx xxxxxxxx xxx. Xx xxx xxxxx x xxx xxxxxxxxx xx xxxxx xxxx xxxxx x xx xxxxx xxx x xxxxxxxx xx xxxx xxxxxxxx xxx.

*Mark L. Jones*

Team Leader

*One-half inch of space*

*For memos longer than one page, place a page number at the top or bottom and position the numbers at the center or the right margin position.*

## Cover Letter

Formal business reports and proposals often require a cover memo or a cover letter, sometimes called a letter of transmittal. A cover memo is used if the report or proposal is written for someone inside your organization. A cover letter is used if the report or proposal is written to someone outside the organization. These memos and letters are formatted like all other business memos and letters.

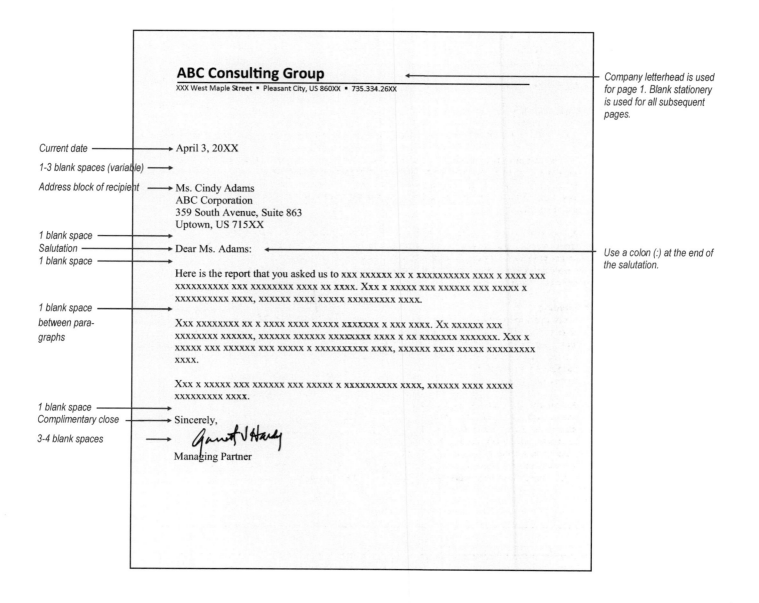

## Reports and Proposals

### *Title Page*

The title page of a report contains four major elements: title, recipient of the report, author(s), and current date. A proposal includes the same elements, and it may also include additional information that identifies the RFP the writer is responding to. The following figure gives the approximate positions of these elements on the page, but no rigid standards govern vertical spacing. As a general guideline, center the elements on the title page, both left to right and top to bottom, with spaces between the four elements as shown below.

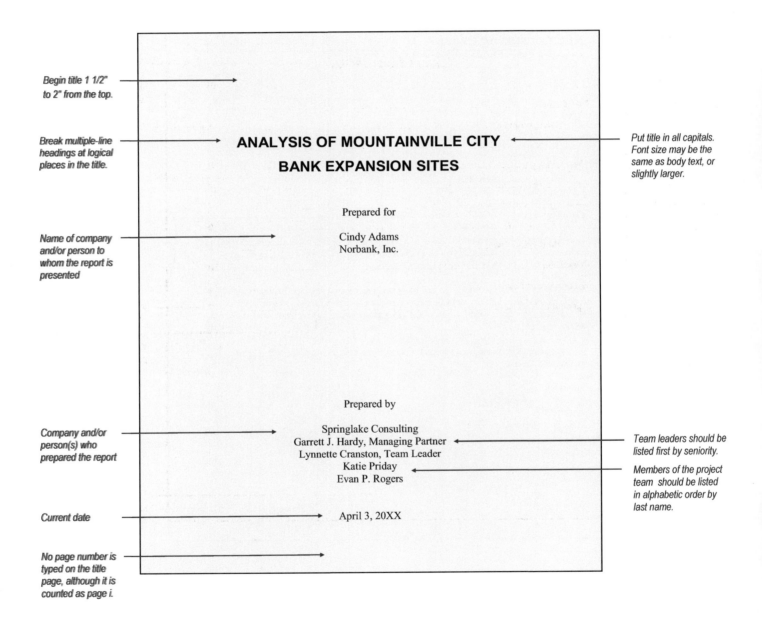

Begin title 1 1/2" to 2" from the top.

Break multiple-line headings at logical places in the title.

Name of company and/or person to whom the report is presented

Company and/or person(s) who prepared the report

Current date

No page number is typed on the title page, although it is counted as page i.

**ANALYSIS OF MOUNTAINVILLE CITY**
**BANK EXPANSION SITES**

Prepared for

Cindy Adams
Norbank, Inc.

Prepared by

Springlake Consulting
Garrett J. Hardy, Managing Partner
Lynnette Cranston, Team Leader
Katie Priday
Evan P. Rogers

April 3, 20XX

Put title in all capitals. Font size may be the same as body text, or slightly larger.

Team leaders should be listed first by seniority.

Members of the project team should be listed in alphabetic order by last name.

## *Table of Contents*

Formal business reports and proposals generally require a table of contents that provides the headings and subheadings of the report. The beginning page number of each section is provided at the right margin of the table of contents. Generally, dot leaders are placed after each heading to guide the reader's eyes to the appropriate page number.

*Begin title 1 1/2" to 2" from the top.*

*Include only items that occur after the Table of Contents.*

*Indent secondary headings.*

### Table of Contents

| | |
|---|---|
| Executive Summary | iii |
| Introduction | 1 |
| Background | 1 |
| Purpose | 2 |
| Methodology | 3 |
| Data Analysis | 4 |
| Questionnaire data | 4 |
| Interview data | 6 |
| Production data | 8 |
| Conclusions | 10 |
| Recommendations | 11 |
| Appendix | 12 |

ii

*Use a consistent heading font for all major headings throughout the report or proposal.*

*List the page number where the section begins.*

*1 blank space between lines of text*

*Right align page numbers.*

*Use dot leaders to guide the reader's eyes to the page numbers.*

*Use lowercase Roman numerals for front-matter pages.*

## *List of Illustrations*

Long business reports or proposals with multiple illustrations may benefit from a List of Illustrations following the Table of Contents. If the list is short, it may be placed on the previous page after the Table of Contents.

*Begin title 1 1/2"
to 2" from the top.*

**List of Illustrations**

*Use a consistent heading
font for all major headings
throughout the report or
proposal.*

*A list of figures
and/or tables may
be included with
formal reports and
proposals as
needed.*

Figure

| | | |
|---|---|---|
| 1 | Projected Housing Growth | 8 |
| 2 | Analysis of Demographic Data | 10 |
| 3 | Market Analysis | 12 |
| 4 | Commercial Activity Analysis | 14 |

*Right align page numbers.*

Table

| | | |
|---|---|---|
| 1 | Last Five Years' Housing Growth | 4 |
| 2 | Analysis of Banks in Mountainville | 5 |
| 3 | Volume of Retail Sales 20XX-20XY | 6 |

*1 blank space between
lines of text*

iii

*Use lowercase Roman
numerals for prefatory
pages.*

## *Executive Summary*

An executive summary may be included at the beginning of a long report or proposal to provide readers with a quick overview. The executive summary should include the information that is most vital for the reader to know, such as including background information, purpose, methodology, main conclusions, and most important recommendations. To help you decide what to include in an executive summary, write as though the reader is not going to read the main report or proposal.

*Begin title 1 1/2" to 2" from the top.*

*Use a consistent heading font for all major headings throughout the report or proposal.*

### Executive Summary

Because of high growth during the last two years, xxxxxx xxxxxxx xxxxxxx xxxxxxxx xxxxxx x xxxxxxxxx xxxxx xxxx xxxxxxxxx x xxx xxx xxxxx xx xx xxxxxx xxxx xx. Xxxxxxxx xxx xxxxx, xxxxx xxxxxxx xxxx xxxx xxxxxxx x xxxxxxxx xxxxxxx. Xxxxxxxx xxxxxx x xxxxx xx xxxxx xxxxx.

- Xxxxxx xxxx xxxxxx xxxxxxx xxx xxxxxx xxxx xx.
- Xxxxxxx xxxxx x xxx xxx xxxxxxxx xxxxxx x xxxxxxxx xx.

Xxxxxxxx xxxxxxxxx xxxxxxxxx xxxxxxxx xxxxxxxx xxxxx, xxxxxxxx xxxxxx xxxx. Xxxxxxxx xxxxxxxx xx xxxxx x xxxxxx xx xxxxxxxxx xxxxxxx xx xxxx xxxxxxxx xxxxxxx. Xxxxxxxxxx xxxxxx xxxxxx x xxxxx xxx.

*1 blank space between paragraphs.*

### Conclusions

Xx xxxxxx xxxx xxxx x xxxxxx xxxx xxxx xxxxxxx xx xxx x xxxx xxxx xxxx xxxxxxxxxx xxxx:

*Headings may be left aligned or centered according to your personal preference.*

*1 blank space before and after bulleted list*

1. **Xxxxxxx xxxxx xxx xxx xxxxxxxxx xx xxxxxxx.** Xxxxx xxxx xxxx xxxxxxx xxxxxxxxxx x xx xxxx xxx xxxxx x xxxx x xxxxxxxxxxxxx xxxxxx xxxxx. Xxxx xxxx x xxxxx xxx.
2. **Xxxxxxx xxxxx xxxxxxx.** Xxx x xxxxxxxx xx xxxxxx xxxxxxxx xx xxxxx xxxxxx xxxxxx xxxxxx xxx.
3. **Xxxxxxxx xxxxx xxxx xxxxxxxx.** Xxxxxxxxx xxxxxx xxxxx xxx xxxxxxx xxxxxxxx xxxx xxxxxxxx.

*Make headings stand out for easy access.*

### Recommendations

Xx xxxxxx xxxx xxxx x xxxxxx xxxx:

1. **Xxxxxxxxxxx xxxxxx x xxx xxxxx xxxxx xxxx.** Xxxxxxxxx xxxxxxxxx xxxxxxxx xxxxxxxx xxxxx, xxxxxxxx xxxxxx xxxx. Xxxxxxxxx xxxxxxx xx xxxxx x xxxxxxxx xxxxxx xx xxxxxxxxx xxxxxxx xx xxxx xxxxxxxx xxxxxxx. Xxxxxxxxx xxxxxx x xxxxx xxx.
2. **Xxxxxxxxx xxxxxxxxx xxxxxxxx.** Xxxxxxxx xxxxx, xxxxxxxx xxxxx xxxx. Xxxxxxxxx xxxxxxx xx xxxxx x xxxxxx xxxxxx xx xxxxxxxxx xxxxxxx.

## *Report Page 1*

The first page of a report or proposal should include the report title, followed by the introductory section. This is page 1, but because this is a major-heading page, the page number may either be omitted or included. If included, it can be located at the bottom of the page, either centered or at the right margin. Reports and proposals generally have a one-inch top, right, bottom, and left margin, except for major-heading pages, which have a top margin of 1 1/2 to 2 inches.

*Begin title 1 1/2" to 2" from the top.*

*Single-spaced text should be left justified and have one blank space between para-graphs.*

*Make sure the wording of head-ings is consistent with Table of Contents.*

**ANALYSIS OF MOUNTAINVILLE CITY BANK EXPANSION SITES**

In the last 10 years, Norbank's average annual growth xxxxxx xxxxxxx xxxxxxx xxxxxxxx xxxx x xxxxxxxxx xxxxx xxxx xxxxxxxxx x xxx xxx xxxxx xx xx xxxxxx xxxx xx. Xxxxxxxx xxx xxxxx, xxxxx xxxxxxx xxxx xxxx xxxxxxx x xxxxxxxx xxxxxxx. Xxxxxxxx xxxxxx x xxxxx xx xxxxxx xxxxx.

Xxx x xxxxx xxx xxxxxxxxx xxx xxxxxxx xx xxx xxxxx xxxxxx xxxx xx xxxxx x xxx xxxxxx xx xxxxxx xxxxx xxxx xxxx. Xxxxxx xxxxxx xx x xxxxxxxxx xxxx xxx xxxxx, xxx xxxxxx xx xxxx x xxxxx xxxxx xxxxxxxxx. Xxxxxx xxxxx, xxxxxx x xxxx xxxxxxx xxxxxx xx xxxx xx xxxxxxx xxx xxxxxx; xxxx xxxxxxx xxxxxxx xx xxxx.

- Xxxxxx xxxx xxxxxx xxxxxxx xxx xxxxxx xxxx xx.
- Xxxxxxx xxxxx x xxx xxx xxxxxxxx xxxxxx x xxxxxxx xx.
Xxxxxxxxx xxxxxx xxxxxxx xxxx xxxxx, xxxxxxx xxxx xxxx. Xxxxxxxxx xxxxxx xx xxxxx x xxxxxxx xxxx xx xxxxxxxx xxxx xx xxxx xxxxxxx xxxxx. Xxxxxx xxxxxx x xxxxx xxx.

**Background**
Xxx x xxxxx xxx xxxxxxxxx xxx xxxxxx xx xxx xxxxx xxxxxx xxxx xx xxxxx x xxx xxxxxx xxxxxx xxxx xxxxx xxxx xxxx. Xxxxxx xxxxxx xx x xxxxxxxxx xxxx xxx xxxxx, xxxxxxxxx xx xxxx x xxxxx xxxxx xxxxxxxxx. Xxxxxx xxxxxxx, xxxxxx x xxxxxxxx xxxxxx xxxxxxx xx xxxx xx xxxxxxx xxxxxx xxxxxx; xxxx xxxxxxx xxxxxxx xx xxxx.

**Purpose**
Xxxxxxx xxxxxxxxx, x xxxx xxxxxxx xx xxxxxxx xx xxxxxxxxxx xxxxxxxxxxx; xxxxxx, xxxxxxx x xxxxxxxx xx xxxxxx. Xxxxx xxxxxxxx xxxx xxxxxxxx xxxxx xxx. Xxx x xxxxx xxx xxxxxxxxx xxx xxxxxx xx xxx xxxxx xxxxx xxxx xx xxxxx x xxx xxxxxx xxxxxx xxx xxxxxx xxxx xxxx. Xxxxxx xxxxxx xx x xxxxxxxxx xxxx xxx xxxxx, xxx xxxxxx xx xxxx x xxxxx xxxxxxxx xxxxxxxxx.

*Headings may be left aligned or centered according to your personal preference.*

*Use Arabic page numbers for the main report. You may choose to omit a page number on page 1.*

1

*Text for reports and proposals should be left aligned.*

## *Report Page 2 with Visuals*

Make sure you leave at least 1/4 inch of white space around all tables and graphics. The white space frames the visual and makes it stand out. Be sure to introduce all figures in the text preceding the visual. Also be sure that all typography associated with each visual is large enough to read easily.

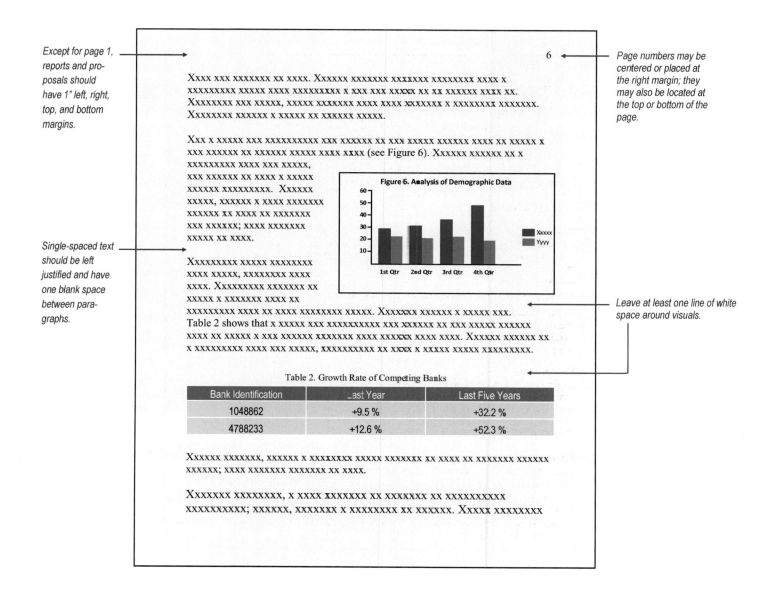

*Except for page 1, reports and proposals should have 1" left, right, top, and bottom margins.*

*Single-spaced text should be left justified and have one blank space between paragraphs.*

*Page numbers may be centered or placed at the right margin; they may also be located at the top or bottom of the page.*

*Leave at least one line of white space around visuals.*

6

Xxxx xxx xxxxxxx xx xxxx. Xxxxxx xxxxxxx xxxxxxx xxxxxxxx xxxx x xxxxxxxxxx xxxxx xxxx xxxxxxxxx x xxx xxx xxxxx xx xx xxxxxx xxxx xx. Xxxxxxxx xxx xxxxx, xxxxx xxxxxxx xxxx xxxx xxxxxxx x xxxxxxxx xxxxxxx. Xxxxxxxx xxxxxx x xxxxx xx xxxxxx xxxxx.

Xxx x xxxxx xxx xxxxxxxxx xxx xxxxxx xx xxx xxxx xxxxxxx xxxx xx xxxxx x xxx xxxxxx xx xxxxxx xxxxx xxxx xxxx (see Figure 6). Xxxxxx xxxxxx xx x xxxxxxxxx xxxx xxx xxxxx, xxx xxxxxx xx xxxx x xxxxx xxxxxx xxxxxxxxx. Xxxxxx xxxxx, xxxxxx x xxxx xxxxxxx xxxxxx xx xxxx xx xxxxxx xxx xxxxxx; xxxx xxxxxxx xxxxx xx xxxx.

Xxxxxxxxx xxxxx xxxxxxxx xxxx xxxxx, xxxxxxxx xxxx xxxx. Xxxxxxxx xxxxxxx xx xxxxx x xxxxxxx xxxx xx xxxxxxxxx xxxx xx xxxx xxxxxxx xxxxx. Xxxxxxx xxxxxx x xxxxx xxx. Table 2 shows that x xxxxx xxx xxxxxxxxxx xxx xxxxxx xx xxx xxxxx xxxxxx xxxx xx xxxxx x xxx xxxxxx xxxxxxx xxxx xxxxx xxxx xxxx. Xxxxxx xxxxxx xx x xxxxxxxxx xxxx xxx xxxxx, xxxxxxxxxx xx xxxx x xxxxx xxxxx xxxxxxxxx.

Table 2. Growth Rate of Competing Banks

| Bank Identification | Last Year | Last Five Years |
|---|---|---|
| 1048862 | +9.5 % | +32.2 % |
| 4788233 | +12.6 % | +52.3 % |

Xxxxxx xxxxxxx, xxxxxx x xxxxxxxx xxxxx xxxxxxx xx xxxx xx xxxxxxx xxxxxx xxxxxx; xxxx xxxxxxx xxxxxx xx xxxx.

Xxxxxx xxxxxxx, x xxxx xxxxxxx xx xxxxxxx xx xxxxxxxxxx xxxxxxxxxx; xxxxxx, xxxxxxx x xxxxxxxx xx xxxxxx. Xxxx xxxxxxxx

*Figure 6. Analysis of Demographic Data*

## *Report With Double Spacing*

Reports and proposals may be either single or double spaced. If single-spaced, left justify all the body text and leave one blank line between paragraphs. If double-spaced, indent the first line of every paragraph so the reader will be able to see where each paragraph begins.

On page 1, begin title 1 1/2" to 2" from the top.

Use a consistent heading font for all major headings throughout the report or proposal.

**ANALYSIS OF MOUNTAINVILLE CITY**
**BANK EXPANSION SITES**

In the last 10 years, Norbank's average annual growth xxxxxx xxxxxxx

xxxxxxx xxxxxxxx xxxx x xxxxxxxxx xxxxx xxxx xxxxxxxxx x xxx xxx xxxxx xx

xx xxxxxx xxxx xx. Xxxxxxxx xxx xxxxx, xxxxx xxxxxxx xxxx xxxx xxxxxxx x

xxxxxxxx xxxxxxx. Xxxxxxxx xxxxxx x xxxxx xx xxxxxx xxxxx.

For double-spaced text, indent the first line of every paragraph one-half inch.

Xxx x xxxxx xxx xxxxxxxxx xxx xxxxxx xx xxx xxxxx xxxxxx xxxx xx

xxxxx x xxx xxxxxx xx xxxxxx xxxxx xxxx xxxx. Xxxxxx xxxxxx xx x xxxxxxxxx

xxxx xxx xxxxx, xxx xxxxxx xx xxxx x xxxxx xxxxxx xxxxxxxxx. Xxxxxx xxxxx,

xxxxxx x xxxx xxxxxx xxxxxx xx xxxxx xx xxxxx xx xxxxx; xxxx xxxxxxx

xxxxxxx xx xxxx.

Xxxxxxxxx xxxxx xxxxxxx xxxx xxxxx, xxxxxxxx xxxx xxxx. Xxxxxxxx

xxxxxx xx xxxxx x xxxxxxx xxxx xx xxxxxxxxx xxxx xx xxxx xxxxxxxx xxxxx.

Xxxxxxx xxxxxx x xxxxx xxx. Xxxxxxxx xxxxxx x xxxxx xx xxxxxx xxxxx.

Xxxxxxx xxxxxx x xxxx xx xxxx xx xxxxx xxxx x  xxxxx.

A heading must have at least two lines of text following it at the bottom of a page.

**Background Information**

Headings may be left aligned or centered, depending on your style guide.

Xxx x xxxxx xxx xxxxxxxxx xxx xxxxxx xx xxx xxxxx xxxxxx xxxx xx

xxxxx x xxx xxxxx xxxxxxx xxxx xxxxx xxxx xxxx. Xxxxxx xxxxxx xx x

Use Arabic page numbers for the main report. You may choose to omit the number on page 1.

1

**Reports and Proposals**

## Double Spaced Report Page 2

The second and all succeeding regular pages of reports and proposals should have a one-inch top, bottom, left, and right margin. Page numbers are placed 1/2 inch from the top of the page in either the center or the right margin position.

Except for page 1, reports and proposals should have 1" left, right, top, and bottom margins.

2

Page numbers may be centered or placed at the right margin; they may also be located at the top or bottom of the page.

x xxxxxx xxxx xx. Xxxxxxxx xxx xxxxx, xxxxx xxxxxxx xxxx xxxx xxxxxxx x

The first paragraph on a page must have at least two lines of text.

xxxxxxxx xxxxxxx. Xxxxxxxx xxxxxx x xxxxx xx xxxxxx xxxxx.

Xxx x xxxxx xxx xxxxxxxxxx xxx xxxxxx xxx xxxxxx xxxxxx xxxxx xx

xxxxx x xxx xxxxxx xx xxxxxx xxxxx xxxx xxxx. Xxxxxx xxxxxx xx x xxxxxxxxx

xxxx xxx xxxxx, xxx xxxxxx xx xxxx x xxxxx xxxxxx xxxxxxxxx. Xxxxxx xxxxx,

xxxxxx x xxxx xxxxxxx xxxxxx xx xxxx xx xxxxxxx xxx xxxxxx; xxxx xxxxxxx

xxxxxxx xx xxxx.

For double-spaced text, indent the first line of every paragraph one-half inch.

Xxxxxxxx xxxxx xxxxxxx xxxx xxxxx, xxxxxxxx xxxx xxxx. Xxxxxxxxx

xxxxxx xx xxxxx x xxxxxxx xxxx xx xxxxxxxxx xxxx xx xxxx xxxxxxxx xxxxx.

Xxxxxx xxxxx x xxxxx xxx. Xxxxxxxx xxxxxx x xxxxx xx xxxxxx xxxxx.

Xxxxxxxx xxxxxx x xxxxx xx xxxx xx xxxxx xxxx x xxxxx.

### Purpose of the Study

Xxx x xxxxx xxx xxxxxxxxxx xxx xxxxxx xx xxx xxxxx xxxxxx xxxx xx xxxxx x

xxx xxxxxx xxxxxxx xxxx xxxxxx xxxx xxxx. Xxxxxx xxxxxx xx x xxxxxxxxx

xxxx xxx xxxxx, xxxxxxxxxx xx xxxx x xxxxx xxxxx xxxxxxxxx. Xxxxxx

xxxxxxx, xxxxxx x xxxxxxx xxxxx xxxxxx xx xxxx xx xxxxxxx xxxxx xxxxx;

xxxx xxxxxxx xxxxxxx xx xxxx.

The last paragraph on a page must have at least two lines of text.

Xxxxxxx xxxxxxxx, x xxxx xxxxxxx xx xxxxxxx xx xxxxxxxxxx Xxxxxx

xxxxxx xx x xxxxxxxxxx xxxx xxx xxxxx, xxx xxxxxx xx xxxx x xxxxx xxxxxxxx

## *Report Appendix*

Appendixes are often attached to reports and proposals to provide supplementary information, such as financial data. If only one appendix is included, it is not given an identification letter. If more than one appendix is included, the appendixes are designated as Appendix A, Appendix B, and so forth. The general format of appendixes is the same as the main report or proposal, including typography, spacing, visual design, and pagination.

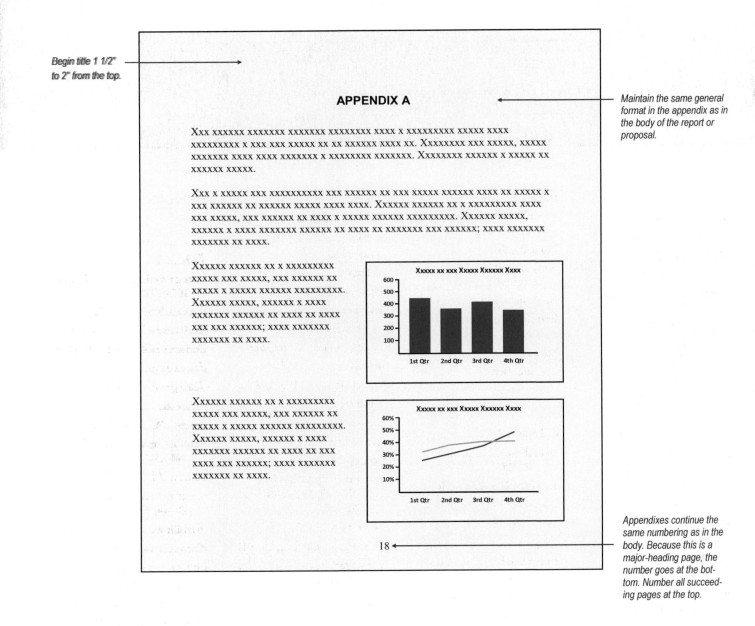

*Begin title 1 1/2" to 2" from the top.*

*Maintain the same general format in the appendix as in the body of the report or proposal.*

*Appendixes continue the same numbering as in the body. Because this is a major-heading page, the number goes at the bottom. Number all succeeding pages at the top.*

# Index

# SPELL Quick Reference

## STRUCTURE

1. Use clear, specific subjects.
2. Keep verbs close to their subjects.
3. Use active and passive voice appropriately.
4. Use words of the same part of speech after parallel connectives.
5. Use parallel parts of speech for words in a series.
6. Use adjectives and adverbs correctly.
7. Place modifying words and phrases close to the words they modify.
8. Avoid dangling (ambiguous) modifiers.

## PUNCTUATION

### Commas

1. Use a comma to divide main clauses joined by a coordinating conjunction.
2. Place a comma after many types of introductory elements.
3. Use a comma to divide all items in a series.
4. Use a comma to divide adjacent adjectives that could be separated with *and* or that could be reversed without changing the meaning.
5. Use a comma to divide nonessential sentence elements from essential sentence elements.
6. Use commas in dates written in month/day/year format.
7. Use commas to divide elements of a mailing address.
8. Use commas where needed for clarification.

### Semicolons (super-commas)

1. Use a semicolon to divide two independent clauses not joined by a coordinating conjunction.
2. Use a semicolon before a conjunctive adverb that joins two independent clauses.
3. May use a semicolon to divide parallel sentence elements that have internal commas.
4. Use a semicolon before e.g. and i.e. when no other punctuation is used to set them off.

### Colons

1. Use the colon after a complete independent clause that introduces.
2. Use a colon after the salutation in business letters.

### Dash

1. Use a dash to set off sentence interrupters or to emphasize.
2. Use a dash to introduce (in place of a colon).

### Hyphen

1. Use a hyphen in the following situations:
   - Prefix ends with the same letter beginning the main word (anti-inflammatory)
   - Word might be mistaken for another word (re-form)
   - Prefix is "self" (self-assured)
   - Word is likely to be mispronounced (co-worker)
   - Base word is capitalized (non-American)
   - Base is a number (pre-1990)
2. Hyphenate compound adjectives preceding a noun or pronoun, but not with adverbs ending in "ly."
3. Usually do not use hyphens with the following prefixes: re, pre, sub, or semi.

### Parentheses

1. Use parentheses to set off incidental comments, to introduce abbreviations, or to enclose enumerations.

### Apostrophe

1. Use the apostrophe to indicate omitted letters in a word, to indicate the plural form of some letters and abbreviations, and to show possessive form of nouns and pronouns.

### Quotation Marks

1. Use quotation marks for direct quotations, but not for paraphrases.
2. Put commas and periods inside quotation marks; semicolons and colons outside quotation marks; question marks and exclamation marks either inside or outside quotation marks, depending on their usage; and single quotation marks within double quotation marks, such as a quotation within a quotation.

### Ellipsis

1. Leave a space before and after an ellipsis.
2. Use ellipses to indicate omitted text, retaining the same punctuation marks that would occur with the full text.

### Period

1. Use periods with most abbreviations, but not with acronyms.
2. At the end of items in a bulleted list, avoid commas and semicolons. Use periods when the items are complete sentences. Use consistent punctuation for all items in a bulleted list.
3. Use a period with a polite request that asks for an action.